Eucharist and Offering

Kenneth W. Stevenson

Eucharist and Offering

Pueblo Publishing Company

New York

Design: Frank Kacmarcik

Scriptural pericopes quoted from the Revised Standard Version of the Bible and the Jerusalem Bible.

Printed in the United States of America.

ISBN: 0-916134-77-6

Contents

Foreword

During the first 1,500 years of the Church's history nobody doubted that the eucharist was a sacrifice. The language of offering and sacrifice was used in the liturgy, and about it, without question. Yet since the Reformation split the western church in pieces, the question of eucharistic sacrifice (Is the eucharist a sacrifice? If so, who offers what to whom and how?) has not only been a matter of dispute among theologians, but it has been one of the markers of division among churches. That is why eucharistic sacrifice, along with the question of Christ's presence in the eucharist, has been on the agenda not only of the Anglican-Roman Catholic International Commission (ARCIC), but of every other ecumenical group the purpose of which is to overcome the divisions bequeathed by the schisms of the sixteenth century. Of the two questions, eucharistic sacrifice and eucharistic presence, sacrifice is perhaps the more difficult and complex because it touches the mysteries of divine grace and human response, and because it touches the nature of the Church itself. How is the self-offering of Christians related to the self-offering of Christ, and how is that to be sacramentally expressed?

ARCIC's method has been to draw on the resources of our shared Christian tradition to express our common Christian faith on matters that in the past have been divisive. ARCIC's judgement that the question of eucharistic sacrifice ought no longer to divide us is now being received and tested in the churches (as is the more comprehensive statement on the eucharist contained in the World Council of Churches' Lima report on *Baptism, Eucharist and Ministry*). One practical value of Kenneth Stevenson's study is that it will help greatly in this process of critical assessment and reception. He demonstrates the variety and richness of our common tradition, a variety much wider than most of us had ever supposed. For our common faith admits of a wide diversity of expression—a diversity that need not be a matter of conflict, but that can and should be a matter of mutual enrichment.

This is an area in which English Anglicans and others have inherited a particular set of anxieties, not so much from the sixteenth as from the nineteenth century. The eucharistic prayers of the Church of England's *Alternative Service Book* show the scars of battles not yet fully healed. If, when the time comes for further revision, we are able to approach this sensitive area with greater confidence and freedom of spirit, it will be largely thanks to scholars such as Kenneth Stevenson, who will have shown us that we need not be so anxious.

So I commend his study not only for its intrinsic interest, but also for its practical usefulness in the life of the Church.

†*Mark Santer*
Bishop of Kensington
29 July 1985

Preface

The idea of writing this book stemmed from two things. When I was a teenager, summer holidays frequently took me all over Europe, so I was able to taste local eucharistic worship in a wide variety of different traditions and cultures. This ranged from French Roman Catholic to Danish Lutheran. Then, when I was a student, I was struck by the variety of ways in which the metaphor of sacrifice found expression in the prayers and hymnody of the various eastern and western churches. There was no liturgical study available on this potentially ecumenical theme.

This study is therefore intended to complete the sequence of books about the eucharist that began with eschatology (by Geoffrey Wainwright), and continued with Holy Spirit (John H. McKenna) and institution narrative (Richard Buxton). Each of these first three is distinctive in scope and style. So is the fourth. (As Dr. Johnson once remarked, one cannot fill one's cup simultaneously from the source and mouth of the Nile.) Although the book sets out to be comprehensive in its overall historical approach, the emphasis falls on the patristic and modern periods. The underlying message is that there is much more *variety* in the whole story than previous studies have shown, and that the contemporary western debate can only really progress if we develop a more imprecise (and eastern) notion of eucharist as "spiritual sacrifice," indeed of *all* worship as sacrificial. Such a broad, ecclesial view of the sacrament of the Lord's Supper is both deeply traditional and startlingly contemporary.

Many people deserve my thanks for helping me to form and digest the ideas in the following pages. These include fellow members of the international *Societas Liturgica;* colleagues in University and Chaplaincy at Manchester; and students at Lincoln Theological College and in the Faculty of Theology here. Above all, my thanks are due to Geoffrey Cuming, who patiently read the draft manuscript and made invaluable and pungent comments. I must also thank Richard McBrien, chairman of the Department of Theology, University of Notre Dame, Indiana, who invited me to take up a visiting professorship for the spring semester of 1983, and who thus provided a stimulating environment in which the book could begin to take shape. Beryl Sweeney and Jenny Haymes deserve my gratitude for producing a clean text. No list of thanks, however, would be complete without mentioning Sarah, my wife, who will remember well the sound of a North American portable typewriter.

I should like to dedicate this book to the memory of my grandfathers, William Reid Stevenson and Christian Julius Skat Hoffmeyer, who may not have shared all my liturgical interests, but whose ecumenical and theological endeavors in Scotland and Denmark earlier in this century would cause them to smile on this offering.

Kenneth Stevenson
Manchester
Ascension Day, 1985

We hail thy Presence glorious,
O Christ our great High Priest,
O'er sin and death victorious,
At thy thanksgiving feast:
As thou art interceding
For us in heaven above,
Thy Church on earth is pleading
Thy perfect work of love.

Through thee in every nation
Thine own their hearts upraise,
Offering one pure oblation,
One Sacrifice of praise:
With thee in blest communion
The living and the dead
Are joined in closest union,
One Body with one Head.

May we thy word believing
Thee through thy gifts receive,
That, thou within us living,
We all to God may live;
Draw us from earth to heaven
Till sin and sorrow cease,
Forgiving and forgiven,
In love and joy and peace.

(From *Hymns Ancient and Modern New Standard*, 1983, no. 266, stanzas 1, 2 and 5, by Richard Godfrey Parsons [1882–1948]; Suffragan Bishop of Middleton, Diocese of Manchester, 1927–1932; Bishop of Southwark 1932–1941; Bishop of Hereford 1941–1948.)

Abbreviations

ACC	*Alcuin Club Collections.*
Anaphoral Offering	K. W. Stevenson, " 'Anaphoral Offering': Some Observations on Eastern Eucharistic Prayers," *Ephemerides Liturgicae* 94 (1980), pp. 209–228.
ATR	*Anglican Theological Review.*
CDI	I. Pahl (ed.), *Coena Domini I*, Spicilegium Friburgense 29 (Fribourg, 1983).
DS	Darwell Stone, *A History of the Doctrine of the Holy Eucharist*, 2 vols. (London, 1909).
EL	*Ephemerides Liturgicae.*
EP	*Eucharistic Prayer.*
FAL	C. O. Buchanan (ed.), *Further Anglican Liturgies*, London, 1975.
GLS	*Grove Liturgical Study.*
JTS	*Journal of Theological Studies.*
Jungmann	J. Jungmann, *Missarum Sollemnia*, 2 vols., Eng. tr., Benziger Bros. (New York, 1951).
LAL	C. O. Buchanan (ed.), *Late Anglican Liturgies*, ACC 66 (London, 1985).
LEW	F. E. Brightman, *Liturgies Eastern and Western, I: Eastern Liturgies* (Oxford, 1896).
LiE	B. Wigan (ed.), *The Liturgy in English*, 2nd ed. (Oxford, 1964).
LMD	*La Maison-Dieu.*
LQF	*Liturgiewissenschaftliche Quellen und Forschungen.*
L'offrande	K. W. Stevenson, "L'offrande eucharistique. La recherche sur les origines, établit-elle une différence de sens?", *La Maison-Dieu* 154 (1983), pp. 81–106.
MAL	C. O. Buchanan (ed.), *Modern Anglican Liturgies* (Oxford, 1968).

Martène	E. Martène, *De Antiquis Ecclesiae Ritibus*, 4 vols. (Antwerp, 1764).
OC	*Oriens Christianus.*
OCA	*Orientalia Christiana Analecta.*
OCP	*Orientalia Christiana Periodica.*
PE	A. Hänggi, I. Pahl (eds.), *Prex Eucharistica*, Spicilegium Friburgense 12 (Fribourg, 1968).
PEER	R. C. D. Jasper & G. J. Cuming (eds.), *The Prayers of the Eucharist: Early and Reformed*, 2nd ed. (Oxford, New York, 1980).
QLP	*Questions Liturgiques et Paroissiales.*
Renaudot	E. Renaudot, *Liturgiarum Orientalium Collectio*, 2 vols. (Frankfurt, 1847).
SC	*Sources Chrétiennes.*
SCA	*Studies in Christian Antiquity.*
SL	*Studia Liturgica.*

Chapter One

Introduction: What Are We Looking For?

When Martin Luther nailed his famous ninety-five theses to the door
of the Castle Church at Wittenberg on October 31, 1517 (as the story
goes), he was doing nothing unusual. In those days, if a young pro-
fessor wanted to stimulate some controversy, he fastened his thoughts
to the university chapel door, which served the same purpose as the
university notice-board does today. Staff and students would come
and go to read and digest what the latest bright mind was producing.
But Luther's action *was* unusual in what those theses contained, for
they amounted to a damning indictment of much of popular medieval
Catholicism. Ever since that date, western Christians have discussed
the eucharist self-consciously. Luther injected into the debate about
the eucharist (which had been going on through the Middle Ages in
various ways) an element of controversy that Christianity had not
known previously. Unlike earlier disputes, what he had to say had
direct liturgical implications; it could not be relegated to the seminar room.

Many forces operate to influence the way liturgy develops. Some
are perceptible, others are not. In the recent work of liturgical renewal
in the West, a recurrent feature is the way in which Protestants increasingly have become ready to see the eucharist in sacrificial terms,
as Roman Catholics have become more ready to describe the eucharist
in ways other than sacrificial.[1] Our knowledge of Christian antiquity
is greater than what our predecessors in the sixteenth century knew,
and there have been developments in theology, spirituality, and liturgy in the twentieth century in which we have walked side by side
and have crossed denominational frontiers in ways that would have
been unthinkable even in the recent past.

Yet the differences of emphasis and approach remain and persist,
and liturgical renewal is one area where the old battles are refought,
although not with the ferocity or ignorance of Reformation and Coun-
ter-Reformation times. Two examples will suffice to show the difference between a liturgy that evolves *self-consciously* because it is
western and post-Reformation, and a liturgy that evolves *organi-*

1

cally because it is eastern and unaffected by controversy. In 1966, the Church of England's Liturgical Commission produced a draft order for the eucharist with a eucharistic prayer based on the anaphora contained in the *Apostolic Tradition* of Hippolytus, in which the words "we offer this bread and this cup" appear in the anamnesis. The text went to Convocations in 1967 with a dissenting vote from one Evangelical, and the eucharistic prayer was altered in the ensuing debate before it was issued for general use.[2] In some ways, it was remarkable that the "offering" words managed to gain an entrance to Anglican liturgy in England at all (it must be remembered that other provinces of the Anglican Communion had been familiar with that kind of language since the eighteenth century);[3] the Protestant culture of England had helped to shipwreck the proposed Prayer Books of 1927 and 1928 through no less a body than Parliament. Yet, as Paul Bradshaw has tellingly described it, Evangelicals in 1967 were "unable to ignore the doctrinal water which had flowed under the liturgical bridge"[4] in the period between the third and the twentieth centuries. In other words, liturgical revision is not a process of turning the clock back to a golden age that existed long before nasty controversies began to rage. The lesson of 1967 in the Church of England was hard for many, and English Anglican liturgy has been affected by it in the period since, up to, and including the *Alternative Service Book* of 1980.

On the other hand, one of the most fascinating episodes in liturgical history is the way in which the anaphora of Basil of Caesarea[5] develops in the various forms that have come down to us. The early text, which probably dates from the late third or early fourth century, is of the greatest interest because it is ante-Nicene, and yet has a skeleton structure identical with the classical Greek West Syrian anaphoras dating from the fourth and fifth centuries. But it contains important theological primitivisms, including the language of consecration at the epiclesis, the commemoration of the departed, and, above all, in the tantalizing use of a past-tense verb at the anamnesis, "we presented." The later Alexandrian version of this prayer amplifies the epiclesis considerably (so that consecration is more explicit), extends the commemoration of the departed, and has a present-tense offering verb ("we offer") at the anamnesis. The Byzantine version extends all these ideas and presents a much richer coverage of the theology of eucharistic offering, consecration, and intercession of the departed. It is beyond doubt that churches in communion with one another (and subsequently out of communion) used these prayers. It is beyond doubt that the respective theologies of these prayers do not contradict each

2

other. But it is nonetheless clear that the emphases are sharpened as the tradition develops.

Liturgical language, of course, is different from the language of a theological document, whether drafted by a council or written as a university dissertation. Liturgical language is inherently conservative, especially as it gets nearer to popular piety. Liturgical language has to "carry" the beliefs of different kinds of people, who come to worship with different levels of understanding and expectation. Moreover, it is frequently the kind of language that a later age can leave untouched but still understand differently from the original drafters. For example, the frontispiece of Charles Wheatly's *Rational Illustration of the Book of Common Prayer* (1720)[6] depicts a High Church Anglican eucharist, celebrated in a classical church, with a priest standing in surplice and academic hood at the north end of a stone altar; up in the clouds stands the Christ figure at the north end of the heavenly altar, part of the same offering and sacrifice. Although Thomas Cranmer's eucharistic views are much disputed even today, they would not have coincided with those of Charles Wheatly, who so readily (and artistically) reinterprets the rite of the 1662 Prayer Book. Another important example of reinterpretation is in the way the Roman Canon increasingly was understood in the later Middle Ages to be exclusively sacrificial,[7] so that its "thanksgiving" (part of the earlier tradition) was downgraded and neglected.

In the following pages, we shall attempt to present a liturgical companion to the various systematic and historical studies of the eucharist down the ages that have appeared in recent years. It will not be our intention to suggest that the liturgy, properly understood (and revised), can solve all history's problems. It is our view that the liturgy opens up many avenues that other studies have not so far taken seriously enough. But first of all, we need to define what we mean by *sacrifice*.

Sacrifice has three main meanings. The first is the basic ritual meaning; the action of offering something material such as an animal or a fruit of the earth to a deity, to burn (or otherwise consume it), in order to reestablish or maintain a relationship with that deity. Sacrifice refers to the whole ritual action; in liturgical terms, it is the whole service. The second meaning narrows down the first; the sacrifice is the thing burnt or consumed, whether it is food or an animal. Both these meanings are ritual in their starting points, and they are part of the religious inheritance of Judaism and early Christianity. It is arguable whether or not they are still part of Christianity's world today.

A third meaning, however, concentrates on the moral aspects of

3

sacrifice, and while at first sight appears to be abstract, is anything but abstract when lived out.[8] A sacrifice in this sense is the destruction or surrender of something valued or desired for the sake of something having a higher or more pressing claim. This kind of sacrifice can be applied both to everyday living and to worship, whether Christian or not, and it is this meaning that gets the most mileage in contemporary Christianity, where sacrifice cannot (in our view) be dismissed as a tired and irrelevant notion. With such a moral and ethical view of sacrifice, Christian living and Christian worship have much in common. This is a view that the early Christian fathers saw in different ways. Perhaps the most dramatic is John Chrysostom, who applied "sacrifice" to all kinds of worship, even to the activity for which he is most famous, preaching.[9]

The Bible knows all three definitions. The story of Cain and Abel[10] at first sight produces the first definition, and the moral of the tale seems to be that God prefers blood to food. Yet the real intention of the Yahwist in his editorial work is to point out that some people are successful in material terms and others are not, and that sacrifice and living require right attitudes and relationships between people. This theme is repeated again and again, most tellingly in Hosea, "I desire mercy, not sacrifice";[11] in other words, "the sacrifice that God wants is not vain ritual, mechanically celebrated, but the sacrifice of mercy between and among ordinary people." When sacrifice is applied to liturgy, it is more wholesome (and, in our opinion, more faithful to tradition) to define *all* worship as sacrificial. Just as ideas about ministry run fewer risks of overlooking certain things when the starting point is the whole ministry of the Church, after which particular ministries within it are examined, so with sacrifice. We can see the eucharist in better perspective if we see it as part of the whole liturgical life of the Church, indeed as part of the whole *ordinary living* of the Church. This supplies useful and necessary foundations, but it is not enough. We need more than this if we are going to say anything new, offer fresh insights, shift traditional perspectives. For this reason, we have adopted three criteria that will recur throughout this study and that will show how the eucharistic prayer in particular and the whole eucharist in general expands and develops, contracts and abbreviates, reforms and deletes, renews and reintroduces certain themes and ideas.

The first criterion is what we call "story." By this is meant the solemn recitation before God of his mighty acts, culminating in the life and work of Christ. Obviously story varies in length and style from one tradition to another. The eastern anaphoras know of no variety *within* the main prayer, although they vary from one prayer to another in the way the story is recounted. On the other hand, the western medieval rites do vary within the anaphora because of the extended use of the preface in pointing up certain principal themes for certain days and occasions. But whether you have invariability with a total recitation of salvation history or variability with a single main idea for the particular celebration, the story is still sacrificial because it highlights the congregation's commitment to certain activities and spiritual insights that are apposite to the occasion. It is pointless to recite the story of God, however it is to be expressed, without being committed to God, just as he is committed to us in the first place. One of the weekday prefaces of the 1970 *Missale Romanum* (which is based on an older Leonine original) defines the nature of that recitation in a pungent and telling manner:

"Father, all-powerful and ever-living God,
we do well always and everywhere to give you thanks.
You have no need of our praise,
yet our desire to thank you is itself your gift.
Our prayer of thanksgiving adds nothing to your greatness,
but makes us grow in your grace,
through Jesus Christ our Lord."[12]

Sometimes it is necessary for the liturgy to define what it is doing in order to remind those who come to celebrate the eucharist that they are not trying to get something out of God, but are doing what they are doing to enable God to get through to them. The sacrifice of praise that the Church offers to God is not just words, mere words, but a solemn commitment to the God who initiates a relationship with his people in order to renew them, pardon them, and help them to grow in the life of faith.

The second criterion is what we call "gift." By this is meant the way in which the prayers describe and treat the bread and wine, whether by offering them or by referring to them explicitly or implicitly as gifts. It is our opinion that gift was the last of the three criteria to enter the early eucharistic prayer explicitly, and that it is a Greek West Syrian and Roman development, which the later medieval West concentrated on in various ways. Gift appears in different guises. One is by the conventional formula encountered for the first time in Hippolytus:

"Remembering his death and resurrection
we offer this bread and cup . . .

and we pray. . . ."[13]

This presentation of the gifts acts as a means of linking the institution narrative with the epiclesis, and it recurs in the Greek West Syrian eucharistic prayers with precisely that logic behind it, sometimes with a reference to the gifts in the epiclesis as "presented here." The Roman Canon takes on a different and more complex structure. But not all anaphoras of antiquity contain an explicit "presentation" of the gifts. We shall draw attention to the Syriac and Armenian anaphoras for their reticence on this matter, although they clearly see the *whole* eucharist as an offering; perhaps they kept something primitive and imprecise where the Greeks and Latins went off on their own elaborations.[14] Moreover, the (Egyptian) anaphora of Mark has a past-tense verb in the anamnesis that must surely refer to some earlier point, either at the start of the anaphora or perhaps to the placing of the gifts on the table before the anaphora begins.[15] Some of these suggestions may be too precise, and it is well known how westerners have looked too logically at eastern euchology. But the eastern prayers have a variety about them over their treatment of gift. The development of the western offertory is an example of a further development of the notion of gift, so that by the time of the Reformation, sacrifice and gift were synonymous, and (to all practical purposes) excluded the other criteria. We shall be arguing that the offertory is essentially preliminary in character, and that if gift is to be explicit in the anaphora, it needs to be associated closely with the epiclesis, as the prayer of consecration of those gifts and the communicants as well.

The third criterion is what we call "response." By this is meant the way in which the Church describes what it is doing in the eucharist. More precisely, however, it means what the Church wants the eucharist to mean and do, as the faithful unite themselves to the sacrifice of Christ. As we shall see, sacrifice first appears as a description of the eucharist in the *Didache*[16] (and not in the prayers themselves) in a moral context. The sacrifice must be pure, and therefore members of the community must be reconciled with one another. Response, therefore, is the "living sacrifice" of the Church and embraces the supplicatory aspects of the eucharistic prayer in the epiclesis and intercessions. Intercession is seen as part of the sacrificial activity of the Church as it offers its concerns to God, and offers the people of God in love and service.[17] The American ecumenical version of the anaphora of Basil of Caesarea in its epiclesis borrows both from the original Alexandrian text and also from the fourth eucharistic prayer of the 1970 Missal:

"Lord, we pray that in your goodness and mercy your Holy Spirit may descend upon us, and upon these gifts, sanctifying them and showing them to be holy gifts for your holy people, the bread of life and the cup of salvation, the Body and Blood of your Son Jesus Christ.

"Grant that all who share this bread and cup may become one body and one spirit, a living sacrifice in Christ, to the praise of your Name. Remember, Lord, your one holy catholic and apostolic Church, redeemed by the blood of your Christ. Reveal its unity, guard its faith, and preserve it in peace."[18]

Many other examples (ancient and modern) could be found to demonstrate the living sacrifice of the eucharist as the response to the mighty acts of God. But the response is far from being the Church taking on where God leaves off, since the response is God's action in us, in our life of discipleship in the eucharist. The spirituality of response is the offering of the whole of our lives anew to God. The essential character of this movement of humanity to God is perhaps what motivated Cranmer to place "self-oblation" *after* communion, where it is in many Anglican rites. But we would also argue that intercession is part of that self-offering also, and that intercession is a legitimate ingredient in the eucharistic prayer, although it is equally sacrificial wherever it is placed in the liturgy.

Story, therefore, provides the *context* of the eucharist. Gift describes the *material* of the eucharist. Response expresses the *action* of the eucharist. But the criteria are not static, since they develop, they mingle, they sometimes cancel each other out. In the medieval Roman West, story is banished from the anaphora and becomes part of the allegorical interpretation of the whole of the Mass; response becomes the psychological devotion of the faithful; gift takes first place in the scheme of things, instanced by the elevation of the host. Some may regard these developments as legitimate; others may prefer something more primitive and wholesome. But the development took place and resulted in fragmentation. The Reformation results in the inevitable pendulum swing against gift, although the notion of offertory rises like a phoenix in some quarters, notably among Laudian Anglicans. This was probably because the ritual actions of the old Latin offertory were too deeply embedded in the corporate memory of many Christians, and such actions could most easily be made symbolic as well as functional and thus provide a useful back door through which an inadequate rite could be reinterpreted. In modern times, eucharistic prayers have been written that emphasize story and response, but the problem of the split epiclesis results in confusion about when the prayer moves from thanksgiving into supplication.[19] The "first" epiclesis (consecration) leads into supplication, when the more logical and primitive pattern would see the institution narrative as part of the thanksgiving and not part of the supplication. This, of course, begs questions about whether or not the narrative is the consecration. But even though that notion is very much part of traditional western piety (whether Catholic, Lutheran, Anglican, or Calvinist), it is clear that modern rites are moving away from emphasizing the narrative, and now concentrate on the epiclesis. It remains to be seen how this works its way into popular piety; many modern hymns are pointing in that direction. Liturgical revision cannot turn the clock back; but renewal that is authentic to the tradition and open to contemporary needs stands a better chance of inculcating a deeper sense of what the eucharist means than a shallow and mechanistic understanding of the worship of God.

In this study, we shall be looking at the way sacrifice is handled in the eucharistic liturgies of churches through the ages, both explicitly and implicitly. The three criteria of story, gift, and response will be used throughout as a means of highlighting developments, new features, exaggerations, and areas of renewal. In the East in particular, we shall be looking for a sequence of ideas within the anaphora. Sometimes this is not possible to discern because of the primitive character of a prayer (e.g., the anaphora of Addai and Mari); at other times, it is apparent and clear (e.g., the anaphora of John Chrysostom).[20] Medieval western developments include the rich catalogue of prayers *Super oblata*, as well as the complex offertory prayers. Post-Reformation insights include the use of the heavenly intercession of Christ as a way of understanding the eucharistic sacrifice, a theme used in abundance in the hymns of the Wesleys. Modern productions attempt to bring out many theological ideas emphasized in twentiety-century writings, including kingdom, Spirit, and the social awareness of the Church. They also attempt to bridge sixteenth-century gaps, so that Calvary is central, but the Church's activity in eucharistic worship is still "real."

Writing about modern liturgical compositions, Leslie Houlden remarked that the problem with "most of the commonest formulations involving sacrificial language is that they start too far up the conceptual ladder; that is, they presuppose more fundamental theological concepts which seem not to be fully clear, like a mountain whose summit is exposed while the lower levels are shrouded in mist."[21] Certainly, the *"retour aux sources"* which has been so much part of reforms before and after the Second Vatican Council must not engender

8

a false enthusiasm that regards anything primitive as containing all the answers to history's difficult problems. Every liturgical expert on antiquity knows that Hippolytus might, conceivably, have been a sham Syrian archaizer, doing his own thing, out of favor with the Pope; Addai and Mari could have been mutilated beyond recognition at the time of Patriarch Iso 'yahb's liturgical adjustments in the seventh century (which involved abbreviations); and the *Strasbourg* papyrus could be a fragment of an early anaphora that went on to include material now lost but quite different in style and content from the later (complete) Greek Mark. With compilers of liturgical texts, all things are possible.

Yet the sacrificial aroma appears to be remarkably adhesive as a useful metaphor to the eucharist, whether it is there from the start, or reappears in a different form, or is banished (or downgraded or reinterpreted). It is probably as well that liturgy is a conservative business, if not in the compilation of texts, then certainly in the way these are understood and digested by the faithful. Formulations about gift are often tortuous and overambitious, whether through repetition (Roman medieval offertory prayers), or through new styles of language (e.g., Mozarabic "holocaust" imagery). What we are suggesting in this study is that once we develop a sense of the sacrificial character of the story and the response, and that the sacrifice is in a true sense spiritual, personal, and ethical, then gift will look after itself. If we are Catholic we can learn to see it in a wider context; if Protestant, we can learn to be less afraid of it. This seems to be the message that history teaches, that the best theology points to, and that the churches of the East still pray in countless patterns and images. So can the spiritual sacrifice of the eucharist be seen for its reality, as part of a life of worship and service.[22]

Chapter Two

The Tunnel: From Bible to Early Text

"For as often as you eat this bread and drink this cup, you proclaim the Lord's death until he comes" (1 Cor 11:26). This is where we must begin for the Christian eucharist. Paul is dealing with a difficult Christian community, and it is probable that only those difficulties caused him to state the tradition about the Last Supper. Much has been made of Paul's use of the "command to repeat."[1] It is significant that he uses the word *anamnesis*, which corresponds to the Hebrew *Zikkaron*, a word that appears throughout Jewish liturgical literature[2] and that is loosely translated by the English "memorial," or "remembrance." But even here, it is used analogously, for in the New Testament and early Christian writers, theological jargon has an element of analogy about it.

Jeremias suggested some years ago that for the early Christians, *anamnesis* meant "that God may remember me,"[3] an explanation that gives overtones rather different from the "dynamic celebration" of commentators in the liturgical school, most notably Dom Gregory Dix.[4] David Gregg has attempted to produce a milder interpretation, using many Hebrew sources in order to back up his case.[5] The fact is that Christians in our time find it hard to think themselves into the mentality of the ancient world, and it is doubly hard to do so in view of the theological presuppositions we bring to that quest. Dix was an Anglo-Catholic scholar, and one finds it hard to dissociate his powerful eucharistic spirituality from his discussion of the New Testament texts; similarly, Gregg is an Evangelical, with a different theological axe to grind. Jeremias may well be nearer the mark because of the eschatological character of this interpretation; it fits in with the context, "until he comes," and it also uses the analogy of "remember" in a dynamic sense, without making the early Christian eucharist seem mechanistic.

We may assume that for Paul, anamnesis was a piece of liturgical jargon that his followers would have understood, not so much from their Jewish background as from the way that background had been reinterpreted through experience of the Christian fellowship at wor-

10

ship, however inadequate (and cliquey) it obviously was. The Christian eucharist is the expression of that fellowship in Christ and with one another, and it therefore requires reconciliation, preparation, care, and a certain degree of order. It is not to be taken lightly, nor is it to become a demonstration of division. Has it, however, sacrificial overtones?

This problem can be made complex indeed, but once again the analogy principle comes to our aid. In the New Testament, sacrificial language abounds, at various levels. There are direct quotations from the Old Testament: "and walk in love, as Christ loved us and gave himself up for us, a fragrant offering and sacrifice to God" (Eph 5:2, cf. Ex 29:18). There are also passages where there is no quotation, but rather a reexpression of the meaning of the Christ event: "For the Son of Man also came not to be served but to serve, and to give his life as a ransom for many" (Mk 10:45).[6] There are, further, many instances in the letter to the Hebrews where sacrificial language is used, but always with a view to explaining the atoning efficacy of Christ over against the Jewish sacrifices.

The reason appears to be simple: sacrifice permeated the ancient world, and it was a fact of life with which any new religion had to reckon. Recently, Robert Daly has made much of this in an account of the origin and development of the idea of sacrifice from the Old Testament to the time of Origen.[7]

In the New Testament, sacrificial words are used with care. The word θυσία occurs frequently, either as a quotation, "Go and learn what this means, 'I desire mercy, and not sacrifice' " (Mt 9:13, cf. Hos 6:6), or as a paradoxical expression, "I appeal to you therefore, brethren, by the mercies of God, to present your bodies as a living sacrifice, holy and acceptable to God, which is your spiritual worship" (Rom 12:1). Here, λογικός means "reasonable" in the Platonic sense of "spiritual." As Sanday and Headlam explain the latter passage, "The relation to the Jewish rite is partly one of distinction, partly one of analogy. The Jewish sacrifice implies slaughter, the Christian continued activity and life. . . ."[8] In both cases, the Christian life is seen as sacrificial, and the New Testament writers are using cultic language in order to show that worship and life in the new covenant are related, in fact are one. Paul turns the sacrificial system of the Old Testament on its head by using the expression "living sacrifice," which at first sight looks like a contradiction in terms because sacrifice had for long implied descruction or death. Already we see what Daly calls the "spiritualization" of sacrifice in early Christian theology following on from the protests of the Old Testament preexilic prophets and late Judaism itself.[9] It is probably with this in mind that the author of the first letter of Peter uses the expression "spiritual sacrifices" (1 Pt 2:5) as the task of the Christian community, by which he means the whole Christian life, focused on worship itself.

The fact remains that nowhere in the New Testament is the eucharist referred to in specifically sacrificial terms. In the concluding part of the letter to the Hebrews, after a long explanation of how the sacrifice of Christ surpasses the sacrifices of the Law, and after a call to the Christian community to persevere in the faith, the writer exhorts his hearers, "Through him then let us continually offer up a sacrifice of praise to God, that is, the fruit of lips that acknowledge his name" (Heb 13:15). Using a technical liturgical term, the "sacrifice of praise,"[10] the author refers to liturgical worship as sacrificial because it implies sincere praise of God, in other words, commitment to him. Because of the centrality of the eucharist to the early Christians, it is hard to avoid the conclusion that the eucharist was regarded as a spiritual sacrifice, as a sacrifice of praise, as, indeed, the embodiment of the living sacrifice, in which the Christ event is celebrated. The sacrificial flavoring, however, is only analogical, because Jesus died once (Rom 6:10, Heb 7:27, 1 Pt 3:18); even here, however, are signs of the need to qualify the once and for all aspect, for in Hebrews, Christ's ministry in heaven is an eternal one, his having died for us (Heb 9: 23ff). What we see here is, perhaps, the need for the Church to assert the necessity of worship and witness in the face of persecution when there was a tendency to fall away from the faith.

The Jewish liturgical background to the eucharist can provide us with further help, thanks to the advance of Jewish-Christian studies in recent years.[11] There was a time when liturgists regarded Jewish euchological formulae as fixed forever, but nowadays scholars are of the opinion that Jewish prayer was developing at the same time as the early Christian traditions.[12] Nonetheless, Jean Laporte has shown strong reasons to believe that "thanksgiving" in late Jewish spirituality and euchology had a sacrificial character, and it may well be more accurate to translate *eucharisteo* as "offer thanks" than "give thanks" within the early Christian liturgy.[13] Once again, we have the process of analogy, for the sacrifice has been spiritualized. Such an offering connotation would also be applied to the Jewish meal blessings, including the *birkat-ha-mazon*, which (it is now generally agreed) forms the basis of the early Christian eucharistic prayers, with their tripartite structure of blessing for creation, thanksgiving for redemption, and supplication for the new Jerusalem.[14] In none of these prayers is there

12

direct reference to sacrifice, which would be inconsistent with the Jewish sacrificial system.

We deliberately began this chapter with the New Testament in order to give our discussion a specifically Christian starting point. We have now reached the point where the Old Testament fills the picture. No one knows exactly why the Jews offered sacrifice, other than the probable historical reason that they (and their neighbors) had long offered sacrifices. The underlying feature of the Old Testament is that no theological reason is given for sacrifice because it is assumed that sacrifices are offered. Sacrifices in both the Old Testament and other religions can be divided into three kinds.[15] *Communion sacrifices* are occasions when the faithful share a feast with the deity (cf. Lv 3 and 7). They are special, festive in character, and require ritual purity. *Gift sacrifices* (Lv 1) are whole burnt offerings and are commonly referred to as "holocausts"; these are the sacrifices of praise offered to God, as tribute to him. Thirdly, *sin offerings* (Lv 4–7) appear to be an extension of gift sacrifices, for the meaning lying behind them is the need to purge the nation of sin. Sin offerings were elaborated considerably in postexilic Judaism. The key lies in the blood (Lv 17:11); the procedures given are complex and cover all sorts of impurity.

There are two other sacrificial rites in Judaism. The first is the passover ritual (Ex 12), which comes near to being a communion sacrifice, but does not really fit into any of the three categories. It is important, however, because of the paschal character of the Last Supper (whether or not the Last Supper was a passover makes little difference to its liturgical aspects). Although the blood of the lamb on the lintel averts the wrath of the deity, the meal itself is a *zikkaron*, a memorial of the mighty acts of God in a formative experience in the nation's self-understanding. Secondly, there is the ritual for the Day of Atonement, with the laying on of hands by the high priest on the goat, which is then cast into the wilderness bearing the sins of the people. The hand-laying also occurs in some holocausts, and this act probably symbolizes a close association between the person making the sacrifice and the animal itself.[16]

The Old Testament gives a rich scheme, and the prophets provide some of its practice with fierce critiques. This is not so much a move in the "anticultic" direction as a challenge to the people, and to their motives and spirituality in worship (Am 4:4 and Jer 7:21). Liturgy seems to live with these problems indefinitely. The Jews lived with an accumulating tradition and (in the words of Michael Ramsey,) "for all its ceremonial elaboration, the system could not conceal hints of an inner scepticism about its own validity."[17] Perhaps this is why the spiritualization of sacrifice began with the preexilic prophets and became so firmly established by the time of Philo.[18] It certainly could not fail to do so after the destruction of the Temple.

The New Testament brings together some of the Old Testament reflection on sacrifice in its description of the meaning of the Christ event. Jesus is the sacrifice for sin, he is the passover Lamb, he is the scapegoat.[19] The ideas are deliberately brought together to mingle in order to point up the essential difference between the New and the Old. As the anamnesis of Christ, the eucharist is a spiritual sacrifice, but no reenactment; it is paschal, in that it commemorates his death; it is a meal, but more than a meal, for Jesus is the bread of life.

This brings us to the *Didache*,[20] a document that poses many problems. Where does it come from? When was it written? Does it describe a eucharist? Is chapter 14 a later addition? The answer to the last question is that 14 probably is an addition, put in to explain 10, which means that what we are faced with *is* a eucharist, and not an *agape*. Thus chapters 9 and 10 give us an account of liturgical procedure "about the thanksgiving," and the formulae written down bear a striking resemblance to the Jewish *berakoth*, with the difference that they are christological and eucharistic, and that they invert the order of creation-redemption. Thus: "We give thanks to you, our Father, for the holy vine . . . we give thanks to you, our Father, for the life and knowledge. . . . As this broken bread was scattered over the mountain. . . ." The community of the baptized eats and drinks. After the (eucharistic) meal, a longer *berakah* gives thanks, again inverting the order of creation and redemption, and again ending with a supplication for the unity of the Church. Care has been taken to reproduce the Jewish conventions, for each short section (9:2 and 3, 10:2 and 3) ends with a *chatimah*(= seal, doxology). Prophets can give thanks "as much as they wish," but the implication is that the text will be followed normally. Chapter 14, however, embodies what seems to be a gloss on the earlier part of the work:

"On the Lord's day of the Lord, come together, break bread, and give thanks, having first confessed your transgressions, that your sacrifice may be pure. But let none who has a quarrel with his companions join with you until they have been reconciled, that your sacrifice may not be defiled. For this is that which was spoken by the Lord, 'In every place and at every time offer me a pure sacrifice; for I am a great king, says the Lord, and my name is wonderful among the nations.'"

Three crucial areas of interpretation are at work in this part of the book. The first is that there is a definite moral imperative for Christian living; confession of sins and reconciliation are to be a regular feature of the eucharistic assembly. Whether this amounted to the kind of confession that later rites developed, particularly from the Reformation onwards, is a matter for debate. But these early Christians, whoever and wherever they were, regarded the eucharist as too important to take lightly, with the result that the author of this chapter regarded it as necessary to warn the congregation(s) using the book as their church order to be reconciled.

The second area of interpretation is that the eucharist is described as a sacrifice that must be "pure" or "undefiled" (cf. Mal 1:11). It is almost as if the author is belaboring this point. How is his description to be interpreted? There seems to be both analogy and moral teaching in it, for the sacrifice is not a "real" sacrifice like the Jewish and pagan cults, but on the other hand the offering must not be spoiled by dissensions in the community. Commentators agree that the meaning of sacrifice is not a precise one: "on aurait tort d'être trop explicite en ce domain."[21] But sacrificial the eucharist certainly is, in a metaphorical sense. Because the word $\theta\upsilon\sigma\iota\alpha$ does not appear earlier, only in this fourteenth chapter, perhaps the sacrificial character is closely associated with that New Testament (and Old Testament) theme that we met earlier, the living sacrifice, the spiritual sacrifice, the need for "mercy, not sacrifice" (Hos 6:6).

Now, the dating and the place of origin of the *Didache* are important for this discussion. Syria, between A.D. 90 and 120 have been the recent answers to these questions, but Joan Walker has suggested a much earlier date (A.D. 40s, in Antioch), although she allows that chapter 14 may be an insertion.[22] Nevertheless, if she is right, it could mean a much earlier date, too, for chapter 14, with its description of the eucharist in sacrificial terms antedating much of the New Testament, and even antedating the destruction of the Temple in A.D. 70, although I would regard this as unlikely.

The third area of interpretation concerns that quotation of Malachi 1:11 (a favorite among later writers),[23] for here we have a bold claim that the Christian faith fulfills the Old Testament prophecy, that all nations offer a pure sacrifice to God, and acknowledge their dependence upon him, in Jesus Christ. (It is interesting that the reference to incense in the passage is not included, although it is among subsequent authors.)

We are left to speculate a great deal. The *Didache* could be early and could have had wide circulation. (We have evidence of the reference to bread on the mountains being used in later Egyptian prayers.)[24] It is tempting to make rather bolder claims for the book than are legitimate. Nonetheless, it fulfills our three criteria in a fine manner: (1) the story is rehearsed as a *eucharistia* (NB so-called); (2) the gifts are referred to in terms comparable to a communion offering ("to us you have granted spiritual food and drink for eternal life"); and (3) the response comes across in the two conclusions to the *berakoth* when it prays for the unity of the Church, as well as in the moral exhortation in chapter 14. Jewish background, Greek culture, and early Christian reflection are all in evidence in this, the most primitive Christian prayer book we have. But the starting point appears to be the spiritualization of sacrifice rather than the Temple, which in any case has been spiritualized as the Christian community (1 Cor 3: 10ff.). The Church is thus seen as "a sacrificial reality,"[25] in the words of Rowan Williams. Although no reference (or allusion) is made to the heavenly offering of Christ, the "pure offering" could refer to the joining of praise with the angels in heaven, which is part of late Jewish spirituality and is also to be found in the book of Revelation (Rv 4:1ff.). Moreover, in apocalyptic, the only altar in the heavenly sanctuary is the incense altar, where no animal offerings are made, but only offerings that are λογικός, again in the Platonic sense of "rational" as "spiritual."[26] This term becomes important later on, both in the East and the West, as a crucial definition of the eucharist as the Christian sacrifice, since it describes in vivid terms the way in which the eucharist joins in the heavenly ministry of Christ, as interceding (eternally), thereby bestowing the benefits of his saving work to his people (in history). The joining of earthly and heavenly become focused on its life of praise (e.g., the Sanctus) and supplication (e.g., epiclesis and intercession). At root, this notion is far from fanciful; it is a way of showing that the eucharist is not just a human activity, but the action of God, in Christ, in his Church, in human history.

There are other sacrificial terms used in the New Testament[27] that are applied to Christ, and that we shall come across later on when they are used to describe the eucharist, either in its various aspects or as a whole. We have already encountered θυσία, both of the work of Christ, and of the response of the believing Christian. Sometimes it is used with the verb προσφέρω ("I bring to . . ."), which has both a general (nonritual) meaning as well as a specific (ritual) application of bringing an offering for sacrifice. In the famous passage that lies behind the Didachist's warning about reconciliation (discussed earlier), Jesus tells his followers that they must be at one with each other before placing their gift on the altar (Mt 5:23f). Here the verb is προσφέρω, used in conjunction with δῶρον (gift). In the fourth gospel, the expression λατρείαν προσφέρειν is used when Jesus warns the disciples that those who kill them will regard themselves as having done God a (sacred) service (Jn 16:2). προσφέρω produces the noun προσφορά, which is used exclusively of sacrifice. The other compound verb is ἀναφέρω, which means "carry up," and which also occurs in a sacrificial sense (Is 57:6, Heb 7:27, Jas 2:21). Yet another verb that later has liturgical overtones is προτίθημι, but in the New Testament it means simply "set forth" or "present," quite neutrally.

From this restricted survey of biblical material, we can see that the Christian understanding of offering was an adaptation of the Jewish (and pagan). Christ is the sacrifice, and in response to his death the Christian is either a living sacrifice (Rom 12:1) or offers "spiritual sacrifices" (1 Pt 2:5). There is a tendency for exegetes of a particular school to expand on the notion of spiritualization to the point where the living sacrifice/spiritual sacrifice is so spiritual that it is, in fact, internalized to the point of being little more than psychological.[28] Nothing could be further from the intentions of the New Testament writers, particularly the author of the letter to the Hebrews. The sacrifices required of the Christian are more real than those performed under the Law (πνευματικός does not mean "abstract"). The spiritualization tendency was long established in Judaism and had been adopted by the Dead Sea communities.

The process of reflection on cultic language continues as time goes on, and until we reach Hippolytus' Apostolic Tradition (and the other archetypes, Addai and Mari and Strasbourg), we do not have much to go on in the way of specifically liturgical texts. In the First Epistle of Clement, we come across reference to those who have "presented the gifts,"[29] in the proximity of the word as meaning the ministry of presbyters (cf. Rom 15:16). How is this little formula to be translated? It seems clear that for Clement, the expression means nothing more or less than "celebrate the eucharist," but it is also clear that "offering gifts" is the way in which that meaning is put together. He is, perhaps, also thinking of the passage in Matthew 5:23. It would be hard to argue for a specific liturgical act within the eucharist, such as the offertory. Whereas the Didache cautions Christians on having a "pure offering," Clement describes the whole eucharist as "offering gifts," and it reads like an early example of liturgical terminology, no more, no less.

In Ignatius is to be found a great deal of sacrificial language, which is christocentric rather than applied explicitly to the eucharist. The worship of Christians is "within the altar," which means "being united with Christ, the altar on which the sacrifice of our prayer is offered."[30] There may be eucharistic overtones in being "within the altar," in communion with the "one eucharist," presided over by the bishop. Ignatius speaks of his death as a sacrifice, an important speculation in view of the possibility that he was a Semitic Christian, who had no sensitivity about referring to more than one sacrifice.

By the time of Justin,[31] more reflection has taken place, although how this has been incorporated into liturgy is hard to tell. Malachi 1:11 is interpreted to refer directly to the eucharist, and Justin brings together (more completely than the *Didache*) the ideas of sacrifice of praise, offering gifts from the created order, and the living sacrifice of Christians. His description of the eucharistic celebration has long been used as an account of the worship of the persecuted church in Rome in the middle of the second century. His account was written for an outsider, however, not for the use of the baptized; we may hazard a guess that, were he to have written for the initiated, he might have included many other details, not least the content of his "prayers and thanksgivings." Nonetheless, in the *First Apology*, we get a glimpse of a formalized liturgy in which there is one unit of thanksgiving prayers, before the eating and drinking:

"Then bread and a cup of water and of mixed wine are brought to him who presides over the brethren, and he takes them and offers praise and glory to the Father of all in the name of the Son and of the Holy Spirit, and gives thanks at some length that we have been deemed worthy of these things from him. When he has finished the prayers and the thanksgiving, all the people present give their assent by saying 'Amen.' "

(Here are Gregory Dix's mingling of word and action.[32]) $\pi\rho o\sigma\phi\acute{e}\rho\epsilon\tau\alpha\iota$ is the verb for "are brought" and $\grave{\alpha}\nu\alpha\pi\acute{e}\mu\pi\epsilon\iota$ is the verb for "offers" of the praise and glory. This latter is not used thus in the New Testament, although we come across it in other early Christian writers. It may be an attempt to convey something of the sacrificial character of giving praise and thanks, for which some modern scholars have argued, but it is not a word that is later used in a restrictive liturgical sense, although it is used in literature in a sacrificial context.[33] Justin's description almost avoids sacrificial language, although $\pi\rho o\sigma\phi o\rho\acute{\alpha}$ and $\theta v\sigma\acute{\iota}\alpha$ are used elsewhere to describe the whole eucharist, perhaps in the total sense that we suggested of the *Didache*.

It is in Irenaeus that we encounter yet further reflection, where the eucharist is both the offering of praise, the offering of gifts, and the living sacrifice of Christians, but he elaborates. In *Adversus Haereses* IV, 29.5 he writes:

18

"But he also advised his disciples to offer the first fruits of his creation to God, not as if God needed them but so that they should not be unfruitful nor ungrateful, and so he took that which is from the creation of bread and gave thanks, saying, This is my Body. And similarly he declared the cup which is from the creation which is our environment to be his blood, and taught the new offering of the new dispensation; this the Church received from the apostles and offers throughout the whole world to God who provides us with nourishment, as the first fruits of his gifts in the new dispensation."[34]

Here we have some theology, indeed; thanksgiving closely associated with the institution narrative, the eucharistic gifts seen as part of the new creation, yet part of the old (and by implication, the Christians who worship), and the identification of the eucharist as the offering of the new covenant. Williams suggests further that Irenaeus defines sacrifice as the response of gratitude for the one sacrifice of Christ, which thus explains why the eucharist can be described sacrificially.[35] Certainly, Irenaeus is a more subtle theologian than Ignatius or Justin; he is a writer with different concerns. We shall come across an even more systematic discussion of the "one offering" and the "many eucharists" in John Chrysostom.[36]

Tertullian builds on this in a significant passage in which he defines the prayer (called *hostia spiritalis*) that Christians offer as a sacrifice:

"We are the true worshippers and the priests who, praying in the Spirit, in the Spirit offer a sacrifice (*hostiam*) of prayer to God, which of course he demanded, which he foresaw for himself. We are bound to offer at God's altar this prayer, dedicated with all the heart, nourished by faith, protected by truth, sincere in its single-heartedness, pure in its chastity, crowned by love and accompanied by good actions along with psalms and hymns—and it gains everything for us from God."[37]

Like Irenaeus, but in a different way, Tertullian is propounding the need for celebrating the eucharist, which it is very hard to exclude from the meaning of such a passage. In other places, Tertullian not only uses *oblatio* (equivalent to προσφορά) but also *sacrificium* (equivalent to θυσία) of the eucharist.[38] Once more, he is affirming the reality of the eucharist, and of the whole Christian life, including all worship, but he repeatedly emphasizes the single offering of Christ. The interchangeability of *oblatio* and *sacrificium* perhaps reflects Christian usage at the time in referring to the eucharist. Again, the verb *offerre* is a liturgical shorthand term for "celebrate." But there is no evidence yet for describing the offering as having a separate reality outside the Christian; rather we see an increasing tendency to combine our three criteria of story, gift, and response.[39]

Paul's living sacrifice of Romans 12:1 is never far from the surface as early Christian theologians grapple with the problems of making real to people what the Christian experience is, and making the link between worship and life. The tightrope that liturgy has to walk is not a problem peculiar to the twentieth century.

We have seen the variety of ways in which sacrifice is treated in the New Testament and among some of the early Christian writers. With the exception of the *Didache*, however, we have not so far dealt with a document that contains a specifically liturgical formulation. Such are, indeed, the *Apostolic Tradition* of Hippolytus, the anaphora of the Apostles Addai and Mari, and the *Strasbourg* papyrus of the anaphora Greek Mark. As we discuss these texts, we shall refer to other liturgical prayers and parallel quotations, including the significant (Coptic) anaphora of Basil of Caesarea, since all these texts could be dated to before the Council of Nicaea.

The eucharistic prayer in the *Apostolic Tradition*[40] of Hippolytus has probably exerted more influence on the twentieth century in its attempts to recover primitive simplicity than it exerted on the ancient world. Long the subject of dispute, and (of course) only a sample prayer for use at an episcopal ordination, its sequence of ideas recalls the structure of the Jewish meal blessing, except that praise for creation has disappeared, and we are left with thanksgiving for redemption and supplication for the eucharist. After the opening dialogue, the president gives thanks for the life and ministry of Christ, which not only includes reference to the Last Supper, but has a brief institution narrative. The key passage follows:

"Remembering therefore his death and resurrection, we offer you the bread and the cup, giving you thanks because you have held us worthy to stand before you and minister to you. And we ask that you would send your holy Spirit upon the offering of your holy Church; that, gathering them into one, you would grant to all who partake of the holy things (to partake) for the fullness of the holy Spirit for the strengthening of faith in truth; and that we may praise and glorify you through your child Jesus Christ, through whom be glory and honour to you, with the Holy Spirit, both now and to the ages of ages. Amen."[41]

Dix's attempt to get rid of the epiclesis is notorious, and we may rest assured that Botte is correct in asserting its authenticity.[42] What is in-

creasingly debated, however, is the relationship between the anamnesis and the institution narrative, a question to which we shall be re-
turning in a wider context. It seems that the anamnesis and the
narrative are insertions into the prayer, since the very nature of the
beginning of the anamnesis ("remembering therefore") reads rather
like a car changing gears. It is conceivable that the older tradition
moved straight from the reference to the death of Christ in the
thanksgiving, to supplication for the eucharist in the epiclesis.[43] Nonetheless, the text as it has been reconstructed by Geoffrey Cuming (and
others) implies a definite logic: "remembering . . . , we offer . . .
and we ask." In other words, the offering of the gifts is associated
closely with the attitude of remembering (giving thanks), and equally
closely associated with praying for the blessing of the Spirit on the
offering of the Church. The original Greek (lost) probably read
προσφέρομεν for "we offer" and προσφορά for "offering." What
is the meaning behind such an archetypal anamnesis and epiclesis?
The anamnesis is bare by comparison with later formulae, which
increasingly include other "saving acts." The epiclesis lacks what
amounts to the later West Syrian reference to consecration and communion, and, of course, the intercessions are not yet present. What is
clear is that such an anamnesis-epiclesis "unit" implies that, for Hippolytus, mildly sacrificial language was used traditionally of the presentation of the gifts and the eucharist as a whole. It is hard to separate too clearly the different sacrificial images of early Christians, and
much more difficult to do so in liturgical prayer, which has to resound
and bear repetition. Yet I would identify "we offer" as meaning the
gifts of the supper, and the "offering" of the Church as referring to
the whole eucharist, in the celebration, in the act of communion, and
in the life of faith as it continues after the eucharist is over.[44] In other
words, so far from carrying some of the distinctly heavier connotations of the later West, this little prayer paints a picture more imprecise and more subtle. That offering is not separate from the people in
their worship, and even though the Greek is probably προσφορά and
the *Didache* uses θυσία, I would argue for an allusion to the sacrifice
of praise, as well as the eucharistic celebration.[45] Furthermore, such
an imprecise interpretation would be supported if the institution narrative–anamnesis (with its more precise reference to the offering of
gifts) were a recent addition to the prayer, amounting to a second
stratum. Elsewhere in Hippolytus, "offering gifts" continues as the acceptable jargon for celebrating the eucharist, and here we may have
an early example of the action in liturgy (placing the gifts on the table) producing a later liturgical formula to express it.[46] The Syriac *Tes-*

tamentum Domini inserts "lāk mqarbūnan hānā qūbāltaybūtā" in the anamnesis ("we offer you this thanksgiving"),[47] which emphasizes further the connection between the anamnesis and the thanksgiving itself, as well as brings out the notion of sacrifice of praise that we saw in Irenaeus and in other earlier writers and biblical quotations. Such an insertion in the tradition may be there to bring out a nuance in the Syriac language; of course, it may be no insertion at all, but an original feature. We shall see in the next chapter how the Syrian Jacobite and Maronite anaphoras elaborate the anamnesis to considerable lengths, an extension of ideas of which the extra formula of the *Testamentum Domini* may be a hint.[48]

The *Apostolic Tradition*, therefore, if looked at from the point of view of what little we know of its background, instead of with hindsight gained from much later formulations, takes on a simplicity and a beauty all its own, a point made many years ago by Walter Howard Frere.[49] Much could be made of the fact that *offerimus* is one of the few main-clause verbs in the entire prayer[50] (the others being "we give thanks" and "we ask"), but the relationships between main clause, subordinate clause, and participle to main verb in the Latin and Greek of the time render that kind of treatment somewhat overprecise.[51] We are dealing with prayer, not doctrinal formulation, in which words and phrases (and other linguistic conventions) flow and mingle with each other, as witness the reinforcement of the notion of thanksgiving in the *Testamentum Domini*. The opening dialogue is a liturgical convention pointing to the importance of the eucharistic prayer, which properly begins with thanksgiving, continues with the offering of gifts from the created order, and prays for the blessing of the Spirit on the eucharistic worship and the unity and whole life of faith of the congregation. None of the problems caused by the later split epiclesis, the overemphasis on the institution narrative, and mechanical notions of consecration are encountered here.

When we turn to the anaphora of Addai and Mari,[52] we come again across dating and textual problems. Most scholars agree that the *Apostolic Tradition* was put together in Rome, about 215; as far as the eucharist is concerned, its influence is more eastern than western. Addai and Mari, however, does not seem to have had any influence outside its own restricted milieu. Some years ago, Ratcliff suggested that the *cushapas* (private prayers of the priest) represented a tradition later than the original, and the researches of Macomber and Spinks have helped greatly to make possible a reconstructed early text,[53] with the important implications that accrue to the history of liturgy and eucharistic theology when such a development takes place. Whereas in

Hippolytus there is a sequence of ideas (however simple), the sacrificial notions in Addai and Mari are less sequential, but rather unitive (as I have argued elsewhere).[54]

The dialogue opens with the peace, then the grace, followed by the clause peculiar to this prayer, "the offering is offered to God the Lord of all," which we find later on quoted in Ephrem the Syrian.[55] After the sequence of the first and second *Gehanta*, each followed by the first and second *Qanona* (although Spinks warns against using these later terms too tightly), the third *Gehanta* prayer follows:

"You, O Lord, in your unspeakable mercies make a gracious remembrance for all the upright and just fathers who have been pleasing before you in the commemoration of the body and blood of your Christ which we offer to you upon the pure and holy altar as you have taught us. And grant us your tranquility and your peace all the days of the world."[56]

It continues with prayer for the mission of the Church, that they may follow in the steps of the holy ones before them, and thereafter:

"And we also, O Lord, your lowly, weak and miserable servants who are gathered together and stand before you at this time have received by tradition of the example which is from you rejoicing and glorifying, and magnifying, and commemorating, and praising, and performing this great and dread mystery of the passion and death and resurrection of our Lord Jesus. May he come, O Lord, your Holy Spirit and rest upon this oblation of your servants, and bless and hallow it, that it may be to us, O Lord, for the pardon of debts and the forgiveness of sins, and a great hope of resurrection from the dead and a new life in the kingdom of heaven with all who have been pleasing before you. And for all your marvellous economy. . . . (Doxology) As we offer up. Amen."[57]

Here is a prayer of a shape different from that represented by Hippolytus, with its identifiable structure of thanksgiving and supplication, suitably clothed in West Syrian institution narrative, anamnesis, and epiclesis. Feeling after an older and more Semitic style of Christian euchology, and uninfluenced by Greek-speaking formulae, Addai and Mari begins with an important statement (lacking in any other traditions) of the unitive sacrificial nature of the eucharist. Its cousin, the Maronite anaphora of Peter the Apostle (often referred to as the *sharar*, from the opening word of a preanaphoral prayer) has what some scholars regard as an older formula, "we offer that pure and holy offering to you."[58] Whether or not this is the case, the fact of mentioning the sacrificial character of the eucharist alongside thanksgiving in the dialogue is a novel idea, and, we may assume, deliberately included in order to juxtapose offering with thanksgiving, as balancing two complementary aspects of the eucharist.

After the thanksgiving in the first and second *Gehantas* and *Qanonas* (we leave aside that vexing question of the authenticity of the Sanctus[59]), the offering image appears for the first time in the context of the shift from thanksgiving to supplication, but with another reference to the whole eucharist, "in the commemoration . . . which we offer . . . upon the . . . altar as you have taught us." Here, again, we have the tension between thanksgiving-commemoration and oblation, subtly held together in an ancient prayer formula, which leads into prayer for the life of the Church. This latter theme becomes the intercessions in *sharar* and in the anaphoras of Theodore and Nestorius, as we shall see later.[60] It is probable that by "altar" is meant the eucharistic table, but it is still possible to see some of the resonances of altar that Rowan Williams drew attention to in Ignatius.[61] Could it be yet another allusion to the whole eucharist, rather than a precise reference to the offertory of the late western Middle Ages? This appears to be supported by the next paragraph, which we quoted, "performing this great and dread mystery of the passion and death and resurrection of our Lord Jesus," which corresponds with the anamnesis of Hippolytus' *Apostolic Tradition.*

At the epiclesis, this notion reappears, in a formula that enriches Hippolytus'. The text is longer ("and bless and hallow it"[62]) with a correspondingly longer series of themes in the prayer; for unlike Hippolytus, which prays for unity and strengthening in the faith, Addai and Mari prays for the forgiveness of sins (cf. *Didache* 14, with the warning about the "pure offering") and the hope of resurrection at the end of time. (The eschatological themes of this tradition are also rich.) The prayer ends on a note of "offering up" praise at the end of the final doxology.

Addai and Mari is a more pastoral prayer than the *Apostolic Tradition.* If recent scholarship is right, what we have seen may well go right back to the third century, if not earlier still. Such dating is not universally accepted, however, and some still argue for an institution narrative, perhaps as one of the items hypothetically removed during the abbreviation of the rite in the seventh century.[63] But the institution narrative's place in the prayer does not affect the way in which the sacrificial character of the eucharist is expressed, which concentrates on two of our three criteria, the offering of thanksgiving and praise, and the benefits of communion in the living sacrifice of the congregation. Our third criterion (the offering of gifts) is weakest here, but perhaps in the Semitic background of the prayer it was not so necessary to express in the body of the anaphora an emphasis on the offering of the gifts. One aspect of *Addai and Mari* consistently under-played is that, although comparative liturgists regard it as a single "anaphora," it is, nonetheless, made up of separate interlocking units, rather like an elaborate piece of furniture. Whereas Hippolytus gives us a single prayer, made up of various related ingredients, Addai and Mari amounts to a more complex arrangement. One senses again and again that this prayer takes us back to a pristine form of Christian euchology, at once wholesome and unitive, when compared with many later texts. It will probably continue to tantalize liturgists, but its unique simplicity over consecration and eucharistic offering, together with its pastoral character, give it a human face, for all the differences of theology and culture that obtain between our own age and the age that produced it. Bryan Spinks[64] has made a study of the offering words in this prayer and suggests that since "the offering" in Syriac is *qurbana*, and this is the word used to translate $\delta\tilde{\omega}\rho o\nu$ in the Old Syriac version of the gospels (at Matthew 5:23f.), we may not only have (more?) evidence for supposing that the passage was early on given a eucharistic meaning, but we also can identify how the Syriac sacrifi-cial terminology in Addai and Mari came from the Hebrew through the Greek. We shall see later on how this prayer's relatives (or deriva-tives) develop some of these ideas.

Of our three archetypes, the Mark tradition represented by the *Strasbourg* papyrus is the most speculative, because not all scholars agree with the hypothesis that it is a complete anaphora in itself. The fragment opens with a blessing for creation, including the creation of man; the text is full of lacunae, and we here reproduce the version given by Jasper and Cuming:

". . . to bless (you) . . . (night) and day . . . (you who made) heaven (and) all that is in (it, the earth and what is on earth) seas and rivers and (all that is) in (them); (you) who made man (according to your) own image and likeness. You made everything through your wisdom, your true light, your Son, our Lord and Saviour Jesus Christ, through whom with him and the Holy Spirit we give thanks to you and of-fer this reasonable sacrifice and bloodless service, which all the na-tions offer you, from sunrise to sunset, from south to north, (for) your name is great among all nations, and in every place incense is offered to your holy name and a pure sacrifice. Over this sacrifice and offer-

ing we pray and beseech you, remember your holy and only catholic Church, all your peoples and all your flocks. . . ."
(The intercessions follow, but with a lacuna; and end with a commemoration of the departed).[65]

The later anaphora concludes these intercessions with the Sanctus and continues the second section of the prayer with a consecratory epiclesis, institution narrative, anamnesis (with the verb in the past tense), epiclesis, and doxology.[66]

An increasing number of scholars agree that the fragment is no fragment, but a complete anaphora, reproducing the tripartite structure of creation, redemption, and supplication.[67]

The offering section is single, complex, and involving a full quotation of Malachi 1:11. But there are new ideas. The first is that the sacrifice is "reasonable" (cf. Rom 12:1—a reasonable offering is one that is not an animal), and the service is "bloodless," thus using paradoxical language. The word for bloodless is $\dot{α}ναίμακτος$, which is not used for sacrifices in the Bible. In the *Testament of Levi* (6:3), it refers to the worship of the angels, and thus represents a further development of the idea of heavenly pure sacrificial worship.[68] But Athenagoras, Origen, and Methodius of Olympus[69] use this term to refer to Christian worship, and it is possible that in a number of these cases, the worship is eucharistic, or, at any rate, does not exclude the eucharist. One of the textual suggestions made by Geoffrey Cuming is to separate "pure" and "offering," thus reading "over this sacrifice and offering. . . ."[70] This makes better sense of the sequence of ideas, leading from thanksgiving to offering, and from offering to intercession.

If the fragment is a complete anaphora, how is eucharistic offering to be understood? We have not encountered the full quotation from Malachi 1:11 before in an anaphora, nor the reference to bloodless offering, nor yet the occurrence of intercessions, although we have seen the beginning of these in Addai and Mari, and we shall see them in a fuller form in the early Alexandrian recension of Basil of Caesarea. It seems that we cannot be precise here, either, and that the eucharistic offering is deliberately expressed once and once only, and soon after the placing of the gifts on the altar. It is later on in Egypt, in Serapion, and in the full form of Mark, that the past-tense verb appears; and we have suggested that in Egypt, the placing of the gifts on the altar is expressed in the anaphora by the past-tense verb in the anamnesis.[71] Others have argued that the past tense refers back not to the placing of the gifts on the altar, but to this "moment of offering" near the beginning of the anaphora, as we have the text in *Strasbourg*.[72] I think that the position of offering in the fragment, so near to the start of the prayer, and leading into supplication, is a subtle interweaving of all three of our criteria, for it can be argued that it is both a sacrifice of praise (especially with the bloodless offering background in Jewish and early Christian literature), *and* a reference to the gifts (recently placed on the altar), *and* a living sacrifice, in that the intercessions follow immediately, thus expressing the concerns of the Christian community at worship.

This discussion rests in part, of course, on the assumption that the fragment is complete. Such a single expression of offering, nuanced as it is, gathers together the three ideas we have seen in different ways elsewhere in such a manner that there is no sequence of ideas here at all but a primitive simplicity. The full quotation from Malachi 1:11 may also be evidence for the later use of incense as a symbol of prayer rather than as a fumigant, and to this we shall return later.[73]

The anaphora of Basil of Caesarea has been studied in its various versions in recent years, and the appearance of the Doresse-Lanne edition of the Coptic fragment, with a retroversion into Greek, has made it possible to bring to light a number of significant issues regarding the origin and development of eucharistic prayers at a critical stage in the story.[74] While the Greek retroversion has been criticized at a number of points by Raes,[75] we nevertheless are left with what most scholars agree to have been an anaphora used by Basil in Egypt when he traveled there as a young man, leaving it behind for the use of Christians there. The text (= *Basil Alex*[1]) bears no trace of the kind of systematic theological overlay that the later Alexandrian and Byzantine versions display; these latter have been identified by Engberding and Capelle.[76] What is of great fascination is the interim character of the prayer, for it stands, as it seems, on the brink of the fourth-century theological developments, but also appears to incorporate earlier traditions within a framework resembling that of the anaphora contained in the *Apostolic Tradition* of Hippolytus and its derivatives.[77] Apart from an interesting handling of eucharistic offering, this prayer has two other (pre-fourth-century?) primitivisms. The first is that at the epiclesis, petition is made for the Spirit to sanctify the gifts "and make them holy of holies"; it is left to the later versions to make this eucharistic consecration more precise. The second is at the commemoration of the departed, where "it is a command of your only-begotten Son that we should share in the commemoration of your saints . . . ," so that God is asked "to remember . . . those of our fathers who have been well-pleasing. . . ." It is similarly left to the later versions to pray with triumphalism in relation to the saints, and with some humility for everyone else.[78] These two theological imprecisions are important for an understanding of the way in which both the theology of eucharistic presence and the theology of intercession and the departed are expressed in the liturgy.

Turning now to offering, we enter a world quite different from Addai and Mari and *Strasbourg*. Although the Coptic fragment of Basil lacks everything in the prayer up to the section before the institution narrative, we may surmise that there was no reference to eucharistic offering in the preface, since nothing appears of that kind in the later Alexandrian version, which is the version actually in use today among the Copts. At four significant stages there are expressions or suggestions of offering. The first is just before the institution narrative, where the eucharist is described as "this great mystery of godliness," which is reminiscent of Addai and Mari's use of "mystery," and which also occurs in a comparable section of that prayer. There does not seem to be any difficulty over this expression; it reappears in the later Alexandrian version, although the later Byzantine version develops it further.[79]

The other three stages begin from the anamnesis, which is worth quoting in full:

"We also, remembering his holy sufferings, and his resurrection from the dead, and his return to heaven, and his session at the right hand of the Father, and his glorious and fearful coming (again), have set forth before you your own from your own gifts, this bread and this cup.

And we, sinners and unworthy and wretched, pray you, our God, in adoration that in the good pleasure of your goodness your Holy Spirit may come upon us and upon these gifts that are set before you, and may sanctify them and make them holy of holies.

Make us worthy to partake of your holy things for sanctification of soul and body, that we may become one body and one spirit, and may have a portion with all the saints who have been well-pleasing to you from eternity.

Remember . . . (intercessions follow).

Remember, Lord, also the weather and the fruits of the earth.

Remember, Lord, those who offer these gifts to you, and those for whom they presented them; and grant them all a heavenly reward.

Since, Master, it is a command of your only begotten-Son (here the commemoration of the departed follows). . . ."[80]

28

At the anamnesis, the Coptic is, without doubt, past tense, which is rendered in Greek by Doresse-Lanne as προεθήκαμεν, which is aorist, so that the Jasper-Cuming text quoted above should, perhaps, be read as "we set forth."[81] Here we encounter for the first time the neutral verb, προτίθημι, instead of the stronger verb, προσφέρω, as in *Strasbourg*. But is the past tense original to the prayer? In other words, is Raes correct in asserting that the aorist verb in the Greek retroversion in an Egyptian "symptom," and that the original Greek had the more conventional present tense, which would read προσφέρομεν?[82] We would prefer to leave the aorist tense, although noting Raes's reservations, since the Coptic is the only original from which we can work. Moreover, it is not pedantic to see in that aorist a reference to the placing of the gifts on the altar, particularly as the anamnesis goes on to stress the creation character of the gifts, and in the epiclesis describes the gifts as "set before you," which could almost be translated colloquially as "lying right here."

The epiclesis is an equally subtle compilation because, although it lacks the imprecision of Hippolytus and also lacks the definition of the later versions of Basil, it prays for the Spirit on the communicants and on the gifts, as if in equal tension. In praying for the benefits of communion, it drifts on into intercession in order to express the intentions and concerns of the Christian community, local and universal. It is interesting to note that the last two petitions for the living refer to the fruits of the earth, and then for those who "offer these gifts," and also for "those for whom they presented them." The creation theme is obviously the strongest in this anaphora, and the verb variation is clearly deliberate, and reproduced in the later Alexandrian version (although not in the Byzantine, another interesting difference).[83] The bringing of the gifts is thus referred to no less than three times in this second part of the anaphora, but is interwoven with the memorial of Christ, the sanctification of the congregation, and the concerns of the congregation. One could say that the development of anaphoral intercession at this stage in Christian history, so far from resembling a manipulation of God, is an expression of the social awareness of the Church. Moreover, there are slight echoes of the exhortation of the *Didache* to keep the offering pure by the inclusion of penitential expressions, which are comparable to Addai and Mari. But these are only parallels, and much as they each include this important area of Christian spirituality, the dominant theme is that of gift sacrifice, into which memorial and living sacrifice are inserted.

We may, then, summarize our analysis of the three archetypes, with the addition of Basil.

Hippolytus's prayer probably dates from the beginning of the third century and was written in Rome, but may have eastern antecedents, and undoubtedly influenced subsequent eastern euchology more than western. The eucharistic prayer contained in it is one of praise and thanksgiving, with the offering of gifts in memory of Christ's saving acts, and with supplication for the blessing of the Spirit on the whole sacrifice of the Church, not one part or aspect of it.

Addai and Mari probably dates from the third or late second century, in East Syria and provides no sequence of ideas, but rather offers the commemoration of Christ, later referring to it as a mystery, and asks for the Spirit to come upon the offering of the Church, which is likewise imprecisely defined, although expressing prayer for forgiveness of sins and participation in the kingdom.

Strasbourg could be complete in itself. It could date from the third or second century, if not earlier, and emanate from Egypt. It provides only one sacrificial formula, at a critical juncture in the body of the prayer, which offers praise and worship primarily, but includes supplication for the life of the Church (and may also refer to the presentation of gifts).

Basil comes from Cappadocia, in all likelihood, and may stem from a tradition before the turn of the third century. It emphasizes the gift sacrifice, but with memorial and intercession as two subsidiary features; it also represents a development from the prayer of the Hippolytan type. Later prayers are noted for their emphasis on one aspect at the expense of others, as we shall later discover.

We have seen how sacrificial and offering nouns and verbs are expressed within what we may regard as the earliest Christian eucharistic prayers, which include not only the archetypes, and Basil, but also the *Didache*. We have also seen how carefully constructed are these prayers, and their concern to point to the reality of the eucharist, without letting it become mechanical. Before parting company with the ante-Nicene Church, it is worth discussing briefly the way in which some other uses of sacrificial and offering formulae appear within and just after the period. The *Didascalia Apostolorum* was written originally in Greek at the beginning of the third century and shows us more of the internal life of the Christian Church than anything else of the time. In chapter 9, the writer contrasts the sacrifices of the Law with the arrangements under the Christian Church, and in the passage betrays how the presence of the Old Testament in the life of the Church (as distinct from being part of the corporate memory of early Christians who were Jewish converts) continues to require clear definitions of how the old is superseded by the new, particularly in worship:

". . . instead of the former sacrifices, offer up now prayers, petitions and thanksgivings. Then there were firstfruits and tithes and special offerings and gifts, but today there are oblations which are offered through the bishops to the Lord God . . .

"And just as it was not lawful for a stranger, that is, for someone who was not a levite, to draw near to the altar or to offer anything without the high priest, so you too shall do nothing without the bishop."[84]

The contrasts are clear. The old sacrifices have gone and are replaced by the acts of worship of the Christian Church, which still have a sacrificial flavor, not in order to point to continuity, but discontinuity. "Prayers, petitions and thanksgivings" probably refer to different kinds of worship, not excluding eucharistic, although by no means excluding noneucharistic either, whereas "oblations which are offered" seem to mean the eucharist (in the way that we have seen earlier, as jargon for "celebrate the eucharist"). The warning in the *Didache* about reconciliation reappears in a developed form in chapter 11:

". . . forgive your neighbour so that you may be heard when you pray, and so that you can offer to the Lord an acceptable offering.

"For this reason, then, O bishops, in order that your offerings and your prayers may be acceptable, when you stand in the church to pray let the deacon say in a loud voice, 'Is there anyone who holds a grudge against his companion?' so that if there should turn out to be present any people who have a lawsuit or quarrel with one another, you can entreat and make peace between them."[85]

The eucharist appears still to be taken seriously as a corporate celebration, in which penitence and reconciliation are aspects of the sacrificial character of the feast. As Michael Vasey has remarked, "In what modern congregation would a deacon dare to call out, 'Is there anyone . . .?' "[86]

Richard Hanson is probably right in drawing attention to the focus on the pure offering that we find in Origen. A typical passage runs thus:

"But we give thanks to the Creator of the Universe and eat the loaves that are presented with thanksgiving and prayer over the gifts, so that by the prayer they become a certain holy body which sanctifies those who partake of it with a pure intention."[87]

31

Here is a description of the bipartite structure of the eucharistic prayer immediately following the presentation of the gifts, with thanksgiving and supplication, the latter expressing the meaning of the eucharistic consecration, for the sanctification of the communicants. Lest he appear to lean heavily on an automatic view of the consecration, we can take comfort in a corresponding passage from elsewhere in his writings:

"Therefore, you ought to offer to God a sacrifice of praise, of prayers, of pity, of purity, of righteousness, of holiness. To offer this aright you have need of clean garments, of vestments kept apart from the common clothing."[88]

Origen seems to bring together the offering of gifts, the offering of praise, and the offering of pure intentions in the life of the Church. Cyprian presents a strong view of offering that we have not met elsewhere.

"For if Christ Jesus our Lord and God is himself the high priest of God the Father and first offered himself as a sacrifice to the Father and ordered that this should be done in commemoration of him, then of course that priest functions rightly in the place of Christ who imitates what Christ did and offers in the Church the full and true sacrifice, if he so begins to offer according to what he sees Christ himself to have offered."[89]

Hanson sees here the beginnings of a doctrine that actually "offers Christ," a tendency he finds regrettable. But perhaps such an interpretation is too literal and does not take into account the subtleties of Cyprian's mind. John Laurance[90] has suggested recently an interpretation of the passage, and others like it, that insists that the eucharist does not reoffer Christ: Laurance regards the use of the word *offerre* as shorthand for "preside at the eucharist," with celebrant identifying himself with Christ in order to make the eucharist real, both for himself and for the communicants. To put Laurance's view in terms of the stage, the spotlight only falls on the priest in order to dramatize the actions of Christ and bring the congregation into them. But whatever interpretation we give to Cyprian, the idea of offering Christ does not occur in the liturgies of antiquity, which again and again stress the memorial aspect of the eucharist in different ways.

The term *anamnesis* we encounter both in the New Testament and in Justin Martyr;[91] the liturgies of the Greek language usually include the command to repeat, followed by the participle, "remembering." The use of the term among early Christian writers is a varied one, and there is an important passage in Methodius of Olympus in which the paschal eucharist, including the baptism, is both the "memorial" (ἀναμνῆσις) and the "representation" (ἀνακεφαλαίωσις) of the passion of Christ.[92] What seems to be in the writer's mind is a desire to define memorial as a dynamic concept and as the work of Christ himself. Perhaps this is why the anamnesis section of the Greek eucharistic prayers invariably follows the pattern of "remembering . . . , we offer . . . , and we pray that. . . ."

Finally, we need to look at two authors who devote some time to the consideration of sacrifice. Eusebius of Caesarea, an influential theologian of his time, deals creatively with the difference between the old and the new covenants.

". . . therefore we both sacrifice and burn incense: on the one hand we celebrate the memorial of the great sacrifice according to the mysteries handed down to us by him, and we proffer thanksgiving for our salvation through pious hymns and prayers to God; on the other hand we dedicate ourselves to him alone and to his high-priestly word, devoted in body and soul."[93]

Gift sacrifice does not take a high profile here; rather the writer concentrates on memorial as dynamic, and on the living sacrifice of the Christian in response to the work of Christ. He cleverly uses "sacrifice" and "incense-burning" as contrasts, the former being a human action, with its risks of impurity, and the latter being the pure action, in the heavenly sanctuary. This is the way in which he stresses both divine act and human response, and he is doing this not by restating a tradition but by wrestling with a problem. This is how the best theology develops.

Ephrem the Syrian, however, takes us near to the point at which the eucharist "offers the offerer," to use the words of Rowan Williams.[94] In a lengthy sermon, Ephrem likens the presentation of Christ in the Temple to the action of the priest in the eucharist.

"But Simeon the priest when he had received Christ in his arms so that he might present (offer) him to God, understood when he beheld him that he was not offering Christ but was himself being offered. For the Son is not to be offered to his Father by a servant; rather the servant is offered to his Lord by the Son."[95]

The passage quoted by Williams reveals the complexity (and the subtlety) of a mind at work in order to make the simple point that the priest offers Christ only in the sense of offering a memorial, so that the action of the Church is, in fact, the action of Christ himself. Perhaps Williams makes rather more of the passage than is warranted, for when we are dealing with sermons, we are dealing with material that was probably used on very few occasions, even though it may represent the thought of a mature mind. The difference between sermons and liturgy is that the latter somehow embodies what the whole Church believes, whereas the former are ephemeral, however profound they may be considered to be, even to the point of expressing theology in a better and fresher fashion than the liturgies themselves.

We have traveled through the Bible, the early Christian writers, and what little we know of the Christian eucharistic liturgies before the Council of Nicaea. It has proved to be a varied scene, with Greek, Semitic, and Latin all working in slightly differing ways to grapple with and pray about the work of Christ and the Church in the eucharist. Our three criteria appear again and again, sometimes with one more emphatic than the others, sometimes with all three held together in a creative tension. What is strikingly clear is that the writers who are quoted are all faced with the task of making the eucharist real to those Christians of that highly productive and theologically fertile and varied era. The actual prayers that we have looked at all have their textual problems, as well as their problems of origin. But being prayers, rather than treatises, they paint varied portraits of the Christian eucharist that hold in tension the offering of thanksgiving for the mighty acts of God in Christ, the offering of gifts of bread and wine as the heavenly food, and the offering of the living sacrifice of a missionary and pilgrim Church. The Jewish Temple tradition and the late Jewish spiritualizing of sacrifice, together with pagan sacrifices among surrounding peoples, these three main influences presented an important background and context in which to fashion a theology and spirituality of worship and living in which the eucharist served as a prime focus, built on the foundations of daily prayer and service. But all this developed because the word "sacrifice," and others associated with it, were common coin in the ancient world, and were applied by Christians both to the work of Christ and to *all* kinds of worship and witness.[96]

CONCLUSIONS

From the foregoing discussion, it would seem that all we can say about eucharistic offering in the early liturgy is that it was imprecisely expressed but understood to be an important metaphor in eucharistic spirituality. But on the basis of the available evidence, we can make some more definite conclusions than this.

1. Despite the questions surrounding the *Didache*, the fact remains that the word θυσία (sacrifice) was added as a way of describing the *whole* action of the eucharist, although specifically sacrificial terminology does not appear in the prayers themselves in a way comparable to the later liturgies.

2. Jewish influence is apparent throughout the early period in the twofold structure of the eucharistic prayer as thanksgiving (story) and supplication (response). These do not exactly correlate, but they prove useful in identifying the nuances of sacrifice in that prayer, in which thanks are offered and the living sacrifice of the church is made, asking for God's blessing upon its eucharist and life of service. Thus the *birkat-ha-mazon* influences the *Didache*, as well as the three archetypes (and *Basil Alex*[1]); late Jewish spirituality is obvious through the influence of the *Testament of Levi* on *Strasbourg*.

3. Paradoxical language is noticeable when speaking of Christian sacrifice. The Didachist warns that the sacrifice must be pure, and *Strasbourg* uses such terms as "reasonable sacrifice and bloodless service." We are into the new covenant, with its different demands and theology.

4. Three archetypes lay the ground for later differences both in the structure of the anaphora and in the way in which sacrifice is treated:

Addai and Mari, with its overtly Semitic structure, has story and response, but does not bring out gift. As we shall see, later East Syrian anaphoras adopt gift in a muted form; later Syriac anaphoras of the Jacobite and Maronite traditions tend to avoid gift at the anamnesis, preferring to link the offering with intercession. This could well be a primitive Syriac resistance to a Greek development.

Strasbourg is similarly Semitic in its structure, stressing story and response; perhaps it included gift only in the later tradition (if the anaphora developed by accumulation, as modern scholars suggest), as witness the past tense in the anamnesis, which we shall see in the next chapter.

Hippolytus is the only one to include all three of our criteria, story, response, as well as gift. It is possible that gift was only a recent addition, and that it was included with the institution narrative–anamnesis in order to link this new "unit" with the epiclesis; "we offer," therefore, for the consecration of the *whole* eucharistic action, which is expressed by the primitive form of epiclesis.

5. These archetypes give us three different regions that correspond approximately to the different areas of Christian initiation recently suggested by Aidan Kavanagh: East Syria (Syriac), West Syria (Greek),

and Rome (whose Canon has similarities of a structural kind with *Strasbourg*/Mark); but the anomalous character of Hippolytus still poses questions about the real origin of the anaphora in the *Apostolic Tradition*. (*Basil Alex*[1] is more reliably Greek in its structure and themes.)

6. The transition of the epiclesis from the kind that we find in Hippolytus to the more developed later forms (e.g., *Basil Alex*[1]) results in a closer definition of the eucharistic action, so that it refers both to the consecration of the gifts and to the sanctification of the congregation (and intercession). This transition is a significant one, because it widens and defines the meaning of "the oblation of the Church"; gift and response are thus sharpened in the way they are expressed in the liturgy. (A similar development is discernible in the Syriac anaphoras, as we shall see in the next chapter, but gift remains less pronounced.)

7. Theologians of the first four centuries were used to describing the eucharist in sacrificial terms, from an early stage. I would suggest a stage contemporary with the New Testament, if the *Didache* and Ignatius are to be taken seriously. But while there are developments in the way in which sacrifice is discussed and understood in relation to the eucharist, what they produce is more in the way of variation on a theme rather than something very new. For example, Irenaeus concentrates on "first-fruits," but he does this as if it were assumed that the eucharist *is* sacrificial. Indeed, his preoccupation with first fruits may well be the result (or the cause) of the inclusion of gift explicitly in the eucharistic prayer; this would explain, perhaps, why the anaphora of Hippolytus (who was influenced by Irenaeus in other respects) is the first to be explicit on this point.

8. Liturgical formulae are remarkably conservative. Even if the past tense in the Greek retroversion of *Basil Alex*[1] is wrong, and the "original" from Cappadocia had a present tense,[97] it still shows that an important verb in the whole anaphora had to be Egyptianized. This suggests that, had it been left in present tense, it would have been deemed unsatisfactory and incongruous. In other words, the offering verb *is* important to the anaphoral tradition. Similarly, when John Chrysostom uses the expression "we offer" of the eucharist (as we shall see in the next chapter), he is using a well-tried liturgical expression that his hearers would have understood.

9. It is significant that of the three criteria, the one that is to prove controversial in later centuries *gift* is probably the last to find itself *explicit* in the eucharistic prayer, and that it properly belongs between story and response:

"we thank you for the story";

"we bring these gifts";

"we pray for your blessing on our eucharist."

Why was it added? Jewish communion sacrifices and an interest in typology could be one reason, but I suspect that it was a Greek development, not a Syriac one (as the liturgical texts show), which resulted from the Church encountering pagan ritual sacrifices and providing a Christian answer.

10. It is equally significant that the archetypes (and *Basil Alex*[1]) betray a more definite reflection on eucharistic sacrifice than on eucharistic presence.[98] (The *Didache* itself is imprecise on both, but it at least describes the whole eucharistic action as a sacrifice.) This suggests that early eucharistic liturgy began with story and response as aspects of the eucharistic spiritual sacrifice, but left formulations on eucharistic presence until much later. Eucharistic presence appears to arrive in more precise terms with the fourth century, as we shall see in the next chapter, with later versions of Basil, among others, and it is centered around the epiclesis. Eucharistic sacrifice in the liturgy is therefore formulated much earlier than eucharistic presence, and has *moral* aspects to it from the beginning.

11. Nonetheless, the expression to "offer gifts" is a recognized way of describing the celebration of the eucharist as early as the time of Clement of Rome.[99] The origin of this expression, however, appears to be derived not from the eucharistic prayer but from Jewish (and possibly pagan) sacrifice, where the devout approaches the altar bringing gifts (cf. Ps 96:8, as well as many other examples). Here is one of the first instances in Christian liturgical terminology of the preliminary doing duty for the entire action, but it is not an offertory procession.

12. If these conclusions are borne out by the evidence, then they have important implications for our understanding of the eucharist today, not least at the level of ecumenical dialogue.

Chapter Three

Flowering: The East

In his work, *A History of the Doctrine of the Holy Eucharist*, Darwell Stone wrote of the fourth century: "As in the earlier period, this constant use of sacrificial language in reference to the Eucharist is unaccompanied by any explicit and detailed explanation of the way in which the Eucharist is a sacrifice."[1] So far so good. But it will have become clear that, although these early liturgies enjoy a certain imprecision over sacrifice, they do reinterpret some aspects of it. Sacrifices in the first three centuries and after were a pagan reality, and probably alive in the memory of those converted to Christianity. In the last chapter, we discussed the three archetypes, and suggested the way in which they have evolved. In the following pages, we shall see how the Hippolytan-Basil pattern, on the one hand, and an adapted form of Addai and Mari, on the other hand, eventually dominate the scene. One of the problems, of course, is how to handle the eastern anaphoras. For our purposes, which are to do justice to theological and literary variety as well as to historical development, we shall deal with these prayers mainly by language divisions. Through our survey, Darwell Stone's "explicit and detailed explanation" may perhaps be seen in a different light; the importance of the Egyptian, Syriac, and Armenian insights will come to the fore, complementing the classical forms of the Greek West-Syrian–Byzantine anaphoras.

GREEK WEST SYRIAN
The anaphora used by the Coptic Church bearing the name of Basil (often referred to by liturgists as *Basil Alex*[2], in order to distinguish it from the earlier Coptic text *Basil Alex*[1]) has been studied by Engberding[2] and others, and it is commonly agreed to have been the work of Basil himself, who updated an earlier prayer form with the theological developments of the fourth century. These developments are trinitarian and christological, so that, for example, *Basil Alex*[2] adds a paragraph after "holy of holies" in the epiclesis in order to specify in what sense the bread and wine are "holy of holies." The two additions refer to the consecration of the eucharistic elements, the first of which

runs, "and make this bread become the holy body of our Lord and God and Saviour Jesus Christ himself, for the forgiveness of sins and eternal life for those who partake of it." But there are remarkably few alterations from *Basil Alex*[1] over eucharistic offering. The reference to the eucharist as a mystery remains before the institution narrative. In the anamnesis-epiclesis-intercessions the changes are small. First, the anamnesis reads the *present* tense, προσφέρομεν, in line with the anaphora in Hippolytus and the other Greek Syrian-Byzantine prayers; if Raes is correct (and Doresse-Lanne are wrong), then this is the authentic reading for *Basil Alex*[1] as well and the aorist there is an "Egyptian symptom."[3] But "we offer your own from your own, in all and through all"[4] is an awkward clause, poetic in style, which causes problems in translation, even though it stresses the themes of creation and the ensuing intercession. Finally, in the intercessions, which are amplified considerably in their scope, the petition for the offerers is slightly expanded (new words are italicized): "Remember, Lord, those who present these *worthy* gifts, and those for whom, *and through whom, and on account of whom* they presented them." There is nothing theologically drastic going on by the insertion of these words, but they emphasize the connection between those who present the gifts (NB present tense) and their prayers and aspirations. It could well be that Basil himself wanted to reinterpret the eucharistic sacrifice along the lines we have already seen, by associating the people with their own gifts, by their own "living sacrifice." There is no sense of seeming to try to manipulate God in a crude fashion; quite the reverse, for the intercessions fill out in *Basil Alex*[2] with many different petitions, for all kinds of human need.

When we come to the later version of this anaphora, which may include further additions by Basil himself (sometimes called Byzantine Basil–Basil Byz), there is yet more evidence of an increasing precision over the sacrificial understanding of the eucharist.[5] The main novel feature comes early on in the preface: "It is fitting and right . . . to hymn you, to bless you . . . the only existing God, and *to offer to you with a contrite heart and a humble spirit this our reasonable service.*" Scholars have noted the resemblance between this new formula and that contained in the anaphora of Greek Mark, which we have already seen in the Strasbourg papyrus.[6] Which of the two traditions is original? It is possible that Basil (or the author) knew the Mark tradition and wanted to include a general reference to the eucharist that would combine the rigors of Psalm 51:17 with the challenge of Romans 12:1. Before the Sanctus, the sacrifice of praise is further strengthened by an interesting combination of words: ". . . the whole reasonable and intelligent creation *does you service and renders you unceasing praise.*" In the other parts of the anaphora (before the institution narrative, and during the anamnesis-epiclesis-intercessions), there are also small differences. The "great mystery of godliness" is recast in order to round off a lengthy account of the life of Christ: "And he left us memorials of his saving passion, these things *which we have set forth* according to his commandments." Here is a neat way of leading into the narrative and the anamnesis that demonstrates the subtlety of the anaphora's internal unity. This is an important little addition because the anaphora was opened with a reference to the sacrifice of praise, and we now have a reminder that the eucharist is also a gift offering. After the institution narrative, the anamnesis contains a small divergence between the tenth-century text represented by Grottaferrata G b VII, and the later manuscripts. In the former manuscript, the offering verb is a present participle ("offering") whereas the later forms give the present indicative ("we offer"). If the participle is authentic, and there is no reason to suggest it is not, the main verb comes in the people's acclamation, "we hymn you. . . ." It is unlikely that any theological importance can be attached to this participle,[7] although it is of undoubted literary significance, particularly as in this later version of Basil the epiclesis also has to begin, "Therefore, Master," so that the unity of the anamnesis-epiclesis is less clear. Moreover, the epiclesis begins with a confession of unworthiness:

"Therefore, Master all-holy, we also, your sinful and unworthy servants, who have been held worthy to minister at your holy altar, not for our righteousness . . . with confidence approach your altar. And *having set forth the likenesses* of the holy body and blood of your Christ, we pray and beseech you, O holy of holies, in the good pleasure of your bounty, that your all-holy Spirit may come upon us and upon these gifts set forth. . . ."

The epiclesis is an adaptation of *Basil Alex*[2], keeping the petitions for consecration, but redirecting the holy of holies to God rather than to the gifts (as in the two earlier Alexandrian versions). But this is all in the context of the eucharistic gifts, which are "set forth" ($\pi\rho o\theta\acute{\epsilon}\nu\tau\epsilon s$—aorist participle passive, and therefore probably not "having," which implies perfect tense), as "antitypes," a word much used of the eucharistic elements. It is clear that "antitypes" replaces "gifts" in the earlier traditions, thus indicating a stronger terminology; they are "memorials" before the institution narrative, but "antitypes" before the epiclesis. I do not think there is a moment of consecration, but the two different words indicate the internal movement of the anaphora:

the narrative recounts *history*, and the epiclesis prays for the present *sacramental reality*.[8]

In the intercessions, the prayer for the fruits of the earth follows the prayer for the offerers, and although the gifts are not "worthy," the same verb is used, "those who *brought*" in each case. The later version of the manuscript adds an ethic dative ("for you"). The author, whether Basil or not, clearly wants to avoid strong verbs at this stage in the anaphora, but wants to maintain the spiritual unity between those who present the gifts with their prayers and intentions.

In the Basil anaphoras, therefore, we see a gradual move from simplicity to complexity, which includes eucharistic offering as well as the famous theological issues of the fourth century. The early Alexandrian version provides the basic foundation with its emphasis on gift offering. This is built upon and elaborated as the anaphora expands, for when an important prayer like an anaphora extends itself in scope, ideas, and length, various expressions have to be inserted to hold the prayer together.

Such, I think, was the intention behind the idea of inserting the offering of "our reasonable service" with "a contrite heart and humble spirit." To see this subtle development is a bit like viewing a series of buildings in the late Romanesque (*Basil Alex*[1]), early Gothic (*Basil Alex*[2]), and later Gothic (*Basil Byz*) styles. There is an obvious common purpose and basic design, but the second stage is the crucial move in the direction of using new design.

With the anaphora of John Chrysostom, however, we are faced with a much simpler scheme. In recent years, the theory that the (Syriac) anaphora of the Twelve Apostles[9] represents an early version of Chrysostom has gained increasing popularity from scholars, and we shall be looking at that hypothesis in relation to eucharistic offering later. The two main versions of Chrysostom in Greek (Barberini 336 and the one in current use) differ very little.[10] There are four sections to look at. The first is just before the Sanctus, where there is no directly sacrificial language, but an obvious general reference to the eucharist: "we thank you for this ministry; vouchsafe to receive from our hands." This probably corresponds to the "reasonable service" in *Basil Byz*. In the anamnesis, we come across a set of ideas very similar to *Basil Alex*[2] and *Basil Byz*, but there are significant differences as the epiclesis approaches:

"We therefore, remembering this saving commandment and all the things that were done for us: the cross, the tomb, the resurrection on the third day, the ascension into heaven, the session at the right hand, the second and glorious coming again; *offering you your own from your own, in all and through all,* (the people respond), we hymn you. . . . *We offer you also this reasonable and bloodless service,* and we beseech and pray and entreat you, send down your Holy Spirit on us and on *these gifts set forth;* and make this bread. . . ."

The offering verb in the anamnesis is in the participle form in the Barberini text (cf. *Basil Byz*), and there is again a reversion to the (older?) reading of the present indicative in the later Greek texts. But it will be seen that the epiclesis begins with the offering of the "reasonable and bloodless service," as in Strasbourg (but omitting "sacrifice"),[11] which is an expression found frequently of the eucharist as a whole in the fourth century, and which we shall meet in the anaphora of James. In the intercessions, this statement of offering is repeated twice at strategic points in the prayers, first at the beginning of the prayers for the departed, and then at the start of the commemoration of the living. In other words, the offering heads each kind of supplication, namely the epiclesis, the prayers for the departed, and the prayers for the living.[12] Whereas the reasonable and bloodless service in the later Egyptian tradition precedes the Sanctus (probably its original position), here in the anaphora of Chrysostom the bloodless offering comes in the second part of the whole prayer and in such a way as to appear more deliberate. Less subtle than Basil, it perhaps reproduces an earlier scheme with the sacrifice of praise as the starting point, but in the context of gift and intercession. If we work on the principle that words rather than shapes migrate easily from one tradition to another in the ancient world, what we have in Chrysostom is a logical extension of that early imprecision that we saw in the Strasbourg papyrus. But it is interesting to note that the noun is $\lambda\alpha\tau\rho\epsilon\iota\alpha$ ("service")—(cf. Rom 12:1 for both these words), whereas we shall come across $\theta\upsilon\sigma\iota\alpha$ ("sacrifice") in the anaphora contained in *Apostolic Constitutions VIII*, and the full expression, "bloodless *sacrifice*," in the anaphora of James. When faced with such a bevy of bloodlessness in Greek West Syria, it is surprising that Basil lacks any reference to it. We may conjecture either that he deliberately avoided it, because he was trying to work out a more developed sequence of ideas on offering within the anaphora, or that it was a later idea altogether.

The anaphora of James[13] is probably the result of a working together of the liturgies of Antioch and Jerusalem at the end of the fourth century. It comes in various versions, including a Greek text and two Syriac translations (both of which are shorter). The textual

42

variants over eucharistic offering are hardly noticeable, however, and not of such importance as they are in the anaphora of Basil. Once again, we are led straight to the anamnesis-epiclesis-intercessions in a series of ideas similar to Chrysostom. Here is a digest of the formulae:

"We therefore, remembering . . . *we offer you this awesome and blood-less sacrifice.* . . .

Have mercy on us, Lord, and send out upon us and upon *these holy gifts set before you* your holy Spirit. . . .

(send down, Master, your all-holy Spirit himself upon us and upon these holy gifts here set before you). . . .

We offer to you for your holy places also, which you glorified by the theophany of your Christ. . . .

(Remember, Lord, the priests who stand around us in this holy hour, before your holy altar, *for the offering of the holy and bloodless sacrifice* . . .)

Vouchsafe yet to remember, Lord, *those who have offered the offerings today on your holy altar*, and those for whom each one offered or has in mind, and those who are now read to you. . . .

The prayer is more prolix than Chrysostom. The portions that are in parentheses do not belong to the earliest stratum, which in our discussion include the repetition of the prayer for the descent of the Spirit (which is probably repeated because of the expanding length of the catalogue of the acts of the Spirit, e.g., at the Jordan)[14] as well as the prayer for the priests (which expresses the tendency to sacerdo-talize the eucharist). We are therefore left with the anamnesis, which describes the eucharist as an "awesome and bloodless sacrifice," an expression that may be intended to refer to the whole celebration rather than exclusively to the gifts themselves. This means that the bloodless sacrifice would have occurred only once in the earliest ver-sion of the prayer, at the beginning of the supplicatory part of the anaphora, where the anamnesis turns into epiclesis. Certain expres-sions (like "holy places") indicate proximity to Jerusalem. But those who offered the gifts appear as before, together with their intentions and prayers. This anaphora has been variously evaluated, and al-though it is long-winded in places, the deliberate use of "bloodless sacrifice" *in the anamnesis* is a striking way of describing the whole eucharistic celebration. The short Syriac version contains features that are more akin to the Syrian Jacobite anaphoras (an addition to the prayer for the offerers referring to those who wanted to be in church but who could not come, and a prayer for the receiving of the offering in heaven). The Armenian version has some characteristics of its own.[15]

The anaphora in *Apostolic Constitutions VIII*,[16] which was probably written about 375 in Syria by an Arian, reproduces a variant of the Chrysostom-James pattern, with nothing as sophisticated as Basil. Once again, we start at the anamnesis and work through epiclesis to intercessions:

"Remembering then his passion and death . . . we *offer you*, King and God, according to his commandment, *this bread and this cup*, giving you thanks through him that you have deemed us worthy to stand before you and to be your priests.
And we beseech you to look graciously upon *these gifts set before you*, O God who need nothing, and accept them in honour of your Christ; and to send down your Holy Spirit *upon this sacrifice*, the witness. . . .
And we entreat you also for *my worthless self who offer to you*, and for all the priesthood, for the deacons and all the clergy. . . .
And we *offer to you also for all* those who have been well-pleasing to you from everlasting. . . .
And we *offer to you for this people*, that you would make them a royal priesthood, a holy nation, to the praise of your Christ. . . .
And we *offer to you also for good weather* and an abundant harvest. . . ."

The author knew the *Apostolic Tradition* of Hippolytus' anaphora, or something very similar to it. We can see evidence for this in the "remembering . . . we offer you . . . this bread and this cup." We have not encountered this description of the eucharistic gifts so far. At the epiclesis the eucharist is described as a sacrifice ($\theta \upsilon \sigma \acute{\iota} \alpha$), again in line with Hippolytus. Just before the prayer for the celebrating priest, there is a prayer for the whole church and for the bishops, but the prayer for "my worthless self" reads awkwardly and could reflect the latest theological and liturgical fashion at the end of the fourth century. Such prayers occur later on but they are not to be found in the classical prayers of Basil, Chrysostom, and James. The fact that "we offer to you" comes three times afterwards does not yield a pattern, but more probably produces a literary variation within the series of intercessions.

This anaphora, attributed to Clement of Rome by its author, enjoyed great popularity in the eighteenth century.[17] Since then liturgiological fashions have shifted as the science of liturgy has developed and the liturgical needs of the churches have changed. The author may have been an adept composer of prayer formulae, but there is something second-hand and unoriginal about it; we can see the background of Hippolytus's sequence, the natural fourth-century expansion of the anamnesis-epiclesis, together with intercessions that include not only prayer for the whole church but also a self-conscious petition for the celebrant. *Apostolic Constitutions VIII* gives us nothing new.

What, then, of these fine Greek originals? Basil works out a complex scheme in order to maintain unity in an expanding prayer, whereas Chrysostom and James use other material within a simpler format. There is nothing theologically contradictory in these prayers, but there is a theological richness stemming from continued reflection on the meaning of the eucharist.

EAST SYRIAN

We have already discussed the anaphora of Addai and Mari. It is now time to look at the two other prayers of the Nestorian Church, the anaphoras of Nestorius and Theodore. There is nothing overtly Nestorian in their christology, even though these prayers were written after the separation of the East Syrian Church from what tradition terms Orthodoxy. Moreover, although both use material from Addai and Mari, the prayer of Nestorius also employs material from Basil and Chrysostom, whereas Theodore's prayer incorporates other material, including parallels from the catechetical homilies of Theodore himself. Both these prayers date from the fifth–sixth centuries. Among the anaphoras used of old by this church was probably the anaphora of the Twelve Apostles, which we shall look at later.

In Nestorius, there are no less than eleven instances of offering.[18] The dialogue expands on Addai and Mari as follows:

1. "The *living and reasonable oblation of our first-fruits,* and the unslain *sacrifice* of the Son of our race, our kinsman, *for all created things* to their utmost bound, *is offered* to God the Lord of all."

These themes are old friends now; although the East Syrian dialogues are different in style and length from everyone else's, because they involve the congregation they are resistant to change. This dialogue fuses together gift, memorial, and living sacrifice in a brilliant manner and is obviously meant to define the movement of the whole eucharistic prayer that follows. (The Urmiah version of the dialogue in Nestorius is even longer, and expands on all three themes.)

In the first *Gehanta* come the next three references:

2. "Do thou, my Lord, give us utterance in opening our mouths, that we may *offer to thee with a contrite heart and humble spirit, the spiritual fruit of our lips, even a reasonable* service."

Here is the corresponding material from *Basil Byz* in the preface, woven together with Ephesians 6:19, placing more emphasis on human praise of God as God's action in humanity (which is reminiscent of the emphases on the δῶρα as God's in the various versions of Basil).

3. "Now to Thee and to thy only begotten Son and to the Holy Spirit *we offer continual praise without ceasing,* because all things are thy work."

This echoes both the doxology in Addai and Mari, and also a section in Basil which has the verb ἀναπέμπω, which we have seen earlier, and which is sacrificial in its overtones.[19]

4. ". . . and we give thee thanks *for this service* and we beseech thee to accept it at our hands."

This echoes a corresponding section of Chrysostom, in which God is asked to "receive" (δέχομαι) the ministry of the eucharist. The notion of accepting becomes important in our subsequent coverage of Syriac anaphoras; in the passage quoted, the meaning seems to be the sacrifice of praise, defined as the eucharist.

The second *Gehanta* contains a further two:

5. (before the institution narrative)
"He left us the commemoration of our salvation, this mystery which we offer before thee."

Once again, the parallel with Addai and Mari is obvious, but the author is also using the reference to the "memorials" that have been presented on the altar from *Basil Byz*, also immediately before the narrative. Basil uses the perfect tense in the verb; whereas Nestorius uses the present tense. Spinks sees some significance in this, which is possible, but in view of our interpretation of the dialogue (as imposing a unity of action on the whole anaphora), this theory seems unlikely. Furthermore, Spinks links the offering of the mystery with the narrative itself, an opinion that has a Latin flavor and seems foreign to the spirit of these prayers.

6. The *Gehanta* concludes with a further offering of praise.

In the *Gehanta* after the narrative come three more offerings:

7. "We *offer unto thee this sacrifice living and holy and acceptable* and glorified and awful and exalted and spotless *for all creatures* and for the holy apostolic catholic church."

There are no exact parallels in the Greek anaphoras, except in the principle of beginning the intercessions with offering, as we have seen particularly in Chrysostom, where that offering begins the epiclesis and the prayers for the departed and the living. James uses the word "awful," which may also be a source. The word "sacrifice" (*debha*) is now being used (rather than "offering"—*qurbana*) by this stage of the anaphora; this may be a deliberate heightening of the tone of the prayer, rather than its theology, but it could also be a simple word variation, as we have seen in the Greek prayers.

8. "And for thy frail servant whom thou hast by thy grace *made worthy to offer before thee this oblation*."

Basil Byz also contains a prayer for the celebrating priest and so does *Apostolic Constitutions*, albeit in a more personal style. We shall come across this theme later.

9. The *Gehanta*, once more, concludes with the offering of praise.

The final *Gehanta* continues the intercessions with two other offerings:

10. "We beseech thee, my Lord, and we make supplication before thee; that thou wilt remember *over this oblation* the fathers and patriarchs, and prophets and apostles. . . ."

This is again reminiscent of both Addai and Mari and Chrysostom in their commemoration of the departed. "Over this oblation" also echoes *Strasbourg*, if we follow Cuming's suggestion. There is nothing theologically novel here, but simply the theme of sacrifice and intercession.

Finally, the epiclesis:

11. "And may the grace of the Holy Spirit come, O my Lord, and may he dwell and rest upon *this oblation which we offer before thee*.[20] May he bless and consecrate it and make this bread and this cup to be the Body and Blood of our Lord Jesus Christ. . . ."

Here we have both Addai and Mari and *Basil Byz*, and also conceivably *Apostolic Constitutions*. And it comes as a climax to the entire prayer.

Spinks remarks, "It would appear, therefore, that while Nestorius may be a skilful conflation of St. Basil and a version of St. John Chrysostom (Twelve Apostles), the offering terminology is mainly derived from the former."[21] Since we have already noted how the ideas of offering used by the Basil tradition are more subtle and complex, we should not be surprised to see them taken into the Syriac style of this anaphora, in an attempt to elaborate on what we may with some justification regard as the East Syrian norm, the anaphora of Addai and Mari. But whereas the Greek West Syrian anaphoras concentrate their offering at the anamnesis-epiclesis-intercessions (and in the case of *Basil Byz*, anticipates some of these ideas in an attempt to hold an increasing length of prayer together in a unity), the pattern of Nestorius is different. It amounts to intercession-epiclesis-doxology, for there is no anamnesis of the conventional West Syrian type. Spinks attempts to work out a pattern for this anaphora, focusing on the institution narrative as the offering, with the elements referred to as a "sacrifice" at the start of the intercessions, and the petition for the consecration only at the end:

Offering of praise (*nqareb, masquin*).

Offering of the commemoration of our salvation (*mqarbinan*) which is performed by the recitation of that salvation as recorded in the institution.

Pleading the sacrifice (*debha*) (death of Christ) which is commemorated.

Petition for the Spirit to make the oblation life-giving to those who receive it.[22]

This pattern looks impressive and is logical, but is it true? The weak unit in the scheme lies in Spinks' emphasis on the institution narrative and in his interpretation of the intercessions. I agree that the placing of the epiclesis at the end has the effect of emphasizing it and of distancing the intercessions from it, unlike the Greek West Syrian order, where the intercessions flow out from the epiclesis. But the notion of pleading seems rather more sophisticated than the text would allow, where Nestorius simply offers the sacrifice for various intentions in order to point out that the eucharist is not just a matter of receiving communion, but also a prophetic sign of the kingdom. Hence the social character of intercessions in respect of both living and departed.[23] This, it seems, is the key to the inversion of intercession and epiclesis, quite apart from its greater affinity with Addai and Mari. And although it is hard to deny to this prayer, and to Theodore, any "sequence or development," my interpretation of an anaphora dotted around with sacrifice of praise, mixed with living sacrifice (but like

Addai and Mari, weak on gift offering), is a simpler one, and avoids looking for moments of offering.

Theodore's anaphora is shorter than Nestorius and may have been compiled in order to allow for an abbreviated prayer.

Brightman and Wagner[24] have suggested that this anaphora may be the work of Theodore himself, but it could be argued that it is the work of someone familiar with the catechetical lectures of Theodore. It contains eleven offerings:[25]

1. The dialogue varies in the textual tradition but the same ideas are expressed as we saw in the case of Nestorius, and Addai and Mari.

The first and second *Gehantas* offer praise:

2. "And thou hast, my Lord, made even the feeble race of mortal man worthy to *offer glory and honor*, with all the companies of those on high, to thy Almighty sovereignty, even with those who at all times before the majesty of thy holiness raise their voice to glorify thy glorious Trinity which in three persons. . . ."

(After the Sanctus):

3. ". . . we *offer praise and honor* and confession and adoration. . . ."

In the second *Gehanta*:

4. ". . . who through the eternal Spirit *offered himself without spot to God*, and hath sanctified us by the offering of his body once, and made peace by the blood of his cross."

Here is biblicism run rife, for the author ingeniously brings together Hebrews 9:14 and Colossians 1:18,20.

5. After the institution narrative, praise, thanksgiving, honor and adorations are "offered."

The third *Gehanta* contains no less than five instances of offering:

6. Praise for being worthy to administer before God "*this awful and divine service*."

7. "We offer before thy glorious Trinity, with a contrite heart and humble spirit this *living and holy and acceptable sacrifice*, the mystery of the Lamb of God. . . ."

8. ". . . that in thy pitifulness *this pure and holy oblation may be accepted* in which thou wast well pleased and reconciled regarding the sins of the world."

In these three quotations, we see the way in which the East Syrian anaphoras deal with what the Greek prayers have in their anamnesis, and the ideas are similar to those in Nestorius. The eucharist is a sacrifice of praise offered by human beings. It is also a memorial of the offering of Christ and is therefore called a mystery. As Spinks says, "a careful link is made between the cross, the Last Supper and the continued performing of the rite."[26]

9. Intercession follows, as in Nestorius, with the same kind of ideas used there.

10. A reference is made to the whole celebration as a sacrifice of praise, "as a good memorial before thee of the righteous of old time," which brings the departed into the offering of praise, a slightly different nuance.

11. In the epiclesis, the Spirit is petitioned to come upon the oblation in a formula nearer to Addai and Mari than to Nestorius.

Although Theodore's ideas are simpler than Nestorius, the same emphases persist. Various theories can be presented for the persistence of the epiclesis at the end. Spinks suggests that the preaching of Theodore may have produced such a scheme, with the epiclesis "resurrecting" the body at the end of the prayer, after the narrative and the intercessions. This could well be the case but it seems to us to be overly subtle. The other important insight that Spinks brings out is that different words for offering occur in these prayers, which can express differences in the Greek between $\pi\rho\sigma\phi\rho\alpha$ and $\theta\upsilon\sigma\iota\alpha$, and can also use offering words of prayer and praise that seem more ordinary in the Greek. Perhaps, as in Addai and Mari, we are really dealing with a language so much nearer to Hebraic thought that such concrete words for prayer and praise can keep their concrete overtones, as compared with Greek, where the words can become more abstract. Although Nestorius and Theodore are more complex than Addai and Mari, the sacrificial ideas are at root similar, with story and response functioning prominently in the prayers, and gift appearing weaker than in the Greek anaphoras (particularly compared with Basil). We are in a different world, a fact that comes out more strongly in Nestorius through the selective use we find there of Greek material. This world bears testimony yet again to the great variety of ways in which eucharistic liturgy is formulated.

EGYPTIAN

Our discussion of *Strasbourg* has already introduced the debate about the origins of the anaphora of Mark. Scholars are apt to approach the eastern prayers with a certain degree of inflexibility, which results in the eucharistic prayers being grouped in overly structural compartments. Although structures may help us, who live in such a different environment from the ancients, it is nonetheless clear that the eastern churches of old (and today) delight in using varying types of anaphoral prayers, which express in different ways the mystery of the Christian faith. Thus the Coptic Church today uses the Alexandrian anaphora of Basil, but also uses that of Gregory Nazianzus; both of these prayers are structured in the Greek West Syrian style. The Coptic Church still uses, occasionally, the anaphora of Mark with its own structure and style. But before we turn to that venerable and complicated prayer, we must first discuss the anaphora contained in the prayerbook of Serapion of Thmuis.

Serapion has been debated by scholars for a long time. Botte regarded him as heretical and the eucharistic prayer inauthentic. Recent studies have tended to rehabilitate him.[27] Certainly his anaphora has idiosyncratic features, but that is an epithet we use because our knowledge of antiquity is so incomplete. We could conceivably come across a collection of Egyptian prayers that casts more fog than light on the euchological scene in that part of the world for those who want the ancients to fit into neat systems. They do not, and Serapion's eucharistic prayer bears this out. Probably dating from the fourth century and in use at Thmuis (whether as a local pecularity or typical of wider usage is impossible to tell), this prayer is entitled ἀναφορά ("offering"), and lacks full intercessions, which may be a factor in assessing it as older than the fourth century.

After the opening catalogue of praise comes a prayer, "give us holy Spirit, that we may be able to speak and expound your unspeakable mysteries," a theme we have encountered in Nestorius. After the Sanctus comes the first epiclesis:

"Full is heaven, full also is earth of your excellent glory, Lord of the powers.

"Fill also this sacrifice with your power and your partaking; for to you *have we offered this living sacrifice, this bloodless offering.*

"To you have we offered this bread, the likeness of the body of the only-begotten.

"This bread is the likeness of the holy body. For the Lord Jesus Christ, in the night when he was betrayed, took bread, broke it, and gave it to his disciples, saying, 'take and eat; this is my body which is broken for you for the forgiveness of sins.' Therefore we also, making the likeness of the death, *have offered the bread,* and beseech you *through this sacrifice:* be reconciled to us all and be merciful, O God of truth. And as the bread was scattered over the mountains, and was gathered together and became one, so gather your holy Church out of every nation and every country and every city and village and house, and make one living catholic Church.

"We have offered also the cup, the likeness of the blood: for the Lord Jesus Christ, taking a cup after supper, said to his disciples, 'Take, drink; this is the new covenant, which is my blood, which is shed for you for the forgiveness of sins.' Therefore *we have offered the cup also, presenting the likeness of the blood."*

The prayer continues with an epiclesis of the Word, a peculiarity, and some short petitions; the full intercessions come earlier in the liturgy. After the commemoration of the departed, which is also short, the prayer ends:

"Receive also the thanksgiving of the people, and bless *those who offered the offerings* and the thanksgivings; and grant health and soundness and cheerfulness and all advancement of soul and body to this whole people." (A doxology follows to conclude.)

A number of features stand out in this prayer. First of all, every single offering verb, whether indicative or participial, is in the perfect tense, and this repetition (to which Capelle draws attention[28]) can only point back to the placing of the gifts on the altar, since these verbs refer exclusively to the gifts. However, the supplication for the people after the epiclesis also has, "for we have called upon you, the uncreated," which presumably refers to the whole prayer rather than to any moment of praise within it.

Secondly, we have the word "sacrifice" at the first epiclesis in an analogous position to that of the anaphora of Mark, which we shall see later. But in what sense is this sacrifice to be understood? Taking into consideration the quotation from the *Didache* (the prayer for the unity of the church, between the two institution narratives), it would seem that the petition to "fill the sacrifice" is not intended to refer to the eucharistic gifts exclusively, especially as these are prayed for in a particular manner later on, immediately prior to the petition for the communicants. The sacrifice, therefore, is the whole celebration, communicants included, perhaps also the eucharistic life of the communicants after the service is over.

Thirdly, in one instance, the offering verb refers to the "bloodless offering" as in *Strasbourg* and the Testament of Levi as well as other early Christian writers.[29] It is hard to identify this as referring to the eucharistic gifts. But it is possible to conceive of the bloodless offering as the hymn of praise (the Sanctus). I would suggest a general reference to the sacrifice of praise, thus bringing it together with the gift offering.

Fourthly, there is the feature of supplication: "we beseech you through this sacrifice," which introduces the themes of reconciliation (cf. *Didache* 14) in the peculiar section between the narrative of the bread and that of the cup. This could be an example of the author (or the tradition represented by this prayer) experimenting with the notions of narrative and anamnesis, which might have been new fashions in anaphoral prayer at the time of writing.

For all the difficulties surrounding the book, Serapion scores high on sacrifice of praise (story), communion (gift), and intercession (response), all of which are brought together in a prayer that has an austerity and a unique flavor about it, as well as some common features with the tradition represented by the anaphora of Mark, to which we must now turn.

In order not to beg the question about *Strasbourg* completeness, it is necessary to quote from all the fragments of Mark.[30]

1. *Strasbourg* (fourth–fifth centuries)
After the Christological thanksgiving:
". . . through whom with him and the Holy Spirit we give thanks to you and *offer this reasonable sacrifice and bloodless service, which all nations offer to you,* from sunrise to sunset, from south to north, (for) your name is great among all the nations, and in every place *incense is offered* to your holy name and a pure sacrifice.

"*Over this sacrifice and offering we pray and beseech you, remember. . . .*"
2. *British Museum Tablet* (eighth century, but confirmed by sixth-century text)
After the Sanctus:
"Full in truth are heaven and earth of your glory through our Lord (and) Saviour Jesus Christ: *fill, O God, this sacrifice also with* your blessing through your Holy Spirit. (Institution narrative.)

"Proclaiming thus, Lord, the death of your only-begotten Son, our Lord and Saviour Jesus Christ, and confessing his resurrection and his ascension into heaven, and looking for his glorious coming, *we offer before you these gifts from your own,* this bread and this cup. We pray and beseech you to send your Holy Spirit and your power on *these* (your?) *gifts set before you,* on this bread and this cup, and to make the bread the Body of Christ and (the cup the blood of the) new (covenant) of our Lord and Saviour Jesus Christ."
3. *The Deir Balyzeh Papyrus* (sixth–seventh century)

After the Sanctus:

"Fill us also with the glory from (you), and vouchsafe to send down your Holy Spirit upon these creatures (and) make the bread the body of our (Lord and) Saviour Jesus Christ, and the cup the blood . . . of our Lord and. . . . And as this bread was scattered on (the mountains) and hills and fields, and was mixed together and became one body . . . so this wine which came from the vine of David and the water from the *spotless lamb* also mixed together became one mystery, so gather the catholic Church. . . ." (Institution narrative, a short part of the anamnesis and part of the second epiclesis follow.)

4. *The Louvain Coptic Papyrus*

After the Sanctus:

"Heaven and earth are full of that glory wherewith you glorified us through your only-begotten Son Jesus Christ, the first-born of all creation, sitting at the right hand of your majesty in heaven, who will come to judge the living and the dead. We make the *remembrance of his death, offering to you your creatures*, this bread and this cup. We pray and beseech you to send out over them your Holy Spirit, the Paraclete. . . ." (First [?] epiclesis and institution-narrative follow.)

5. *The John Rylands Manchester Papyrus* (sixth century)

After the Sanctus:

"Full in truth are heaven and earth with your holy glory through the Lord and God and our Saviour Jesus Christ. *Fill, O God, also this sacrifice with* the blessing which is from you through your holy Spirit."

When it comes to the full text, the two main versions (Greek and Coptic, the latter a translation of an earlier and lost Greek text) do not present any substantial differences over offering. There are four distinct places where offering is mentioned in the anaphora. First, after the christological thanksgiving:

". . . through whom with him and the Holy Spirit we give thanks to you *and offer this reasonable and bloodless service, which all the nations offer you*, (Lord,) from sunrise to sunset, from south to north, for your name is great among all the nations, and in every place *incense is offered* to your holy name and *a pure sacrifice, a sacrifice and offering*."

(The Coptic adds "*sacrifice*" after "reasonable"; and after "and a pure sacrifice" it adds, "*And over this sacrifice and this offering we pray and beseech you*" . . . (both insertions as *Strasbourg*. Later Coptic versions direct the use of incense now, as the intercessions begin.)

Second, after the commemoration of the departed, before the second intercession:

"Receive, O God *the thank-offerings of those who offer the sacrifices,*
at your (holy and) heavenly and intellectual altar in the vastnesses
of heaven by the ministry of your archangels; of those who offered
much and little, secretly and openly, willingly but unable, and *those
who offered the offerings of* today; as you accepted the *gifts* of your
righteous Abel, (the bishop censes and says) the sacrifices of our father Abraham, (the incense of Zachariah, the alms of Cornelius), and
the widow's two mites; receive also their thank-offerings, and give
them imperishable things for perishable, heavenly things for earthly,
eternal for temporal."

Thirdly after the Sanctus:

"Full in truth are heaven and earth of your holy glory through (the
appearing of) our Lord and God and Saviour Jesus Christ: *fill, O God,
this sacrifice also* with a blessing from you through the descent of your
(all-)holy spirit. (Institution narrative follows.)

Fourthly after the institution narrative:

"Proclaiming,
(Master,) Lord, Almighty, (heavenly King,) the death of your only-begotten Son . . . we *have offered before you from your own gifts;* and we
pray. . . ." (NB in the second epiclesis, the gifts are referred to as
"these loaves and cups.")

Such fragmentary evidence as can be assembled testifies to a common
tradition in which variations are easily discernible.

First, *Strasbourg* and the complete texts witness to the offering of
the "reasonable sacrifice and bloodless service" in the preface, together with the quotation from Malachi 1:11, but "sacrifice" has been
dropped after "reasonable." We have already discussed the meaning
of this passage, and there is no need to repeat it here; the same interpretation is possible, whether or not the *Strasbourg* papyrus is a complete anaphora. The offering is that of the whole eucharist.

Secondly, although all the other fragments are at one with the full
text in having some kind of epiclesis after the Sanctus, there are differences. The BM Tablet, the Rylands fragment, and the full text all
ask for the completion of "this sacrifice" as a preliminary to the institution narrative, whereas the Deir Balyzeh papyrus and the Louvain
papyrus both pray more explicitly for the consecration of the bread
and wine, with no explicit sacrificial language in the former (except
the use of material from the *Didache*, with its paschal overtones), but
with the offering of the gifts in remembrance in the latter. These are

important differences because they point to an instability surrounding the sequence of first epiclesis, institution narrative, anamnesis, and second epiclesis. All this makes the completeness of *Strasbourg* more attractive, a theory explaining the evolution of the Egyptian liturgy. The elements are also described as "bread and cup" (cf. Hippolytus) in the anamnesis.

Thirdly, although the later text uses the aorist tense for the offering verb in the anamnesis, the BM Tablet does not (it uses the present), and of course, the Louvain fragment has the present participle ("offering") after "we remember," although this comes before the institution narrative.

All this leaves much for speculation, but the full text of Mark has a clear sequence of ideas, and it is to be noted that in it we have yet another position for the intercessions,[31] after the offering of the "bloodless service." The four occurrences of offering material amount to an offering of the whole eucharist (after the christological thanksgiving); the offering of gifts, including reference to noneucharistic gifts (after the commemoration of the departed); and the offering of the memorial (in the first epiclesis and in the anamnesis, but in the latter the past tense points back). What, then, of that past tense, "we presented," "we offered"? Some would translate it as present tense, but this is to strain the Greek and do severe injustice to the tradition.[32] Others would point it back to the offering of the "bloodless service."[33] I have suggested elsewhere that it refers back to the presenting of the gifts on the altar,[34] and the petition for accepting the "thank offerings" seems to corroborate this view. Gregory Dix made liturgists somewhat skeptical of his "offertory theology," but when he wrote that the church "looks back to the offertory and expresses the meaning of that. It looks forward to communion and prays for the effects of that,"[35] he was wrong to try to suggest some universality for his theory, but may well have been near the truth if this analysis were to be applied to the anaphora of Mark. One can add to this view the special emphasis placed on intercession in the full text (together with the use of incense) as well as the sacrificial way in which these intercessions are introduced, the identification of the people of God with the universal concerns of the Church *as well as* with the memorial of Christ and the gifts of bread and wine. The evolution of Mark will continue to cause liturgists problems, but it has some unique features that are only understood when looked at on their own. Whatever that evolution may have been, Mark represents no haphazard pile-up of euchology,[36] but a delicate and pastoral understanding of the meaning of the eucharist within an anaphora whose internal unity gives it a special character.

The Coptic Church nowadays uses Mark only once a year, and although its normal eucharistic prayer is *Basil Alex*[2], it uses a third anaphora, Gregory Nazianzus, on a few special occasions. Its most obvious peculiarity is its address to Christ throughout, a factor that persuaded Jungmann that it was a late and Monophysite composition. This theory has been challenged recently by Gerhards, who argues that it antedates the Monophysite controversy.[37] Although the prayer has other peculiarities as well, its treatment of offering is no more than a variant of *Basil Byz*. Thus, before the Sanctus, "ten thousands present (προσάγουσι) to you their service (λειτουργίαν)." Before the institution narrative, the celebrant says "I offer you these symbols of my freedom"; this combines *Basil Byz's* way of referring to the elements before the narrative with the first person singular, as in *Apostolic Constitutions*. (Gregory moves back and forth from we to I at several stages of the anaphora.) At the anamnesis, the present participle, προσφέροντες, and the epiclesis refer to the gifts as "set before you," in the traditional manner. In the intercessions, the longer version of the prayer for the offerers (*Basil Byz*) occurs.

We must also look briefly at some Ethiopic prayers. The anaphora of the Apostles[38] has a simple anamnesis formula similar to the *Testamentum Domini*, "we offer you this bread and this cup, giving thanks to you." It is noteworthy that, as in some of the texts in the Mark tradition, the gifts are described directly as bread and cup in the anamnesis. The prayer of Our Lord[39] is more allusive; using the same form as the Apostles in the anamnesis, it adds, "we offer you this eucharist" in the epiclesis, and refers to the elements as "this gift which we have presented to your holiness," once again referring back to the offertory. The anaphora of John, Son of Thunder[40] has a unique scheme; the offering is that of the shepherd Christ, and the intercessions also begin with the offering of sacrifice, this time as a pure offering, but there is a difference. The priest denies any offering of material things, leading up to the claim that "we offer you your humanity, we offer you your divinity, we offer you your apparition"; the intercessions follow. The anamnesis asks for the offering to be received and refers to the sacrifices of the Old Testament. Reminiscent in structure (and in some themes) of Mark, this prayer is a masterpiece of prolixity and biblical ideas. Among other Ethiopic prayers, there are some that have no explicit offering material at all, others that do, but there is little that is entirely new in them.[41]

The Maronite Church uses some anaphoras in conjunction with the Syrian Jacobite, and it also has its own version of Addai and Mari. This provides us with yet more proof of the Semitic background of Syriac-speaking Christians, however much they were affected by the classical Greek-speaking formulae of West Syria. The anaphora of Peter the Apostle,[42] commonly known as the *sharar* (from the opening word in a prayer immediately before the anaphora), is clearly related to Addai and Mari, and it has been the subject of much study in recent years. The dialogue begins with a long definition of the ensuing eucharistic action similar to the Urmiah version of Nestorius. Early on in the prayer there is an offering of incense, which is described in sacrificial terms, "we offer that pure and holy offering to you." This section is a later addition to an earlier core, but it is interesting that it should be inserted near the beginning of the anaphora in a way similar to *Strasbourg* and to the Egyptian tradition of Mark. It also provides proof that not all liturgies that adopted incense merely took over the practice as a fumigant, but rather attempted to give it a theological interpretation. (Coptic versions of Mark add incense at the start of the intercession, another point of comparison here.)

In the body of the prayer, at the end of the second *Gehanta*, we have:

1. "Let us *offer to you glory,* and honour in your holy church before your propitiatory altar."

The second *Gehanta* comes in for some expansion, opening with a definition of the celebration in terms very similar to the Addai and Mari tradition:

2. ". . . in the commemoration of your body and your blood, *which we offer to you upon your living and holy altar as you,* our hope, have taught us. . . ."
3. "We make, O Lord, the memorial of your passion as you have taught us. . . ."
4. "We remember . . . to be a *propitiatory sacrifice* . . . and to sanctify the unclean *through your sacrifice.*
. . . and *offer this oblation* to your divinity. . . .
. . . and *may this oblation be acceptable before you;* which we offer on your atoning altar in memory of your passion.
May the glorious Trinity be pleased by this *incense and by this oblation* and by this chalice. . . .

and upon me, feeble and sinful, who offered it, may the mercy of the glorious Trinity shine forth. . . ."

The intercessions in the second *Gehanta* contain the following:

5. "We offer before you, O Lord, *this oblation in memory of* . . . (departed).
Remember, O Lord God, at this moment *those who offer oblations, vows, first-fruits and memorials.* . . .
. . . and for all who participated in this *eucharist which was offered upon this holy altar.* . . .
. . . and, O Lord, may this eucharist *be as a memorial of our dead."*

The epiclesis, as in the East Syrian anaphoras, comes as the climax:

6. "And may he come, O Lord, . . . and dwell and rest *upon this oblation* of your servants."

The first, second, third, and sixth correspond with material in Addai and Mari. The fourth and fifth, however, increase the length of the prayer but do not complete the ideas in the prayer. The fourth is an anamnesis of sorts, remembering the sacrifice of Christ and praying for the work of that sacrifice in the Church through God accepting the offering of the eucharist. The prayer by the priest for himself repeats what we saw directly in *Apostolic Constitutions,* and which we have seen elsewhere. The intercessions begin with the departed (as Chrysostom and other anaphoras); it probably connects with the notion of the acceptance of the offering in heaven, which is a notion we shall see among the Syrian Jacobite prayers and one which we have already seen in Mark. Like Nestorius and Theodore, *sharar* maintains the epiclesis at the end, but I do not think there is a subtle sequence of ideas to "resurrect"[43] the bread at the end. Rather it is the commemoration of the sacrifice of Christ (which *sharar* defines more clearly than Addai and Mari), prayer for the acceptance of the offering, leading into commemoration of the departed, supplication for the living, and, finally, the epiclesis. I suspect that the tradition of epiclesis at the end was so strong that the compiler of this prayer decided to extend the central part of the prayer instead. As in Addai and Mari, gift offering is weak; sacrifice of praise and the living sacrifice of intercession have been developed and fused together in the notion of acceptance of the offering, as we shall see in some of the Syrian Jacobite anaphoras.

The anaphora of the Twelve Apostles[44] has been referred to earlier in our discussion because a theory has gained popularity among liturgists that this prayer is an earlier edition of the anaphora of Chrysostom. If this is so, then it represents a veritable landmark in the history of eucharistic prayers because of its relative silence regarding offering material. All the Syriac prayers contain the kind of general offerings of praise that were noted in the East Syrian anaphoras. But what of other types of offering? In the anamnesis of Twelve Apostles, the only theme is thanksgiving, leading into supplication; there is no offering verb at all. At the epiclesis, prayer is made to send the Spirit "upon these offerings set before you, and show" them to be the body and blood of Christ. It is only at the start of the intercessions that we come across the formula: "we therefore offer to you, almighty Lord, this reasonable sacrifice for all men. . . ." It also includes a brief prayer for the offerers. In other words, while the anamnesis is dominated by the theme of remembrance and the epiclesis describes the elements as offerings, the intercessions open with the offering of "reasonable sacrifice," this latter being the same formula as those that open the intercession in Chrysostom (although in Chrysostom the offering is also "bloodless" at the beginning of the epiclesis). Twelve Apostles gives us a scheme that we shall encounter again in other Syrian Jacobite, Maronite, and some Armenian prayers. It is indeed a simple one: the sacrifice of praise lies behind the whole anaphora, at the epiclesis the gifts are described as offerings, and then the intercessions begin with a reference to the whole eucharist, along the lines of the "living sacrifice" of the whole congregation, in offering their concerns to God.

The question remains, of course, was Twelve Apostles written by Chrysostom himself? It is conceivable that it was, but the absence of the offering verb in the anamnesis (and its overall similarity with other Syrian Jacobite, Maronite, and Armenian anaphoras) marks it off from the Greek West Syrian prayer forms, which are more explicit in their handling of offering material in this aspect. Assuming some antiquity for Twelve Apostles, it is somewhat ironic that Syriac euchology should not require a stronger sacrificial character; certainly, as we saw in Addai and Mari, the offering aspect is weak when set alongside celebration and remembrance, and if Twelve Apostles was once used also by the East Syrians, then we have identified something common between Syriac-speaking Christians, which is of considerable importance from a linguistic as well as a theological point of view. The softer understanding of sacrifice in Addai and Mari and the way in which this may have been taken over by the author of Twelve Apostles could provide the foundation of the offering themes in these Syriac anaphoras.

For example, the anaphora of Eustathius of Antioch,[45] which exists in several versions, is economical in the way it covers the main themes of salvation history. The post-Sanctus "offers threefold sanctifications" to God (i.e., sacrifice of praise), the anamnesis has no offering verb, the epiclesis prays for the Holy Spirit on "these offerings set before," the intercessions pray "through this sacrifice," and towards the end, asks for the offerings to be received, "which are offered for" the intentions in the intercessions. Eustathius develops the anamnesis in such a manner as to pick on the notion of the second coming (from the institution narrative) and to pray at length about it, so that it hardly seems an anamnesis at all. This is a feature of many of the Syrian Jacobite and Maronite prayers, which either concentrate on the second coming or work backwards to Bethlehem, so that the anamnesis is of the whole life of Christ. Thus, John the Evangelist[46] (Maronite) leads towards the second coming; in the intercessions it prays for those who offered gifts on the altar; it also prays that the eucharist will be received on the "spiritual altar" in heaven, which is a variation on the theme of angelic ("pure") worship and the acceptance of the eucharist.[47] On the other hand, Marutas of Tagrit[48] (Maronite) works out a complete "curriculum vitae" of Christ, starting with the Virgin birth. It is interesting that the first part of the thanksgiving in these prayers becomes brief (or perhaps the tradition was reticent at this point from an early stage), while the anamnesis develops in both chronological directions.

The anaphora that appears in the *Euchologion* of the White Monastery (attributed to John of Bosra[49]) is indeed a prolix composition. In the section before the Sanctus are two allusions to the sacrifice of praise, by the angels as well as by humans (who offer "the testimony of fear"). Immediately following the institution narrative is a lengthy *midrash* on the narrative (another feature of the Syriac prayers) that describes the celebration of the eucharist as a "mystic institution," but there is no offering of gifts. The elements are referred to in the past tense, the bread "prepared," the wine "mixed." However, in the following (anamnetic) section, the nature of Christ's sacrifice is worked out along the lines of the letter to the Hebrews ("not made with hands," "once," "not alien blood").[50] In the epiclesis, the prayer denies offering the blood of bulls and works up to a magnificent climax in language again reminiscent of Hebrews, "we offer to you the same person, as a sacrifice and oblation without blemish . . . we pray . . . that this reasonable sacrifice may be for those who receive for perfect salvation. . . ." This is a detailed sequence of ideas, indeed! The offering is not of animals, nor of fruit, but of the Savior, who made himself a sacrifice. The eucharist is a means whereby the benefits of that sacrifice can be received by the faithful. This is one of the most original prayers we have so far seen, and it betrays a background of theological apologetic with a Hebrews christology, in order to express how the eucharist is sacrificial. The key is not the Church's reoffering of Christ, but the Church offering a reasonable sacrifice in commemoration of that one offering. A later Maronite prayer attributed to Chrysostom[51] uses material from this anaphora as well as Eustathius and in the preface insists that the offering is not of bulls; in the intercessions it prays for the acceptance of the sacrifice. It contains no offering verb in the anamnesis.

Two reticent prayers so compress the institution narrative as to cause (in one case) some consternation to the Latin-minded editor. Thomas of Heraclea[52] has a brief anamnesis (compared with Marutas of Tagrit), but still alludes to the incarnation. At the epiclesis it only describes the eucharist as "mysteries"[53] (rather than something more material), which the Holy Spirit is to "complete," another allusive expression. The intercessions ask that "these oblations which we now offer for . . ." should be accepted. Here is yet one more variation in which the intercessions begin with offering of material gifts, not the bloodless sacrifice or reasonable service. Dionysius of Amid[54] also has a compressed institution narrative; an anamnesis that simply described the Church as "performing the memorial"; an epiclesis "on these oblations set before"; and intercessions that begin, "we offer to you, Lord, this sacrifice for. . . ." Whereas Thomas of Heraclea has some new features, Dionysius of Amid reproduces the same series of ideas that we see in Twelve Apostles.

Philoxenus appears in three versions that vary the sacrificial material. The first two demonstrate this clearly.[55] In both, the anamnesis extends back to the birth of Christ and also forward to the second coming, praying fervently for the faithful to be among the elect. Whereas in the former "we offer praise and exaltation" and "this sacrifice," in the latter we only "commemorate." At the epiclesis, the former uses "sanctify these mysteries," whereas the latter has "on these oblations which are offered to you." At the intercessions both pray for the acceptance of the sacrifice, but the former adds "for you are the receiver of sacrifices and oblations." Thus, the first version of Philoxenus stresses sacrifice rather more, as if trying to define how it functions in the prayer and indeed as a feature of eucharistic faith and practice.

Dioscurus[56] refers on more than one occasion to the placing of the gifts on the altar in past-tense terms and for the acceptance of the offering after the epiclesis. A fine prayer is James of Edessa.[57] In the preface, we have the sacrifice of praise, "you taught us voice of glorification and thanksgiving, which we offer to you." The anamnesis is very long. Not only does it look forward with awe and trembling to the second coming, but it begins with a significant redefining of what anamnesis means, "your supernatural dispensation we inscribe on the tables of our hearts, and we discern with the eyes of our minds, O Word of God, the famous mysteries of your wonderful deeds."[58] In the intercessions the sacrifice is offered "for" and the priest also prays that the oblations be received "from my hands." The offerers are prayed for with the words, "remember in this time of this sacrifice."

There are two particularly important anaphoras in the Syrian Jacobite repertoire. Severus of Antioch,[59] which may go back to the seventh century, if not earlier, begins the anamnesis with "Therefore, completing this bloodless sacrifice, O our Lord Jesus, we ask you for your love towards men on account of which you gave your very self for us." It goes on to pray about the second coming at length. In the epiclesis the sacrifice is asked to be received "on your reasonable and supercelestial altar as a sweet savor" and the Holy Spirit is to come "on these oblations set before"; in the intercessions, there is prayer for the offerers. Like John of Bosra, but in a different way, Severus of Antioch needs to describe in what sense the eucharist is sacrificial; the petition for the offering to be received in heaven is an easy idea to work into the prayer just after the second coming has been mentioned, with its theme of the presentation of the Church on that day at Christ's right hand.

Timothy of Alexandria,[60] which may go back even earlier than the sixth century, offers laud and honor in the post-Sanctus. In the anamnesis, which works from the birth of Christ through to the second coming at some length, it describes the eucharist as "this reasonable and bloodless sacrifice which we offer to you," and goes on: "do not despise a contrite and humbled heart, Lord, but receive this sacrifice on your reasonable altar," which latter idea is linked with the prayers of the saints. The epiclesis prays for the Spirit on "these oblations which are offered"; the intercessions begin, "we offer you, Lord, for . . ." (and these include prayer for the offerers).

The Maronite anaphora of John of Saba,[61] which may go back to the seventh century, is reticent on offering; in the anamnesis, the church is mindful of the saving acts, and therefore "with this mystic sacrifice offers penitential and lamenting voices" to God. In the intercessions, God is asked to "remember . . . over this spiritual and bloodless sacrifice. . . ." On the other hand, the Maronite prayer of Xystus[62] mentions no offering until the epiclesis, when the Holy Spirit

63

is to come upon "this eucharist set before, and sanctify it . . . and sanctify those oblations . . . and rest upon this oblation of your servants." The tradition represented by that anaphora may go back indirectly to the kind of prayer we saw in Addai and Mari. Here it finds some definition, so that the people are directly associated with the eucharistic sacrifice, which is not a separate entity from themselves.

The total Syriac tradition of anaphoras (both Syrian Jacobite and Maronite) comes to over ninety-five. What we have seen is a selection from a most complete collection of eucharistic prayers. From them, we can discern the following features.

First, the absence of an offering verb in the anamnesis.[63] This only seems to be contravened when the author is defining closely the nature of sacrifice (e.g., Timothy, Severus, and John of Bosra). Twelve Apostles is used by both Jacobites and Maronites and may be an archetype.

Second, the offering of praise is a nuance that is easier to express in Syriac[64] than in Greek, as we have already seen in the case of the East Syrian prayers. But there are instances where this comes out more strongly than usual and is defined in sacrificial terms (e.g., Eustathius, John of Bosra, and Timothy).

Thirdly, while the eucharistic elements are sometimes referred to as oblations at the epiclesis, the universal place to offer is at the beginning of the intercessions, as we saw in Twelve Apostles. This offering is sometimes "reasonable" and/or "bloodless," and sometimes refers to the eucharistic elements themselves, although I would suggest that the latter is a subsequent tradition, and actually understood to refer to the whole eucharist rather than to just one aspect of it.

Fourthly, sometimes this notion of offering at the intercessions is reinforced by prayer for its acceptance during the epiclesis, immediately prior to the intercessions. This is a notion already seen in (Egyptian) Mark of the thank offerings and referred to somewhat imprecisely as a ministry in Basil. *Sharar* provides the archetype for this idea.

Fifthly, the anamnesis is a very flexible entity in the tradition. It is interesting to observe how the opening thanksgiving series is brief when the anamnesis is considerably expanded, whether this expansion is backwards in time to the birth of Christ, or forwards to the day of judgement.[65] The historical and the eschatological mingle happily and are not mutually exclusive when the anaphora contains both emphases.

Sixthly, there is a tendency among a few anaphoras to redefine anamnesis itself, in a way which we may term "psychological." This is yet one more example of the process of making the eucharist real for the people of the time.

Seventhly, the essential link between those who have offered gifts with the intercessions as well as with the ensuing communion is never entirely lost. The early tradition represented by Twelve Apostles shows this, as well as much more elaborate prayer forms such as John of Bosra.[66]

Finally, while theological emphases may vary from one prayer to another, the notion of sacrifice is nonetheless in the background, whether brought out in the form of praise, or gift, or intercession. What is beyond dispute, however, is that the "remembering . . . we offer" is not really part of the Syriac tradition but is a notion more akin to Greek West Syria. This may explain why gift offering is the weakest of the three criteria in these prayers. Perhaps this was not an idea needing so much emphasis.

ARMENIAN

The Armenian liturgy is being taken much more seriously by liturgists today.[67] The consensus emerging is that the roots of the Armenian rite lie with the old Syrian liturgy. What we see from Armenian anaphoras is a mixture of Syriac reticence and Greek West Syrian precision over offering.

The Armenian anaphora of James[68] provides us with a good example of adaptation, being an abbreviation of Syriac James. It may, indeed, be paralleled in the way in which Twelve Apostles was "Syriacized" (if it comes originally from the Greek West Syrian tradition). At the anamnesis, which is shorter than both the Syriac and the Greek, we remember the saving acts, and then "shout and say: spare us, Lord . . . ," leading into the epiclesis, where the bread is "set before." After the petition for consecration, the priest prays that God "receive from our hands the gifts of your body and blood." The intercessions follow, and they contain prayer for the offerers (past tense, like other examples we have seen).

The scheme reads very much like some of the Syriac anaphoras we saw earlier, apart from the petition for God to receive the body and blood, which is yet one more kind of liturgical shorthand for accepting the eucharist. The absence of the offering verb is in line with so many of the Syriac prayers, where prayer for the acceptance of the eucharist and, more commonly, the offering at the start of the intercessions are the norm. Another example of adaptation is that the angels "offer proclamation" of the glory of God in the preface.

The anaphora of Cyril[69] refers to the eucharist as "this triumphal mystery" in the post-Sanctus, a theme repeated in the anamnesis, where "we always offer for our redemption the terrible and fearful mystery." At the epiclesis, the Spirit is to come "over these offered gifts," and prayer is made in the intercessions for peace for the departed "through the immortal sacrifice," which surely refers to the sacrifice of Christ, remembered in the eucharist. Sacrifice is once more treated in a different (and subtle) way, echoing the mystery theology we have met in some of the Syriac anaphoras.

The anaphora of Sahag[70] in similar fashion describes the eucharist as "this holy present mystery" before the institution narrative. At the anamnesis we have another Syriac-looking compilation, with the insistence that "through your love you ordered this single sacrifice to be offered to you, not from the blood of animals according to the Old Testament. . . ." At the epiclesis the Spirit is to come upon "these gifts set before," a Grecism in the text. In the intercessions, prayer is made for offerers with another Grecism from Basil. Here is textual selectivity indeed! With a few Greek words, intended as direct quotations, and with Syriac ideas, the Armenian anaphora adapts to its own way of understanding the eucharist. It uses paradoxical language ("this single sacrifice to be offered") to show that the eucharist is sacrificial and to point to the unique character of the sacrifice of Christ (hence the allusions to Old Testament procedures). The parallels with the Syriac anaphoras are striking.

The anaphora of Athanasius is more complex.[71] During the post-Sanctus, "we offer thanks to you . . . you gave us your only-begotten son . . . victim and anointed, lamb and heavenly bread, archpriest and sacrifice. . . ." This is deliberately paradoxical language, building on the tradition of the New Testament reflection on the meaning of Christ's death. However, at the anamnesis we encounter the Basil formula, "we offer you your own from our own, in all and for all," but this is after the eucharistic action is described as "offering before you this mystery of the saving body and blood of Christ" (cf. Addai and Mari). The epiclesis prays for the Spirit "on these gifts set before" and the intercessions refer repeatedly to "by this sacrifice." Toward the end the deacon makes his own interjection, "we offer . . . thanks for the holy and immortal sacrifice, which is on this holy altar," and prays for the priest who offers it and for the departed. This is probably a later addition. All in all, Athanasius amounts to an interesting and original composition, bringing together both Greek and Syriac features; among the latter is the reference to the eucharist as "this mystery."

The anaphora of Gregory Nazianzus[72] is the most Greek-looking of all the Armenian prayers so far. In the post-Sanctus the priest prays, "let us offer this sacrifice as an odor of your sweetness" (Phil 4:18, also used in Syrian rites). The anamnesis begins with "we offer you, Lord, these oblations given to us by you on this altar" (cf. Addai and Mari). It goes on to record the saving acts and includes a remembrance of the three persons of the Trinity; "we offer blessing and glory to the holy Trinity," and "with everlasting glorification we offer this sacrifice and confess this to be the deified body and blood." The epiclesis is brief, twice referring to the "memorial." The intercessions plead "through these gifts" and "through these things" on four occasions. But in spite of the offering in the anamnesis, Gregory Nazianzus still contains some significant Syriac features, including the dialogue, the expanded anamnesis, the stress on sacrifice of praise, and the sacrificial references in the intercessions.

The anaphora of Gregory the Illuminator,[73] thought to be an early form of the anaphora of Basil has the same sacrificial material in the dialogue as we have seen in Athanasius. The anamnesis only mentions placing the "figure" of the body and blood of Christ on the table; this corresponds with the antitype in *Basil Byz,* also at the end of the anamnesis, but after the verb "we offer," and the participle, "having presented." In the epiclesis, the Holy Spirit is sought "on us and on this sacrifice which is placed before your divinity," an expression reminiscent of Hippolytus, Addai and Mari, *Apostolic Constitutions,* and some Syriac prayers. The intercessions include prayer for the offerers, the celebrant, and the departed. Gregory the Illuminator thus brings together different elements and provides yet one more example of reticence over gift offering in the conventional Greek West Syrian manner at the anamnesis. Indeed, if it really *is* an Armenian version of Basil, then the gift offering verb has been deleted.

The anaphora of Ignatius is a translation of the Syriac version.[74] No offering verb appears in the anamnesis, and the epiclesis simply refers to the bread and wine, without any allusion to their presentation on the altar. The intercessions begin thus: "We make before you each day, Lord, the memorial of this sacrifice, which is carried out and completed through the holy rite, so that you may watch over the Catholic Church. . . ." They include prayer for the celebrant, the congregation (in their offering of thanksgiving), the offerers, and also those who have offered first-fruits and other oblations. The intercession for the departed similarly begins with the theme of "making the memorial," presumably to correspond with the prayers for the living. A feature of this anaphora (and many of the Syriac ones also) is the way in which narrative-anamnesis, epiclesis, and intercessions flow easily from one to the other, thus casting some doubt on the use of these conventional terms for structural analysis when they result in a piecemeal approach to the prayer itself.

As time goes on, we may one day be in a position to judge with more clarity the origin of both the Armenian and the Syriac anaphoras. But from our examination of these five prayers of the Armenian Church (only Athanasius is in use today), it is clear that, so far from giving us an offbeat variant of Byzantinism, these prayers offer some highly significant variants of old Syriac euchology. They show a greater sensitivity to the sacrificial character of the atonement than the classical prayers of the Greek West Syrian tradition. In particular, through painting a picture of contrast between the Old Testament and New, we meet paradox and counterstress (e.g., Gregory's anamnesis *sacrifice* immediately followed by epiclesis *memorial*), which adds yet one more feature to a varied scene.

ANAMNESIS VARIETY AND ITS IMPLICATIONS: A SUGGESTION

How has this literary variety come about? A case could be argued for a decisive role taken by our archetypes. Hippolytus represents the Greek West Syrian type, with the "remembering . . . we offer"[75] logic at the anamnesis-epiclesis. This is also shared by the fourth-century anaphoras of Alexandrian Basil, Chrysostom, James, and (as we shall see) the Roman Canon. *Strasbourg* shows the early Egyptian tradition, with a general offering after the short thanksgiving series prior to intercession; "we offer this reasonable sacrifice and bloodless service . . . we offer *for*. . . ." The Roman Canon shares some of this logic, too.[76] Addai and Mari has a unitive notion of offering (perhaps the most primitive of all), which subsequent Syriac euchology develops either in the manner of *sharar*, or of Theodore and Nestorius, or again of the many other prayers represented by the Syriac traditions, of which Twelve Apostles is a prime example. In this latter category, the anamnesis is a critical element, but the offering is associated with intercession (as *Strasbourg*). The Armenian prayers are more Syriac than Greek, but they develop in their own way with their own interests, notably in christology.

It is now possible to suggest that the effect of the inclusion of the institution-narrative anamnesis into the anaphora was a varied one. Greek West Syria and Rome opted for adding an offering, which in the Greek tradition was associated closely with consecration through the ensuing epiclesis. East Syria was reluctant about either (or both) the narrative and the anamnesis[77] because the christological material is well expressed elsewhere and in other ways. Egypt opted for a past tense because of the powerful language at the juncture of the thanks-giving series and intercession. The other Syriac tradition (Jacobite-Maronite as they later came to be called) did not universally adopt the Greek pattern because of its inherent Semitic attachment to the sacrificial character of supplication in the intercessions.

It seems as if at every stage the Jewish background of the eucharistic prayer is being adapted and appropriated. There is no uniformity. Coptic, Syriac, Armenian, and Greek go their own ways.

LITERARY EVIDENCE

Cyril's *Mystagogical Catecheses* contain many allusions to the liturgy but only two references to offering, both of which are in the fifth lecture:

"Then, having sanctified ourselves with these spiritual hymns (i.e., the Sanctus), we beseech God, the lover of man, to send forth the Holy Spirit *upon (the gifts) set before him. . . .*

"Then, after the *spiritual sacrifice, the bloodless service has been perfected,* we beseech God *over that sacrifice of propitiation, for the. . . ."*[78]

It has recently been argued that the Jerusalem liturgy was of the Egyptian kind rather than of the Antiochene type.[79] For our discussion this makes little difference. The epiclesis that Cyril quotes looks as if it could be either Egyptian or Antiochene (i.e., either Mark or something like James), although the word "over" does point to Mark as the liturgy behind the second quotation.[80] The purpose of the author, who is the preacher, is to quote the liturgy, since the work is a mystagogical catechesis.

When we turn to the anaphora described in the *Hierarchia Ecclesiastica*,[81] sacrificial language is limited; celebrating the eucharist is referred to in such terms ταύτης ἱερουργίας and ἱερουργεῖ τὰ θειότατα. But the reference to offering comes in regarding the nature of the divine presence, "through the symbols set before in a priestly manner."

The anaphora alluded to by Theodore of Mopsuestia,[82] on the other hand, is rich in sacrificial imagery, as we might expect from such a preacher. The deacon says, "behold the offering," at the beginning of the dialogue, and the bishop "begins the offering of the sacrifice" (meaning the anaphora). But the sacrifice is defined as "the memorial of the sacrifice and death of the Lord." The elevation is performed of "the oblation of the sacrifice and the sacrifice of communion," another double emphasis on the unique character of Christ's death and

69

the corporate nature of the memorial in the eucharist. The eucharist is also a sacrifice of praise ("at all times offer praise and hymns").

After the Sanctus the bishop "offers pity . . . for us." In the epiclesis, the eucharist is described as "the gift of Christ . . . through which those (gifts) which are offered. . . ." The bishop "offers prayer to God" for the Spirit to change "the bread and wine which are offered . . . which is the memorial of immortality," once more stressing the theme of anamnesis. The epiclesis is linked to intercession, both the living (offering supplication for all) and the departed ("then he goes on to the commemoration of those who have died, because this sacrifice can guard both us in this world and also those who have died in faith . . ."). The main sacrificial themes in Theodore's lectures add nothing new to our discussion of anaphoras so far, but supply us with corroborative detail.

Literary evidence from the other eastern Fathers is not lacking. Basil of Caesarea, for example, speaks of the priest as "completing the sacrifice," in language that is liturgical jargon for celebrating the eucharist, although the term "complete" does not appear in the anaphora bearing his name.[83] Gregory Nazianzus suggests "let us sacrifice ourselves to God" and is concerned with relating sacrifice to eucharist:

"I know of another altar. . . . It is at this altar that I will stand, and I will *sacrifice acceptable offerings, sacrifice oblations and burnt-offerings. . . .*"

Also:

"I know that no one is worthy of the great one, who is God and sacrifice and high priest, *who has not first offered himself to God as a living sacrifice* and holy, and displayed the rational service which is acceptable, and has sacrificed to God *a sacrifice of praise,* and a contrite spirit. . . . How then was I to make bold to offer to him the external sacrifice, *the antitype of the great mysteries?*"[84]

Gregory's concern relates the Old and the New covenants and the work of Christ with the celebration of the eucharist. A similar line of thought is to be found in the writings of John Chrysostom:

"It is not the name who makes the *gift of the oblation* to become the body and blood of Christ, but Christ himself. . . . The statement transforms the oblations . . . makes *complete the sacrifice* at every table. . . ."

Perhaps most significant of all:

"We *offer every day, making a memorial of his death.* This is one sacrifice, not many. And why? Because it was offered once. It resembles in this the sacrifice which was taken into the holy of holies. This (Jewish) sacrifice is a type of that sacrifice (of Christ). We always offer the same person . . . the same oblation; therefore it is one sacrifice. . . . By the same token, the offering of the sacrifice in many places does not, of course, mean that there are many Christs. Christ is everywhere one, entire in this place and that, one body . . . and so one sacrifice. . . . *We offer now what was offered then,* an inexhaustible offering. . . . We offer the same sacrifice: or rather, *we make a memorial of that sacrifice.*"[85]

Chrysostom takes the line of thought in Gregory one stage further. Unlike Cyril, who is describing the liturgy and supposing some familiarity with it, the golden-mouthed teacher of Antioch is defining principles. Nonetheless it is hard not to see some kind of allusion in the second passage to the anamnesis, "we offer, making a memorial." His overriding interest is to show how Christ supercedes the Jewish sacrifices and how the eucharist is not part of the same sacrifice of Christ but is a memorial. Chrysostom is dealing with a difficult theological paradox. He is not the first to do so.

Perhaps more interesting than any of those Greek writers is Theodoret of Cyrrhus. Commenting on the notions of eucharistic sacrifice he has definition, apologetic, and liturgical allusion in the following passages:

"Christ is a priest . . . *who does not himself offer anything, but he acts as the head of those who offer.* For he calls the Church his body, and through it he performs *the office of priest as man, while as God he receives the offerings.* The Church offers the symbols of his body and blood, sanctifying the whole mass through the first-fruits."

Also:

"If the priesthood established by the law has come to an end, and the priest who is 'in the order of Melchisedek' has offered his sacrifice, and has made all other sacrifices unnecessary, why do the priests of the new covenant perform the mystical liturgy? Now it is clear to those instructed in divinity that *we do not offer another sacrifice, but perform a memorial* (ἀναμνήσις) of that unique and saving offering. For this was the Lord's command: 'Do this in remembrance of me.' So that *by contemplation* we may recall what is symbolised, the sufferings endured on our behalf, and may kindle our love towards our benefactor, and *look forward* to the enjoyment of the blessings to come.[86]

Many of the ideas contained in these two passages we have come across before. Theodoret is continuing in a long succession of theologians who stress both the unique nature of Christ's offering as well as the memorial reality of the eucharist. He also makes Christ the offerer, in order to ensure that reality and not reduce the eucharist into a mechanistic ritual. But he also gives us a clue to the two developments that we have seen in many of the Syriac anaphoras. In the first passage, Christ as God "receives the offerings," and in the second passage, "by contemplation we may recall what is symbolised." In the Syriac eucharistic prayers, we have noted two important trends that are absent in the Greek anaphoras. One is the prayer for the acceptance of the offering in many an anamnesis, prior to the epiclesis ("receive this offering . . . and we pray that your Holy Spirit . . ."). Another trend is the way in which the notion of anamnesis itself is redefined in a psychological manner ("through the eye of the mind"). Theodoret was a bishop in the Syriac-speaking part of Syria, and it is probable that he was brought up as a native Syriac-speaker himself.[87] In these passages we may find these two native Syriac theological features of many anaphoras.

AUTHENTICITY AND PSEUDONYMITY

So far we have only allowed for the authenticity of the anaphora bearing the name of Basil, and that only with the qualifications made by some recent scholars. But in recent years, other anaphoras have been defended for their authenticity. Georg Wagner has suggested that much of the anaphora of John Chrysostom is the work of that great teacher himself.[88] Gabrielle Winkler[89] has suggested the same for the Armenian anaphoras, of Gregory Nazianzus himself. Raes has taken the debate on the relationship between Chrysostom and Twelve Apostles even further by suggesting Twelve Apostles to be much earlier.[90] Parallels between the anaphora bearing the name of a writer with the actual writings of that author have convinced Capelle as well as Engberding that *Basil Alex*[2] and *Basil Byz* were the work of the great Cappadocian.[91] Connolly did the same with Hippolytus. Brightman did the same with Theodore.[92]

All this can be great fun, but at the end of the day it must prove to be at least partially inconclusive. As Geoffrey Cuming has pointed out, authors can quote liturgy without that liturgy being their own work.[93] And although eucharistic presidents were early on constricted by certain conventions, at least by the time of Origen,[94] those conventions did not serve as severe laws, on the one hand, nor as opportunities for license, on the other hand. Many a modern preacher knows how effective it can be to quote the liturgy, especially in a society in which the Bible is either not very familiar or else known in many different translations. The conclusion to be drawn from these anaphoras—Greek, Coptic, Syriac, and Armenian—is that they underwent a long process of development, which probably coincided with times of their richest theological life.

For example, the three Byzantine anaphoras probably date from the fourth and fifth centuries, as do the Coptic-Greek prayers; whereas the Syriac and Armenian may well date from the fifth-seventh centuries, although even here recent studies suggest an earlier date for the origins of the Syriac and Armenian rites as a whole. If Twelve Apostles is early, is the absence of an offering verb a "Syriac symptom," or is it an ancient feature, similar to Addai and Mari and the Maronite *sharar* (which offer commemoration, but not gifts)? If, on the other hand, Twelve Apostles dates from the seventh century, the absence of an offering verb in the anamnesis could indeed be a "Syriac symptom," and we are left to conclude that it originally had one, as does Chrysostom. I am not here arguing for great differences in theology, but for literary variety, reflecting on different theological emphases.

The theories of modern scholars, claiming authenticity for their choice anaphoras would, indeed, be wonderful if true. But the question must remain, for the time being at least, an open one. When great figures in the church disappear from the scene, their works, (whether liturgical, homiletical, architectural, or other), tend to become enshrined and embroidered in the minds of the faithful. It is good that all the eastern churches (not least the Syriac, Nestorian, Jacobite, and Maronite) associate their eucharistic prayers with great and holy men. But liturgy is a conservative business that changes sometimes imperceptibly, sometimes forcibly. Whenever and however, and by whomever all these many anaphoras were written, their ways of dealing with offering language vary from one tradition to another. This is because they had different, although complementary, perceptions of what the eucharist is, and because expressing those perceptions is a process which never really stops. Whether one is dealing with the gift offering mentality of a Basil of Caesarea; the sacrificial christology of a John of Bosra; the "total" anamnesis of the Christ event (starting with Bethlehem) in a Marutas of Tagrit; or the repeated paradoxes of living sacrifice, memorial sacrifice, and sacrifice of praise of a Gregory Nazianzus . . . all these liturgical nuances show that minds were alive and fertile.

Chapter Four

Flowering: The West

When it comes to dealing with the West, frustration sets in because of a lack of continuous evidence, and because we do not encounter anything like the literary and theological variety of the eastern anaphoras. But, as if to compensate for this, the Roman Canon, (which eventually dominates western medieval eucharistic euchology) has an almost single-minded attachment to the notion of offering. Through it, and through the themes of the various prayers *Super oblata* ("over the oblations") at the offertory, we shall see a logical progression of ideas that, step by step, works up to a crescendo at the end of the anaphora. Variability within the Canon (the *Hanc igitur*) and before it (the *Super oblata*) enrich the picture. The Ambrosian prayers provide their own variation on this basic structure. But it is in the Mozarabic prayers (especially in the *Post pridie* units within the anaphora) that a real literary and theological difference is to be seen, which probably points back to the old Visigothic rite of the fifth and sixth centuries, with its own style. As in the case of the eastern prayers, the picture is only complete when all the minority groups are looked at properly. The total scene is inadequate if we think that Roman and Byzantine prayers say all there is to be said.

AMBROSE OF MILAN, AND THE ROMAN CANON

In the fourth book of the *De Sacramentis*[1] (now no longer disputed as the work of Ambrose), the great teacher of Milan explains the meaning of the eucharist. The treatise at this point contains several allusions to the liturgy then in use at Milan, and these allusions are both strikingly similar to and significantly different from what we know to be the later Roman Canon. Although Ambrose is known to have been influenced by eastern theology, notably John Chrysostom and Basil of Caesarea, the liturgy he used takes us into a world different from the one we have seen. The relevant portions of Book 4 are worth quoting in full:

"14. Perhaps you will say, 'My bread is common (bread).' But that

bread is bread before the words of the sacraments; when consecration has been applied, from (being) bread it becomes the flesh of Christ. And by what words and whose sayings does consecration take place? The Lord Jesus'. For all the other things which are said in the earlier parts (of the service) are said by the bishop:
Praise is offered to God, prayer is made for the people, for kings, for others; when the time comes for the venerated sacrament to be accomplished, the bishop no longer uses his own words, but uses the words of Christ. So the word of Christ accomplishes the sacrament."

"21. Do you wish to know how consecration is done with heavenly words? Hear what the words are. The bishop says:
Make for us this *offering approved, reasonable, acceptable,* because it is the figure of the body and blood of our Jesus Christ; who, the day before he suffered. . . ." (Institution narrative follows, with explanation.)

"27. And the bishop says:
Therefore, remembering his most glorious passion and resurrection from the dead, and ascension into heaven, *we offer you this spotless victim, reasonable victim, bloodless victim,* this holy bread and this cup of eternal life; and we pray and beseech you to *receive this offering on your altar on high by the hands of your angels,* as you vouchsafed to receive the *gifts* of your righteous servant Abel, and the sacrifice of our Patriarch Abraham, and that which the high-priest Melchizedek offered to you."

The basic outline of the anaphora is clear. It begins with praise, which is offered. It moves into intercession for various topics. The prayer reaches a particularly solemn point when the preacher is moved to quote from the liturgical text rather than describe its movement of ideas, at which the offering is to be acceptable as the "figure" of the body and blood of Christ. Then comes the institution narrative, about which Ambrose stresses that the bishop is not using his own words, but the words of Christ (even though the bread is "broken"). Great emphasis is placed on these words and they supply the foundations for the later western concentration on the narrative as the words of consecration.[2] Ambrose has already (in chapter 14) spoken of "when the consecration has been applied." We are already a far cry from Theodoret of Cyrus's priestly invocation. After the narrative, the anamnesis gives us familiar territory, with the convention of "remembering . . . we offer," but what is offered is a "victim," which is rhetorically described as "spotless," "reasonable," and "bloodless," the second and third of which are words we have met before in reference to the whole sacrifice of the eucharist. But here the victim is the bread and cup. This short anamnesis leads into another prayer for the acceptance of the offering, this time asking for it to be taken to the heavenly altar by an angel, and backed up by a reference to the sacrifices of Abraham and Melchizedek. Ambrose's anaphora, therefore, consists supremely (but not necessarily solely) in the offering of praise, followed by intercession, followed by consecration. The consecration is closely associated with the acceptance of the sacrifice. In this scheme, we have no need to define the nature of the sacrifice, except in the anamnesis, where paradoxical language is used by the juxtaposition of "victim" with various adjectives, to be followed immediately by bread and cup.

Like Hippolytus, there is praise, but this time it is followed by intercession. Like Hippolytus, there is an institution narrative followed immediately by an anamnesis, but these are sandwiched by petitions for the acceptance of the offering.[3] Like Hippolytus, the prayer ends with a doxology. Where does the notion of acceptance come from? We have encountered it before, in the Egyptian tradition of the anaphora of Mark and in several of the Syriac anaphoras (Jacobite and Maronite). In Theodoret of Cyrus we have seen explained the logic of God receiving the offering as well as being the originator of that offering. It is just that we do not find the idea of the acceptance of the *offering* in the Greek West Syrian and Byzantine eucharistic prayers. However, this elaboration must have been the result of a long tradition, in which apologetic demands of a society that knew pagan sacrifices played an important part. As Ralph Keifer has put it, "the notion of votive offering influenced the Roman understanding and verbal expression of offering."[4] At root, Ambrose's prayer is a Roman one from a theological standpoint, even though there are discernible parallels with the East. The gift offering of the Old Testament has of necessity been infected with the pagan votive offering, in order to make the eucharist real for people of yet one more different culture.[5] Ambrose does not mention the Sanctus, and it could well be that this was a subsequent insertion into the tradition. In Egypt, the Sanctus[6] came in as a logical development from the allusion to the heavenly worship and the offering of the bloodless service (as *Strasbourg*). Its presence in the East Syrian tradition probably reflects early Semitic roots, and even (in the case of Addai and Mari) an original use. Here, however, the sequence of ideas precludes it, for the moment.

The Roman Canon, on the other hand, both supports and amplifies the liturgical quotations of Ambrose of Milan. Whereas Ambrose tells us something of the Milanese liturgy in the second half of the fourth century (probably towards the end), the Canon's text dates from much later (the eighth century), although the form in which it appears in the Old Gelasian Sacramentary probably contains the text as it was used at the time of Gregory the Great. The studies of Botte, Willis, and others[7] enable us to probe further behind the text and to establish the earliest appearance of some of the paragraphs, especially at the time of Innocent I, whose letter to Decentius of Gubbio in A.D. 416 is a valuable piece of correspondence. Here is the full text[8] of the relevant portions of the Canon, from the Sanctus to the doxology:

Te igitur: "We therefore pray and beseech you, most merciful Father, through your Son Jesus Christ our Lord, *to accept and bless these gifts, these offerings, these holy and unblemished sacrifices;* above all, those which *we offer to you for your holy* Catholic Church: vouchsafe to grant it peace, protection, unity, and guidance throughout the world, together with your servant *N.* our pope, and *N.* our bishop, and all orthodox upholders of the catholic and apostolic faith."

Memento: "Remember, Lord, your servants, men and women, and all who stand around (us), whose faith and devotion are known to you, *for whom we offer to you or who offer to you this sacrifice of praise for themselves and for their own,* for the redemption of their souls, for the hope of their salvation and safety, and pay their vows to you, the living, true and eternal God.
"In fellowship with (a list of saints)."

Hanc igitur: "Therefore, Lord we pray you graciously *to accept this offering made by us,* your servants, and also by your whole family; and to order our days in peace; and to command that we are snatched from eternal damnation and numbered among the flock of your elect; through Christ our Lord."

Quam oblationem: "Vouchsafe, we beseech you, O God, *to make this offering wholly blessed, approved, ratified, reasonable, and acceptable;* that it may become to us the body and blood of your dearly beloved Son Jesus Christ our Lord;
Who (institution narrative follows)."

Unde et memores: "Therefore also, Lord, we your servants, and also your holy people, have in remembrance the blessed passion of your Son Christ our Lord, likewise his resurrection from the dead and also his glorious ascension into heaven; *we offer to your excellent majesty from your gifts and bounty a pure victim, a holy victim, an unspotted victim,* the holy bread of eternal life and the cup of everlasting salvation."

Supra quae: "Vouchsafe to look upon them with a favourable and kindly countenance, and accept them as you vouchsafed *to accept the gifts of your righteous servant Abel,* and the sacrifice of our patriarch Abraham, and that which your high-priest Melchizedek offered to you, a holy sacrifice, an unblemished victim."

Supplices te: We humbly beseech you, almighty God, to bid them be borne by the hands of your angel to *your altar on high,* in the sight of your divine majesty, that all of us who have received the most holy body and blood of your Son by partaking at this altar may be filled with all heavenly blessing and grace; through Christ our Lord."
(Prayer for departed)
(Commemoration of more saints)
(Doxology).

The dialogue appears in Hippolytus in a slightly different form, and instead of the thanksgiving series contained in it, the Canon has variable prefaces, which may have first appeared in the fourth century when it was thought appropriate to emphasize a particular aspect of the saving acts of God in Christ. At any rate, with the second part of the prayer developing through the fourth and fifth centuries, it is perhaps understandable that the first part should develop also. The inclusion of the Sanctus could have played an important role in this. *Some early* prefaces do not seem to lead into the Sanctus[9] at all, yet one more example of the conservative character of the Roman liturgy at this time.

Te igitur and *Memento* are both mentioned by Innocent I in his letter to Decentius of Gubbio, which means that they were in circulation in 416.[10] Neither is quoted by Ambrose, however, although something resembling them has been used as the intercession in the earlier part of the anaphora he describes. The first list of saints (*Communicantes*) probably comes from the mid-fifth century and is a natural development from the preceding paragraph. Both *Hanc igitur* and *Quam oblationem* appear in Ambrose, but they are conjoined and have some linguistic differences so that we are left to suggest that Ambrose is describing an earlier version of both these prayers, a single archetype. The *Hanc igitur* is, of course, a variable prayer (like the preface); the Leonine Sacramentary has ten, the Old Gelasian no less than forty-one, whereas the Gregorian has six, thus showing a tendency to abbreviate and simplify.[11] (It should not be surprising to the twentieth-century liturgist to note that the Canon allows of variability at two separate foci within the prayer, namely thanksgiving and supplication, each of which are foundations for the basic shape of the eucharistic prayer in its Jewish antecedents.) The institution narrative (*Qui pridie*) occurs in all the main sources, including Irenaeus, Hippolytus, and Ambrose, although the words of Christ in the Canon are simpler than in Ambrose.[12] The following paragraph (*Unde et memores*) is the most similar to Ambrose, along with the narrative, but the differences include the way in which the victim is described, although the victim is still treated with rhetorical repetition. Common but indirect parentage with Hippolytus is suggested. Ambrose conflates the next two paragraphs (*Supra quae* and *Supplices te*), and Botte has shown how the latter was probably brought together by a Gregorian editor in the sixth century. The prayer for the departed originally did not take place on Sundays, and the commemoration of further saints probably dates from the sixth century, but the doxology is comparable to Hippolytus and Ambrose, although there are again differences and additions.

We are left with a bare minimum of prayers either alluded to or actually described by Ambrose, of which all can be fitted somewhere into the later Canon, but allowances must be made for the independent character of the Milanese liturgy. The Canon itself, however, provides us with a lengthy series of supplicatory themes centered round the institution narrative and anamnesis. These supplicatory prayers are all sacrificial in their tone and can (at least in principle) be traced back to the period from the end of the fourth century through the fifth to the sixth. This is the era in which the Roman tradition of liturgical prayer was developing through the *libelli missarum*, which are those local books of improvised prayers written down for use on various occasions, and which lie behind the later sacramentaries. It is significant that of the *four* paragraphs (*Hanc igitur* and *Quam oblationem, Supra quae* and *Supplices te*), Ambrose gives us *two* conflations, which are probably earlier versions or earlier local variants. But having allowed for this, what are we to make of the sequence of prayers in the Canon?

Various attempts have been made to make sense of them, whether by medieval commentators[13] or scholars (like Frere[14]) who found the paragraphs disjointed and illogical. Recently, Ralph Keifer has made a study of the Canon, and he comes up with a simple pattern:[15]

Vere dignum-Sanctus	We praise you
Te igitur	We offer (for the whole church)
Memento	We offer (for particular persons)
Communicantes	We offer (in union with . . .)
Hanc igitur	We offer (for special needs)

Quam oblationem	Accept our offering
Qui pridie	Because Christ commands it
Unde et memores	In his memorial, we offer
Supra quae	Accept our offering as you did those of the old covenant
Supplices te	Make it pleasing and beneficial for us

Once it is assumed that the praise can be *offered* (as Ambrose had so described the preface), then the *igitur* of *Te igitur* falls into place, because the logic of the whole prayer is, as Keifer puts it, "we offer you praise which is an oblation; we *therefore* ask that you accept it." Apart from dispensing with the difficulties surrounding that *igitur*, such an analysis is along the lines we have earlier suggested of different approaches to sacrifice, approaches of praise, of intercession, and of gift. There can be no doubt that the Canon concentrates on offering to the exclusion of much else that we have seen in other anaphoras, notably the work of the Holy Spirit. As Gy has put it: "the Roman Canon is of all the anaphoras the one which places the most importance on offering. Its sequence of ideas, without being wrong, has something of its own character, much more than the transition from Greek to Latin has separated the two aspects of the eucharist, namely thanksgiving and consecration."[16]

Moreover, the similarity with the Egyptian tradition is noticeable because of the link made between the intercession and the prayer for acceptance of the sacrifice, a different emphasis from the Greek West Syrian and the Syriac notions we saw in the previous chapters. But it cannot be denied that both Ambrose and the later Canon place considerable weight on the narrative itself by the way in which it is introduced and also by the language with which the eucharist is described in the *Unde et memores,* as victim, "pure," "holy," and "unspotted." Admittedly, the paradoxical character of this language is heightened by the addition of words in the Canon that are not in Ambrose, "from your gifts and bounty." The theme of gift sacrifice has been transformed into something much stronger than we have so far seen. Some key quotations from Ambrose and Augustine reflect this direction in thought. First, from Ambrose:

"We have seen the High Priest coming to us; we have seen and heard him offering his blood for us. We priests follow, as well as we can, so that *we may offer sacrifice for the people.* Though we can claim no merit, we are to be honoured in the sacrifice; for, although Christ is not now visibly offered, yet he is himself offered on earth, when the body of Christ is offered. Moreover, it is made clear that *he himself offers in us,* since it is his words which sanctify the sacrifice which is offered."

Also:

"Formerly a lamb was offered, and a calf; now Christ is offered. But Christ is offered as man, accepting suffering; and he offers himself as priest, so that he may forgive our sins; here, in symbol; in reality, there, where he intercedes for us as an advocate before the Father."[17]

In the first passage, we note some of the concerns that we saw earlier in the *De Sacramentis.* The celebrant has a duty in following liturgical procedures because of the serious nature of the task, to "offer sacrifice for the people," once more alluding to the eucharist as both inter-cession and consecration (and communion). Ambrose sees the eucha-rist in dynamic terms and interprets the eucharistic action not as the Church obeying a command so much as the work of Christ in his people, "he himself offers in us," and he repeats his insistance on procedure, "since it is his words. . . ." In the second passage, Am-brose is more concerned with the theological apologetic of sacrifice, a theme we encountered in the East, both in anaphoras and also in teaching. In the old days animals were offered, but Christ has put an end to all that by his life ("accepting suffering"), by his death ("so that he may forgive"), and by his eternal intercession ("as advocate before the Father"). Such notions of eucharistic sacrifice are strongly christocentric because they link the eucharist with the saving work of Christ and try to point to the way in which the eucharist continues that work, although that work is not the Church's but rather the work of Christ himself. Already, we see a different approach to these issues from that expressed in the eastern anaphoras. The apologetic concern of Ambrose is not to insist on the memorial character of the eucharis-tic sacrifice (as we saw in Chrysostom and Theodoret[18]), but to show how Christ is the agent of the sacrifice. Augustine takes these ideas further:

"The offering of sacrifices of animal victims by the Fathers in ancient times . . . is to be understood as having just this purpose: to symbo-lize all our endeavours to be united with God, and our concern to achieve the same end for our neighbour. A sacrifice therefore is the *visible sacrament of an invisible sacrifice;* that is, it is a sacred sign. . . . 'A sacrifice to God is a contrite spirit.' . . . Mercy, too, is a real sacri-fice. . . . After all, the divine instructions concerning sacrifice in the service of the tabernacle or temple are by their symbolism directed to-wards love to God and neighbour. . . ."

Also:

A true sacrifice is every act which is performed so that we may be united with God in holy fellowship. . . . *Although this sacrifice is made or offered by man, still the sacrifice is a divine act. . . .* The whole redeemed community, the congregation and fellowship of the saints, is offered as a universal sacrifice to God by the great High Priest who offered himself in suffering for us in the form of a servant, that we might be the Body of so great a Head. This form of a servant he offered, in that he was offered; for in this he is mediator, priest, and sacrifice. So the apostle exhorted us to 'present our bodies as a living sacrifice . . .'; we ourselves are the whole sacrifice. . . . This is the sacrifice of Christians. . . . *The sacrifice the Church celebrates is the sacrament of the altar,* which the faithful know well, where it is shown to her that in this thing which she offers she herself is offered."[19]

Parentage with Ambrose is clear but Augustine takes time to define terms and to quote scripture. In the first passage, we have a moral interpretation of sacrifice, with God-ward and man-ward implications. Then in the second passage, the writer insists that the eucharistic sacrifice is the act of God himself, as is the sacrifice of Christ's life and death. The response of Christians is to be a living sacrifice, which, I would suggest, is fidelity in good works, including the eucharist itself. It seems that behind all these four passages lies an assumption that the eucharist *is* a sacrifice, but, instead of propounding the concept of memorial, which is weaker in the Roman Canon than it is in the eastern anaphoras, we have by contrast a strong and dynamic view of the eucharist as the life of God in the faithful now. It is likely that Augustine's liturgy resembled that of Ambrose, for we know that North Africa followed Rome in liturgical practice. What Augustine is doing, therefore, is defining a concept in a new way, because it is an assumed part of Christian worship and part of a long tradition. Augustine's strong notion of Christ in the eucharistic sacrifice harks back to some of the language we saw in Cyprian's writings. Such weighty imagery stemmed from a spirituality built upon a eucharistic liturgy in which the sacrificial dimension was greater than any others.

By the time of Gregory the Great, similar ideas appear, with less theological acumen but with an obvious pastoral concern:

"For this victim in a unique way saves the soul from eternal destruction, which in mystery renews for us the death of the only-begotten Son, who . . . yet . . . *is again sacrificed on our behalf in this mystery of the sacred oblation. . . .*"

Also:

"The mere reception of the Sacraments of our Redeemer is not enough really to consecrate the mind unless good works also be added. . . .

"*We must offer ourselves to God with a penitent heart,* because we who celebrate the mysteries of the passion of the Lord are bound to imitate the rite which we perform. Then will it be really a sacrifice to God on our behalf, when we have made ourselves a sacrifice. . . ."[20]

Gregory may well be thinking of the inner meaning of *ite, missa est* at the end of the eucharist when he preached those telling words of the living sacrifice. Gregory is wrestling with the meaning of the memorial in a way that we have not seen in Ambrose and Augustine. It seems to me that Gregory saw the word "victim" as an allusion to the Canon; and by "victim" he is referring both to Christ and to the eucharist.

In our discussion, we have noted the main parallels, but, of course, Hippolytus's *Apostolic Tradition* (even if Roman) need not give us the *norm* for all Roman Christians at the start of the third century. The trouble is that the commonality between Hippolytus's eucharistic prayer and the later East is considerably stronger than with the later West, and we shall be continuing to clutch at liturgical straws if we fail to accept this discontinuity and the uncertainties that surround the background of the Canon. Yet the Canon has a sequence and development that may well go back to a time considerably earlier than Ambrose himself, at least in principle, particularly as the internal unity of the Canon rests on the assumption that the eucharist is a sacrifice of praise and a sacrifice of gifts, which will only do God's will if they are accepted by him in heaven.

There is a great deal of subtlety in the way the material has been put together, as witness the assignation "bloodless" of the "victim," a notion that the East would not yet have used. On the other hand, the East stresses the divine economy, whether in the thanksgiving series (e.g., Basil) or the expanded anamnesis (as in some Syriac anaphoras), and relies on the Holy Spirit for the sanctification of both gifts and people. The Roman Canon, by contrast, takes us toward heaven and uses bread and wine and the work of Christ in the faithful now as the means of doing this, together with an elaborate sacrificial system with which to express it. The pagan background, single-mindedness, and logical sequence of ideas we see in this eucharistic prayer are to be paralleled in the nuptial blessing of the same tradition. As

Keifer writes, "whether the resulting pattern of eucharistic prayer is found appealing or not is another question, but it cannot be denied that on its own grounds it is coherent."[21]

THE SACRAMENTARIES: HANC IGITUR AND SUPER OBLATA

Ambrose does not mention the *Hanc igitur* directly, although he prays for the offering to be acceptable. The point of the separate prayer, however, is to ask God to "accept this offering" for a particular intention. It seems likely that (like other prayers in the Mass) these were originally prayed *extempore* according to set norms. Indeed, the structure of the *Hanc igiturs* as they appear in the sacramentaries would suggest precisely such an origin. This short paragraph focuses on a special theme of prayer in the Mass.

We have already noted that the Leonine book contains ten, the Old Gelasian no less than forty-one, but there are only six in the Gregorian (to be reduced to three in the Missal of 1570). In the Gregorian, the occasions are (apart from the usual form in the Mass for all other occasions): the ordination of a bishop (although this is entitled *praefatio*), Maundy Thursday, Eastertide (starting with the Vigil Mass), the ordination of a presbyter, and the nuptial Mass.[22] It would seem that Gregory the Great had in mind pruning down the use of the *Hanc igitur* to a minimum. The Supplement and its subsidiary manuscripts contain many more, which are mostly paralleled in the Old Gelasian, and most of these are for the votive Masses,[23] which of course are absent in the *Hadrianum* text sent to Charlemagne. This is an important pastoral point because it demonstrates the different conditions under which the eucharist was celebrated in Rome by the Pope and north of the Alps by ordinary priests, for in the Frankish lands, the eucharist was increasingly celebrated "for" many various needs and circumstances. (It was probably his perusal of these countless votive forms that inspired Gregory Dix in this century to write his immortal paragraph in the final chapter of *The Shape of the Liturgy*, "Was ever another command so obeyed . . .").[24]

There is little theological variety in the *Hanc igitur* because the second part of the prayer usually states briefly the pastoral needs and aspirations of the celebration. For example, the prayer for the nuptial Mass prays for the bride, who has lived to see her wedding day, that she may be made worthy of being joined to her husband. In the context of the old nuptial Mass with its precommunion blessing, such a prayer necessarily points forward to that blessing and to the ensuing communion.[25] By adding the prayer for peace and preservation from damnation to the common form, Gregory the Great himself perhaps expressed the turbulent circumstances of the time.[26] I would myself see the *Hanc igitur* as the result of a lengthy evolution, perhaps with as much variety and variation as the preface.

With the *Super oblata*, however, we are on different ground. Unlike the *Hanc igitur*, which belongs within the Canon, the *Super oblata* immediately precedes it. When did this prayer first appear?

The sacramentaries usually call it "over the oblations," but this is a seventh-century title and one that soon gave way (due to influences from the Gelasian books) to the later title, *Secreta*. "It is doubtful whether it appeared quite as early as the Collect, which we have seen reason to trace back to the time of St. Leo,"[27] writes Willis. He notes that the Ascension Mass that Capelle attributed to Leo has no such prayer in the Mass set, nor have the Pentecost Embertide Mass sets.[28] Willis goes on to suggest that the prayer came into regular use between the time of Leo and Gelasius, which puts it between 461 and 492. Even though this may well be the case, Willis begs the question from the start of his discussion about the *function* of the prayer, whose purpose (he claims) "is to commend the offerings to God, and to ask him to receive them."[29]

David Holeton has challenged this traditional view in a study of the liturgical terminology employed by Leo in his preaching. He has put up a strong case for concluding that such words as *munus* and *oblata*, so far from referring exclusively to the gifts presented on the altar, in fact are imprecise expressions which encompass the whole eucharistic celebration.[30] While some of Holeton's quotations from Leo and the *Super oblata* prayers in the sacramentaries may seem to stretch the evidence a little, in many cases his interpretation appears sound. Liturgists need to have cherished assumptions questioned, and the long line of interpreters of offertory prayers[31] have a considerable task to refute Holeton's analysis. It cannot be doubted that these prayers were understood subsequently to refer to the gifts, as our discussion will show within the development of this prayer in the sacramentary tradition. But that is another matter. In liturgy we are so often dealing with the gap between the original intentions of the author or authors and the way in which those prayers are later heard by priests and faithful.

The vocabulary of the *Super oblata* is varied, and it is worthwhile to take a closer look at these prayers as they occur in the sacramentaries to see how sacrificial language and imagery are employed within them. The words are usually *munus* (gift), *oblatio* (offering), *sacrificium* (sacrifice), *hostia* (victim), *mysterium* (mystery), together with such verbs as *offerre* and *deferre*, and sometimes *celebrare* and *immolare*. The

Leonine Sacramentary is rich in the mixture of all these, and we find little real theological consistency in the collection, which is hardly surprising in view of the number of prayers that occur in the book. For example, an early prayer in the collection[32] does not mention any gifts, but the *praeces* (prayers) that the faithful bring to the altar. It asks that the intercession of the saints may protect them. Frequently, the theme of the sacrifice of praise occurs, with or without reference to the gifts, however these latter are to be interpreted. Sometimes, the dynamic notion is expressed in a verb such as *occurimus* (we come to meet). This could refer to the presentation of the gifts, but it is more likely an image borrowed from the procession at the start of Mass.

There seem to be three categories of prayers. First, there are those which are imprecise and only speak of *vota* (vows), or of *solemnia celebrare* (celebrate the solemnities); these sum up the entire celebration.[33] Then there are those that have more overt sacrificial imagery, but that are patient of Holeton's interpretation; these often speak of a *munus oblatum* (gift offered, or presented) or *haec dona* (these gifts, presents).[34] Thirdly, there are those that explicitly refer to the eucharistic gifts; they use such language as *victimam spiritalem* (spiritual victim), and *in hoc altari proposita* (which have been placed on this altar).[35] The offering verb varies a great deal, sometimes in the present tense, sometimes in the past tense, and we even come across the present participle. Unlike our discussions of the eastern anaphoras, such variation is the result of a need to enrich vocabulary, for we are not here dealing with whole eucharistic prayers, but rather with individual prayers that are to be used on numerous occasions, and which, therefore, should use formulae that have a wide range of meaning.

I would suggest that these three types of *Super oblata* in the Leonine Sacramentary embody a definite shift from imprecision to precision. In other words, they start life as prayers that express the whole eucharist and eventually become prayers that refer explicitly to the bread and wine. If such a view contains any veracity, then the *Super oblata* has a varied and uncertain history behind it, more subtle than just a desire to use different vocabulary. In fact, its history perhaps betrays some confusion about its original purpose. Sometimes the language is nothing short of quaint (*per haec caelestis vitae commercia* = "through this exchange of heavenly life"),[36] and there are occasions when the offerers (*offerentes*) are referred to as well. There is also a preface (no less) which has *hostias tibi laudis offerimus* (we offer you victims of praise).[37] But behind even the different understandings of this prayer lies a ready acceptance of sacrificial imagery, which can use verbs such as "immolate" and nouns such as "victim" that are sometimes offset by qualifying terminology, such as *sacrificium singulare* (single sacrifice)[38] and constant references to the sacrifices and offerings of praise and devotion. There are also allusions to receiving holy communion (*sacri participation mysterii* = "through participation in the holy mystery").[39] The eucharist can still be described as an immolation, a term that has been reinterpreted as a liturgical shorthand for a theological truth; the spiritualization of sacrifice never seems to stop, especially in the Latin West.

The Old Gelasian Sacramentary uses many (but not all) of the *Super oblata* in the Leonine, and it is interesting to see which themes recur in this collection. The same basic vocabulary persists, but the *Super oblata* tend to use language that refers explicitly to the gifts. Holeton's thesis cannot work so easily here and the language tends to be stronger. For example, *immolare* and its cognate *immolatio* occur more frequently. *Munus* is still the favorite noun for the prayer, as it is in the Leonine book, although there are discernible shifts in the collection towards using *oblatio* and *sacrificium* as substitutes. The offering verbs *offerre* and *deferre* occur with less frequency. We also note a tendency to describe the effects of the eucharist in inner dispositions, such as *expiatis mentibus* (with expiated minds).[40] While *hostia* (victim) sometimes appears with *placatus* (be pleased), we also see *mysterium* (mystery) alongside *gerimus* (perform, do). There are also occasions when the assembly "offers the sacrifice *for*" (*pro*) some cause.[41] This last feature could be a late stratum in the tradition. Certainly the Old Gelasian *Super oblata* prayers show a move toward specifically eucharistic ideas, referring to the eucharistic gifts, a process that may have been caused by the fact that the Gelasian books have *two* prayers before the *Super oblata*, which thus provide more possibilities for general prayer on the theme of the day, earlier in the Mass.[42]

The Gregorian Sacramentary uses many prayers that also appear in the Leonine and the Old Gelasian; in fact, the majority of them appear in the Old Gelasian. This means that the same vocabulary recurs, including verbs like *immolare* and *caelebrare* (celebrate).[43] The seasonal concerns of the prayer find expression, as is to be expected. But it is in the Supplement[44] that there is a discernible shift away from the three strands in the Leonine book. The Supplement and its derivative manuscripts bring together material from the Gelasian of the eighth century and earlier Frankish liturgical traditions. The theological tendency of these ancillary collections is even stronger still, and we can observe two tendencies.

First, *pro* (for) occurs more frequently, and we also encounter *ut* (in order that).[45] It is a harmless linguistic convention but it shows a more defined purpose in the prayer. The second tendency is more important, namely, the first-person singular[46] in the verb of the prayer, *offero*, which occurs once in the Supplement, in a votive Mass for the priest himself, and no less than eleven times in the ancillary documents throughout various other votive formulae. It could be conceded that when a priest is offering a votive Mass for himself, he should use the first-person singular, but when that linguistic convention is spread to other votive Masses, the conclusion is clear that the *priest* is doing something that the congregation is *not*. He is exercising more than a function of liturgical presidency; in fact he is a kind of mediator. The *Super oblata* is by now recited silently, which perhaps provides the context for this shift from a communitarian conception of the prayer to a privatized understanding. The shift has a great deal of pastoral theological significance about it.

Moreover, the prayers in the Supplement tradition include eccentric compositions that express various ideas, from an epiclesis, to a reference to the offering of incense (an idea present in a prayer in the Old Gelasian also). We can also note a slight shift away from *munus* to *sacrificium* and *hostia*, as well as the recurrence of *immolare* and its cognates. One prayer lacks any reference to the gifts and refers to God as "receiving the prayers." This may be an old prayer dating from an earlier tradition or else modeled on some of the prayers in the Leonine collection.[47] But this is an exception; the Gregorian Sacramentary does not involve any great theological or literary variation from the Old Gelasian;[48] the Supplement and its derivative manuscripts bring us beyond that older tradition. In sum, therefore, we note the following tendencies in the evolution of the *Super oblata*:

1. An early stratum that treats the whole eucharist as an offering; these are found in the Leonine.
2. A later stratum that refers specifically to the eucharistic gifts through what are obviously literary conventions; these are found in all the sacramentaries.
3. A stratum similar to the previous one, which employs stronger language such as *immolare* and *hostia*; these are found in the Old Gelasian and the Gregorian.
4. Another similar stratum, which develops themes of inner purity and the benefits accruing from the celebration of the eucharist; these are also found in the Old Gelasian and Gregorian.
5. A later stratum of prayers in the first-person singular that are priestly in their style; these are to be found in the Supplement and its ancillary manuscripts.

6. Another overall tendency is for early prayers (in the Leonine) to be short, whereas many of the prayers in the Supplement tradition are lengthy and repetitious.

Such, then, may be the story of the *Super oblata*, which expresses many different kinds of aspirations for the eucharist. The first-person singular prayers are our link with the growing cluster of invariable offertory prayers that we shall see in the following chapter.[49] The whole prayer tradition, however, points to how words must interpret acts, especially when those actions are repeated at a small altar, at a silent and private Mass. Theologically, these prayers take us from the fifth century of Leo the Great to the early ninth century of Alcuin of York. In that span of more than three centuries,[50] the context in which the eucharist was celebrated changed considerably. Developing euchological formulae both carried and expressed that development. The principle of variability has its high moments as well as its dangers, but it is a wonderful vehicle for expressing how people perceive the eucharist. We have traveled from imprecision through precision to priestly professionalism. Whether or not that development was legitimate is another matter, but we have the eloquence of an exceedingly rich prayer tradition as one of our main witnesses to that complex journey.

Before we move to the Gallican and Mozarabic rites, a word should be said about the early Ambrosian tradition, represented by the Bergamo Sacramentary,[51] dating from the eleventh century. Many of the *Super oblata* (which are so-called in the text of the prayers) are paralleled in the collections we have already looked at. These come after a collect as well as the *Super sindonem*. Some of them only occur in the Ambrosian books, however, and they are of great interest because of the theological imagery they employ. One of them prays in general terms for the benefits of communion and makes no mention of offering gifts, or, for that matter, of offering the whole eucharist: *ut sacramenti dominici nobis operante virtute* ("by the virtue operating in us of the sacrament of the Lord").[52] Another alludes to the *vota* (vows) of the eucharist. Yet another prays for the help of the intercessions of the martyrs. A charming little prayer for Epiphany says the gifts are not gold, incense, or myrrh, but the eucharistic gifts.[53] We also come across a prayer that begins with giving thanks for the life of the Church and asks for future benefits. Another is a short consecration epiclesis that does not mention the Spirit.[54] It is hard to tell what lies behind these compositions, except that there are various ideas that are different, though complementary. Brevity is not necessarily proof of antiquity, but all these prayers are in the standard length of the older sacramentaries. None of them reaches the prolixity (or priestliness) of some of the Supplement's compositions. Their function in the Milanese rite is not uniform. While they can loosely be called prayers over the gifts, they are more in the form of prayers of "interlude" rather than of offertory. Such an analysis at least holds good for those prayers in the Bergamo Sacramentary which do not appear in the other books and (we may hazard a guess) are germane to the Ambrosian tradition, having perhaps some antiquity as well.

GALLICAN AND MOZARABIC TRADITIONS

Germanus became archbishop of Paris in 555, and a commentary on the Gallican liturgy has long been attributed to him. Sacrificial language is not consistently used, but there is no lack of it. Unlike Augustine (whose concern is to define sacrifice), Germanus assumes that people will understand that sacrifice is a legitimate word to use of the eucharist. He affirms that "the mystery of the eucharist is offered in commemoration of the passion of the Lord,"[55] so that beneath his references to the eucharist *hostia* and *sacrificium*, and his strong view of the symbolism of the offertory procession (taken from the Byzantine Great Entrance), his notion of eucharistic offering is still that of a memorial-sacrifice. We are into liturgical commentary, with the kind of ceremonial concerns that this entails. Perhaps through the pages of Germanus's commentary we come close to the heart of how many folk understood the eucharist in Gaul during the sixth century. It was long before the romanization of the liturgy. Unfortunately, we have little liturgical literature to go on in order to clothe Germanus's fine words of explanation with actual texts used when the liturgy was celebrated. We do have four books, however, which together give us a fairly good picture of Gallican liturgical formulae from the seventh to the early ninth centuries, although they grow in Roman symptoms as times progress.

First of all comes the *Missale Gothicum*,[56] which dates from the seventh century and was probably written in Alsace. The two main variable prayers in this book give us a good idea of the kind of sacrificial imagery employed. They are the *Post nomina* (a prayer used after the names of those for whom Mass is offered have been read out), and the *Post mysterium* (corresponding to a variable anamnesis-epiclesis). The style of Latin is different from anything which we have seen before because it is more repetitious, fulsome, and personal.

The *Post nomina* prayers are of a different genre from the *Super oblata* in that their purpose is to link those whose names have been declaimed with the eucharistic celebration. This is a more complex idea than it sounds, and the prayers contained in this book (and in the others that we shall see later) are a complex interweaving of ideas. One *Post nomina* describes the eucharist as *sacrificium laudis oblatum* (the sacrifice of praise which has been offered), whereas another says nothing about offering but dwells on the theme (St. Agnes). Another again concentrates on the various gifts (*diversis oblationibus*) and refers back to the offerers. The "*sacrificium laudis*" recurs, although it would be hard to argue that as late as this time the original connotations remain. It is more likely a linguistic variation, with a slight overtone of praise, and a useful safeguard against the idea that the sacrifice is a real sacrifice in the pagan sense.[57]

The *Post mysterium* compositions are more complex still. For the feast of the Epiphany, there is an insistence on eucharistic gifts (and not gold, incense, and myrrh) that we saw in the Bergamo Sacramentary. Another prays for the descent of the *coaeternus et cooperator paraclytus spiritus* (coeternal and co-worker Spirit the Paraclete), so that the oblation may be blessed and consecrated, *quod obtulimus pro delictis* (which we offered for sins). Another prays less precisely for the Holy Spirit *supra haec sollemnia* (on these solemn things), *ut fiat nobis legitima eucarista* (so that this eucharist may be legitimate for us); this latter notion occurs frequently in the Gallican rites.[58] Yet another is called *Post secreta* and combines material from the Canon with the eastern idea of epiclesis:

"Remembering the most glorious passion of the Lord, and his resurrection from the dead, we offer you, Lord, this unspotted victim, reasonable victim, bloodless victim, this holy bread and saving cup, asking you to allow your Holy Spirit to pour on it, with us eating eternal life and drinking the perpetual kingdom."[59]

Two other prayers employ a similar sequence of ideas, and we may conjecture that the author knew both the Roman Canon and the Byzantine rites.[60]

Before we leave the Gothic Missal, we should also note that in two prefaces (called in one case by the Gallican term, *Immolatio*), the mixture of sacrificial imagery goes into yet one more variant. In the first, the eucharistic memorial is defined as a *devoccionen . . . immolamus tibi . . .* victimam laudis (we immolate to you the devotion . . . the victim of praise). The longer a preface becomes, and many Gallican and Mozarabic prefaces are long, the more tempting it is to leave christological events and move into descriptions of what the eucharist is. In the second, the definition is succinct; *immolationem effigiem in sacrificio spiritali, Christo offerente* (an immolation, likeness, as a spiritual sacrifice, Christ offering). It goes on to include the offered gifts and the intentions of the offerers.[61] Here we have all three of our criteria, the memorial sacrifice, the gift sacrifice, and the living sacrifice of intercession.

The Gothic Missal gives us an interesting variation on the theme. We have different prayers, which have various emphases. The *Post nomina* prayers link sacrifice with intercession. The *Immolatio* offers praise and thanksgiving. The *Post mysterium* offers the gifts in memory of Christ and asks for consecration, sometimes with an eastern-type epiclesis. Unlike the Roman Canon (but like the Syrian anaphoras), the institution narrative is part of the thanksgiving and not the supplication. Through such flexibility, seasonal material also can be introduced into the sequence of ideas. We shall see some of this operating again.

The Bobbio Missal[62] also dates from the seventh century but comes from the north of Italy. It seems to have had a mixed origin and was probably a Mass book for itinerant priests. Because of the mélange of material, it is hard to note any particular trends. We shall confine ourselves to drawing attention to a few special items in the collection of prayers. A prayer *Ad pacem* (before the eucharistic prayer) describes the eucharist as *sacrificium . . . celebrandum* (a sacrifice to be celebrated). On St. Stephen's Day, the protomartyr "showed the very first oblation of the new confession." Another *Ad pacem* asks God to "receive the prayers of your people with the oblations of victims." Yet another talks of "this sacrifice" with *offero* (I offer), along the lines of the *Super oblata* discussed earlier, which lends support to the idea that the first-person singular type of prayer originates north of the Alps within the Gallican tradition, from which it began to infect the Supplement tradition. Many of these prayers offer "for" something or other, but this is the same notion that we encountered in the Gothic Missal. Finally, a *Contestatio* (preface) addresses Christ in rhetorical terms: *tu verus agnus dei quaesitus ad victimam per cuius sanguinem* . . . (you are the true lamb of God sought as a victim through whose blood . . .).[63]

Two more Gallican books deserve some attention. The first is the *Missale Gallicanum Vetus*,[64] which dates from the eighth century and shows signs of romanization. *Oblatio* is a favorite word compared with *munus*, and many of its prayers are also found in the Gothic and Bobbio books. Two prefaces (one is called *Immolacio*, the other is described as *Contestatio*) are of interest. The first is from an Eastertide Mass set; it deals with the Passover and then becomes christological, "he is the lamb which was immolated . . . whose passion and resurrection we celebrate." Among the *Masses of Mone*, a *Contestatio* alludes to baptism as a sacrifice, *filicitas baptismi offertur* (the fruitfulness of baptism is offered). The Rutland fragment contains what is a priestly offertory prayer, *suscipe, sancta trinitas, hanc oblationem, quam tibi offero* (receive, holy Trinity, this oblation, which I offer to you). We shall come across this prayer again.[65]

The second book is the *Missale Francorum*,[66] which dates from the early ninth century and has also been romanized. The *Super oblata* contain nothing new, except that one of them combines the notion of *differentias hostiarum unius sacreficii* (diversity of victims of the one sacrifice) and the gifts of Abel that God received of old. Another such prayer identifies the offering with the vows of the people.[67]

It is difficult to know what to make of these books. The Gothic is probably a complete Mass book and has affinities with the Mozarabic Sacramentary, which we shall see next. On the other hand, the Bobbio, the *Missale Gallicanum Vetus* (together with the *Masses of Mone*), and the *Missale Francorum* appear to have had a more provisional use, as well as draw from traditions that differed somewhat in the way they described the various prayers of the eucharist. But they are of intrinsic interest, for they show an important tangent to the total story, in which sacrifice and eucharist continue to be defined and celebrated with an increasing reliance on biblical precedents. The language of these books is less legal than the Roman sacramentaries.

Before we go on to the Mozarabic Sacramentary, we should look briefly at the teaching of Isidore of Seville regarding the eucharistic sacrifice. Isidore became archbishop of Seville about 600 and died in 636. It was an era of great development in the old Visigothic Church. His concern with all matters of doctrine and church procedure in general is considerable, and among these are to be found some clear teaching on the eucharistic sacrifice. Like some of the themes in the prayers we have looked at, typology is an obvious concern:

"A type of this sacrifice was shown before in the priesthood of Melchisedek. . . . 'Thou art a priest for ever after the order of Melchisedek,' that is, according to the rite of this *sacrifice which Christ completely offered in His passion*, and which He commanded that His Apostles also should have as His memorial. . . . Christ, the Wisdom of God, has made for Himself a house, that is, the holy Church, in which He has offered the sacrifice of His body, in which He has mingled the wine of His in the cup of the divine Sacrament, and has made ready a Table, that is, the altar of the Lord, sending His servants, the apostles and teachers, to the foolish, that is, to all nations ignorant of the true God, saying to them, 'Come, eat My bread, and drink the wine which I have mingled for you,' that is, 'Receive the food of the holy body, and drink the wine which I have mingled for you, that is, Take the cup of the sacred blood.' "

Also:

"The sacrifice which is offered by Christians to God, Christ our Lord first instituted as Master. . . . Though these things are visible, yet being sanctified by the Holy Ghost, they are changed. . . ."[68]

Isidore thus brings together imagery from the Old Testament and gives a kind of doctrinal liturgical homily. Less concerned with first principles (as was Augustine), he is still anxious to show from the Bible in what sense the eucharist is a sacrifice. For him, typology and memorial are key concepts.

When we turn to the Mozarabic Sacramentary,[69] we find some of Isidore's concerns reappearing, together with common themes, and indeed, whole prayers from the Gothic Missal. In this book, the *Post pridie* is the title for the variable prayer after the institution narrative. A good example of Isidore's typology is in such a prayer for Easter Monday that is quite lengthy, where Abel and Abraham and Melchisedek are mentioned as precedents for the offering of sacrifice, and God's blessing is invoked *in Patrum hostiis invisibiliter descendebat* (as it descended invisibly [a favorite word in these prayers] on the victims of the Fathers). The eucharist should be an *odor suavitatis* (an odor of sweetness) and the prayer continues with both the themes of God accepting the sacrifice and the descent of the Holy Spirit. This latter combination of ideas seems happily to marry the Roman Canon and the Greek epiclesis. On the other hand, the Epiphany *Post pridie* reproduces what we have already seen in the Gothic Missal and Bergamo Sacramentary, the idea no doubt stemming from a common tradition.[70]

The vocabulary of these prayers is quite different from the Roman *Super oblata. Munus* is rare, as is *oblatio,* but *sacrificium* and *hostia* are frequent. Moreover, *deferre* (which does occur in the sacramentaries) does not appear once, for *offerre* is deemed sufficient. *Libamina* (libations) and *victima* (victim) are frequent ideas. But there is one entirely novel idea that we see regularly, and that is *holocaustum* (holocaust).[71] It does not occur again in known western eucharistic prayers, although it appears in the ordination rite of a presbyter in the Maronite rite. To use such a strong terminology of the eucharist implies a great confidence in the agility of minds to translate liturgical shorthand, although one can hazard a guess that this was now an easy exercise since holocausts were centuries out of date. The psalms provide sufficient inspiration for this. The Mozarabic liturgy entitled the offertory chant as the *Sacrificium*, and these short ejaculatory songs are sometimes classic in their implied theology. One example is from the Eastertide section of the book:

"Offer to the Lord your holocausts and victims, the tithes and firstfruits of your hands, your vows and gifts; and eat from them in the sight of the Lord. So that the Lord your God may bless you. Alleluia!"[72]

We are left in no doubt that the theology of holocaust is related to all other kinds of offerings in order to strengthen what is an offertory theology. The movement of ideas is plain, if the language recondite: the people of God offer all their gifts, all that they have, which amounts to bread and wine, so that they may eat in his presence and be blessed by him.

The Mozarabic liturgy prefixes its eucharistic prayer dialogue with the antiphon from Psalm 42 ("I will go to the altar of God") and ends with the bidding to "offer fitting praise and thanks."[73] The antiphon is a direct liturgical quotation from the Psalter. It could hardly be altered, being a venerable text, but its movement and logic look back to the *Sacrificium*, while the sacrifice of praise is implied for the ensuing preface (*Illatio*). One *Illatio* runs as follows:

"It is fitting and right, almighty Father, that we should give you thanks through your Son Jesus Christ, the true high priest for ever, the only priest without spot of sin; for by his blood, which cleanses the hearts of all, we sacrifice to you the propitiatory victim, not only for the sins of all people, but also for our offenses, that by the intercession of our high priest for us, every sin committed by the weakness of the flesh may be forgiven. . . ."

Here we have a fine liturgical statement of Isidore's high priest christology and eucharistic spirituality. In bold phrases, biblical in inspiration, the eucharistic celebration is defined from one particular angle, but with no hint of adding to the one sacrifice, which is eternal.

One of the shorter *Post pridie* prayers reproduces ideas similar to those expressed in the Roman Canon:

"Bless Lord, this victim that is offered to you in honor of your name, and sanctify the minds and purify the wills of those who partake of it. Amen. By your gift, holy Lord, for you create, sanctify, quicken, bless, and provide for us your unworthy servants all these truly good things, that they may be blessed by you, our God, to the ages of ages. Amen."

Sometimes, the *Post pridie* will mention a feature of the day's celebration, as on the commemoration of St. Eulalia, whose body was miraculously preserved through the fire of persecution.[74] A good example of a holocaust theme is on the feast of St. Stephen:

"Serving these your gifts and precepts, Lord, we place on your altar the holocausts of bread and wine; asking the most profuse piety of your mercy, that by the same Spirit, through which Virginity conceived you in flesh uncorrupted, the undivided Trinity may sanctify these victims; so that when they shall have been received by us in fear no less than veneration, whatever lives ill against the soul may perish, and whatever shall perish may no longer live again."[75]

There is a warmth and tenderness about these prayers that complements the clipped and neat style of the Roman compositions, and one is sometimes led to think that they are hardly in the same language. The story of western eucharistic euchology is limited if our survey were confined to the classical sacramentaries. In these venerable Mozarabic prayers, many of which probably go back to the time of Isidore himself, we see displayed a confidence in the use of language and a penitential approach to God that contrasts with the subtle and dry compositions of Leo, Gelasius, or Gregory the Great. The liturgist finds reading many of these prayers a tantalizing affair, simply because it is difficult to tell with any degree of certainty what lies behind them. The Mozarabic Sacramentary is a ninth-century collection of prayers. Even though it has much in common with Gothic and Bobbio (and to a lesser extent with *Missale Gallicanum Vetus* and *Missale Francorum*), we are left to conjecture its precise origins. On the basis of comparison of texts and the ideas contained within them, however, the many ingredients that lie behind them contain a number of linguistic conventions concerning the eucharistic sacrifice that are sufficiently distinct from the sober Roman formulae to merit more attention than they have hitherto been given.

In the following chapter, we shall pursue a number of features that help to transform the patristic Mass into the medieval one all over Europe. A new genre of prayer writing is on the way that combines the personal and individual characteristics of some of these Gallican and Mozarabic prayers with entirely new features, and among these, the lengthy priestly *Super oblata* of the Supplement tradition provide the material as the eucharist slips onward into a devotion of the priest, watched by the faithful.

CONCLUSIONS

The prayers of the medieval West that we have seen so far take us into a world different from the East. It is not just difference in *language*, it is also one of *style* and *emphasis*. Because of the contrasts between the Roman and Mozarabic traditions, we can sum up their salient features as follows:

1. In the Roman tradition, offering dominates the prayer at an early stage, probably long before the text of the Canon was fixed. Even if Hippolytus's anaphora is authentically Roman and third century, it is not beyond the bounds of possibility that two (or more) different types of anaphora were in use among the Christians of Rome at the time. My suspicion is that the strongly sacrificial character of the Canon dates from the time when the Roman Church changed from Greek to Latin.[76]

2. The Canon diminishes story through the use of the proper preface, because of its particularity. The only other parts of the prayer that tell the story are the narrative-anamnesis, which, however, are not as integrated to the prayer as they are in the eastern anaphoras, where they appear as a unit in the course of a life of Christ. Through its very construction, therefore, the Canon brings together gift and response in a way we have not so far seen. Its initial logic has something in common with the early Egyptian tradition represented by *Strasbourg*.

3. With story in decline, and gift and response fused together, the preanaphoral prayer subsequently called *Super oblata* has a somewhat confused history, starting life as a general prayer, offering the whole eucharist and perhaps even summing up the whole of the fore-Mass. It then takes on a more specific role as an offertory prayer in order to find a precise task within the whole rite. The sacramentary traditions and the principle of variety for occasions may well have encouraged this process.

4. With gift taking on a prominent role in the eucharistic prayer's second part, and with the presentation of the bread and wine on the altar often accompanied by elaborate ceremonial, it is clear that gift has to be extended, a process that eventually leads to the "stratum three" prayers of the later Middle Ages (as we shall see in the next chapter). Gift lies deep in the corporate memory that produced the

Roman Canon in the first place, but it is always linked with prayer. I would suggest that when the *Super oblata* become specifically gift-oriented, they do this as a duplication of the Canon. (Contrariwise, the eastern "prayer of the veil" in the Syriac traditions duplicates the anaphora only in the sense of a more general understanding of eucharistic offering as a spiritual sacrifice.)

5. The *Mozarabic* tradition, on the other hand, has a markedly different vocabulary. Although including an elaborate offertory rite before Rome did, the Mozarabic rite has prayers that demonstrate by their juxtaposition of diptychs and *Post nomina* that offering gifts and offering intercessions are closely connected. Here is a grandiose variant of what we see in a much simpler form in the Roman tradition itself. But the variant is as near the eastern anaphoras in their concern to pray for those who have offered the gifts during the anaphoral intercession. Here are separate developments of a common theme.

6. The principle of variety within the eucharistic prayer itself results in a continuing reflection upon the way sacrifice is expressed, both in the *Illatio* (sometimes) and also the *Post pridie* (always). This means that, through the very need for variety admitted in the principle itself, different expressions and language are required, so that many of these *Post pridies* can include elaborate anamnesis themes (along eastern lines) as well as complex petitions for acceptance of the offering, with or without explicit epiclesis themes. The accumulative effect of this rich tradition is perhaps the reason for such high-flown expressions as holocaust. Do the *Illatio* and *Post pridie* ever stray beyond their task of expressing thanksgiving and supplication? Sometimes the *Illatio* wanders into sacrificial descriptions of the eucharist; perhaps this represents a later tradition. But their linguistic styles are distinct. The *Illatio* is proclamatory and repetitive; the *Post pridies* are more precisely formulated.

7. A feature of the Mozarabic *Sacrificium* chants at the offertory and of the *Post pridies* is the use of Old Testament typology, in particular libations and holocausts. In the East, we have not so far seen such an undiluted use of psalmic material. When the Old Testament is used, it is usually given the kind of selective treatment that appears in the letter to the Hebrews. But some of these Mozarabic prayers do not undergo this process. Why? I would suggest that the Old Testament allusions to libations and other offerings start life as offertory chants, and from there slowly enter the anaphoral tradition. The offertory chant is a chant sung by several voices and therefore in some sense is a popular entity within the liturgy. (Amalarius of Metz's response to the *Orate Fratres* uses similar material.)[77]

8. In spite of the use of this kind of language, the Mozarabic prayers through their fulsome character and devotional style avoid concentration on the theme of sacrifice that the Roman tradition deliberately espouses. By their variety, they show an adventurous spirit in the face of Roman austerity; in spite of the problems of dating these prayers, norms for improvising an *Illatio* or a *Post pridie* are discernible, in which the offering of the story and the gift and the response mingle freely. Gift and response duplicate before the anaphora at the offertory, and they also find expression in the *Post pridie*. But the *Post pridie* is often so elaborate that its story is fulsome, too, including a rich catalogue of Christ events. These events have usually been included among many others in the *Illatio* as well.

9. There are fundamental differences between Mozarabic/Gallican prayers and Roman ones having to do with the internal unity of the eucharistic prayer. Mozarabic and Gallican traditions keep story in often lengthy *Illatio* compositions, and then move from thanksgiving into supplication after the institution narrative, with the *Post pridie*. The Roman tradition, on the other hand, plays down story through the decline of the preface; because of its strongly supplicatory character, which begins immediately after the Sanctus, the narrative is already part of that supplication.[78]

10. In what sense, then, can these eucharistic traditions be called "impetratory"? If there is a distinction between eucharist as solemn intercession and eucharist as asking repeatedly for something that the faithful expect to get,[79] then the answer must be that the old Mozarabic and Gallican traditions are *not* impetratory, but that the Roman tradition becomes impetratory at that point when the votive Mass takes over from the temporal Mass as the dominant eucharistic diet of priest and faithful. If this is so, then we are describing the ninth-century Carolingian monastic Mass and the Supplement's euchological tradition.

PRAYER FOR THE DEAD: AN APPENDED NOTE

Christians in the early centuries soon gathered for special eucharists for the departed.[80] The second-century evidence comes from Aristides and the *Acts of John* and moves into the third century with Tertullian and Cyprian and on to the fourth with Chrysostom, Ambrose, and Augustine.[81] But the terminology which they use (*offerre pro*, offer for) amounts to no more than "celebrate the eucharist for," since as we have seen the normal expression in the second, third, and fourth centuries for the celebrating of Mass was to "offer." The early Christians, fired by admiration for their martyrs and later for their holy men and women, regarded it as important to ritualize both the fact of death and the hope of the resurrection in the communion of saints. But we do not encounter explicit prayer for the dead in the eucharist until the early Coptic version of the anaphora of Basil of Caesarea, whose primitive "resurrection at the end" theology we have already noted. The significant aspect of that possibly very early prayer is that it does not divide the dead into saints and everyone else. Nor do the classical anaphoras of the Greek West Syrian tradition. *Basil Alex*[2] reproduces almost exactly the same language of *Basil Alex*,[1] except that the conclusion of the prayer is slightly different: "To those indeed, Lord, whose souls you have received, grant rest there [i.e., in the communion of saints, mentioned previously], and grant them a share in the kingdom of heaven."[82] The anaphora then concludes with a prayer that the assembled community may also share in the kingdom, together with a final doxology. Renaudot's Latin translation gives a complex periphrastic rendering of "grant them a share" that involves the notion (alien to the Greek text but no doubt familiar to Renaudot's mind) of the dead being "transferred" to the kingdom.[83]

Basil Byz, however, inverts the order of living/departed-and-saints to departed-and-saints/living. After the epiclesis, there is prayer for fellowship with the saints: "And remember all those who have fallen asleep in hope of resurrection to eternal life, and grant them rest where the light of your countenance looks upon them."[84] This is a slight move toward regarding those who have died in separate contexts; the church can rejoice in the fellowship of saints and ask for rest for those who have died whom it perhaps knew better. But I would not interpret the prayer as envisaging the two contexts as separate places, as this puts the Church in the position of making theological judgements that are alien to the tone of the prayer. The anaphora of John Chrysostom retains the order of *Basil Alex*[1] and *Basil Alex*[2], starting each section, with: "We offer you also this reasonable and bloodless service for. . . ."[85] Like Basil, although in a different way, "those who rest in faith" are in the same paragraph and category as "all the righteous spirits perfected in faith" as well as "this saint whose memorial we are keeping." The same ideas are reflected in the other eastern anaphoras, the Syriac tradition witnessed in Addai and Mari and *Sharar*, the Armenian represented by Athanasius and Gregory Nazianzus.[86]

If these prayers date from the fourth and fifth centuries, they echo the comparable treatment of the Roman Canon, where, however, the distinction is stronger. The first list of saints (*Communicantes*) follows the *Memento*. It dates from the fifth century. After the narrative (*Qui pridie*), anamnesis (*Unde et memores*), and prayers for acceptance of the offering (*Supra quae* and *Supplices te*), the priest prays:

"Remember also, Lord, the names of those who have gone before us with the sign of faith, and sleep in the sleep of peace. We beseech you to grant to them and to all who rest in Christ a place of restoration, light, and peace."[87]

The context is so different now and the two categories so far apart in the prayer itself that it is tempting to see in the Roman Canon the germ of later developments, although they are not yet explicit.

The East never lost the nonjudgemental stance of the early anaphoras that we have just looked at, whereas the Latin traditions from the ninth century onwards pray much more specifically about the forgiveness of the sins of those who have died, so that there is a consequently higher expectation of what the eucharist can do for the dead.[88] By contrast, the earlier formulae in the Leonine Sacramentary pray for peace and light as the Christian community both mourns the loss of loved ones and rejoices in the paschal mystery of Christ.[89] The Supplement tradition brings a much more specific element, including *Hanc igitur* prayers such as:

"Therefore, Lord, we pray you graciously to accept this offering, which we prayerfully show to your love, for the souls of our faithful ones; that through these holy mysteries they may be forgiven of all their sins, and made partakers of eternal blessedness."[90]

From the ninth century onwards the themes of forgiveness of sins and its attendant ideas become more pronounced in the burial rites. One only has to look at the list of contents of the Gregorian Sacramentary and compare it with the Supplement and its related documents to see how offering Mass for the dead was in France a well-established and oft-repeated business. Repeated Masses for various dead is a different idea from celebrating Mass at someone's funeral. Sicard has shown how the primitive gave rise to the later custom.[91] Bereavement and the need to ritualize relationships with those who have died are the two features that initiate the practice of celebrating Mass for the dead, and Paulinus of Nola expresses both these in a fine *Carmen*.[92] However, once liturgical prayer introduces (or is interpreted as conveying) the notion of the eucharist actually remitting the sins of the dead, we are into a different theological world, which requires its own justification, and one that the East and the primitive West cannot provide.

Chapter Five

Accumulation In The Later Middle Ages

In the previous chapters we examined the eucharistic prayer material as this appears in the main eastern and western servicebooks and probed into the origins and development of the variable preanaphoral prayer in the main western rites. Some differences have come to light, some of them long since known among scholars, others new, others again more tentative. These include the fact that whereas eastern eucharistic prayers are units in themselves, western eucharistic prayers have variable units within a fixed form, so that for all the differences in tone and language that obtain between the Roman Canon and the Mozarabic prayers, they share a basic approach to the composition of an anaphora. Our underlying conclusion, however, is that both East and West demonstrate a fundamental variety of language, which reflects differences of culture and language (Greek, Syriac, Armenian, Roman-Latin, Frankish-Latin, Visigothic-Latin) as well as the way words are used and the way their use is developed within those traditions.

In order to handle material that is by its very nature and scope highly complex, we intend to deal now with a number of features that contribute to the idea of eucharistic offering as the Middle Ages progress. These include ordination prayers for the making of new presbyters, in the East and West; the eastern preanaphoral and western offertory prayers; other private oblatory prayers in other parts of the eucharist; and allegory and reinterpretation of the whole eucharist. Some trends are discernible whereas others are more subtle and ambivalent.

ORDINATION
The *Apostolic Tradition* of Hippolytus contains ordination prayers for bishops, presbyters, and deacons. It should come as no surprise that the prayer over presbyters makes no mention of eucharistic celebration, whereas the prayer over a bishop alludes directly to the eucharist in the second part:

"to propitiate your countenance unceasingly,
and to offer to you the gifts of your holy Church.
. . . *offering to you a sweet-smelling savour;* through. . . ."[1]

Similarly, the prayer over a deacon runs: "and to present in your holy
of holies *that which is offered* to you by your appointed high-priest to
the glory of your name."[2] There are textual problems in this latter
prayer, since the second part of the prayer only occurs in the Ethiopic
version. Of the two possible interpretations (presenting gifts at the offertory or administering communion), the second idea is the most attractive, although it cannot be said that the prayer is at all clear.[3]
Nonetheless, the bishop's function is to offer the gifts of the church;
this formula is an old friend, for we came across it in our discussion
of ante-Nicene terminology. We shall come across it again.

Gy has drawn attention to the variety of function between the
bishop and presbyter in a small rural diocese in Antioch, an urban
set-up like Rome, and a large diocese in the north of Gaul.[4] The fact is
that when we look at the eastern ordination prayers, we see some variety between bishop and presbyter but the use of the same kind of
language as in Hippolytus. Thus, the Coptic rite speaks of the presbyter "completing the work of a priest," whereas the bishop "offers you
gifts in holy churches."[5] The early Byzantine rite uses liturgical terminology for the presbyter, "to offer you gifts and spiritual sacrifices,"
which is exactly paralleled in a Syrian Jacobite prayer.[6] Bernard Botte
suggested that both these prayers may have a common parent in a
short and imprecise formula in an early Palestinian prayerbook.[7] In
Syria it seems the priest has already begun to regard celebrating the
eucharist as a regular liturgical task, whereas this is not the expectation of Hippolytus's church order. The East Syrian (Nestorian) rite
elaborates on this theme. Before the ordination of the presbyter, the
archdeacon prays: "that they *may offer you peaceable sacrifices without
taint.* . . ."[8] The ordination prayers, which are fulsome in style, repeat the theme: "*offering to you oblations of prayers and sacrifices of
praises.* . . ." Once again, the ordination rite reinforces what we have
seen of the eucharistic prayers. The East Syrian tradition lives easily
with imprecise sacrificial language, which encompasses both the offering of praise, prayer (of intercession?), and the eucharistic gifts.

The Armenian and Maronite rites are richer still. The Armenian ordination of a presbyter at one point prays: "that he may *complete the
terrible and holy sacrament* of the body and blood of our Lord and Savior Jesus Christ for the forgiveness of sins of those who communicate worthily." In another prayer: "and to *offer you praise* for grace

received."[9] Imprecision over eucharistic offering lies at the heart of these Armenian prayers, as well as explicit references to the eucharistic celebration and the attitude of communicants. The Maronites, on the other hand, use more lavish language:

"to *perform the priesthood* and to show the ministry in the divine mysteries . . .
to stand before your holy altar, and *to offer gifts and spiritual sacrifices* . . .
and offer to *you completed sacrifices* . . .
and offer *good sacrifices and perfect holocausts and spiritual oblations* . . .
and to *offer you pure oblations with vows and first-fruits and good incense and pleasing smells.* . . ."[10]

Although these images refer to liturgical ministry in a fuller fashion, they do not constitute a significant theological development. The background of general sacrificial worship is the context in which to interpret these fine formulations.

However, when we turn to the West, we immediately see discontinuity with Hippolytus and a greater preoccupation with typology and priestly office. The Leonine Sacramentary ordination of presbyters makes no mention of sacrifice but is more concerned with "the office of the second dignity."[11] It is, however, in the north of Europe that sacrificial language comes into the picture. The *Missale Francorum* refers to the establishment of "propitiation and, sacrifices, and rites" in an address before the ordination of a bishop. At the ordination of priests, the same book prays for "sacerdotal gifts."[12] The Mozarabic rite shares with the Gallican rite prayers for the life-style and spiritual growth of the presbyter, but also includes a reference to the "tabernacle of thy temple," and, after the ordination itself, a short address to the newly ordained with the following: ". . . have, therefore, access and power to approach the altar of God." This, surely, is an allusion to the opening part of the prelude to the eucharistic prayer, "I will go to the altar of God."[13]

The Gallican rite, however, also included an anointing of the presbyter, with a special formula: "May these hands be consecrated and hallowed by this unction and our blessing, so that whatever they bless may be blessed and whatever they hallow may be hallowed."[14] The scope of this prayer includes the eucharist but also any other blessing. This anointing gained entrance, with varying formulae, into the ordination rites of northern Europe, for it appears in the Gelasian

Sacramentary of Angoulême and appears in the Roman Pontifical from the twelfth century.[15]

The most sacrificial custom starts life in the mid-tenth century in the Romano-Germanic Pontifical when the bishop hands to the newly-ordained presbyter a paten and chalice for the ordination Mass that follows.[16] It seems innocuous at first, merely expressing a liturgical ministry that was, perhaps in need of emphasis at a time when the concelebration at ordinations was becoming more ceremonial than real. The accompanying formula, which appears in later pontificals, is explicit to the point of crudeness: "Receive the power to *offer sacrifice to God,* and to celebrate Mass as much for the living and for the dead."[17] Such an idea is an extension of the exercise of "priestly power," which we have seen in the earlier western ordination rites, and is also written in the literary genre of imperative formulae, which have also accompanied the giving of the stole and the clothing with the chasuble immediately prior to the anointing. The history of the ordination rites of the late medieval West is told elsewhere,[18] but it is worth noting how late and circumstantial is the formula for giving the paten and chalice. Its symbolism is heavily eucharistic and expresses eloquently how the priesthood was understood in the latter part of the Middle Ages. By contrast, the eastern rites, by their very conservatism and their reluctance to privatize the Mass, keep to patristic imagery, although not without other kinds of elaboration, as in the case of the Maronites.

PREANAPHORAL PRAYERS

Robert Taft[19] has finally laid to rest the traditional view that in the eastern rites those prayers that immediately precede the anaphora are offertory prayers. Through a thorough examination of the available evidence and a comparative study of other liturgies, he has demonstrated that the prothesis before the liturgy of the catechumens is what corresponds to the offertory, and that what takes place immediately before the anaphora is a functional exercise of placing the gifts on the altar, with a preparatory prayer that points forward to the whole anaphora. The relevant portions of the texts in these preparatory prayers are worth looking at closely.

First, in *Basil Byz:*

"Out of the abundance of your mercy accept us who draw near to your holy altar, so that we may be worthy *to offer you this spiritual and bloodless sacrifice* for our own sins and for the faults of the people.

"Receiving it as a fragrant aroma on your holy and heavenly and spiritual altar, send down upon us in return the grace of your Holy Spirit.

"Look with favour on us, O God, and behold this worship of ours and accept it as you *accepted the gifts of Abel, the sacrifices of Noah, the holocausts of Abraham, the priestly services of Moses and Aaron, the peace-offering of Samuel. . . ."*[20]

In the anaphoral tradition of Basil, some of these ideas are old friends but one of them, the notion of accepting the sacrifice, has not appeared before and can be compared with the passage in the complete anaphora of Mark before the commemoration of the departed.[21] Some reservations have been expressed over the antiquity of this prayer. Mateos has even suggested that it was originally two prayers, the first being one of access to the altar, and the second (starting at "look with favour") being perhaps a real offertory prayer.[22] Taft uses the unstable character of the text to support the idea that, although it could mean offertory, it is not original to the tradition.[23] The liturgy of James uses most of the material of this prayer but has it towards the end of the prayers of the faithful, which hardly mixes well with the ideas of the prayer.[24] However, at a date before the ninth century, but perhaps not very long before, the idea of God accepting the sacrifice as he did the Old Testament sacrifices entered the Basil tradition. We have come across this idea in Mark and it could be the result of influence from there. Alternatively, it could be just the result of a prolix prayer-writer ransacking the Bible for obvious sacrificial themes.[25]

The Chrysostom prayer is simpler, although it is not without problems of meaning:

"O Lord God almighty
who alone are holy
who alone accept the *sacrifices of praise* from those that call upon you
    with (their) whole heart;
accept also the prayers of us sinners
and bring us to your holy altar
and enable us *to present to you these gifts and spiritual sacrifices*
for our own sins
and for the faults of the people;
and make us worthy to find favour in your sight
that *our sacrifice may be acceptable to you*
and that the good spirit of your grace may rest upon us
and upon *these present gifts*
and upon all your people."[26]

The interpretation of this prayer stems from its function within the whole liturgy. It is preparatory, it looks forward to the anaphora, and while it does include reference to the gifts (as does the prayer previously looked at in *Basil Byz*), it does not look back to an offertory as many of the western *Super oblata* do (although this is in a liturgy where the gifts are in fact prepared immediately before the eucharistic prayer). Taft writes: "the whole prayer is in intimate relation to the offering (anaphora) to come, but is not in itself an offering. That is, we do not offer now, but pray that the offering we are about to make in the anaphora will not be vitiated by our unworthiness to approach the altar. The direct object of the petition is worthiness to offer; the acceptance of the coming offering is a consequence of this."[27]

This puts the Basil and Chryostom liturgies in a different category from both the western rites (particularly the Roman), and also the Syriac rites. First, the western prayers *Super oblata* by their very nature look back, whether to the placing of the gifts on the altar, or (if Holeton is correct) to the offering of the whole eucharist, and may also look forward to the Canon. They do both. But some of the Syriac liturgies already contain a prayer for the acceptance of the offering, between the anamnesis and the epiclesis, to reinforce the movement of the anaphora at that point. As we shall see, some of them also contain a petition for the acceptance of the offering in the preanaphoral prayer, but that inevitably places the prayer in a somewhat different light.[28]

The Greek liturgies of Chrysostom, Basil, James, and Mark include sacrificial language at other points in the eucharist. Apart from a concern with incense symbolism in Mark, they all seem to use this language at three points, namely at the prothesis, the Trisagion, and the prayer of the faithful. At the prothesis, *Basil Byz* asks God to "bless this offering, and receive it on your heavenly altar," which reappears in the later Chrysostom, although it is lacking in the Barberini 336 version. James speaks eloquently of the bread and wine as a sacrifice, while Mark also prays for acceptance "on your heavenly *and reasonable* altar," perhaps echoing the reasonable sacrifice of the anaphora. In all of them, the priest's prayer before the Trisagion includes solemn praise, which we "send up," a verb already encountered in Justin and Chrysostom that may have sacrificial overtones. The Trisagion is a particularly solemn part of the liturgy of the catechumens and a sacrificial interpretation is appropriate at this point.[29]

Incense is also given sacrificial symbolism. In all the Greek liturgies, an incense prayer refers to the ceremony as "for a sweet-smelling-savor" (James) or by the simpler expression, "we offer this incense"

(Chrysostom, Basil, Mark). However, James also refers briefly in an incense prayer to God "accepting this incense" and Mark also offers incense at the Trisagion and at the Cherubikon. None of them refers to Malachi 1:11, except the anaphoral tradition of Mark. This lends support to the notion that the use of text antedated the use of incense in Christian worship but later suggested it; Mark (and *Sharar*) have anaphoral intercessory incense offerings, which we have already discussed.[30]

Thus we may summarize sacrificial language in the Greek anaphoras as coming (1) at the prothesis, referring to the whole service and the gifts; (2) at the Trisagion, referring to the offering of praise and solemn worship; (3) at the preanaphoral prayer, looking forward to the anaphora itself (referring to the unworthiness of the people); and (4) at various points in the liturgy where incense is offered. This adds up to a deliberate picture and builds on the idea of all worship as sacrificial, not just a particular moment within the eucharist. The deliberate nature of the way in which such sacrificial allusions are spread through these venerable liturgies is further evidence of the rich character of eastern spirituality. Perhaps the saving grace of these rites is that there is, indeed, no offertory, with all the ritual and theological complexities of that very western act. Even when sacrificial language occurs at the prayer of the faithful, it inevitably points forward to the anaphora and to the acceptance of human worship by God.

The Syriac liturgy of James has a prayer before the anaphora similar to the Greek that probably goes back to a common tradition. In the prothesis, not only is incense treated in a more fulsome manner, but a prayer is recited by the priest over the chalice in such delicate terms as these:

"O pure and spotless Lamb *who offered to the Father an acceptance offering* for the expiation and redemption of the whole world: *vouchsafe us to offer ourselves to thee a living sacrifice well-pleasing* unto thee and like unto thy sacrifice which was for us, O Christ our God for ever."[31]

Addressed to Christ, this prayer expresses some of the redefining of eucharistic sacrifice that we have seen in many of the Syriac anaphoras. In the East Syrian liturgy, similar theological concerns are reflected in the prayers, which include at the prothesis a prayer to Christ, "who was an acceptable and spotless sacrifice." Also incense is offered in prayer both at the preparation at the beginning of the liturgy of the catechumens and at the presentation of the gifts. When the gifts are placed on the altar before the anaphora, the theme of memorial-sacrifice is once again expressed:

108

"May Christ, who was sacrificed for our salvation and who commanded us to make a memorial of his death and burial and resurrection, *receive this sacrifice at our hands* by his grace and mercy for ever."[32]

Syriac James and the East Syrian liturgy have also in common a bidding by the priest for the congregation to pray for his worthiness. James has it before the anaphora, whereas the East Syrians place it earlier:

"My brethren and my master, pray for me *that my sacrifice may be accepted*" (James).

"Pray for me, my brethren and my beloved, that I be accounted worthy *to offer* before our Lord Christ *this sacrifice living* and holy for myself and for all the body of the holy church by the grace of his compassion for ever" (East Syrian).[33]

Liturgists can label self-conscious formulations as late in comparison with early traditions. They also build upon the potential spirituality that is connected with many of these sacrificial prayers. The *cushapas* (private prayers by the priest) in the anaphora of Addai and Mari are not, strictly speaking, preanaphoral, but they are agreed to have been later insertions, reflecting a different kind of liturgical tradition. They are very priestly and contain an element of penitence and a sense of the transcendent that the earlier prayers of the anaphora lack altogether. The first *cushapa* prays, "may we accomplish this living and holy service with our consciences clean"; the second takes up the theme of unworthiness from Isaiah 6, suggested by the Sanctus, which has just been sung; and the third asks God to "accept this offering for . . . ," in the context of intercessions.[34]

Before we leave the Syriac orbit, a word needs to be said about the prayers of the veil, which come immediately before the anaphora in the Jacobite and Maronite anaphoras. Their sacrificial language comes in three different ways. The first is simply to state that "we offer this sacrifice," as in prayers like Cyril, Dioscorus, Matthew the Pastor, and the Holy Teachers.[35] The second is to pray that God accept the sacrifice, which is what we find in Twelve Apostles, Marutas of Tagrit, Philoxenus of Herapolis, and Moses Bar Cephas.[36] The third is not to have any sacrificial imagery at all, but just to pray for worthiness in the ensuing anaphora and communion.[37] We have already noted how some of the Syriac anaphoras include a petition for the acceptance of the sacrifice between anamnesis and epiclesis; there is no discernible pattern between anaphoras that have such a petition in the anaphora and those that include this theme in the prayer just preceding the anaphora. In the final analysis, none of these prayers is in any sense an offertory prayer. They all point forward to the anaphora itself.

The Armenian liturgy combines material that we have so far seen in Byzantine and Syriac traditions. In the preparation, before the prothesis: ". . . we draw nigh in great fear and trembling to *offer this reasonable sacrifice. . . .*" Also ". . . we are taught that it is by prayer and the incense of a godly life that we are united with thee. And forasmuch as one of the Trinity is *being offered and another accepteth . . .* do thou receive our supplications. . . ."[38] The Armenians begin on a note of penitence and express it in terms of personal inadequacy and christological truth. At the prothesis, the prayer over the gifts and the incense prayer are both taken from Chrysostom, although the latter is altered to "I offer."[39] However, both at the Trisagion and during the Cherubikon, Basil is the source.[40] In the prayer before the anaphora, however, we have a very Syriac-looking composition:

"Lord God of hosts and maker of all beings,
who didst bring all things into existence out of nothing,
who also in love towards mankind didst honour our earthly nature
by raising us to the estate of ministers of so awful and inexplicable a
    mystery:
thou, O Lord, *to whom we offer this sacrifice,*
accept from us this presentation and consummate it into the mystery
    of the body and blood of thine only begotten
and grant this bread and cup for a remedy of forgiveness of sins to
    us that taste of it."[41]

A fine and beautiful prayer, it also shows that when preanaphoral aspirations develop into complexity, they begin to anticipate main themes in the eucharistic prayer. But it just stops short of that apparent offense and distinguishes between presentation and consummation.

Eastern liturgies are as rich and varied in their use of sacrificial language outside the anaphora as they are within it. What is beyond doubt is that the *whole* celebration is regarded as sacrificial. In this sense these prayers seem to arise out of what we have already learned of the wide application of sacrifice by the fourth century in Greek Christian theology and also of the rich evocations of offering-language in Syriac. While the Greek rites themselves do not include within the anaphora any overt prayer for the acceptance of sacrifice, they do before it, as witness Basil, Chrysostom, James, and Mark. All

110

these rites employ sacrificial language in a deliberate manner, at the prothesis, the Trisagion (if it occurs), the preanaphoral prayer, as well as the anaphora itself. To these can be added prayers of preparation before the prothesis, prayer during the Cherubikon, and various incense prayers in the course of the liturgy. If we use the comparative method, the internal logic of the whole liturgy becomes apparent in all the different traditions. They have a basic similarity, for all that the Syriac liturgies (and Greek James and Mark) make much more of incense. But they also develop this language in their own way, even though we see material from Basil and Chrysostom at times borrowed by James and the Armenian liturgy. Taft has written in gnomic fashion, "it is impossible to interpret unless one knows what one is interpreting."[42] If one approaches the eastern liturgies expecting to find a confused and amorphous mass of jumbled items, in contrast to slimlined western logic, then one remains in a fog. However, when western presuppositions are cast to the winds and the various eastern liturgies are looked at on their own terms, a coherent picture emerges, although it is not without occasionally excessive accumulations. Sacrifice is the whole service (preparation); sacrifice is the gifts (prothesis); sacrifice is praise (Trisagion); sacrifice is intercession (prayer of the faithful); sacrifice is the anaphora itself (the preanaphoral prayer). Then, within the great prayer itself, various rich images are used freely. The eastern liturgies bring the faithful into participation in the sacrifice of Christ by the living offering of worship and service. This is a picture that is both biblical and deeply rooted in the Fathers.

These prayers are in most cases probably later than the time of the composition of the anaphoras, even those that immediately precede the anaphora itself. In the Byzantine and Armenian rites, we can date many of them to the Barberini 336 manuscript, but not all of them. It is also in the ninth century that many of the ceremonial directions for the prothesis rite are first encountered, including the use of Lamb imagery (e.g., Jn 1:29) of the loaf of bread.[43] The prothesis is originally a prerogative of the deacon because of its preparatory role, but it eventually becomes so important that the priest must do it himself; this is an example of anticipation. Each Syriac anaphora in the Jacobite and Maronite collections has its own preparatory prayer. These prayers also have the same meaning as the Byzantine and other eastern rite prayers. This is evidenced by a remarkable common mind over function in the liturgy. They are definitely *not* offertory prayers. But we must now turn to these as they occur in the medieval Roman rite.

The various local missals of the western Middle Ages betray a common core (the Ordinary of the Mass), together with a great deal of variation in the private prayers of the priest before mass, at the altar steps, before the gospel, at the offertory, and before and after communion, as well as after the dismissal. At all these stages, the priest used a collection of prayers that served to turn the Mass into a private devotion for himself. Much has been written on these prayers, which Dix dubbed "stratum three." In order to see what is happening to the Mass, and to do justice to the extent of this variety, it is perhaps appropriate to start at the end of the story with those prayers that appear in the Missal of Pius V after the Council of Trent in 1570.[44]

Suscipe sancte pater: "Receive, holy Father, eternal God, this *unblemished offering* which I, your unworthy servant, *present to you*, my living and true God, *for* my innumerable sins, offences, and negligences; *for* all who stand round, and for all faithful Christians, alive and dead; *that it may avail* for my salvation and theirs to eternal life."

Ds q humanae substantiae: "O God, who in a wonderful way created human nature in its dignity and more wonderfully restored it; grant us through the mystery of this water and wine, to share his divinity who vouchsafed to share our humanity, Jesus Christ, your Son, our Lord; who. . . ."

Offerimus tibi: "*We offer you, Lord, the cup of salvation,* and pray that of your kindness it may ascend in the sight of your divine majesty for our salvation and that of the whole world, in a sweet-smelling savour."

In spiritu humilitatis: "Receive, Lord, our humble spirits and contrite hearts; and *may our sacrifice be performed today in* your sight so as to please you, Lord God."

Veni sanctificator: "Come, Sanctifier, almighty, eternal God, and *bless this sacrifice* prepared for your holy name."

Per intercessionem: "Through the intercession of blessed Michael the archangel, who stands at the right of the altar of incense, and of all the elect, may the Lord vouchsafe to bless this incense and receive it as a *sweet-smelling savour;* through. . . ."

Psalm 141:2–4

Psalm 25:6–12

Suscipe Sancta Trinitas: "Receive, holy Trinity, this *offering which we offer you* in memory of the passion, resurrection, and ascension of our Lord Jesus Christ; and in honour of the blessed ever-virgin Mary, and blessed John the Baptist, and the holy apostles Peter and Paul, and of . . . all saints; *that it may avail to* their honour and our salvation. May they vouchsafe to intercede for us in heaven, whose memory we celebrate on earth, through. . . ."

Orate fratres: "Pray, brothers, that *my sacrifice and yours* may be acceptable to God, the almighty Father."

Suscipiat: "May God *receive the sacrifice from* your hands to the praise and glory of his name, and to our benefit, and that of all his holy church."

This series of prayers has been studied in detail by Jungmann, Willis, and Tirot,[45] together producing a full complement of medieval precedents and texts, and showing how the main theological themes of these prayers bring out ideas that are to be found in the Canon. Most of the later medieval rites contain something resembling this scheme for the offering of bread, the mixing of the chalice, the offering of the chalice, a prayer for the congregation, a prayer for the whole sacrifice, the blessing of incense, the offering of incense, the washing of hands, another prayer for acceptance of the offering, and the final dialogue. The sources are fascinating to catalogue:

Suscipe sancte pater: the prayer-book of Charles the Bald (875–877).

Ds q humanae substantiae: adapted from a Christmas collect in the Leonine Sacramentary, and appearing from the eleventh century, starting in Italy.

Offerimus tibi: the *Missale Mixtum,* therefore Mozarabic; in many local missals from twelfth century.

In spiritu humilitatis: cf. Daniel 3:39–40. Willis notes its appearance in the *Missale Mixtum;* Jungmann catalogues its varied position, either here, or just before the *Orate fratres,* from the ninth to the eleventh centuries.

Veni sanctificator: Also Mozarabic; Bernold of Constance knew of it (eleventh century); it is found in *Ordo Romanus* VI, 10, and also appears in the ninth-century Stowe Missal. The present form is a modification of the Visigothic original.

Per intercessionem: The altar was censed at the offertory in many rites from the eleventh century; this formula dates from the thirteenth. Liturgists are agreed that the original source is the incense prayer at the Great Entrance in the liturgy of James.

Ps 141:2–4: Eleventh–twelfth centuries.

Ps 25:6–12: Eleventh–twelfth centuries.

Suscipe sancta trinitas: Carolingian, ninth century, a substitute for the diptychs, which commended the offerers to God and which was suppressed by Charlemagne.

Orate fratres: Also ninth century, although the response first appears only in the eleventh.

A number of features relevant to our quest underline the use of the prayers in the late Middle Ages. First, they varied from one tradition to another, both in form and sometimes in order. For example, whereas some late medieval French books include virtually all of these items, the English missals of Sarum, Bangor, York, and Hereford lack *Veni sanctificator, Per intercessionem,* as well as *Ds q humanae* and *Offerimus tibi. In spiritu humilitatis* comes later, before *Orate fratres.*[46]

Secondly, while some of the prayers show obvious signs of anticipating material in the Canon, not only in principle but in the actual words, there are signs in some of them that do not appear in the Tridentine Missal (but that emanated from the Cluniac tradition) of the allegorical interpretation of the Mass in immolation language.[47]

Thirdly, the opening prayer, *Suscipe sancte pater* (Rhenish in provenance) contains the telltale first-person singular "which I . . . present to you." It is significant that the Council of Trent suppressed other such first-person singular prayers by the priest.[48]

Fourthly, there does not appear to be an internal logic of ideas of sacrifice in these prayers, as we saw in the Canon itself. Sometimes, the prayers appear to interpret the actions and can do so in a heavily sacrificial sense. Other prayers, the *apologiae,* are unrelated to liturgical actions, and are purely penitential in tone and function. Both these tendencies highlight the pastoral context of the private Mass, offered by the priest.[49]

Fifthly, in the local medieval service books that luxuriated in this genre of prayer, the *Suscipe sancta trinitas* (Frankish in provenance) often appeared in alternative forms to suit different circumstances, such as offering Mass for the priest himself, for the congregation, for the dead, or a Mass of the saints. This prayer begins to correspond with votive Masses, which were frequently in use, and has a function in the rite reinforcing the variable *Super oblata.*[50]

Sixthly, whereas some local rites are austere in their offertory prayers, others are lengthy. For example, an early thirteenth-century missal from Gregorienmünster, Basel, has a lavish series of *apologiae*, with protestations of unworthiness by the priest,[51] whereas the late medieval Sarum Missal is much simpler.

Finally, it is in the evolution of the bidding and the response (*Orate fratres*) that we see a debate about the role of the priest vis-à-vis the congregation. I have noted elsewhere some variety of interpretation in the late Middle Ages within the rites of marriage over what the priest is there to do. (Does he hand over the woman to the man? Does he join the couple together? Does he solemnize the union? Does he witness the consent and give the blessing?) In *Orate fratres* some responses are definite, whereas others are lacking altogether. Some rites address the bidding only to the other ministers, whereas some make it to the whole congregation. This means that although the bidding was popular in the late Middle Ages, it was interpreted to function within the eucharistic action in different ways. For example, the same Basel rite rubricates that the priest asks the ministers to pray for him and then includes a lengthy response in which the Lord is to "be mindful of your sacrifice," which is also described as a "holocaust" in terms reminiscent of Amalarius. This latter word recurs, for example, in the fifteenth-century rite of Toul.[52]

While the prayers themselves simply accompany actions and vary in their imagery and in length, the bidding and response have theological overtones that are far more important than the mere fact of being paralleled in comparative terms by eastern practice. The variety in the textual traditions must be interpreted theologically and not brushed aside as embodying no more than local linguistic traditions. There is in this bidding a self-consciousness about roles that defines what the priest is there to do and what the congregation is there to do. It is a moot point as to whether *meum ac vestrum* means "it is *your* sacrifice as well as mine," or "it is *my* sacrifice as well as yours,"[53] but the very fact that the formulation was made indicates the final breakdown of the eucharist as the corporate offering of the whole Church. Taken together with the language of immolation, we are now well into priestly sacrifice. It cannot be emphasized too strongly what effect the offertory has on the whole eucharist by its very position, particularly when compared with the eastern rites (particularly the Byzantine), which have the offertory material before the liturgy begins. By contrast, medieval western rites, whether fulsome (like the Basel monastic book of the thirteenth century) or comparatively bare (like the fifteenth-century Sarum Missal), throw a great deal of weight onto the offertory as being no longer the oblations of the people, but a performance by the priest on their behalf. Bernard Botte used to make the comment that the Middle Ages saw the gradual usurpation by the priest of all the acts that by ancient tradition had been performed by the laity, with one sole exception, the handing of the bread and the cruets to the priest at the offertory. One is led to muse over how different this story would have turned out had medieval priests been able to grow a third hand.

Actions and priestly devotions, then, seem to lie behind all these prayers, including even the *Orate fratres*, particularly as it starts life as a direction and precedes the one variable prayer which lacks *oremus*, namely the *Super oblata*. Liturgical history is full of subtle ironies. We have been watching the way in which the eucharist is reinterpreted by the accumulation and insertion of new material. With the hindsight of the twentieth-century experience of liturgical revision, it is perhaps as well that no one thought of composing a new liturgy *de novo* in these euchologically rich centuries.

THEOLOGY, DRAMA, AND PIETY

If in the medieval West the dominant themes of the priest's private prayers through the Mass are sacrifice and penitence, the main point at issue in theological disputation in the eucharist was the nature of the presence of Christ. While Gregory, Germanus, and Isidore do not actually say that in the Mass "we offer anew to God" the sacrifice of Christ, the western emphasis on sacrifice was considerably stronger within theology and liturgy than it was in the formative period in the East. It was Alcuin who insisted that there is one sacrifice, on the cross, in heaven, and on the Christian altar, but so far from suggesting that in the eucharist that sacrifice is repeated, the intention of that statement is to bring together the fragmented ritual practices of an age in which the eucharist was being celebrated with ever greater frequency, in order to give it an historical and eternal foundation.[54] Offering is an outward act, consecration is an invisible one, according to Theodulf of Orleans, so that by offering he means the act of celebrating the eucharist that the congregation can see.[55]

The Carolingian theologians assume "offer" as the dominant theme in the eucharist. This is how the words of the liturgy would come across to anyone reading the text of the Canon and the variable *Super oblata*. Paschasius Radbertus and Rabanus Maurus provide a "strong memorial" interpretation of offering in the eucharist, although Ratramnus of Corbie attempts to spiritualize this tendency by pointing to the sacrifice as a figure of things past.[56] Hincmar of Reims, however, simply states that the church's sacrifices are real, doubtless with an eye to dangerous liberals like Ratramnus. Ratherius of Verona goes as far as to say: "If it is a mystery, it cannot be grasped; if it is of faith, it ought to be believed, but not to be investigated."[57] We saw how the language of *Super oblata* and the offertory prayers became more pronounced as time went on, in particular from the Leonine Sacramentary through to the time of the Supplement documents (ninth century). The same process is discernible in theological reflection. Fulbert of Chartres (1029) talks of "the appeasing sacrifice," and Lanfranc, who championed the traditional view against Berengar of Tours, asserted that whereas "on the cross Christ offered himself as a sacrifice for redemption . . . the real flesh . . . and blood . . . are offered on the Lord's Table."[58] What is happening here is not so much an overt stress on eucharistic sacrifice for its own sake, but rather an emphasis on sacrifice in the interests of promoting a doctrine of the real presence of Christ. Durandus of Troarn takes up the same theme in a different way: ". . . in the reality of his divine nature he receives the prayers of his faithful people and in his divine power and majesty grants their prayers." Here we have medieval theology and spirituality of the eucharist in a nutshell! Durandus of Troarn gives us the view of the eucharist that is not only strong but almost mechanical, with a high doctrine of presence and intercession. Witmund of Aversa insists that "our sacrifice is not a shadow . . . ," although he is making that statement in a somewhat different theological and liturgical context from the writer of the letter to the Hebrews.[59]

Peter Damien and Anselm take a different approach. Damien defines the eucharist as a sacrifice of praise whereby earthly and heavenly are brought together. Anselm takes up the theme of the union of earthly and heavenly by pointing to the presence of the angels in the sacrifice. These interpretations are more liturgical in their stance and based on an inner reflection on the Canon itself.[60] Odo of Cambrai, Ivo of Chartres, and Alger of Liège try to combine the foregoing ideas in their liturgical commentaries by stressing the realness of the sacrifice of the cross and the union of the Mass with the sacrifice in heaven. Alger of Liège extends the typological approach to sacrifice by saying that at the *Te igitur*, the priest enters the holy of holies, an observation that expresses the fragmented spirituality of the eucharistic prayer, with the sacrificial concerns of his age.[61]

The thirteenth-century commentators of France, however, advance the whole debate even further. Hildebert of Tours, Honorius of Autun, and Stephen of Autun[62] take as their starting point that the Mass is a mystical representation of Christ's passion. Christ died once and is daily offered in the Church. They do not have quite the same theological interests as the preceding writers, for they are part of a tradition of allegorical interpretation to which we shall return when we have completed the theological survey. Hugh of St. Victor questions the idea of "I offer" in the words of the priest and insists that "we offer"; the Mass "recalls the sacrifice of Christ not only in mind but also by the sign of the cross."

Hugh could only have written these words if two special circumstances had prevailed.[63] The first is a common understanding that the priest offers the sacrifice, rather than the priest on behalf of the people. The second is the ever-pervading issue of making the notion of anamnesis live in the kinds of people who in culture and thought are far distanced from the world of the historical Jesus.

With typical theological precision, it is Peter Lombard who sums up the debate. He states that what is presented and consecrated by the priest is called a sacrifice and an oblation because it is the memorial and representation of the *real* sacrifice.[64] Lothar Conti (afterwards Innocent III) has obvious concerns over eucharistic presence, which led him to the quaint suggestion that the Canon should conclude with the institution narrative (because these are the words of consecration). He takes up the protest of Hugh of St. Victor, that "we" (and not "I") offer the eucharist, which is an offering directed to God as a sacrifice of praise.[65] Peter Damien used the notion of sacrifice of praise, but by this time the original meaning of this concept was all but lost and was merged into a mélange of sacrificial expressions for describing the eucharist.

In the same century, William of Auvergne tries hard to define sacrifice in more philosophical terms and builds on the idea of the meal sacrifice as the means of communion with God and of associating with others in the communion. Although these concepts show the same preoccupation with eucharistic presence, they form one of the most original ways of understanding eucharistic sacrifice in the Middle Ages.[66] It is left to Thomas Aquinas to redefine the eucharist.

He defines sacrifice as belonging to natural law. Sacrifice includes both the outward sacrifices and "the inner spiritual sacrifice whereby the soul offers itself to God." Then he comes to the crux of the matter; "a sacrifice is so called because man makes something sacred." The eucharist "is called a sacrifice insofar as it represents the passion itself of Christ; and it is called a victim insofar as it contains Christ Himself who is the saving Victim."[67] Bernard Capelle studied the three variable prayers for the feast of Corpus Christi. He has compared the ideas contained in them to writings of Aquinas on the eucharist and suggests that the threefold notions of memorial, unity of the Church, and prefiguring of future glory form three vital areas of reflection on the eucharist for Aquinas. It is certainly a neat sequence of ideas. But sacrifice does not seem to enter the picture. Aquinas obviously thought that memorial (in the collect) was sufficient.[68]

The tale of western medieval eucharistic theology is told elsewhere, but we have shown how varied were the notions of eucharistic sacrifice among the writers and thinkers of medieval Europe. Few of them betray any real doubt about sacrifice. The controversy over eucharistic presence provoked varied interpretations of how Christ is present in the bread and wine, which were based on argument and experience of the celebration of mass. The same could be said to be the case regarding eucharistic offering. For these theologians, the Canon provided a daily means of confrontation with the sacrifice of Christ in a series of prayers that from a comparative point of view produces a one-sided picture of the eucharistic action.

There is, however, a shift toward an even stronger view of sacrifice expressed by Gabriel Biel (c. 1420–1495), who really adds the final touches to the sacramental edifice soon to be demolished by the Reformers. Biel goes the whole hog and says that at the *Unde et memores* in the Canon, the priest offers the body and blood of Christ to God himself.[69] It is very doubtful if Aquinas would ever have gone that far.

What these are trying to define is the memorial-sacrifice of the eucharist. But they are doing this in a context in which the votive Mass is the most frequent type of eucharistic celebration. The question is not just "how does the sacrifice of Christ relate to the sacrifice of the Mass," but also, "what does the sacrifice of the Mass do." This question is not really asked because it is assumed. It is true that one age should not project its own concerns upon another. But it is hard to underestimate how great was the accumulative effect of the oft-repeated votive Mass on the medieval understanding of the eucharist. If you continually "offer Mass *for*" all sorts of concerns (many of them laudable), you are steeping the eucharist in the external and internal concerns of the Christian community.

For the medieval Mass, our three criteria have been somewhat upset. Gift has been subsumed, in spite of the elaborate nature of the offertory prayers, for the simple reason that popular reception of communion has declined. Response has been transmuted into the many votive forms of Mass, which (as some of the formulae for the *Suscipe sancta trinitas* show) were often votive Masses for the dead, of the saints, and for the priest himself. The votive forms did express the concerns of the Christian assembly, whether they were actually present at Masses offered for them or not. But the transmutation provides a context in which exaggeration can be born. Finally story has become attenuated with the decline of the thanksgiving series, which in Rome had disappeared long ago and had become the proper preface of the sacramentaries. For the votive Mass, the mystery for which thanks were given did indeed provide a proper preface, but it was a reduced affair when compared with the riches of the whole economy of salvation. In order to understand the full dynamics of the transmutation of story, we have to return to the 9th century.

Amalarius of Metz[70] frequently is regarded as the man who invented the allegorical interpretation of the Mass. As far as the West is concerned, he deserves the prize, but he has some eastern antecedents, including Theodore of Mopsuestia. Amalarius had the genius to provide for the Middle Ages the only way in which story could live. He interpreted the whole Mass as an allegory of the life of Christ for the spiritual benefit of the priest and also for the faithful. Amalarius was no theologian in the narrow sense; he was, rather, an imaginative ritualist with a complex mind. This comes across in the way he interprets the Mass.

In the Mass, all that precedes the gospel reading is Christ's life from the time of his birth to the last journey to Jerusalem. The introit is the Old Testament prophets foretelling the coming of the Messiah. The Kyrie corresponds to the recent prophets, especially Zechariah and John the Baptist. The Gloria, only said on certain occasions, proclaims the nativity. The collect, whatever the occasion, is Christ in the Temple at the age of twelve. The epistle or Old Testament reading is the preaching of John the Baptist. This first part of the allegory ends with the gospel, which represents the words and deeds of Christ in his ministry.

The second part of the allegory starts with Palm Sunday and ends with Pentecost. The offertory prayers and Canon are the prayers of Jesus in the garden of Gethsemane. These lead through his trial, crucifixion, death, and burial. The commixture is the resurrection. The peace is the greeting to the disciples and their knowledge of the resurrection. The fraction is the breaking of the bread by Christ at Emmaus.

This is the scheme produced by Amalarius in his *Eclogae de officio missae*.[71] It is assuredly an ingenious interpretation of the eucharistic celebration, in which the whole salvation history of Christ is called to mind. It has its faults, in that the original ideas for the function of various ingredients in the eucharist, chiefly the eucharistic prayer, are glossed over in order to travel through a complicated "story" in the mind of the worshipper. But for all its faults, this was how the low

120

Mass of the Carolingian age was best interpreted, with the ritual actions of the priest at the altar telling the congregation where he was in the Mass. Liturgists of more recent times continue to see the anaphora as a unit, but that is not how the ceremonialists from the ninth century onward perceived it in practice.

Although Florus the Deacon[72] attacked Amalarius's scheme, he (and his followers) did not succeed in erasing these new notions of eucharistic celebration from the minds of people who were ready to accept them. It is so often the case that a great mind will sum up and express what the people of a given age want to hear. In succeeding ages (though with differences) this allegorical interpretation was established and became the way in which the Mass was explained by many. As Hardison has aptly described it: "the role-playing demanded of the congregation by Amalarius exemplifies what can only be called 'sliding-time'."[73] Amalarius went on to compose an even more elaborate scheme in his *Liber officialis*, in which the older basilican (episcopal) Mass is given a similar treatment, but in more detail. This interpretation requires for its effectiveness a particular architecture, a large open Romanesque building, whereas the earlier sequence of ideas (in the *Eclogae*) could be applied to any low Mass at a small side altar.

The subsequent history of liturgical commentaries includes both adaptation and extension of Amalarius's ideas. Ivo of Chartres regards everything before the *Super oblata* as the Old Testament and everything thereafter as the life of Christ.[74] The three twelfth-century Frenchmen (Hildebert, Honorius, and Stephen)[75] concentrate more on the mystical representation of the passion. Rupert of Deutz[76] combines the liturgical with the mystical. Bonaventure provides a devotional commentary in which the priest is seen to imitate the actions of Christ. But the name associated particularly with developing the allegorical interpretation of the eucharist is Durandus of Mende, who sees numerous symbolisms in the actions and words of the Mass as an imitation and rehearsal of the central events of salvation.[77]

We can see that story has changed somewhat from the solemn recital of salvation history in the anaphora. With Amalarius, it becomes the mental devotion of the individual on salvation history through the celebration of Mass itself. The liturgical purist may scoff at the sometimes devious minds that helped inculcate a spirituality of mental prayer and meditation during the medieval Mass. But its advantages in a popular low Mass cannot be overemphasized. The story has lost its verbal dynamic and has become a mental exercise, with the various cues for change given by the actions, rather than the words, of the priest at the altar. Set against a strong view of eucharistic sacrifice, already present in the old Latin prayers of the Mass, and the subtleties of the theological writings of the age, it all adds up to an increased emphasis on the sacrifice and passion of Christ that is being celebrated, renewed, and represented in the minds of devout worshippers who seldom receive communion.

Vernacular piety echoes much of what we have said. The *Layfolks Mass-Book* (as it was used in fourteenth- and fifteenth-century England) contains the following rhymed devotion for use after the *Orate fratres:*

"When the priest goes to his book
His privy prayers for to look,
Kneel thou down and say then this. . . .
'God receive thy service
And this most solemn sacrifice,
For the priest and for us all
That now are here or here be shall,
This Mass to hear or worship do,
The sacring to see or pray thereto;
And for all that live in God's name,
That they have help from sin and shame,
And for the souls that hence are past,
That they have rest that aye shall last. Amen.' "[78]

The passive character of the individual worshipper is apparent from the tone of this kind of language. It also reinforces the priestly character of the sacrifice of the Mass. The *Orate fratres* is the culmination of the invariable offertory prayers, leading into the prayers from "his book," i.e., the *Super oblata*, the dialogue, preface, Sanctus, and Canon. The notion of solemn intercession is not absent either because the worshipper thinks about both the living and the dead. The corresponding material for use during the Canon concentrates on the consecration and elevation, with the necessary attitude of adoration that this climax to the Mass must induce in the faithful. Dom Gregory Dix has made much of the fifteenth-century Mass devotions, *Langforde's Meditations in the Time of the Mass*, which continue the same individualistic piety, concentrating on the sacrifice of Christ and the faith-response of the worshipper. Once again, the offertory is the most sacrificial:

"Have meditation how our Lord, the Saviour of all mankind, most willingly offered Himself to His eternal Father, *to be the sacrifice and oblation for man's* redemption; and *offer yourself to Him in return both body and soul,* which He so dearly bought. Rendering in recognition of the same to His grace by devout meditation all the thanks of your heart, that it would please His goodness to be the ransom for your trespass and sins."[79]

In this short passage, we have the themes of story and response. For all the exaggeration of offertory prayers, once again the theme of gift is conspicuous by its absence.

The medieval western rites following the Roman (rather than the Mozarabic) uses demonstrate what happens when one of the three criteria is exaggerated and overshadows the other two. The roots of this isolation of story into a very strong notion of commemoration can be traced far back to the language of Cyprian and Gregory the Great. But this, I think, is more an instance of the difficulty we have already seen in the East of translating the anamnesis, although the eastern rites tackled it more constructively. In the West, the sacrificial character of the eucharist becomes embedded in the Canon. The story loses the force it has in all the eastern anaphoras because the preface becomes so "proper" that it loses its connection with what follows. Late medieval ceremonial elaboration merely divides preface and Canon even further. The internal unity of the eucharistic prayer has broken down and the story has to reappear in dramatic terms through the preaching and popular piety of Amalarius of Metz and men like him. Vernacular piety internalizes this process further so that the worshipper meditates on the whole mystery of redemption. Past Protestant polemic has written off the later medieval pious worshipper in semi-Marxist terms as an oppressed peasant under the power of the clergy. This is not a wholesome view, and much of the modern "rhetoric of participation" serves to underline that popular sharing in the eucharistic action need not be the noisy, bustling business of post-Vatican II worship. But the pileup of the medieval West progressively exaggerates the sacrificial character of the eucharist. Story detaches itself from the anaphora in real terms, allowing the Canon itself to carry a very strong view of anamnesis. The prayers that lead up to the Canon and many of the medieval theologians reinforce this view. Individually, these features do not add up to a great deal. Together they serve to turn the Mass into something different from the dynamic preaching of Leo the Great or Augustine of Hippo.

Through these "stratum three" prayers at the offertory, we get a glimpse of the piety of many of the medieval priests, although not all medieval local uses went in for offertory prayers that were either

123

lengthy or couched in "I" language. Nonetheless, in spite of the protests of Hugh of St. Victor against that first-person singular, the Mass priest was content with that personal focus in the Mass.

Francis Clark has written on the medieval background of the English Reformation vis-à-vis eucharistic sacrifice and has suggested that the English Reformers, whom we shall be looking at in the next chapter, knew exactly what they were doing in repudiating the "Catholic" view of the eucharist, in offering Christ.[80] Clark's work was an important thesis to bring to the ecumenical movement, but it is at root an unsympathetic analysis of the intentions of the Reformers, whose first and basic protest against the late medieval Mass was its *pastoral practice*: ever-repeated masses for the dead, or for one or other good purpose, with few if any communicants. It is noteworthy that even lay brothers in religious communities were reluctant to receive communion more than a very few times in the year.[81] Ironically, it is Aquinas whose theology of eucharistic sacrifice is more traditional than the dynamic "re-presenters."[82] This is expressed not only in his theological writings and the Mass prayers for the feast of Corpus Christi, but also in the eucharistic hymns that bear his name. *O salutarius hostia* is a hymn to Christ with a eucharistic context; it is not a hymn to the eucharist with a christological context.

What of gift and response? We have already seen how gift has become theoretically exaggerated through the offertory prayers, but at the same time isolated from its purpose, namely to offer gifts to God for consecration in order to receive them back for communion. That simple internal logic of the eucharistic prayer and the eucharistic action has slipped from the corporate mind and becomes even more of a problem in the Reformation era, when the founding fathers insist on regular communion but cannot remove the practice of not communicating that had been there for centuries. Response remains, theoretically, in the Canon and also within the *Suscipe sancta trinitas* prayer. But it loses its intercessory character by embodying a single theme rather than including a whole recital of the concerns of the Christian community. (Once again, we look to the East and find the wholesome patristic ideal still present behind later overlay, as in the Byzantine liturgy.) Response is to be seen in the vernacular piety, but it is more in the sense of looking at Christ and making a psychological response than of offering up the intentions of the *life* of the Church.

Much of our discussion on theology, drama, and piety has been concerned with the medieval West, largely because it was an expanding Church, bubbling over with ideas, theology, architecture, and a rich Christian civilization. The East, by comparison, did not live in such luxurious surroundings. When we look to the East, we see the patristic notions of eucharistic offering still present in the liturgy. It is true that the Byzantine commentaries on the liturgy from the seventh century emphasize the prothesis and the Great Entrance, but none of this distorts the three criteria of story, gift, and response. All of them insist that Christ is the sacrifice, from Maximus, through the *Historia Ecclesiastica* of Germanus, the *Protheoria* of Nicholas of Andida, down to Nicholas Cabasilas and Symeon of Thessalonica. It is not so much an exaggeration of eucharistic sacrifice that is the eastern problem as the anticipation of eucharistic presence at the Great Entrance, a feature of popular piety that Nicholas Cabasilas has to explain.[83] Back in the time of Justin II, in the sixth century, Patriarch Eutychius preached a memorable sermon that attacked those who taught the veneration of the unconsecrated elements at the Great Entrance.[84]

However, there was controversy in the Orthodox Church in the eleventh century concerning the interpretation of the priest's prayer during the Cherubikon.[85] We have deliberately left this until now because of its comparatively late date and because it is in a different genre from the other preanaphoral prayers that we dealt with earlier. The prayer first appears in the Barberini 336 text of Basil. It thereafter occurs in southern Italian texts of John Chrysostom, but only appears in Constantinople at the end of the tenth or beginning of the eleventh century. It is rare in the Byzantine liturgy for being phrased in the first-person singular; the priest is praying for himself. It is also a long prayer,[86] and we quote here the relevant portions.

"No one bound down by the desires and pleasures of the flesh is worthy to come to you. . . . And yet because of your ineffable and boundless love for mankind . . . and as master of all you bestowed on us the holy celebration of this *liturgical and unbloody sacrifice.*

"By the power of the Holy Spirit enable me, clothed as I am with the grace of the priesthood, to stand before this your holy table and *offer your sacred and immaculate body and precious blood.*

"It is to you, then, that I come . . . : do not turn away your face from me, nor reject me from among your children, but rather allow these gifts to be offered to you by me, your sinful and unworthy servant.

"*For you are the one who offers and is offered,*[87] *who accepts and is distributed,* Christ our God, and to you we send up glory with your eternal Father. . . ."

The logic of this composition is clear. The priest is praying in a penitential tone for the grace of God to overcome his unworthiness as he approaches the most solemn part of the liturgy, which is defined as "this liturgical and unbloody sacrifice." The theme of bloodless sacrifice we have already encountered in the anaphora of James among the Byzantine eucharistic prayers, although we have seen it elsewhere. Here it is presumably a reference to the whole eucharistic action, focused on the anaphora.

Then the priest prays more specifically for the grace to handle the sacred bread and wine, which is described in the strongest terms we have so far seen in the Byzantine rite, "offer your sacred and immaculate body and precious blood." The context seems, at this point, to refer to the handling of the sacred species after the anaphora, for in the next paragraph, he repeats the theme, and in the concluding paragraph, Christ is identified as "the one who offers and is offered, who accepts and is distributed." The background of this prayer appears to be a strong doctrine of the eucharistic presence rather than a strong doctrine of eucharistic sacrifice. The eleventh-century controversy was provoked by this prayer, a fact that is illuminated by its comparatively recent inclusion in the Chrysostom liturgy; by the eleventh century it was in regular use in that liturgy at Constantinople. The controversy was settled after councils held at Constantinople in 1156 and 1176. The theological question at issue was whether Christ offered himself on the cross to the Father and the Holy Spirit only, or also to himself as the Son. The liturgical aspects of this controversy are not important, except that they illustrate the connection between the earthly and the heavenly liturgies.

The important liturgical parallel of this prayer is with the "I" prayers of the medieval West, but we may hazard a guess that the contexts are different. The Eastern prayer seems to have begun life as a devotion during the singing of the Cherubikon, whereas the western compositions are part of the accumulation of prayers at the offertory. Nonetheless, the theology of the prayer itself, embedded as it is in a dramatically and psychologically important part of the Byzantine rite (the Great Entrance), does not contradict the earlier tradition. Rather, it parallels other developments in the medieval West. But it cannot be claimed to rest entirely on a patristic theology or piety. It is a symptom of the Great Entrance, and if Taft's restoration of the Entrance to some noble simplicity were ever to be carried out, presumably this prayer would go, or would be made optional.

126

CONCLUSIONS

Was the medieval era in the East and West a pileup? The answer to this question depends on theological, liturgical, and devotional presuppositions. Not everything primitive is necessarily pure, and we are left to speculate whether the western and eastern developments would have been very different had their social histories been reversed, with the West constantly struggling against invaders, and the East luxuriating in expanse and development. Dix's description of the evolution of the western rite inevitably leads to the conclusion that the "stratum three" prayers are a clutter and that many of them serve no real theological purpose. I would add that they fasten on to an already dominant theological theme of sacrifice and give it an even higher profile within the theology and spirituality of the eucharist than it had already.[88] But private prayers are not, per se, a useless exercise, since they usually serve to help the celebrant concentrate on ritual actions, whereas the more subtle (and perhaps primitive) idea of ritual actions being performed in silence involves more concentration. Nonetheless, by their very inconsistency (whether they are expressed in "I" or "we"—language, and what they imply about the theology of the eucharist in the *Orate fratres*), the West does deserve the attribution of piling high sacrificial language and penitential prayers in the Mass. Moreover, the ordination rites of the West reflect a growing concern that the priest's primary function is to "offer mass." These interests are not so strong in the much-neglected euchological traditions of the old Gallican and Mozarabic rites. From the point of view of liturgical genre, many of these prayers are of the collect type, either economically phrased or elaborated in such a way as to include sentiments and repetitions in the style of a vernacular devotion. But the Supplement tradition extends the normal length of prayers of the *Super oblata* kind, and it would seem that these many local compositions for use at the offertory were intended to express a perceived theology of what the priest is there to do. It would indeed be hard to argue for different theologies at this point among the many western rites, but it is possible to discern a creeping ambivalence about these prayers. For example, not every European rite contained either the length or the variety of the *Missa Illyrica*,[89] which was composed in Minden in the eleventh century. Indeed, the relative paucity of offertory prayers in the fifteenth-century Sarum Missal bears witness to the need to keep these prayers short and to the point. But already in Germany and Hungary in the fourteenth and fifteenth centuries, this whole section of offertory prayers was being described as the "little canon,"[90] thus expressing a duplicatory character in relation to the Canon itself.[91] Moreover, the Canon itself undergoes its own development, as popular allegory and theological interpretation place it in the center of the eucharist, with elevation serving as substitute for communion, institution narrative seen as words of consecration, and the beauty of the sacrificial notions that make up its original genius obscured rather than interpreted by priestly silence and sanctuary ceremonial. The ambivalence of the offertory is heightened when the variety of text and response in the *Orate fratres* is taken into account. The late medieval western prayers do not exactly contradict each other if we compare one tradition with another, but they do prove the recurring truth discernible in twentieth-century liturgical development that liturgy does need a theological critique, especially when local improvisation is not only permitted but actually encouraged.[92]

However, the eastern rites cannot be awarded the same analysis. We have seen how eastern ordination prayers kept and elaborated patristic imprecision in the way they allude to eucharistic sacrifice; the presbyter is there to lead the people of God in their offering of spiritual sacrifices. Moreover, many ordination prayers in the East also allude to the pastoral and teaching aspects of the presbyteral office. In the eucharistic liturgies of the East, however, the preparation of the gifts assumes a high importance and can do so because it takes place *before* the eucharist proper begins. The Great Entrance becomes a fine liturgical spectacle, giving vent to the abilities of liturgical mystagogues and commentators. But within the prayers used before the anaphora (the prayer of the veil in the Syriac tradition) lies a determination to look forward to the anaphora. They are preparatory prayers, and many of them may well be much older than the earliest texts, particularly as their themes and their linguistic style (especially in the Syriac books) suggest an earlier custom of improvisation according to set norms. Although they are written in the first-person plural, their preparatory nature bears comparison with the East Syrian *cushapas*. Other prayers before the anaphora (during the liturgy of the catechumens) express appropriate sentiments in interpreting the whole action of the liturgy, and they keep alive the notion of the whole eucharist as sacrificial in a general and spiritual sense. The enduring message of the East is that by its conservatism, it holds together story, gift, and response, and keeps them in balance, unlike the West, even though both East and West were accumulating more and more and could have done with some legitimate pruning.

Chapter Six

The Reformation and Its Aftermath

When Thomas Aquinas wrote that the eucharist is "at once a sacrifice and a sacrament," he was trying to bring together (among other
things) the sacrificial and the sacramental aspects of the Mass: "it has
the nature of a sacrifice in that it is offered, and of a sacrament in that
it is received."[1] We have seen how varied were the interpretations of
both presence and sacrifice in the later Middle Ages, although none of
these variations found direct liturgical expression in the prayer formulae within the Mass. But the Reformers one by one reject the sacrificial
character of the eucharist in the way that they understood the western tradition to have received it. For the first time that we know of,
large portions of Christendom were engaged in controversy concerning eucharistic sacrifice. It is not a question of defining details, of reinterpreting a tradition, nor yet of adjusting certain aspects of the way
in which Mass is celebrated. The western Reformation is in part an
intellectual break with the Middle Ages by its leaders, and in part a
gut reaction against the pastoral context in which most Masses were
celebrated.

It is hard to be objective about the Reformation even in an ecumenical age, and the fact that we now know more about the origins of the
eucharist than did Luther, Zwingli, Calvin, or Cranmer, makes us a
little wary of pronouncing value judgements on their liturgical and
doctrinal work. Moreover, in giving account of that work, it would be
easy to do so from the point of view of the twentieth-century liturgical movement, with its post-Dixian four-action shape, and its espousal
of the Greek West Syrian kind of eucharistic prayer. (Even though Dix
has been proved somewhat exaggerated in his claims for offertory,
and the ongoing progress of the study of origins is teaching us more
about Semitic Christianity, most contemporary liturgiologists are from
churches that are heirs of recent liturgical revision along those lines.)

But liturgical scholarship was only beginning in the sixteenth century, and the Mass was not understood in strata that would be clearly
identifiable. The late medieval literate layperson would attend Mass,
devoutly kneeling, with a book of devotions for use as meditations

while the priest celebrated the sacred rite with his back to the congregation, and in community of prayer with the devout only in the sense that nonverbal contact was the norm. As we are now rediscovering, such methods of building up community and spirituality have their uses. The priest offered Mass for various intentions, the layperson rarely communicated, and the words used by the priest, both at offertory ("stratum three") and consecration ("stratum one and two"), emphasized the sacrificial character of the Mass, to the exclusion of other aspects. Story has migrated from the preface to the mind of the worshipper as the Mass unfolds as an allegory of Christ's life. Gift remains, but loses its essential pristine link with communion. Response becomes a psychological development in the faithful worshipper as an individual. When it comes to analyzing the motives and work of the Reformers, we must take care to see the context in which they were operating and realize above all that the sixteenth-century explosion was the very first time that the way in which the eucharist was celebrated was to be debated on such a grand scale. Bishop Alan Clark, who was the Roman Catholic co-chairman of the first Anglican-Roman Catholic International Commission, and who made eucharistic sacrifice the subject of his thesis at the Gregorian University in Rome many years ago, once addressed an ecumenical conference of seminarians in an English cathedral city. Before his address, he had gone into the cathedral (a magnificent medieval edifice), and had sat down in the choir stalls pondering the visual expression in that building of both continuity and discontinuity at the Reformation. Speaking of both sides of the quarrel, he recounted this experience to his audience and professed his intention of both accepting and probing "that explosion of ideas which happened in the sixteenth century."[2]

LUTHER

In 1520, Luther wrote his influential *Babylonian Captivity*, in which he outlined the current needs as he saw them of the Church. He also preached a sermon *On the Lord's Supper*, in which he propounded the true doctrine of the eucharist. Both these compositions give us a clue to the restless mind and forceful modes of expression of this great German Reformer. The *Babylonian Captivity* begins its negative comments on the eucharist with an attack on the practice of withholding the cup from the laity, and a strong criticism of the doctrine of transubstantiation. It is interesting that the items come in that order, for his third point then emerges as follows:

"The third captivity of this sacrament is by far the most wicked abuse of all, in consequence of which there is no opinion more generally held or more firmly believed in the church today than this, that the mass is a good work and a sacrifice. And this abuse has brought an endless host of other abuses in its train, so that the faith of this holy sacrament has been turned into merchandise, a market, and a profit-making business."[3]

Luther turns his mind to the bread and wine first, and only then to what he sees as an underlying irrelevant and distracting doctrine that is poisoning the proper understanding and celebration of the other two. Secondly, the doctrine of sacrifice is "firmly believed," and one senses Luther's despair in his desire to eradicate it. Thirdly, the doctrine of sacrifice (Luther thinks) is inextricably bound up with the notion of celebrating Mass for various causes, including the dead; in other words, that the mass is "a good work." Fourthly, this abuse has had the effect of depreciating the eucharist, so that its context (a meal at which all receive) becomes entirely different (noncommunicating attendance, and concentration on the intention for which Mass is offered). As has recently been said, "what the scholastics joined together [i.e., sacrifice and sacrament], Luther put asunder."[4]

The sermon *On the Lord's Supper*, however, is markedly different in tone, as one would expect. Strongly christological, it contains such analysis and reflections as these:

"Such prayer, praise, thanksgiving, and offering of ourselves we are not to present before the eyes of God on our own account, but we are to lay them on Christ and leave it to him to present them to God. . . . If the mass is called a sacrifice in this sense, and so understood, it is all right. Not that we offer the sacrament, but that we through our thanksgiving, prayer, and offering implore him and give him occasion to offer himself for us in heaven and us with himself."

Also:

"Faith I call the true priestly office which makes all of us priests and priestesses. Through faith we place ourselves, our misery, our prayer, praise, and thanksgiving in Christ's hands, and through Christ offer it all to God in the sacrament. Thus we offer Christ to God, that is, we give him occasion and move him to offer himself to us, and us with himself."[5]

Luther is still, it must be remembered, using a Latin Mass. This may be the key to such phases as "prayer, praise, and offering of ourselves," and "through our thanksgiving, prayer, and offering." The former may be a reference to the response of the congregation, for Luther is certainly an heir of vernacular piety; the latter is more than likely to be his interpretation of the Canon, for "thanksgiving" could refer to the preface, "prayer" to the first part of the Canon, and "offering" to the second part. His earlier insistence that "if the mass is . . . so understood" can then be seen as implying that *this* interpretation (of the Mass, and the Canon itself) is the correct one, whereas other interpretations are wrong.

The second quotation has been described by Regin Prenter as appearing to be "very un-Lutheran."[6] But it comes from the horse's mouth, nonetheless, and Prenter provides a convincing interpretation, that the offering of Christ is going on all the time, in heaven, and that it is at the eucharist that the faithful can be brought into that offering, but that this is through the action of Christ himself. The idea of the heavenly altar is in the Canon, and we have seen how this theme is in the East a secondary one, except in the anaphora of Mark. Luther, for all his latent desires to reform the Mass, is trying to reinterpret along New Testament lines. You can only offer anything if you first ask Christ to offer it for you: "we give him occasion and move him to offer himself for us, and us with himself."

There is a self-consciousness about both these quotations that is not present in the *Babylonian Captivity*, where Luther can let his mind leap ahead in the manner of a discourse. His sermon, on the other hand, is carefully tailored to liturgical context and pastoral need. A third quotation from that sermon is worth citing as well:

"The bread and the wine are offered in advance for benediction in order that they may be sanctified through the word and the prayer. But having been blessed and consecrated they are no longer offered, but rather received as a gift from God."[7]

Once again, Luther's definition of the action of the eucharist and his interest in pastoral context are manifestly clear. First of all, the bread and wine are "offered in advance." Here, he refers to the offertory prayers, and the *action* of preparing the gifts. Secondly, they are sanctified "through the word and the prayer." It seems clear that by these terms he means the institution narrative and the ensuing prayers, asking God to receive the offering in heaven. Thirdly, there is no further "offering," but, instead, the gifts are "received as a gift from God." In other words, we do not offer the gifts apart from ourselves, but we actually receive them. Herein lies the whole thrust of Luther's eucharistic protest, that the bread and wine are on the altar waiting to be received by the faithful; they are not there for the sole purpose of offering to God, then to be consumed by the priest alone.

Neither the *Babylonian Captivity* nor the sermon *On the Lord's Supper* can be relegated to being merely early Luther, for they were both written in 1520 when he was launching out into the deep and preaching the reformation of the church. Prenter takes care to discuss the full implications of the sermon for ecumenical dialogue, to which we shall return later.

So much for Luther's teaching. We now have to look at the *Formula Missae* of 1523 and the *Deutsche Messe* of 1526.[8] It is interesting that Luther took as long as he did to do his liturgical revision; his conservatism over the externals of worship (including the elevation) is well-known. Much of it survives in parts of Germany and Scandinavia today.

First, the *Formula Missae:*

". . . there follows that complete abomination, into the service of which all that precedes in the Mass has been forced, whence it is called *Offertorium*, and on account of which nearly everything sounds and reeks of oblation. . . . Therefore repudiating all those things which smack of sacrifice and of the offertory, together with the entire *canon*, let us retain those things which are pure and holy, and then we will order our Mass in this fashion.

"The bread and the wine having been prepared, let the order be in this manner:

Dialogue
Preface
Institution narrative
Sanctus
Lord's Prayer . . . omitting *Libera nos*
Peace
Communion with *Agnus Dei*
Post-Communion prayer

"This is the way we think about the Mass. . . ."

Secondly, the *Deutsche Messe:*

"Institution narrative
Elevation
German Sanctus, or *Gott sei gelobet*, or *Jesus Christus unser Heiland*
Lord's Prayer
Communion."

The two schemes are different in some respects, but similar in others. The principal liturgical criteria are stated in the *Formulae Missae*, where Luther states his intention to get rid of the offertory prayers, as well as the sacrificial prayers of the Canon, so that we are left with the placing of the gifts on the altar (either during the Creed, or at the narrative itself), followed by the preface, the narrative, and the Sanctus, thus placing the narrative in a novel position. Private prayers thereafter disappear, except that if they are used, they must be turned into the first-person plural. The postcommunion prayer is not from the variable collection because of sacrificial language, but is to be one or the other of the private prayers of the celebrant, again turned into first-person plural. The *Deutsche Messe*, on the other hand, apart from being in German (the *Formulae Missae* was in Latin), omits the preface, and further suggests that the communion be administered separately after each narrative. Luther is obviously sensitive about defending the elevation and calls in the example of the elderly (who might be confused by its disappearance) in order to support his conservatism.

But what was his intention? Had his theology altered since 1520? A number of theories have been suggested. The traditional view of the more liturgically-minded scholars is that Luther did what amounted to a hatchet job on the Roman Mass. Brilioth and Reed[9] (and others) have worked on that assumption, concentrating on the negative side of his work, while pointing up the difficult context in which he was working. When you compare these schemes with what went before, you cannot fail to notice that a number of items have disappeared; moreover, when comparative liturgy is our method, the absences far outweigh the additions. But this is oversimplifying things. Luther added the communion of the people, in both kinds, and he included vernacular hymnody during the communion and elsewhere as an essential aspect of the liturgical action. He also wanted the institution narrative to be chanted so that it could be heard by all, a practice that survives in some places to this day. No alteration is made to the posture or the clothing of the celebrant, although the vesture was gradually simplified in time.

If the 1520 sermon is interpreted in the way we have suggested, then it is hard to see how Luther's theology has altered in a matter of years, for both the *Formula Missae* and the *Deutsche Messe* place a strong emphasis on thanksgiving for the work of Christ and invocation of his presence. But our three criteria have shifted noticeably. Story has become isolated in the preface, which is perhaps one reason why in the Swedish rite of Olavus Petri in 1531,[10] the preface is carefully written in order to lead into the institution narrative. But the preface does not appear in the *Deutsche Messe*; it is optional in Bugenhagen's Brunswick Order of 1528, and does not appear in the conservative Brandenburg-Nuremberg Order of 1533.[11] However, Luther places strong emphasis on preaching and on the reading of the word in the vernacular. Secondly, gift has lost any symbolic overtones, other than those associated with the consecration and communion. This is a step forward because the weakness of the late medieval scheme was that there were many offertory prayers, but the gifts were not actually eaten and drunk by the communicants, who hovered in faith and devotion, adoring a real but abstract presence at the elevation. Gift offering has taken on a new meaning; the meal is solemn, and it is a testament, but it is not a sacrifice. The strongly christological character of Lutheran piety and eucharistic hymnody needs to be taken into account when assessing the overall effect of this new liturgy, especially with regard to the presence of Christ.

Thirdly, response has moved into the inevitable metamorphosis required by the doctrine of justification by faith alone. The Christ-event has done it all, and continues to do it all, so that, as with story and gift, we see a considerable widening and simplifying of the eucharistic action, in which the sacrificial character is exclusively Christ-centered.

From a comparative liturgical point of view, of course, Luther's isolation of the institution narrative must be seen against the background of the later Middle Ages,[12] which saw the gradual usurpation by that narrative of much of the force of the rest of the prayer, so that the elevation itself is not just a showing, but also an offering, which is probably why it was repugnant to many other Reformers. Moreover, Luther allows two well-known priest's prayers for use immediately after communion, but he does not allow the variable ones because of the language they use. In this, yet again, is the late Middle Ages, with its "stratum three" mentality, taking over the Reformation?

Such an analysis is true, but only in part. Comparative liturgy is not the answer to all our problems about understanding the past. It is important to look also at the context of these reforms. The narrative comes immediately after the thanksgiving (in *Formula Missae*, the Swedish rite, and others), and the consecration ends with a note of solemn doxology in the German Mass, with everyone singing the German Sanctus, or some other hymn. Moreover, for someone living at the time, the act of communion by the congregation would take on the aspect of a radical innovation, comparable to the changes English travelers noticed in attending Mass in French and German cathedrals through the 1960s as the Vatican II reforms entered the piety of many Roman Catholics. Spinks[13] champions Luther against his liturgical detractors and insists that his liturgical work was not reductionistic. This is true up to a point, but when you deliberately set out to delete something, the absence is known and felt. Even when there are other compensations, the truncation of the eucharist that we see in the German Mass assuredly reduces the Christian story, gift, and response to an individual level, so that it is seen that they can no longer be entrusted to the action of the Church. One can see why the reaction took place, and the fact that Luther has a two-stage program of liturgical revision (1523 and 1525) makes him comparable to Zwingli and Cranmer. For Luther, the Church is not wholly trustworthy, so that sacraments must be propounded as the activity of God himself, through Christ. In that sense, Luther deserves to be regarded as a serious Reformation liturgist.

Subsequent Lutheran development is a tale of reform, of controversy and eventual decline,[14] as the eucharist becomes an occasional celebration. This was not Luther's fault; it was due to the inability of Christendom to unlearn eucharistic habits that had been set in their ways over several centuries. Pietism brought its own effects on the liturgy, but that is another story. In any case, it does not involve substantial change to Luther's liturgical scheme, except yet further emphasis on the preached word and a further erosion of liturgical features of the eucharist.

ZWINGLI, BUCER, CALVIN, AND KNOX

Justification by faith was the preaching of both Luther and his followers, and the other Reformers. When we come to look at their liturgical work, we can see how they dealt with the eucharist. The same themes recur that we saw in Luther: a strong emphasis on the work of Christ himself, eating and drinking the bread and wine, within the context of a simplified liturgy. From the aesthetic point of view, Luther was the most conservative of all. But Zwingli, Bucer, Calvin and Knox, who were all much more severe over the presentation of the liturgy, give us a real glimpse into vernacular liturgy.

Zwingli's *Epicheiresis*[15] of 1523 leaves much of the foremass intact (as Luther), and during the Nicene Creed, the elements are prepared, keeping traditional custom at High Mass. Immediately comes the dialogue and preface and Sanctus; the Canon is then replaced by the four following prayers: these prayers are lengthy, and include material such as:

1. "In accordance with this promise, when the appointed time was fulfilled, *you offered your Son, our Lord Jesus Christ,* who took our flesh through the pure and ever-Virgin Mary, that *he might become for us perfect priest and perfect victim,* unique among the human race. He gave himself to be *the sacrifice for those who were lost:* and not content with this, so that we might lack for nothing, he gave himself to be our food and drink. So, most blessed Father, we pray that your goodness may constantly be on our lips: and, although our deepest gratitude can never match your kindness, we pray that in your constant and unfailing goodness you will make us worthy *to sing your praises continually with our hearts and lips and in our deeds,* and to ask for nothing that would be alien to you. In confidence, therefore, *we shall offer you prayer and praise in* accordance with your will . . ." (Lord's Prayer).
2. "We would eat the flesh and drink the blood of your Son in vain, if we did not firmly believe above all things the faith of your word, that your Son our Lord Jesus Christ was *crucified for us and atoned for the sins* of the whole world. . . ."
3. "Therefore, O Lord, . . . And as we believe that your Son, *once offered for us, made reconciliation to the Father,* so we also firmly believe *that he offered himself to be the food of our souls under the forms of bread and wine;* so that the memory of his generous deed may never be abolished. . . ."
4. "Through him be ready to hear our cry, 'O Lamb of God, you take away the sins of the world, have mercy on us.' . . . O Lord, draw our hearts by your gracious light, that we may worthily and faithfully join in the sacred banquet of your Son, of which he himself is both our host and our most delectable food" (institution narrative and communion).

This is strong material, verbose in style, with biblical allusions throughout. Christ is at the center, and the faithful come to God through him. It is interesting that the central events of salvation are alluded to in all four of the prayers, although the first prayer is the one that makes it most explicit. *Christ* is the sacrifice, and he offers himself to his people; the eucharist is not a dynamic action, but a preached and perceived assurance of faith. There is a tenderness in Zwingli's language that is paralleled in genre in some of the private offertory prayers and layperson's devotional prayers during the medieval Mass. Particularly in the first prayer, the themes of story and response are strong because it is a solemn recitation of salvation through Christ, which points forward to the living sacrifice of the faithful after eating and drinking the bread and wine. (This is paralleled with Cranmer's 1552 scheme, where self-oblation comes after the communion.) But this sacrifice of the people is one of gratitude as well as one of "deeds," thus safeguarding justification by faith! What is engaging about all these prayers is that for all their emphasis on Christ, there is a like emphasis on the faithful; "for us" is a theme spread over these devotions.

But just as Luther opts for a more radical abbreviation in his second reform, so does Zwingli. In the *Action oder Bruch*[16] (Action or Use), the liturgical structure remains as of word and sacrament, but the euchological content is severely reduced, with the result that the eating and drinking is preceded by the Pauline narrative, and little else. Zwingli draws the congregation together, in order to place them around the table. The story, the gift, and the response have become located in the preached word and the solemn eating and drinking, but they have lost their specifically eucharistic reference. Dix did damage to ecumenical convergence in his parodying of the Reformers, in particular through his description of Zwingli as teaching "the real absence." A simple liturgy does not necessarily produce a simplistic piety. What we see in Zwingli is an emphasis on the action of eating and drinking together that we have not seen perhaps since the New Testament and in the eucharistic background of the ante-Nicene Church. It cannot be denied that Zwingli's scheme is the most extreme Protestant we have so far seen, but that does not mean that for Zwingli the eucharist lacked importance. His theology is novel in its repudiation of Luther's strong understanding of eucharistic presence, but his mode of expression is a straight form of vernacular piety.

Meanwhile, in Strasbourg, there was a deliberate attempt to conserve by Diebold Schwarz, and later to mediate between Luther and Zwingli, by Martin Bucer. Schwarz's[17] Mass was first celebrated in 1524 and amounts to a vernacular translation and adaptation of the old Latin mass. What he keeps and what he does not keep is of great interest. After a simplified foremass, the bread and wine are prepared immediately following the Nicene Creed. Instead of the offertory prayers, Schwarz provides a cunningly wrought version of the *Orate Fratres:*

"Brothers and sisters, pray God the Father, through Jesus Christ, our Lord, that he will send us the Holy Ghost, the Paraclete, to make our bodies a living sacrifice, holy, acceptable unto God, which is our reasonable service. May this happen to us all."

You cannot get more strong a hint than this that the liturgy is to carry a notion of self-oblation that the old Mass had not emphasized! The dialogue immediately follows, together with preface and Sanctus, after which come the lavabo and silent prayers (a new position), and the remainder of the Canon, with some of the sacrificial material remaining but toned down considerably. The precommunion prayers have been similarly simplified. Schwarz's liturgical sense dictated placing oblatory-type prayers together, hence the position of offertory prayers (now no longer silent) after the Sanctus. Subsequent editions of Schwarz's Mass made alterations, including further reduction of offertory prayers and the Canon itself. But Maxwell is right to draw attention to the fact that at Strasbourg, at least initially, the Canon was kept "*qua* Canon," even though altered; it was not dispensed with (as Luther), nor did the Bidding Prayer of Prone take over (as Zwingli, and later Reformers).

However, Martin Bucer's[18] influence soon became felt at Strasbourg, so that the scheme represented by Schwarz was increasingly simplified, especially in the Canon, which, however, continued to contain supplicatory and intercessory material. Late in 1525, a new position was accorded to the narrative, just before the eating and drinking. The adapted *Orate Fratres* persisted until 1537; its survivial that long is significant, and its general invocatory character perhaps more in line with its ninth-century ancestor than some of the late medieval formations. Vestments and altar vocabulary eventually disappear.

The form of service eventually in use at Strasbourg was largely the work of Bucer himself, and the 1539[19] text demonstrates the conservative character of the Strasbourg tradition, although it has moved on considerably from the early days of Schwarz. After the preparation of the elements in silence, the minister "stands behind the Table," and makes a long prayer. Three samples are given, the third about half again as long as the other two, but a very Vatican II-type direction beforehand says "with these or similar words." These prayers begin with intercession and lead into supplication for communion. They are not so aggressively christological as Zwingli, nor does one feel preached at when one reads them. The first describes the work of Christ as "*to offer and give himself so that he may live in us, and we in him, as members of his body, serving you fruitfully in every way.*" The second, with more feeling, prays: "Help us to grasp by true faith how great is your love for us, that *you have given your dear Son to die for us. . . .*" The third ends christologically:

"And since, for our sake, he *has not only offered his body and blood* upon the cross to you for our sin, but also wishes to give them to us for food and drink unto eternal life, grant that *we may accept his goodness and gift* with complete longing and devotion. . . .

". . . so that we may at all times *give thanks and praise*, and glorify your holy name *in all that we say and do*."

The minister ends the prayer with the Lord's Prayer (compare Zwingli's *Epicheiresis*) and proceeds to the institution narrative, after further warning about the meaning of the Supper (if not already done earlier). As with Zwingli, there is strong emphasis on eating and drinking together, but the eucharistic theology of Bucer's prayers is less guarded, although we still have the theme of building up the faith of the believer as the prime movement in the eucharist itself.

When John Calvin was minister to the exiles in Strasbourg between 1538 and 1541, he was so impressed with Bucer's liturgy that he used it himself, with few alterations. By the time of the 1542 Geneva *Form of Church Prayers*,[20] Calvin's liturgical program had reached some maturity. The elements are placed on the table, following the Creed; there is "the Prayer," which is like one or other of the lengthy prayers in Bucer's collection. A long exhortation follows, beginning with the institution narrative, moving on to excommunicate "all idolaters," asking all to examine their consciences, and asserting that "this sacrament is a medicine for the spiritually poor and sick . . . let us receive this sacrament as a *pledge that the virtue of his death and passion is imputed* to us for righteousness." It ends with a call to "raise our hearts and minds on high, where Jesus Christ is, in the glory of his Father," and by euchologically denying a localized presence in the bread and wine. The eating and drinking follow.

Calvin's liturgical ability may not have been up to the standard of Bucer, but in his theological writings, we find that he does not waste his words in going straight to basic questions. Rejecting any sense of impetration in the eucharist, he writes:

"The apostle . . . teaches us that the sacrifices of the Law were abolished by the death of Christ because there was remembrance of sins in them. It is clear from this that this kind of application (of Christ's sacrifice) which they (Catholics) invent has disappeared."[21]

Like Luther, and in the new prayers that we have seen so far, Calvin insists that Christ, and no one else, is the agent of the eucharist, as he pleads his own sacrifice.

Christ is continually doing this because he rose from the dead for this purpose. Similarly, the *Institutes* exude the same kind of assured doctrine, mixed with a rigorous summary of theologians of the patristic and medieval eras. Strongly christological, Calvin's arguments insist on the presence of Christ as strong and powerful, but Christ is in heaven, and since he puts so much emphasis on Christ's presence in heaven, the eucharistic action of pleading the sacrifice is his, and his alone. Calvin's concern is to deny transubstantiation and also to avoid Zwinglianism. He includes a summary of the bare necessities of a eucharistic rite.[22]

Knox's Genevan service book of 1556 makes a few changes.[23] Significantly, the narrative of the institution is read from the pulpit by the minister at the end of the sermon service, thus placing it in what Barkley describes as a prophetic relationship with all that follows; the bread and wine have been placed on the table during the psalm immediately prior to the reading, a significant piece of drama. The minister comes down from the pulpit and reads a fairly long prayer in which thanks are given for redemption and for the forgiveness of sins, and for being able to come to the Lord's table. There is no question but that the sacrifice has taken place:

". . . whom of very love thou didst give to be made man, like unto us in all things (sin except) that in his body he might receive the punishments of our transgressions, *by his death to make satisfaction to thy justice.*

". . . O Lord the blind dullness of our corrupt nature will not suffer us sufficiently to weigh these thy most ample benefits: yet nevertheless at the commandment of Jesus Christ our Lord, *we present ourselves to this his table (which he hath left to be used in remembrance of his death until his coming again)* to declare and witness before the world, that by him alone we have received liberty, and life: that by him alone, thou dost acknowledge us thy children and heirs: that by him alone, we have entrance to the throne of thy grace: that by him alone, we are possessed in our spiritual kingdom, to eat and drink at his table."

The bread and wine are consumed by the communicants, and the service concludes with a prayer of thanksgiving, a psalm, and a blessing.

This form also appears in the *Book of Common Order* of 1564[24] of the Scots Presbyterians.

CRANMER

The liturgical work of Thomas Cranmer has been much debated and often described. His theological views have more often reflected the views of his interpreters than views that he may have held himself, although Gregory Dix's charge that he was a thoroughgoing Zwinglian from 1549 (not just 1552) has not yet been refuted adequately.[25]

Before looking at the first Prayer Books, it is necessary first to glance at the sequence of ideas in the ill-fated rite contained in Hermann Von Wied's *Simple and Religious Consultation* of 1545,[26] which Cranmer used. After the foremass, which ends with the Creed, the Offertory (*sic*), and a warning against unworthy reception, the people should "make their oblation," and then go "nigh to the altar." The priest recites the preface (preceded by a dialogue, in the usual manner), which is very Lutheran-looking (even Oriental); the ideas in the preface range from creation through the incarnation, and end with the response of praise: "and that we *should glorify and exalt thee here and evermore in all our words and deeds,* and sing unto thee without end with all thy holy angels and beloved children." The Sanctus follows, leading straight into the institution narrative, and the service proceeds along Lutheran lines.

The two significant features of this rite are, first, that the people must make an offering, and this offering is called an oblation; and secondly, the preface ends on the theme of the living sacrifice of praise of the people, thus making the Sanctus even more significant in its doxological position, prior to the recitation of the institution narrative. We shall return to both these features in due course. For our discussion, we must go immediately to the Prayer Book of 1549,[27] whose "Canon" has recently been restudied by Geoffrey Cuming. Laying aside for the moment the theology of the rite, it is of prime importance that the sequence of ideas within the prayers, and the way Cranmer uses his sources, is set out clearly.

After the foremass, which ends with the exhortations (optional), and the offertory (with sentences), the eucharist proceeds as follows:

1. "While the Clerks do sing the *offertory,* so many as are disposed shall offer to the *poor men's box,* everyone according to his ability and charitable mind. And at the offering days appointed, every man and woman shall pay to the Curate the *due and accustomed offerings.*"
2. "Then shall the Minister *take* so much bread and wine as shall suffice for the persons appointed to receive the holy communion. . . ."
3. Dialogue, preface, with propers, Sanctus.
4. Prayer: "We humbly beseech thee most mercifully to receive these our prayers, *which we offer unto thy divine Majesty. . . .* And especially we commend unto thy merciful goodness this congrega-

142

tion, which is here assembled in thy name, *to celebrate the commemoration of the most glorious death of thy Son."*

5. Prayer continues: "O God, heavenly Father, which of thy tender mercy didst give thine only Son Jesu Christ to suffer death upon the cross for our redemption; *who made there (by his one oblation once offered) a full, perfect, and sufficient sacrifice, oblation, and satisfaction, for the sins of the whole world;* and did institute, and in his holy gospel command us to celebrate a perpetual memory of that his precious death, until his coming again . . ." (institution narrative follows).

6. "Wherefore, O Lord and heavenly Father, according to the institution of thy dearly beloved Son our Saviour Jesu Christ, *we thy humble servants do celebrate and make here before thy divine majesty, with these thy holy gifts, the memorial which thy Son hath willed us to make;* having in remembrance his blessed passion, mighty resurrection, and glorious ascension. . . ."

7. "And here we *offer and present unto thee (O Lord) our self, our souls and bodies, to be a reasonable, holy and lively sacrifice unto thee;* humbly beseeching thee, that whosoever shall be partakers of this holy communion may worthily receive the most precious body and blood of thy Son, Jesus Christ. . . ."

8. "And although we be unworthy (through our manifold sins) to offer unto thee any sacrifice, yet we beseech thee to accept *this our bounden duty and service,* and *command these our prayers and supplications, by the ministry of thy holy angels, to be brought up into thy holy tabernacle,* before the sight of thy divine Majesty; not weighing our merits. . . ."

9. Lord's Prayer, penitential rite (from 1548 Order), communion.
10. Postcommunion prayer refers to "good works."

These prayers are a subtle interweaving of new and old, and they repay examination.[28]

1 and 2. While the "people's offertory" had not died out in the Middle Ages, it was an occasional affair, but in any case the innovation is not so much in principle as in kind.[29] Here is no offering of bread and wine (although these must be provided by the parish), but rather the offering of money. It is significant that the people are exhorted strongly to contribute (by the tone of the rubrics, although, as Bucer was to point out, not often in practice).[30] The money is not offered at the altar, but the bread and wine are to be placed on the altar, although without prayer. The singing of the offertory chant is a functional item, allowing musical establishments to air their talents.

3. Nothing new; but there are a few proper prefaces.

4. Prayer offered to the divine majesty for the Church can be paralleled in Hermann, and also the *Te igitur*. The (later) prayer for the congregation (NB just before the commemoration of the departed, and after the general prayer for Church, state, Church leaders, people, and sick) can be paralleled from the Litany of 1544, Hermann, and also the *Memento* of the Canon, but Cranmer has filled out these secondary sources.[31]

5. The opening part of the prayer commonly described as consecration (but not by Cranmer) hammers home the point that Christ died once for all on the cross. The Köln *Antidagma* of 1544 and the *King's Book* similarly contain material to that effect. The Canon does not, because it has other concerns. It is, moreover, interesting that in the "epiclesis" that precedes the institution narrative, the bread and wine are described as gifts and creatures that can be paralleled in the *King's Book*, and perhaps in the Roman Canon.[32]

6. The anamnesis avoids any oblation of the gifts, but the Canon is obviously at the back of Cranmer's mind, if only for negative reasons (*Unde et memores*).

7. The self-oblation is also found in Hermann. Cuming suggests a remote parallel from the Sarum prayer before the Peace, but this seems a little far-fetched;[33] Cranmer introduces the theme of forgiveness of sins, which is not prominent in the Canon.

8. Prayer for the acceptance of the sacrifice can be found in the *Nobis quoque* and the *Hanc igitur*; the idea of "bounden duty" also appears in the Litany.[34]

10. For "good works," cf. Ephesians 2:10.

What are we to make of this conflation and composition? Scholars of Brightman's generation tended to see in Cranmer (especially in the 1549 book) a more gentle Reformation than those of the era following Gregory Dix. For instance, Brightman[35] suggested that for Cranmer, there are three sacrifices: (1) the Church's commemoration of Christ's oblation on the cross; (2) a sacrifice of praise for the benefits of the passion; and (3) the offering of the faithful of themselves in response to Christ. Cuming, however, compares these ideas with the writings of Cranmer himself and comes to the conclusion that Brightman's first can stand, but that his second and third are really one and the same.[36] Later theology thus interprets the Prayer Book, but that is not the point. Cuming reaches the conclusion that Cranmer does have three offerings, but the first is that of prayer, at the start of the intercession, the second is Christ's sacrifice, and the third is the self-oblation of the people.

My own analysis would accept Cuming's criticism of Brightman, who may at this stage have allowed his tractarian exegetical tendencies to run away with him. But I think that Cranmer's "offering" of prayer at the start of the intercession is of great importance because it sets the tone of what follows. We have already seen how the Greek ἀναπέμπω (send up) appears both in Justin and in the Greek liturgies, and how Syriac can easily accommodate sacrificial overtones in making solemn prayer. Moreover, coming so soon after the dramatic actions of the offertory (is this the Christmas game, as Gregory Dix suggests),[37] the meal aspect of the eucharist is emphasized through the realness of the bread and the wine (placed on the altar without an offertory), and in the eating and drinking afterwards. They are "gifts and creatures," functionally displayed, solemnly prayed over, consumed with faith.

Bucer's criticisms of the 1549 Prayer Book are well known. He did not like the residual Catholicism hinted at by some of the language, for instance the acceptance of the offering in heaven, which he feared would be interpreted in Catholic terms. He wanted more emphasis placed on the offering of alms because he observed that not many parishioners took it seriously enough. (Perhaps Bucer should be made the patron saint of stewardship campaigns.) He wanted stronger emphasis placed on the people's oblation. Of the end of the Canon, he writes with Protestant conviction and real insight into Cranmer's motives in masking Reformed theology beneath traditional symbolism:

"It is sufficiently clear that the authors of the book intended at this point to preserve some kind of reference to the traditional prayers in which there are numerous references to sacrifices and oblations, although today the sacrifices to which the holy Fathers understood these words to refer are no longer there at the Lord's table; that is to say, the gifts for the poor. It is to be noted how the Papists have twisted those words, and we should therefore avoid language of this kind rather than imitate it."[38]

You cannot get a stronger hint than this that further revision is needed; and when we look at 1552,[39] the process of revision is taken still further. Apart from the abolition of vestments, except the surplice, the altar is now described as the table, and it is set alongside the people in the chancel to avoid any sacrificial symbolism connected with traditional orientation. (Luther had got away with the retention of vestments in many places, and also with the custom of orientation.) The scheme looks like this:

1. "Then shall the Church wardens, or some other by them appointed, *gather the devotion of the people*, and put the same into the poor men's box, and upon the offering days appointed, every man and woman shall pay to the curate the due and accustomed offerings. . . ."
2. Nil, except by implication.
3. After intercession and penitential rite.
4. Prayer: "We humbly beseech thee most mercifully to (*accept our alms* and) to receive these our prayers which we offer unto thy divine majesty."
5. No change, other than stylistic, but "of himself" added after "one oblation."
6. The old anamnesis has been subsumed into a petition for "consecration" before the institution narrative: "Hear us, O merciful Father, we beseech thee; and grant that *we, receiving these thy creatures of bread and wine, according to thy Son our Saviour Jesus Christ's holy institution, in remembrance of his death and passion, may be partakers* of his most blessed body and blood.
7 and 8. These follow in a single prayer, without change, after the communion: the reference to the heavenly presence is deleted.

Some have contended that Cranmer was Calvinist in 1552, having been Lutheran in 1549, and doubtless Catholic at some time before.[40] Dix's contention that he was Zwinglian from 1549 onwards is based on a careful examination of Cranmer's own work on the Lord's Supper in 1550, together with his replies at his trial, as well as a thorough study of the two Prayer Book rites.[41] There is no doubt that 1552 is a much more austere rite than 1549, but as far as eucharistic offering is concerned is there any substantial difference? The offering of alms is now supervised by certain persons and seems to hold a stronger place in the liturgy. It is ritualized in the prayer of intercessions: God is to accept prayers and money (the implication being, but nothing else except what is closely defined hereafter . . .). That the anamnesis should go in the interests of following the institution narrative closely with the eating and drinking should not surprise, especially as Bucer's own Strasbourg rite invariably followed the sequence of long prayer, including intercession, narrative, and eating and drinking. But what has altered drastically is the *order*. The people are at the heart of the drama, so that having made their offering of money and having offered solemn intercession, they are exhorted and confess. They give thanks and pray humbly about communion. The bread and wine are set apart in a carefully worded manner, again placing the emphasis on the people ("that we," contrasted with the 1549 epiclesis). The elements are immediately consumed, after which the people *either* give thanks for communion, looking forward to good works, *or* they pray for the acceptance of the sacrifice of themselves (without any reference, this time, to the tabernacle in heaven). If 1549 were ambiguous, 1552 is clear in its "shape," and that shape is nothing to do with taking, blessing, breaking and sharing the elements, although it must be admitted, neither had the late medieval Mass, obscured as it was beneath that overlay of late euchology, allegorical interpretation, and vernacular piety. It is the people who "do" the eucharist, but in a manner that stresses the fact of redemption, with self-oblation after communion. It may be that 1549 could be interpreted in Catholic terms, as Gardiner tried, but the second book got rid of so much that was familiar in context and language that 1552 (which does not even refer to the placing of the bread and wine on the table, although it assumes that the elements are there) does not conceal anything.

However, does its notion of eucharistic offering differ? In emphasis, yes, but not in kind. The liturgical context of the prayers is different, and so, therefore, is the theological balance. The Prayer Book of 1549 still has a church-centered focus through the context of the prayers and the careful weaving together of sacrificial ideas. That of 1552, on the other hand, aggressively points to the communicants as the Church, to be prepared for eating and drinking, but at the expense of any objective activity. Dix has made much of the psychological character of medieval piety and has compared Langforde's *Meditations* with the Reformers' theological emphases, where divine worship is a phase of life rather than a corporate activity.[42] But being a phase of life is no bad thing in itself,[43] and had Dix shown a little less delight in teasing Cranmer-lovers, and more care in trying to understand the intentions of the Reformers, then Anglicans (and others) would be more able to look critically at their sixteenth-century roots through the eyes of liturgiology, both comparative and historical. Even though many of the Reformers did have a two-stage program of liturgical revision, it is hard to determine whether or not Cranmer knew what he wanted to have before 1549, and simply put forward that book as an interim, what Dix describes as a "ballon d'essai." In 1552, Cranmer makes story into a heavenly event, gift remains unsymbolic, functionally on the table, but response is strong, focused in the postcommunion event, but also stressed in the intercession. The eucharist is about the concerns of the people, so these concerns must be enumerated with considerably more detail than the old Canon allowed. If Cranmer trusts the Church to do anything, then it is to repeat the actions of Christ as simply as possible, within a liturgical context dominated by the read and preached word, the penitential preparation and subsequent self-oblation of the communicants. All in all, it is a brilliantly constructed liturgy of anthropocentrism, bringing the people before God to remind them of the saving event of Christ and to eat and drink together.

Those who are ready to label Cranmer Zwinglian forget that Cranmer takes more care to use traditional liturgical sources than virtually any other Reformer, and it may be that it is for this reason that his critics, like Bucer, wanted the Reformation to go further than 1549 had allowed. It cannot be doubted, however, that the kind of psychological stirrings of the devoted and penitent heart that he saw in medieval piety would be fed by such a liturgy, and perhaps could be commended to them, even though the Prayer Book of 1552 was short-lived because of Edward VI's untimely death. The Prayer Book of 1552 represents a landmark in the development of eucharistic offering, with the dual foci of Christ in heaven and human beings on earth; Christ has bridged the gap, and it only remains for the Church to make it obvious.

We have seen how many and varied were the medieval western and eastern churches' attempts to express anamnesis in the eucharist, from "remembering . . . we offer" in Greek anaphoras, through the imprecise "reasonable and bloodless service" in Egypt, to "accept this sacrifice in heaven" in Rome. One is left to speculate what Cranmer would have done had he been faced with another anaphoral tradition. I suspect that something equally man-centered would have emerged, but I doubt he would have been so averse to gift, since that theme takes its place alongside the others in the East. It is most obviously at the presentation of the bread and wine that Cranmer is belligerently silent; the bread and wine are there, but people matter more. Bucer, Cranmer, and Calvin all knew their Fathers and the patristic treatment of offering, but they could not face up to the ancient imprecision of language because the context in which they were working was theologically much more explosive and therefore required the liturgy to deal with sacrifice in a self-conscious manner. We are now away from the organic development of liturgy and well into the era in which definition is in order; many modern eucharistic prayers of an experimental kind bear the same marks, especially those that seek to work out an Auschwitz theology, dwelling on the agony of Christ, suffering in his world today, and on what should be the response of the people of God in loving action. Alan Clark once referred to the notion of "excommunicating ideas—temporarily";[44] with an eye to the western Reformation, Clark points up the sixteenth-century predicament with understanding and candor. Luther, Zwingli, Calvin, and Cranmer, with their contemporaries and associates, felt obliged by the combination of tradition and their experiences of theological debate to excommunicate the notion of eucharistic offering because of the exaggerated position it had developed in the western medieval Mass. We have seen how untraditional was this accumulation and how much more wholesome was the treatment of the various eastern churches. We shall return later on to the lessons that can be learned from this sad tale. For dynamic memorial of the Church in offering gifts, that supremely simple movement of ideas in the early anaphoras, we now have the eucharist as the action of Christ from heaven, to penitent and obedient hearts. The starting points are different. But there are just as many dangers inherent in trusting too much in the Church's activity as in concentrating on preparation and confession and being worthy.

THE LATER PRAYER BOOKS
Subsequent Prayer Books[45] betray the tug-of-war between differing factions in England and Scotland, some wanting more Reformation, some wanting a return to 1549, some wanting things to stay the same. The Prayer Books of 1559 and 1604 add little to the story for our purpose, save to say that in 1559, the words of administration from 1549 ("the body of our Lord Jesus Christ . . .") and 1552 ("Take this . . .") were run together. It was in the Scottish Prayer Book of 1637 that the High Church party managed to secure a strong base, as Gordon Donaldson and Richard Buxton[46] have shown in their studies on the theological and liturgical background of this remarkable but ill-fated book. For the purposes of comparison, we shall use the tabulation of items as in our treatment of Cranmer.

1. "While the Presbyter distinctly pronounceth some or all of these sentences for the Offertory, the Deacon or (if no such be present) one of the Churchwardens shall *receive the devotions of the People* there present in a bason provided for that purpose. And when all have been offered, he shall reverently bring the said bason *with the oblations therein,* and deliver it to the Presbyter, who shall humbly present it before the Lord, and set it upon the holy Table. *And the Presbyter shall then offer up and place the bread and wine prepared for the Sacrament* upon the Lord's Table, that it may be ready for that service."

4. Prayer of intercession; with "(*to accept our alms,* and)". The prayer for the communicants (1549) is to be omitted when there is no celebration.

(Penitential material, as 1552, with changes.)

5. "Then the Presbyter, standing up, shall say the *Prayer of Consecration,* as followeth. . . ."
Prayer as 1549, complete with epiclesis, and manual acts.

6. "Immediately after shall be said *this Memorial or Prayer of Oblation,* as followeth."
Prayer as 1549.

7 and 8. As 1549.

There is much to be said about these schemes, which was clearly the result of the "Laudian" school, although the nickname "Laud's Liturgy" is a misnomer since it was more the work of Wedderburn. The directions for the offertory combine the ritualizing of the alms-giving in 1552 with a move back to 1549 (and earlier) in the direction for the presbyter to "offer up" the bread and wine. There is no offertory prayer (that is to come later in the Scottish tradition), but the compilers clearly saw a need to make the action of placing the elements on the table more than merely functional. The other changes, which are a reversion to 1549, also include important liturgical descriptions: the prayer of consecration is so-called (it was not in 1552), and the prayer following this is called "Memorial or Prayer of Oblation." This latter is a little puzzling, since it betrays a certain self-consciousness about the prayer itself (doubly so in view of the conscious *restoration* of the 1549 format); but once the sequence of ideas in the prayer is clear, then the two titles are self-explanatory, for the first part of the prayer is an anamnesis, and the second part is the oblation of the communicants. It is also noteworthy that the Scottish book avoids priest and minister by going back to the patristic "presbyter."

Donaldson has made clear that, while Knox's rite lacked an epiclesis, ministers frequently inserted one, and Puritans did not object to the prayer of oblation after the consecration.[47] What is new, however, is that the prayers are defined carefully in the rubrics, and the presbyter "offers up" the bread and the wine. But Laud's enemies used his eucharistic preferences against him, and it could well be that it was his emphasis on offertory and his espousal of the 1549 rite that provided opportunity for the question of eucharistic sacrifice to be brought up at his trial. Laud countered his critics on this point by asking how *sacrificium laudis* could possibly be *oblatio corporis?*[48] But Laud's theology was not the principal reason for his execution. We shall return to the question of different interpretations in eucharistic theology among Anglicans later. Suffice it for the moment to state with Buxton that the 1637 rite "represents more or less the ideal eucharistic liturgy according to the mind of the Caroline divines of the early seventeenth century."[49] This is all the more obvious when we come to look at the proposals that the High Church party wanted to be included in the 1662 Prayer Book.

The "Durham Book" is an edition of the Prayer Book dated 1619 into which copious amendments have been written and which was the work of John Cosin, incorporating his own suggestions for revision as well as those of Matthew Wren. As the editor notes, "whereas neither had previously so much as mentioned the Scottish Liturgy, it is quite obvious that they now had it open on the table in front of them."[50] Thus, there is a proposal for the priest to "offer up and place upon the Table so much bread and wine as he shall think sufficient," an idea taken straight from the Scottish book and supported by such notables as Andrewes and Jeremy Taylor. In the intercessions, the words "and oblations" are inserted after "alms," a disputed addendum, but one that John Dowden has demonstrated to have meant "other devout offerings" and not the bread and the wine.[51] The prayer for the communicants in 1549, which was deleted from the intercession in 1552, should return, but in brackets (again following Scottish 1637). The remainder of the eucharistic rite follows the 1552 pattern until after the prayer of humble access, when once more, Scottish precedent is followed in that the prayer that had been widely interpreted as consecration is so-called. Moreover, Cosin wants the 1549-Scottish petition for consecration, and the manual acts are brought in, too. The 1549-Scottish pattern is again followed in the inclusion of the memorial-oblation prayer immediately after the narrative of institution, although it is not so described as in the Scottish book. Other proposals included more details, such as provision for additional consecration.

The Durham Book as a whole did not win the day for many reasons, including a lethargy about liturgical revision after the long, dark days of the Commonwealth. But the additions of placing the bread and wine on the table, the reference to oblations, and the title "consecration" were all included in the 1662 book,[52] thus indicating that, however Zwinglian Cranmer may have been, many Anglicans did not use his liturgy in that way, preferring a stronger accent on the Church's corporate action in the eucharist. But the liturgical pundits could not dislodge what was now a time-honored sequence of prayers. The story is an interesting example of the tension between the original drafters of a liturgy and subsequent generations' understanding and implementation of it. Such a phenomenon is not new to our study, for we have already observed it in the medieval West over the understanding of the Canon and the inclusion of supplementary prayers to make the offertory rites more meaningful. Ironically, some seventeenth-century Anglicans wanted to have their cake and eat it; they were intent upon the offering of money *and* the solemn placing of the elements on the table, whereas, it could be suggested, the intentions of Thomas Cranmer were for the medieval offertory of bread and wine to bite the dust ritually, and to appear as nothing compared with the general activity of the congregation in collecting alms for the good purposes of the Christian community. Puritan exceptions mentioned at the Savoy Conference included both a suggestion for the deferral of the collection until the end of the service and dissatisfaction with the consecration as "not here explicit and distinct enough."[53] Here, perhaps, we have an un-Anglican but Calvinist theology; there is no point in suddenly collecting money in the middle of the service (could the collection conceivably be linked in their minds with post-communion self-oblation?), but we still need to say what we are doing when reciting the institution narrative.

THE WESTMINSTER DIRECTORY AND THE "SAVOY" LITURGY
If Charles I failed to secure a strong foothold for his High Churchmanship in Scotland in 1637, he was also the indirect cause for the triumph of Presbyterianism in 1645 with the *Directory*.[54] Bare as it is from a liturgical point of view, it nonetheless shows marked theological confidence in places where Cranmer's prolix rite was vague by comparison. After the ministry of the word and the exhortation, there is "the Prayer, or Blessing of the Bread and Wine." The *Directory*, of course, does not provide forms of prayer, but lays down what themes should be used; here are some portions from this "Prayer."

"With humble and hearty acknowledgement of the greatness of our misery. . . .

"To give thanks to God for all his benefits, and especially for that great benefit of our redemption, the love of God the Father, *the sufferings and merits of the Lord Jesus Christ the Son of God, by which we are delivered;* and for all means of grace, the Word and Sacraments, and for this Sacrament in particular, by which *Christ and all his benefits are applied and sealed up* unto us. . . .

"Earnestly to pray to God, the Father of all mercies, and God of all consolation, to vouchsafe his gracious presence, and the effectual

152

working of his Spirit in us, and so to sanctify these Elements of Bread and Wine, and to bless his own Ordinance, that we may receive by faith the Body and Blood of Jesus Christ crucified for us, and so to feed upon him, that he may be one with us, and we with him. . . ."

Then comes:

"The Elements being now sanctified by the Word and Prayer, the Minister . . . is to take the Bread . . ."* (here follows the institution narrative, with manual acts).

The *Directory* opts for the pattern of solemn prayer with narrative and manual acts thereafter, immediately prior to the eating and drinking.[55] What is interesting is that the thanksgiving prayer (a *eucharistia* if ever there was one) is vague about its content but precise in its sacramental effects, whereas Cranmer's rite is the opposite, in being precise as to content, but vague as to effect. While the doctrine of the presence is strong by comparison with the more extreme Reformers we have seen already (including, let it be said, John Knox), there is no doctrine of eucharistic sacrifice whatever. A collection is taken at the end as a response to the whole service, but it is functional, as in Cranmer, and no need is felt to place it within the liturgy in such a way as to replace consciously the old offertory rites, which are now gone forever. The *Directory* represents a mature flavor of British Puritanism, with a strong sense of order, decency, and confidence in the activity of God among his people. But while the eucharist is a memorial of Christ, the sacrifice has happened and causes the people of God to come together in him, to feed on him by faith, in the power of the Spirit.

When we turn to the ill-fated "Savoy" rite of Richard Baxter,[56] we see an adventurous Puritan formulary that satisfied neither the Prayer Book supporters nor the anti-Prayer-Book group. We have had occasion elsewhere to commend Baxter's work as of intrinsic interest. His eucharist shows originality within the confines of a basically Puritan rite and is centered on three prayers, addressed to the Father, the Son, and the Holy Spirit.

1. The first prayer acknowledges God as creator and redeemer, and the work of Christ:
". . . who hath ratified the new testament and covenant of grace with his most precious blood; and hath instituted this holy Sacrament *to be celebrated in remembrance of him till his coming."*
It concludes with a brief prayer for consecration.
2. The Pauline institution narrative is read out.

3. The minister declares the elements "sacramentally the body and blood of Christ."

4. The second prayer is a tender meditation to Christ on his work for the faithful:

". . . and hath instituted this holy Sacrament to be used *in remembrance of thee till thy coming; we beseech thee, by thine intercession with the Father, through the sacrifice of thy body and blood,* give us pardon of our sins, and thy quickening Spirit, without which the flesh will profit us nothing. *Reconcile us to the Father. . . ."*

5. The minister takes the bread and breaks it before the people, saying:

"The body of Christ was broken for us, *and offered once for all to sanctify us: behold the sacrificed Lamb of God,* that taketh away the sins of the world."

6. The minister pours the wine, saying:

"We were redeemed with the precious blood of Christ, as of a Lamb without blemish and without spot."

7. The minister then prays to the Holy Spirit:

"Most Holy Spirit . . . shed abroad the love of God upon our hearts, and draw them out in love to him. *Fill us with thankfulness* and holy joy, and with love to one another. Comfort us *by witnessing that we are the children* of God. Confirm us for new obedience. Be the earnest of our inheritance, and seal us up to everlasting life."

Baxter's rite does not waste a single syllable, and in this respect we are encountering a euchological conciseness that we have not seen since the *Didache* or the *Apostolic Tradition* of Hippolytus. Baxter's brillant sense of image and meaning even provide him with the chance to combine eucharistic spirituality with the doctrine of the Trinity, although the themes of the prayers prevent a mechanical view of the Trinity, with separate roles for each member. Like a hymn writer, too, he includes the devotional aspects of the penitent coming to eucharist. But, of course, his liturgy (doubtless used by himself in one form or another) did not, and could not, win the day. Like the *Directory,* it is precise where Cranmer is not, although the number of words he uses is considerably fewer than Cranmer's. Ratcliff praised Baxter's work for its conciseness of style and Catholic theology.

Within this rite, he combines both story, gift, and response by holding together the doctrines of eucharistic thanksgiving and memorial, by a bold frankness in speaking of the elements, and by a piety that both rejoices in the mighty acts of God and looks forward to service afterwards. What is particularly interesting is his reference to the intercession of Christ, for the eucharist is the action of Christ, and it can only be understood in Baxter's terms with such a theological proviso. Moreover, his Lamb imagery, also used in his marriage rite,[57] combines a strong doctrine of the presence of Christ and an insistence that Christ is in heaven. He also invents a symbolic action for the wine, pouring, to correspond to the breaking of the bread. Baxter's rite gives us a glimpse of a kind of Low Church sacramentalism that is often lost sight of in reflections about the eucharist. While the Establishment was about to bask for a long while in the rolling periods of Cranmer's prose, one cannot fail to notice that Baxter was both more radical and more traditional.[58]

Are any differences discernible between Luther, Calvin, and the other Reformers, over their doctrine of eucharistic offering as it finds expression in the liturgy? There are no essential divergences, for all agree that the sacrifice has already taken place, and that, in consequence, the eucharist is one of "pleading"[59] only, the very act of pleading being the work of Christ in the believer. But the liturgies that they produced work out this theology in different ways. Luther tells the story in the great doxological periods, founding a hymn tradition unprecedented in western Christianity. Within the eucharist this makes his preface almost superfluous. His handling of gift and response are similarly straightforward; the gifts are treated functionally, and the response is one of faith rather than in expressions of intercessory concern.

Calvin's liturgy owes a lot to Bucer in its euchological material wherein the sacrifice is again that of Christ interceding in heaven. The story is not doxological, it is homiletic in its direction, although none the worse for that. The gift and response are once again functional and faith-centered, respectively.

Cranmer provides the richest euchological scheme, but follows Zwingli in a man-centered rite (in 1552), attempting to eliminate the offertory of bread and wine by the ceremony of taking the collection. His story is partial, since Christ's resurrection is only mentioned on Easter Day (in 1552), and it is generalized; his gift is that of money for the poor, so that is generalized, too; his response is generalized like the other Reformers into acts of faith. None of this can be reduced to the level of the merely psychological, as Gregory Dix would have us believe; you can try out that line and interpretation with any liturgy, if you set out to do so.[60] Better liturgists than Calvin who nonetheless followed his theology managed to keep more than Cranmer did of patristic insight into the question of eucharistic offering, a salient example being Richard Baxter. It is by Luther's instrument of eucharistic hymnody that the earlier Christian tradition is opened up, through a brilliant combination of Hebrews christology and a liturgical medium of song that was trusted much more by certain churches of the Reformation than the more traditional medium, that of set prayer. It need hardly be added that ordination rites of the Reformation reflect these concerns,[61] although, as we have seen, the early ordination rites of presbyter in East and West were reticent on eucharistic sacrifice, preferring to use the code expression of "offering gifts" for presidency at the Lord's Supper, without any notions of offering Mass for living and dead.

ANGLICAN INTERPRETATION

There can be little doubt that even though Cranmer had deliberately not called the prayer containing the institution narrative the prayer of consecration, most Anglicans interpreted it to be so. Hence the trouble caused by Johnson in 1573 when he failed to repeat that prayer on an occasion when the elements were consumed before all communicants had received the sacrament.[62] John Jewel, who represents classical Elizabethan Churchmanship and who was bishop of Salisbury from 1560 to 1571, is strong on eucharistic presence and remarkably precise on eucharistic sacrifice. Speaking of the relationship between the sacrifice of Christ and the eucharist, he writes: "This sacrifice is revived, and freshly laid out before our eyes in the ministration of the holy mysteries." Also: "We offer up Christ, that is to say, an example, a commemoration, a remembrance of the death of Christ." Perhaps most telling of all:

"The ministration of the Holy Communion is sometimes of the ancient fathers called an 'unbloody sacrifice,' not in respect of any corporal or fleshy presence . . . but for that it representeth and reporteth unto our minds that one and everlasting sacrifice that Christ made in His body upon the cross. . . . This remembrance and oblation of praises and rendering of thanks unto God for our redemption in the Blood of Christ is called of the old fathers 'an unbloody sacrifice.' . . . Our prayers, our praises, our thanksgiving unto God for our salvation in the death of Christ is called an unbloody sacrifice."[63]

From these and other passages, it is clear that Anglicanism was already developing a critical and erudite approach to early Christian tradition with the kind of struggling for definition in contemporary terms that the term "anamnesis" requires, which we have seen worked out liturgically in the Syriac and Armenian anaphoras. Edwin Sandys has similar interests, but is anxious to define all worship

156

as sacrificial: "Sacrificing is a voluntary action whereby we worship God, offering him somewhat in token that we acknowledge Him to be the Lord, and ourselves His servants."[64] Richard Hooker, on the other hand, shows reluctance to accept sacrificial imagery of the eucharist in any but the sacrifice of Christ on the cross, the sacrifice of thanksgiving, and the sacrifice of the people, although his notion of sacrifice of thanksgiving is stronger than Cranmer's because he has a more powerful doctrine of the eucharistic presence.[65] In the section on the sacraments added to the Catechism in 1604 (the work of John Overall), the doctrinal shift away from Cranmer is noticeable in the way in which the presence of Christ is more obviously defined. The reason for the eucharist being celebrated is: "For the continual remembrance of the sacrifice of the death of Christ, and of the benefits which we receive thereby."[66]

The seventeenth century was full of reinterpreters. Lancelot Andrewes, whose thought is not always easy to follow, is clear in repudiating both Zwinglianism and Romanism over the eucharistic presence. Defending the use of the term "altar" for the holy table, he writes: "The Holy Eucharist being considered as a Sacrifice (in the representation of the Breaking the Bread and pouring forth the Cup), the same is fitly called an Altar."[67] More central in theology is Richard Mountague, who defines the eucharist in patristic terms as "only representative, rememorative, and spiritual." Thomas Morton, on the other hand, defines four areas of Protestant sacrifice. The first three are his interpretation of the prayer of oblation at the end of the eucharist: the sacrifice of mortification ("we offer . . . ourselves"); the sacrifice "Eucharistical" ("accept our sacrifice of praise and thanksgiving"); and the sacrifice "latreutical" ("our bounden duty and service"). It would be hard to distinguish the first from the third, and it is noteworthy that his fourth type does not base itself on liturgical quotation, the "sacramental representation, commemoration and application" of Christ's all-sufficient sacrifice.[68] John Bramhall, however, takes the logic further:

"We acknowledge a representation of that sacrifice to God the Father; we acknowledge an impetration of the benefit of it:
we maintain an application of its virtue: so here is a commemorative, impetrative, applicative sacrifice."[69]

It is perhaps as well that this kind of language did not gain an entrance into the English liturgy.

Similar ideas can be found in the writings of Herbert Thorndike, John Cosin, and William Laud. Laud, of course, places more emphasis on the role of the priest, insisting that the priest offers the commemorative sacrifice, the priest and the people offer the sacrifice of praise and thanksgiving, and each faithful believer offers himself. Here, the notions of anamnesis and eucharistia are far apart and are to be distinguished by who is the agent.[70] William Forbes, first bishop of Edinburgh, bases his thinking on Hebrews christology. He feels after what he terms the "more moderate Romanists," in that the eucharist is not only a sacrifice of thanksgiving, "but also propitiatory in a sound sense, and is profitable to very many not only of the living but also of the dead." Forbes saw that the term "propitiatory," which was to be used at Trent, did not mean repeating Calvary, but was a way of describing the eucharist in dynamic terms. Forbes's theology deserves more attention from scholars.[71]

Jeremy Taylor was strong on sacrifice too. His writings breathe a profound belief in the realness of the eucharistic action, as well as the way in which the believer can appropriate eternal act through sacrament; his liturgical writings, however, are less happy:

"The people are sacrificers too in their manner: for besides that, by saying Amen, they join in the act of him who ministers, and make it also their own."

Also:

"As it is a Commemoration and Representation of Christ's death, so it is a Commemorative Sacrifice. . . . There he sits, a High Priest continually, and offers still the same one perfect Sacrifice; that is, still represents it as having been once finished and consummate, in order to perpetual and never failing events. And this also His ministers do on earth. They offer up the same Sacrifice to God, the Sacrifice of the Cross by prayers, and a commemorating rite and representment. . . ."[72]

The Hebrews christology is apparent. When it comes to his liturgy, we see a conflation of Chrysostom (all worship as sacrificial, in the opening prayer of approach), Cranmer (the offering of alms), and in the anaphoral prayers, a combination of Anglican High Churchmanship and patristic scholarship:

"We Sinners thy unworthy Servants, in remembrance of thy life-giving passion, thy cross and thy pains, thy death and thy burial, thy resurrection from the dead, and thy ascension into Heaven, thy sitting at the right hand of God, making intercession for us, and expecting with fear and trembling . . . ; *do humbly present unto thee, O Lord,*

158

this present Sacrifice of remembrance and thanksgiving, humbly and passionately. . . ."[73]

Taking Cranmer to his logical conclusion, Taylor offers intercession, in sacrificial terms, within the context of self-oblation after communion. We have not encountered this combination so far, but it shows that Taylor connected self-offering with intercession. He makes nothing of the placing of the elements on the table. If some of his language is quaint, his liturgical principles are of great interest in their logic and originality.

Anthony Sparrow's *Rationale* was influential as a commentary on the Prayer Book of 1604. He makes much of the term "oblations," referring to the offering of alms only, and taking the opportunity to deal with the biblical background for offering money. He only briefly describes the prayer of oblation:

"The Priest offers up the Sacrifice of the holy Eucharist, or the Sacrifice of Praise and Thanksgiving for the whole Church, as in all the old Liturgies it is appointed; and together with that is offered up that most acceptable Sacrifice of our selves, Souls, and Bodies, devoted to God's service."[74]

Once again we have a patristic interpretation of the eucharist, but this time without the logical trimmings. Central Churchmen like Thomas Comber and William Nicholls interpreted the oblations (only inserted in 1662) as referring to the offering of money, but there is evidence of some High Churchmen reinterpreting it as the eucharistic gifts, the first of whom was Bishop Patrick, in 1669.[75] Non-Jurors followed in his trail.

One interesting point in connection with offertory is the fact that the English coronation service includes an English form of the *Super oblata* that makes it abundantly clear that the bread and wine are being offered and are to be consecrated. It was first used at the coronation of Charles I and has been used with some modification ever since. Perhaps here, in Erastian England, do we find one of the more telling examples of Baumstark's Law, whereby special occasions embody primitive customs and are therefore the most resistant to change.[76]

The eighteenth-century High Churchmen provide further development. Charles Wheatly's *Rational Illustration*[77] was another popular commentary on the Prayer Book. Buxton identifies an increasingly Catholic-ward trend in his theology in the successive editions of this book, from 1710, through 1718, to 1720. He knew his eastern liturgies and clearly wanted a return to 1549. In 1710, the offertory rubric is important: "to the intent that we may plead for all the World by the memorial of that Oblation which contained Mercy for all, and by which Christ now intercedes for all in heaven." Nothing new here, except perhaps an attachment to the act of placing the gifts on the table. But by 1720, the book is longer and includes a luscious frontispiece, portraying a priest standing at the north end of a classical altar with a cloud in heaven above it, and Jesus standing at a similar position in relation to the heavenly altar. Wheatly thus depicts the High Church road back to eucharistic sacrifice *via* the epistle to the Hebrews. Most influential on Non-Jurors and those like-minded who remained within the Establishment was John Johnson's *The Unbloody Sacrifice*. His offertory theology (like Wheatly's) provides the basis for his thinking:

"We offer the Bread and Wine, separate from all other oblations of the people; we offer them, as having been solemnly pronounced by the words of institution to be full representations of Christ's Body and Blood. And we make propitiation with them, after God has first, by the illapse of the Holy Spirit, perfected the consecration of them."[78]

This is quite a jumble, for it conflates the chronology of offertory, consecration, and communion, and draws together Cranmer's rite and eastern interpretations of consecration by the Spirit; it also emphasizes that it is God who consecrates. But Johnson has moments of greater clarity, defining five aspects of sacrifice:

"That material bread and wine . . . were by a solemn act of oblation in the Eucharist offered to Almighty God in the primitive Church. . . .

"That the Eucharistical bread and wine, or body and blood, are to be offered for acknowledgement of God's dominion. . . .

"That the Communion Table is a proper altar.

"The bishops and priests are the only proper officers for the solemn offering and consecrating of the Christian Eucharist.

"That the sacrifice of the Eucharist is rightly consumed by being solemnly eaten and drunk by the priest, clergy, and people."[79]

Johnson is repeating a theme and a Churchmanship rather than going back to first principles, but the new feature here is the one hinted at in the previous quotation, that the consecrated bread and wine are offered to God, although he nowhere suggests that we offer Christ's body and blood in the eucharist. This additional offering seems to be connected with consecration in order to make it effectual. We shall come across this idea in the Catholic Apostolic rite in the next century.[80]

Robert Nelson, on the other hand, keeps his language moderate but also uses the act of offertory as the basis for his idea of eucharist sacrifice: ". . . the Christian sacrifice, wherein bread and wine are offered to God, to acknowledge him Lord of the creatures . . ."[81] Daniel Waterland, however, fastens on the notion of anamnesis and links this with the sacrifice of intercession by Christ in heaven. Buxton suggests that this was the more typical view of Anglicanism.[82] It certainly starts more authentically from the text of the consecration prayer, rather than attempting to reinterpret the act of placing the bread and wine on the table. The two starting points are distinct. We have seen them before; one we have called story, the other gift. Cranmer has indeed been reinterpreted and the eucharist is recovering some of its dynamic patristic past, although both these aspects have come in, as it were, by the back door. I think that through Hebrews christology, this was achieved as an effective reinterpretation of Cranmer's prolix but static rite. It does not express the ideas of a fringe group, but a wide spectrum within Anglicanism.

ANGLICAN EXPERIMENT

It is one thing to interpret Cranmer; it is another to compose your own liturgy. Grisbrooke has edited a collection of various liturgies, all dating from the seventeenth and eighteenth centuries, which form an interesting backdrop to the kind of definitions we have discussed hitherto. Symbolically, Grisbrooke frames these liturgies with the 1637 Scottish and 1764 Scottish rites.[83] We have already discussed Jeremy Taylor's work. Our first three are equally unofficial.

Edward Stephens[84] probably wrote his liturgies around 1696, and there is evidence that (at least in the case of the first one) they were used at daily celebrations at Cripplegate, where he was a member of the congregation. His first liturgy is virtually that of Scottish 1637. The second draws considerably on the *Apostolic Constitutions*, thought at the time to be work of Clement of Rome and therefore "apostolic." The anamnesis is a verbose composition: ". . . that this our *Unbloody, Reasonable, and Spiritual Sacrifice* may be acceptable and well Pleasing . . . and look upon this Token and Memorial of the Covenant. . . ." Yet more eastern-looking is this third liturgy. It has an *Orate Fratres:* "Assist me, Brethren, with your Prayers, and pray to God for me, that *my and your Sacrifice may be acceptable with God* the Father Almighty." The offertory defines the eucharist as the "Memorial of the great Propitiation." But the anamnesis states that we "do offer unto thee, by *this Pure and Immaculate Offering.*" Stephens appears to be more western in his handling of sacrifice in his second and third liturgy for all his "unbloody" language. This is an interesting aspect of his thinking and shows how through western ideas he can repeat didactically the once and for all nature of Calvary as well as the real quality of the eucharist as an action of the Church. His theological theory is more satisfactory than his liturgical practice.

William Whiston[85] produced a liturgy in 1713, after having professed his confidence in the *Apostolic Constitutions;* the liturgy's anaphora is in the main a rearrangement of Cranmer along the lines of 1549, but with a significant insertion in the prayer of oblation. After the anamnesis, expanded to encompass the second coming, and prayer for the benefits of the passion, it runs:

"And here *we offer and present unto thee, O Lord, these thy Gifts, as Memorials of* the precious body and blood of thy dear Son; beseeching thy divine Majesty to have pity upon us, and hear all our Supplications which we put up unto thee in his name; and together with them, *we also offer and present unto thee, ourselves. . . .*"

This scheme is of considerable interest. First of all, Whiston would have been sufficiently familiar, through *Apostolic Constitutions,* with the fact that the offering verb normally appears in the anamnesis. His anamnesis is an expanded one compared with 1549, and like the Syrian Jacobite and Maronite anaphoras (which expand the anamnesis considerably more), the offering comes later in the prayer in the context of pleading for the benefits of the passion and of self-oblation. In other words, while the oblation is not of the body and blood of Christ (Whiston is not espousing a moment of consecration), he is trying to associate the people with the gifts in a patristic manner. Reading his text, it is hard to avoid seeing Cranmer intercalated with eastern and idiosyncratic ideas. His handling of eucharistic offering is clearly in parallel with many of the Syriac anaphoras that we saw in an earlier chapter.

John Henley[86] broke with the Church of England and produced in 1726 a liturgy for use in his oratory. His eucharists were said to be picturesque. In his other writings he models himself very much on the *Apostolic Constitutions,* but his anaphora fortunately does not go in for the length of that document.

The "Oblation" runs as follows:

"Therefore, in remembrance . . . according to his works: WE OFFER TO

THEE, our king and our God, according to his Constitution, this bread, and this cup, giving thee thanks thro' him, that thou hast thought us worthy to stand before thee, and *to sacrifice unto thee*. Amen."

The "Invocation" begins:

"And we beseech thee, that thou wilt mercifully look down upon these gifts, *here set before thee*, O thou God, *who standest in need of none of our offerings;* and do thou accept them to the honour of thy Christ; and send down thine holy Spirit, . . ."

The prayers "For the whole Church" include:

"We farther pray, and *offer unto thee, for* thy whole Church. . . . We farther pray to thee for me, who am nothing, who offer to thee. . . .
We farther offer unto thee . . ." (four times)

Henley is more aware of liturgical structure than the other writers, hence the titles to the subsections of his anaphora. *Apostolic Constitutions* is at the back of his mind throughout, notably in the anamnesis and the intercessions, and his capitalization of the offering words is of great importance for some later rites that he obviously influenced. The epiclesis is also taken from the Constitutions, including the petition for God to look upon the sacrifice. Self-consciousness rears its head in the need felt by Henley to define "offer for" by "pray for," which shows both the passage of time and Henley's eager desire to be primitive.

The Non-Jurors come next, with their two important liturgies. That of 1718[87] is less adventurous than 1734 and includes an offertory prayer resembling many of the preanaphoral prayers of the veil that we saw in the Eastern rites:

". . . that we may be worthy to offer unto thee *this reasonable and unbloody Sacrifice for our Sins and the Sins of the People.* Receive it, O God, *as a sweet smelling savour* . . . : so of thy goodness, O Lord, vouchsafe to *receive these Offerings from the hands of us sinners,* that being made worthy to minister at thy Holy Altar without blame, we may have the reward. . . ."

This prayer has followed an explicit placing of the bread and wine on the table. The eucharistic prayer is remodeled along lines of the *Apostolic Constitutions*. The transition in the anamnesis to the epiclesis is an interesting conflation, showing parallels with Henley's interests:

"Wherefore, having in remembrance . . . ; *we Offer to Thee, our God,* according to his holy Institution, *this Bread and this Cup:* giving thanks to thee through him, that thou hast vouchsafed us the honour to stand before thee, *and to Sacrifice unto thee.*

"And we beseech thee to look favourably on these thy Gifts, *which are here set before thee, O thou self-sufficient God;* And do thou Accept them to the honour of thy Christ; and send down thine Holy Spirit, the witness of the passion of our Lord Jesus Christ, *upon this Sacrifice. . . .*"

This reads very much like Henley, but there are slight changes. No reference to offering occurs in the intercessions, which further shows how difficult it is to reintroduce the notion of offering into the euchological formulae of a much later age. But there is no doubt that the anamnesis-offering-epiclesis has been restored, and the language is the most "Anglican" so far.

The 1734 rite[88] has the deacon bid the congregation to "present our offerings" to God, which seems to refer to the money only, as is the meaning of the offertory prayer, which mentions "offering gifts." The anaphora is considerably longer than 1718, but the anamnesis-epiclesis offering material is identical with 1718, a point of great interest, showing that the priorities in 1718 were to express a theology in accord with their own concerns and to defer further enrichment. One cannot help realizing in 1734 a more logical treatment of the offertory, although the distinction between money and the bread and wine seems somewhat contrived.

Thomas Rattray's liturgy of 1744[89] was a private production made with copious patristic references. Like the English Non-Jurors, he makes the deacon begin the offertory with a bidding, but his offertory prayer is the prayer in 1 Chronicles 29:10ff., which becomes embedded in subsequent Scottish liturgies: "Blessed be thou . . . Thine, O Lord. . . ." Rattray's eucharistic prayer is an amalgam of Greek material. The anamnesis is lengthy, looking forward to the second coming: "Wherefore in Commemoration of his life-giving Passion . . . we Sinners *offer to Thee, O Lord, this tremendous and unbloody Sacrifice. . . .*" Moreover, the intercessions begin: "We *offer to Thee, O Lord, for thy* holy. . . ." They revert to "Remember" in subsequent petitions, but at the end of the commemoration of the living comes:

"Vouchsafe also, O Lord, to remember *those who have this Day offered these Oblations* at thy holy Altar, and *for whom* or for what Ends every one *has offered*, or has in his Thoughts, (and those whose names we have lately read before Thee)."

Rattray is thus the first to use the 1 Chronicles passage, and the first to include a prayer for the offerers, although his translation is remarkably clumsy, even given the fact that the meaning is not easy to convey in English terms.

The climax to this little part of the whole story comes in 1764 with the Scottish Communion Office.[90] The Non-Juror background (the Scots Episcopalians were Non-Jurors anyway) and Rattray's scholarship give us a veritable landmark in the long drift away from Cranmer, even when reinterpreted by 1662 and subsequent Caroline divines. The presbyter (NB 1637 terminology) or the deacon begins the offertory with the bidding, "Let us present" (Non-Jurors 1734 and Rattray), and the 1 Chronicles passage is read out as a prayer over the money only. The presbyter then "offers up" and places the bread and wine, as 1637. Christ's "oblation" is his "own" (and is not "one," nor made "there" on the cross), thus smoothing out Cranmer's somewhat preachy description of the work of Christ. The anamnesis-epiclesis is short by comparison with what we have recently seen:

"Wherefore, O Lord, and heavenly Father, according to the institution of thy dearly beloved Son our Saviour Jesus Christ, we thy humble servants do celebrate and make here before thy divine majesty, with these thy holy gifts, WHICH WE NOW OFFER UNTO THEE, the memorial thy Son hath commanded us to make; having in remembrance. . . ."

These oblatory words appear in various editions from as early as 1735, and were introduced under the influence of another liturgically-minded Scotsman, Gadderar. But they appear invariably from 1764 onwards, with the seal of approval of all the Scottish bishops, supported by Rattray's scholarship. The influence of Henley is apparent in the capitalization of the offering words, but I think that the formula as it appears in 1764 is more subtle still. A case could be made out for it embodying three Byzantine features: (1) the verb "we offer" in the anamnesis; (2) "these gifts set forth" in the epiclesis; and (3) the priest's *ekphonesis* at these very words.[91] Moreover, the whole section is described as "the oblation" in small print in the margin of the text in a way similar to the directions for the manual acts, where "This is my body/blood" and "Do" are also capitalized. The Scottish Episcopalians have a eucharistic liturgy far distant from 1552, since their anaphora is a unity with an eastern-positioned epiclesis; the intercessions follow all this, so bringing length and antiquity in one single stroke.

There is evidence that presybters raised the bread and cup at the offering words, which in a small Episcopalian chapel would have lent a little drama to a rite usually celebrated with the minimum of outward fuss.[92] While liturgiologists may prefer to term the items that follow the institution narrative as anamnesis, epiclesis, and so on, the use of the title "oblation" must be seen to hark back to 1637, although it is significant that the 1764 revisers opted for "oblation" over against "memorial," which was the alternative title in 1637. The fact that such a decision was taken demonstrates how the compilers of the 1764 rite intended it to be understood, that there is an oblation in the eucharist, but it belongs not at the offertory (which is no more than a functional action, however solemn and necessary), but rather within the anaphora itself, where it can be seen to follow closely on the notion of memorial. Perhaps the capitalization is unnecessary, although pastors know well that in a long prayer it is often a good idea to point to salient themes and ingredients in order to safeguard the attention of the weary and young. It would seem that Rattray and his colleagues intended no notion of magic words. Nonetheless, they got their patristic theology back into the eucharistic prayer, thus giving expression to the aspirations of those who regarded the eucharist as sacrificial in the sense of embodying story, gift, and response, all of which mingle together in the anamnesis-epiclesis and subsequent prayers for acceptance of the thanksgiving and the offering of the communicants' lives. For the gifts are closely associated with the story, and the people are inextricably bound up with that movement of thought, with its attendant eucharistic spirituality. At long last, the memorial-sacrifice theology of the classical form of Anglicanism could be explicit, and not merely implicit, in an official Anglican liturgy.

Through the consecration in Aberdeen of Samuel Seabury as first bishop for the Episcopal Church in the United States of America in 1784, an unofficial concordat was signed between the Scottish Episcopalians and the Americans. Much has been made of Seabury's work in the production of the first American Prayer Book in 1789. Marion Hatchett has recently redressed the balance by suggesting that William White, among others, had just as much a part to play in the gradual introduction of the Scottish-type anaphora in that church.[93] His communion rite "recommended to Episcopal congregations in Connecticut," published in 1786, certainly reproduces the 1764 service, but he did not get his own way automatically. On one or two details Seabury had reverted to the 1662 form, notably over "one oblation" for "own" and the reintroduction of made "there" on the cross. This may have been because of the difficulty in changing time-honored formulae, since that part of the prayer resembles Cranmer very closely, unlike the anamnesis-epiclesis, which is new. Some of the Americans wanted a 1637-type anaphora, but Seabury felt very strongly about 1764: "To confess the truth, I hardly consider the form (i.e., 1637) . . . as strictly amounting to a consecration."[94] The 1786 Proposed book contained an adapted 1637 prayer, but Seabury together with Bishop White and others secured a form of the 1764 prayer in the 1789 book, although a rearguard action made the epiclesis-consecration formula less overt. Since the book was to be issued with a selection of hymns, no doubt popular under Wesleyan influence, the 1789 book ends the anaphora with a direction that a hymn should be sung immediately after it. This is a significant addition, the first official one of its kind in Anglican liturgy. (It had been suggested in the preface to the 1786 book.) In the Standard edition of 1792, another rearguard action succeeded in printing "which we now offer unto thee" in ordinary letters, and in including "and Word" after "Holy Spirit" in the epiclesis, thus trailing the coat of 1637.[95] It is clear that Seabury did not bully a reluctant faithful into an unwelcome liturgy. Many people were ready for it, and it is equally clear that anti-Tory sentiment would have played at least an indirect part in the use of a new liturgy that was different from England. As Echlin notes, "with the promulgation of the 1789 Communion Service, a long and complicated evolution reached a consummation,"[96] and he goes on to muse that George Washington himself was Episcopalian and would have used this American rite when attending eucharistic celebrations.

THE WESLEYS

In our discussion of Lutheran liturgy, we took note of the important place played by hymnody in eucharistic worship. England provided its own version of this tradition in a remarkable compilation that first appeared in 1745, entitled *Hymns on the Lord's Supper*.[97] Many have been the attempts to describe the theological stance of John Wesley. He had much that was Puritan, and much that was High Church, and much that was leading Methodists away from a narrow-minded Establishment. On the eucharist John Wesley was strong, having been a daily communicant in the days of the "holy club" at Oxford. The hymns that he and his brother wrote are arranged carefully into six groups:[98]

1. As it is a Memorial of the Sufferings. (nos. 1–27)
2. As it is a Sign and a Means of Grace. (nos. 28–92)
3. The Sacrament a Pledge of Heaven. (nos. 93–115)
4. The Holy Eucharist as it implies a Sacrifice. (nos. 116–127)
5. Concerning the Sacrifice of our Persons. (nos. 128–157)
6. After the Sacrament. (nos. 158–166)

It will be immediately apparent that the second section merited the most hymns, but that is appropriate in a sacramental and evangelical movement. Vincent Taylor drew attention to the importance of Wesley's sacrifical hymnody of the eucharist when he wrote:

". . . no modern presentation of the doctrine of the Atonement is likely to be satisfactory which ignores, or deals imperfectly with, the doctrine of the Eucharist. . . .

"Before the Oxford Movement of the last century, it was recognized by John and Charles Wesley as their collection of *Hymns on the Lord's Supper* shows:

'This Eucharistic Feast
Our every want supplies,
And still we by his Death are blest
And share his Sacrifice.' "[99]

By these headings the Wesleys promulgated a new way of looking at the eucharist in the liturgy itself, and that is by theological genre. This had not happened before, except in prayer formulae and perhaps in preaching. By grouping the hymns in this manner, the Wesleys provided a unique way of looking at the eucharist from different angles. Hebrews christology permeates much of this fine liturgical poetry, especially in hymns that plead the sacrifice and speak of the union between Christ in heaven with the believer on earth through the eucharistic celebration. Indeed, one is left to ponder that the great advantage of these hymns is that they do not localize particular liturgical actions, but rather speak by their very medium of the total celebration of the eucharist.

"Ye Royal Priests of Jesus, rise
And join the Daily Sacrifice,
Join all Believers in His Name
To offer up the Spotless Lamb.

168

"On Him, who all our Burthens bears
We cast our Praises and our Prayers,
Ourselves we offer up to God,
Implung'd in His Atoning Blood."[100]

Sometimes the imagery of these reaches a stage where vividness is powerful:

"We need not now go up to heaven,
To bring the long-sought Saviour down;
Thou art to all already given,
Thou dost even now Thy Banquet crown:
To every faithful soul appear,
And show Thy real presence here!"

Also:

"For us He ever intercedes,
His heaven-deserving passion pleads,
Presenting us before the throne;
We want no sacrifice beside,
By that great Offering sanctified,
One with our Head, for ever one."[101]

The theology of these prayers leans heavily on the presence of Christ in heaven interceding for humankind, into which the eucharist fits itself as a pleading of that sacrifice. A simple hymn in the fifth section (the "Sacrifice of our Persons") perhaps sums up the whole of Wesleyan spirituality:

"Jesu, to Thee in faith we look;
O that our services might rise
Perfumed and mingled with the smoke
Of Thy sweet-smelling sacrifice.

"Thy sacrifice with heavenly powers;
Replete, all holy, all Divine;
Human and weak, and sinful ours:
How can the two oblations join?

"Thy offering doth to ours impart
Its righteousness and saving grace,
While charged with all our sins Thou art,
To death devoted in our place.

"Our mean imperfect sacrifice
On Thine is as a burden thrown;

169

Both in a common flame arise,
And both in God's account are one."[102]

There is a tenderness and a strength of biblical allusion in these
hymns that mark them off as among the finest to have been written about the eucharist. There is nothing new of theology in them, for
they all combine story and response, although their handling of gift is
the least strong of the three criteria, probably because in hymnody
this might be taken to imply eucharistic adoration; solemn eating and
drinking does occur as a theme in other hymns. But the genius of
them all is that they refer to the whole eucharistic celebration as an
objective activity of the Church into which the believer is brought
as Christ fills the celebration and the life of faith with their true
meaning.

It could be said that such a strong accent on the doctrine of atonement, and a regular practice of holy communion, together with a flair
for hymn-writing—these are the three forces at work in the production of hymns at once powerful and human.[103] John Wesley's liturgical program, the Sunday Service of 1784,[104] did involve an abbreviation of the Cranmer services, no doubt because many thought them
worthy of abridgement (and Wesley was a popularizer). A subsidiary
reason could be that his hymns were taking an important part in
the worship of Wesleyans, and the liturgy needed pruning in consequence. In fact, his abbreviation of the eucharist did not affect the
sacrificial material. To the contrary, if you add Cranmer's rite to Wesley's hymnody, you have quite a combination of liturgy, theology,
and spirituality. The Wesley hymns give expression to much of the
kind of High Church Anglican speculation about the eucharist as a
sacrifice, and also deal with apologetic problems such as the nature
of memorial, the union of Christ with the believer, and the way in
which the eucharist is an action of the whole Church.

ROMAN CATHOLIC THEOLOGY BEFORE AND AFTER THE COUNCIL
OF TRENT

The Council of Trent met in order to settle external disputes faced by
the Catholic Church. In the second session (under Paul IV) in 1551,
transubstantiation was dealt with, but the matter of eucharistic sacrifice was deferred. It was not until the third session (under Pius IV)
in 1562 that the subject of the sacrifice of the Mass was finally discussed, in the course of which the Dominicans and the Jesuits (only
founded in 1540) quarreled over details of interpretation. The Dominican line, which could trace itself back to Aquinas, had been popular-

170

ized by Melchior Cano, and it defined principles closely. The Jesuit view was being championed by Alphonso Salmeron, who was actually present at the Council. Salmeron's emphasis on sacrifice was stronger, since it held that the sacrifice consists of the offering of the body and blood of Christ at the consecration. Salmeron has four actions in the eucharist (consecration, oblation, fraction, and consumption), but he identifies the sacrifice with the consecration in neat, clipped prose. The Council itself pronounced on the fact that in the Mass the victim is closely identified with the cross, and that the eucharist is a bloodless offering of a propitiatory kind in which Christ offers himself "by the ministry of priests."[105] The Council approved of the sequence of prayers in the Canon and recommended regular communion to the faithful. It subsequently rested all liturgical power in the hands of the Pope in 1563 and approved of the reform of the Missal. The Tridentine Mass book appeared in 1570. It swept aside many of the medieval offertory prayers, providing the forms that we discussed in the previous chapter. In addition, the Missal allowed a 200-year rule for those dioceses and religious orders that wanted to continue their own usages, but in practice most dioceses adopted the new book. The number of votive Masses was reduced and Catholicism settled down to what Klauser described as "the era of rubricism,"[106] in which the role of the liturgist was to probe how to get the words and actions right rather than to investigate the historical background of present euchological forms. Of course, this latter role was not to come onto the scene for some time to come.

Post-Tridentine Roman Catholic theology on the eucharist is a complex story.[107] It is interesting to note the way in which this story unfolds itself. Gabriel Vasquez (another Jesuit) distinguishes between the "absolute" (the cross) and the "commemorative" (the Mass) sacrifices of Christ, in which Christ is offered but in different ways. Catholic emphasis on the objective character of the offering insists on the fact that Christ is offered, rather than that Christ offers himself. Robert Bellarmine, on the other hand, starts with the spiritual altar in heaven. He takes delight in quoting from the Fathers (including Irenaeus and Augustine) and stresses the intercession. (Bellarmine, who was a Jesuit also, was much read by Anglicans, such as Laud.) Leonard Leys, also a Jesuit, describes the words of consecration as functioning "like a sword" in the sacrifice, perhaps with an eye to eastern prothesis ceremonies, but inevitably he went for a more realistic notion of eucharistic offering.

Three Oratorians, de Condren, Oliver, and Thomassin, take the debate further and insist that the sacrifice of the Mass is the same as that of the cross, and in consequence speak much of the heavenly altar. Subsequent theologians place considerable stress on the notions of representation and the separate consecration of bread and wine as effecting the sacrifice. There are considerable subtleties of language employed by these theologians, but the message is clear; behind apparent differences (the Dominican, Jesuit, Oratorian), the emphasis on correct doctrine of presence and sacrifice means that the eucharist is seen primarily in those terms. It could almost be said that the identification of the sacrifice with the words of consecration (alien in the original spirit of the Canon, be it noted) may have resulted from a sacrificial rather than a demonstrative interpretation of the function of the elevation of the host and chalice. What is of great interest is that although Catholic and Protestant differed in great measure from each other, both sides tended to emphasize the heavenly altar and the intercession of Christ. The era that fell upon the western churches after the Council of Trent was no ecumenical age. Nor was it a particularly "traditional" one, if the early traditions of the Undivided Church are taken into account. We have to wait until the age of recovery for the debates of the sixteenth century to be seen in their true light and for pastoral and theological progress to be made in common. Meanwhile, what this chapter has proved beyond dispute, from Anglican, Roman Catholic, and other points of view, is that the interpretations of subsequent ages can be far removed from the intentions of those who originally compose prayers. Liturgical history has its ironical lessons.

CONCLUSIONS

It is not the purpose of a liturgical historian at this stage to try to prove that black is white, and that the Reformers really wanted to have a doctrine of the eucharistic sacrifice after all. But the liturgical picture is, in a sense, more complicated than the theological one. From the disparate character of the medieval Mass books, which were on the whole uniform over the Canon but varied over the offertory prayers, it is interesting to note how the different Reformers handled their inheritance.

Luther, whose native Germany knew elaborate offertory prayers (the *Missa Illyrica* was compiled in Germany) deliberately excludes the offering of gift, but substitutes the biblical notion (as he sees it) of feasting together in the presence of the Lord. Subsequent Lutheran hymnody builds on this idea,[108] although Luther himself had little use for specifically eucharistic hymnody other than metrical versions of the Ordinary of the Mass, and a few other compositions.

172

In Strasbourg, in spite of an initial conservatism (witnessed to by Schwarz), the offertory has to go, even when redefined, and more thoroughgoing reform robs the liturgy of the externals that Luther himself liked and wanted to keep, although supplicatory prayers replacing the Canon persist. But a similar theological emphasis is apparent. Story and response remain, although they are separated, and gift only survives in the feasting together.

In Geneva, Calvin works along similar liturgical lines. Unlike Luther, who eventually simply rejects eucharistic offering, however, Calvin attempts to define it, although this redefinition gets into Calvinist piety when this is the specific interest of subsequent preachers and theologians.

In Scotland, Knox's followers introduce the solemn carrying in of the elements by the elders, which comparative liturgists inevitably liken to the eastern Great Entrance; this is a quaint example of liturgical conservatism.[109]

In England, Cranmer eventually opts for sacrifice after communion in the curiously worded prayer of oblation, in which the offering of the sacrifice of thanksgiving and the offering of the people's oblation are expressed definitively. This position, together with the absence of a placing of the gifts on the table in 1552, is on a comparative level a series of negatives. We are *not* offering gifts, we are *not* offering Mass, but we *are* offering ourselves. Through the elaborately worded character of his liturgy, it is left to subsequent commentators and theologians to reinterpret this scheme. It is interesting to note how some of them use the placing of the gifts, restored in 1662, or the sacrifice of thanksgiving after communion as two starting points. One bases one's doctrinal scheme on the liturgy itself, and therefore has a good chance of getting the laity to digest it. We saw a variant of this process in the medieval West, where theologians used the Roman Canon and the offertory prayers to base their ideas upon, in greater or smaller measure, a liturgy not intended to carry such strong notions of sacrifice. This tendency carries on after the Reformation in Catholic theology and piety.

The Reformation carries further the separation of prayers in the eucharist into different compartments and units. That process had already begun in the medieval development, as witness the "little canon," with all the liturgical and theological implications of that title. This inevitably means that the opportunity for keeping together story, gift, and response was lost. The Reformers knew something of ancient liturgy (Melanchthon approved of offering in the Byzantine rite),[110] but not as much about the era of origins as the reformers of

173

the twentieth century. Work begun leads to new questions, and although not everyone was happy with subsequent attempts at recovery (instanced in the Non-Jurors), the more historically-minded were able to see that the authentic and wholesome traditions of the East had something to teach the West. The enduring lesson of this sad era is that words can be made to mean what you want them to mean; even "representation" as a definition of eucharistic anamnesis can carry a psychological and a realist and an "intermediate" meaning. It is just as well that liturgical prayer never had to use such a term. In the British Isles, the pressure towards placing the gifts on the table in 1662 and the Kirk's grand procession of elders bear witness to the conservative character of liturgical actions. The enthusiasm for this solemn act, variously interpreted, proves to be the back door through which some western Protestant churches make a recovery of the *presentation* of gift.

The sixteenth century was not an era in which to walk securely in matters theological, certainly not regarding the eucharist. Luther put asunder sacrament and sacrifice. Calvin distinguished between latreutical and propitiatory sacrifice (he was happy with the former, but not the latter). Zwingli went the whole way and drove a wedge between remembrance and sacrifice. Theological and liturgical reconstruction took on an unprecedented form, and it was left to subsequent generations to assimilate and adapt their work.

Chapter Seven

Renewal In The 19th And 20th Centuries

The era of recovery really begins in the nineteenth century, which is set in motion by a conscious search for the roots of Christianity in several communions, that include Anglican Tractarians, the Catholic Apostolics, and many others. At the time they all encountered opposition because of their "Catholic leanings"; their teaching and liturgical programs involved considerable reinterpretation of the traditions they had inherited. Later on, liturgical revision becomes inevitable in Anglicanism, but as late as the first part of the twentieth century this work is still in the shadow of the fourth-century West Syrian pattern of eucharistic prayer that the Non-Jurors and their contemporaries espoused. Finally, the work of liturgical renewal takes on an unprecedented energy, focused on the Roman Catholic Church's Second Vatican Council, whose Constitution on the Sacred Liturgy in 1963 and Missal of 1970 bring in a new era of reform based on a more critical search for origins in a world that had changed a great deal.

FORETASTE 1: THE TRACTARIANS
Tractarian preoccupation with the doctrine of the eucharistic presence inevitably put eucharistic sacrifice into second place, but the founding fathers of the movement had some important things to say about it, nonetheless. In his *Origines Liturgicae*,[1] William Palmer (who was later to become a Roman Catholic) observed that the eucharist in the primitive church was a "mystical and commemorative sacrifice," and insisted that the eucharist was not just a verbal oblation but also an act of oblation. One can see the Protestant context within which these protestations were made and the Catholic tradition of Anglicanism that Palmer is continuing, stretching back to the sixteenth and seventeenth centuries. Interestingly enough, Palmer refuses to accept that the oblation in the eucharist is of the consecrated elements. John Henry Newman's early teaching[2] was less advanced than his later thinking, for he tries consciously to steer a middle course between the sacrifice in "a literal sense" (the Roman Catholic position, as he per-

ceives it), a sacrifice "aiming at salvation without their own personal exertions" (the Protestant position), and also the Liberal notion, which he describes as "the expediency of virtue." It was in the sophistry of Tract 90 that Newman tried hardest to explain away the English Reformation, which was an exercise too much for him.

Edward Pusey, more of an historian than Newman, catches a vision of the primitive church that is more compatible with Anglicanism.[3] Bread and wine are placed on the table (Pusey never uses the word "altar") at the offertory, but that is not the eucharistic oblation, for this oblation is the commemorative sacrifice of the eucharist, the sacrifice of praise and thanksgiving. Both Palmer and Pusey realized that Roman exaggeration, as they saw it, was caused partly by linking eucharistic sacrifice with transubstantiation, so that the oblation is impetratory and propitiatory, rather than commemorative and (in a mental sense) representational. However, Pusey later on goes further. He describes the Reformers of the sixteenth century as teaching a eucharistic sacrifice that is "prominently merital," and therefore a spiritual act of the worshippers; the Non-Jurors, he said, taught that the sacrifice is "prominently material" of the bread and the wine; but the primitive Church regarded the sacrifice as "the continuance of the One sacrifice." One could quarrel with him on his oversimplification of the Non-Jurors, and his description of the primitive concept could have been more precise. But he is preaching a sermon, not expounding a complex treatise. In subsequent correspondence with Manning, then still an Anglican, he fastens onto the notion of pleading the sacrifice of Christ, therefore approaching God with "pledges of his love," and also of linking the eucharist with the heavenly sacrifice of Christ, the eucharist then being an image of the heavenly liturgy. We have seen these ideas before; "pleading the sacrifice" and the "heavenly liturgy" are post-Reformation back doors through which previous writers have come to eucharistic offering, although the heavenly worship is also a primitive notion.[4]

R. Wilberforce[5] found such understandings inadequate and identified the victim of the eucharist with the victim of the cross. He suggests that there are three answers to the question, "what is offered in the eucharist?" First, the devotion of the communicants; this is the nominal answer, the Protestant Reformation one. Secondly, the bread and the wine, which is the traditional High Church notion. But both these are inadequate, and Wilberforce opts for the third, which is nothing less than the offering of Christ himself. By oversimplifying the Protestant and High Church cases, he leaves himself no option but to go for the strongest notion of all, and it is perhaps because of these high views that he became a Roman Catholic.

But what of Tractarian piety? It is well-known that the early Tractarians were not interested in that preoccupation with liturgical presentation that later generations made their own. But the Oxford Movement, with its theological bias, and the Cambridge Movement, with its architectural interests, were bound to come together. There is a famous painting in Pusey House, Oxford, of a eucharist celebrated in Margaret Chapel in 1849 (the predecessor to All Saints, Margaret Street). Three ministers—in surplice, scarf, and hood—are kneeling at an altar, facing eastward. The celebrant is in the middle, the two assistants at either end of the footpace. Decrying the north end position of the celebrant, which had been the norm in Anglicanism since the seventeenth century, the parish clergy produced by the new movement needed to express in ritual form the aspirations and the teaching of their mentors. In the same year, a devotional manual called *Eucharistica*[6] was produced, consisting of "Meditations and Prayers on the most holy Eucharist from Old English Divines." The basis of the little book is the Prayer Book eucharist, but it is intercalated with many of these devotional prayers and quotations, interpreting offertory, consecration, and oblation in a High Church (Caroline) manner.

Eucharistica was produced by a more traditional High Church group, and its foreword was written by Samuel Wilberforce, bishop of Oxford. But it demonstrates the kind of piety being stirred by the Movement. For liturgical presentation, the *Directorium Anglicanum* (1858) contains the Tractarian combination of Oxford and Cambridge Movements in all the medieval dressing that was fashionable in those circles. Full directions are given for the provision of vestments and altar furnishings. Particularly interesting, however, is the way the Prayer Book is interpreted. The Offertory is immediately circumscribed in a footnote as follows: "The Sacramental elements *are* the oblations, and all other kinds of oblations at this time grew, merely and purely, out of this one." This provides the excuse for describing the subsequent action as "The Oblation of Bread and Wine, commonly called the First Oblation."[7] In the course of the ritual presentation of the gifts on the altar, "all bread and wine destined for this holy use should be set apart with prayer for the purpose." Again in a footnote there is a translation of one of the prothesis prayers from the Byzantine liturgy, including the words, "Thyself bless this oblation, and receive it to Thy Altar." The footnotes are full of quotations from the Fathers, and also from writers such as John Johnson. In the Prayer for the Church Militant, the priest is to distinguish between "alms and oblations":

". . . having first verbally oblated the alms, he will take the chalice with the paten thereon with both hands, and will offer the sacrifice to God, holding the chalice and paten before his breast.
"The following form of *Secreta*, (which is quite a model,) from the Hereford Missal, is strongly recommended to be said *secreto* during the pause at the oblation of the elements." (Here follows the Hereford version of "Receive, O Holy Trinity.")

The consecration is called "the Canon"; some Roman ceremonial directions are introduced, and footnotes include much Prayer Book history. The elevation is directed, and dubious legal grounds are given for it thus:

"The ostension or elevation of the chalice, *after* the consecration, which was the ancient English custom, was prohibited by a Rubric in Edward VI's First Prayer Book, but this rubric has been omitted at all the subsequent revisions, therefore the prohibition falls to the ground."

After the consecration come *Preces Secretae*, which "may be said," and which consist of the Roman Canon, from the *Unde et memores* through to the *Per quem*. An interesting observation comes in the discussion about supplementary consecration, where the author observes that the Sarum *Cautelae Missae* directed that only the institution narrative was needed for consecration (in the event of defect), thus providing precedent for *"un-oblated* elements" (author's italics) being consecrated.[8]

The *Directorium Anglicanum* holds together a number of different sources for this material. First, there is an obvious desire to include Roman Catholic material where this is lacking in the Prayer Book. Thus, we have the alleged *Secreta* at the oblation of the bread and wine, the use of the term "Canon," together with ceremonial directions, and the optional use of the second part of the Roman Canon, albeit silently. Secondly, the Prayer Book is adapted considerably in the way in which it is interpreted, hence the use of "oblations" to refer to the bread and wine, and the precedents followed for the elevations. Thirdly, a discreet introduction of eastern material rears its head with the prothesis prayer. What we see at work is a medieval orientation of the eucharist; the Roman directions are all culled from pre-Reformation English sources. For the ritual (as opposed to the theological) mind, the *Directorium* offers the teaching of the Tractarians, by stretching the Prayer Book further than we have so far seen.

Less ambitious than the foregoing is *The Priest to the Altar*[9] (1861), a compilation more judicious in its use of sources, with the Prayer Book rite and its propers forming the central part of the text, but supplemented with variable secrets, post-communions, and seasonal blessings taken from medieval texts; all this appears together with the 1549, Scottish, and American eucharistic rites. No clearer hint could be given that the main aspiration of the compiler is to purify the English rite by a careful introduction of new material.

Into the text of the Prayer Book come the following features at the offertory: (1) a final "sentence" is added, in square brackets, which is the Scottish liturgy's offertory prayer; (2) while placing the chalice and paten on the altar, the priest is to recite the *In spiritu humilitatis* from the Sarum Missal; (3) while the gifts are being placed on the altar:

"the Assistants shall at the same time pray secretly for him, saying, The Grace of the Holy Ghost enlighten thy heart and thy lips, and the Lord graciously accept this sacrifice of praise at thy hands, to the glory to His Name, and to the benefit of us sinners, and of all His holy Church."

This last prayer is a translation of the response to the *Orate Fratres* in the Sarum Missal. It is made into a private devotion by the assistants to stand on its own, but is contextualized by the ritual action of the priest. However, like the Scottish liturgy's offertory prayer, both the priest's *In spiritu humilitatis* and the assistant's prayer for him are printed in brackets, in order to show that they do not belong to the official rite. (This latter could hardly be in doubt.)

After the Prayer of Humble Access, and before the consecration, the celebrant is to say "the Secret" (yet another misunderstanding of the term). This consists of: in the Name of the Father; The *Te igitur*, part of the *Hanc igitur*, and the *Quam oblationem*. But an alternative to this eclectic use of the Roman Canon is a short quotation from the epiclesis in *Apostolic Constitutions VIII*:

"Most Merciful God, look graciously upon the Gifts now lying before Thee, and send down Thy Holy Spirit upon this Sacrifice: that he may make this Bread the Body of Thy Christ, and this Cup the Blood of Thy Christ."

While this is being said secretly at the altar, the assistants "may pray for him" (again), with some verses from Psalm 20, "according to the ancient Use of York." The consecration prayer itself is clearly regarded as defective, since immediately after it the priest "may add secretly the Prayer of Oblation" either from Sarum (the *Unde et memores* and the *Supra quae*) or from 1549 (but only including the anamnesis). The Agnus Dei and Sarum precommunion prayers are also printed. After communion, the prayer of oblation is described by margin rubrics to begin with "the oblation," followed by "the oblation of ourselves" at "And here we offer and present unto Thee. . . ." It is interesting to note that the 1549, Scottish, and American texts are not subjected to any reinterpretation or expansion.[10]

The Priest to the Altar considerably adds to the Prayer Book rite, but is less concerned with externals than the *Directorium*. Particularly intriguing is the selective use of Latin material at the offertory and in the Canon (which latter does not involve intercessions, since the Prayer Book rite already has these). Whereas the *Directorium* allows a prothesis prayer from the East, *The Priest to the Altar* permits an *Apostolic Constitutions* epiclesis, but placed before (and not after) the consecration. There is also a self-consciously English desire to find additional material from pre-Reformation sources, but this was the way in which the Tractarians often commended more elaborate liturgical presentation to their people.

Orby Shipley's *Ritual of the Altar*[11] (1870), however, goes the whole hog and freely inserts Roman material into the Prayer Book text, without any differentiation of source, thus paving the way for the later *Anglican Missal* and *English Missal* traditions. The 1570 Roman offertory prayers are reproduced in full, in somewhat wordy translations, including the alternative *Suscipe, sancta trinitas* for use at Masses for the dead. The sequence of prayers ends with *Orate fratres* and the Secret (which is now at long last properly understood). After the Prayer of Humble Access, there is a left-hand page entirely taken up with a picture of the crucifixion, and the "Canon of the Mass" begins, with the entire text of the Roman anaphora translated into English, only allowing for the Prayer Book consecration prayer to come where the Latin has the *Qui pridie,* so that even the (supposedly) inadequate petition for consecration is supplemented by the Roman *Quam oblationem.* The intercessions in the Canon remain, too, as do the precommunion prayers of the celebrant.

One could say that the *Ritual of the Altar* represents the inevitable, but selective, use of Latin and Greek material in the *Directorium,* and *The Priest to the Altar* witnesses to the fact that some of the Tractarian liturgiologists were ready to *adapt* rather than simply *imitate,* a liturgical principle that we shall see in the Catholic Apostolic liturgy. Trac-

180

tarian hymnody also demonstrates an increased awareness of eucharistic sacrifice. John Mason Neale[12] is the name associated with the work of translating many fine hymns, and these include those eucharistic hymns attributed to Thomas Aquinas for use at the Feast of Corpus Christi. *Hymns Ancient and Modern*[13] included eucharistic hymns from the start. But a hymn such as Charles Wesley's "O thou before the world began" was altered in some versions, in order to soften the imagery and loosen the link between the eucharist and the heavenly liturgy of Christ.

George Hugh Bourne's "Lord enthroned in heavenly splendour" was first published in 1874 and evokes the kind of imagery that many traditional High Churchmen would have found acceptable.[14] But the most poignant of all Tractarian hymns was originally written as a poem and was subsequently used in abbreviated form (the usual version only contains stanzas three to six); William Bright's "And now, O Father, mindful of the love" brings together the eucharistic themes of anamnesis, invocation, and intercession, which heeds the protests that the sacrifice of Christ is one and unrepeatable. The whole hymn has a christocentricity that places it among the most human and yet the most objective of all eucharistic devotions:

"And now, O Father, *mindful* of the love
That bought us, once for all on Calvary's Tree,
And *having with us him that pleads above,*
We here present, we here spread forth to thee
That only offering perfect in thine eyes,
The *one* true, pure, immortal *Sacrifice.*

"Look, Father, look on his anointed face,
And only look on us as found in him;
Look not on our misusings of thy grace,
Our prayer so languid, and our faith so dim:
For lo, between our sins and their reward
We set the passion of thy Son our Lord."[15]

The success of the hymn lies in its ability to handle the Reformation issue without preaching at the worshipper. Christ's offering is once and for all, yet the eucharist presents it to the Father, participating by being caught up in the heavenly offering. The criticism of Pelagianism is beautifully met by the famous clause, "And only look on us as found in him." Interestingly enough, the hymn goes on to intercession, so that it brings together both story, gift, and response, although the gift aspect is the weakest of the three. The same theological ideas recur in Bright's earlier hymn, "Once, only once, and once for all," which was published in 1866, and in that year also appeared William Chatterton Dix's famous "Alleluia, sing to Jesus,"[16] which picks up the Hebrews christology so beloved of the Caroline divines and places the action of the eucharist firmly within the context of the heavenly liturgy, and in a dynamic manner that recalls the writings of the Fathers.

Although not exclusively within the interests of the Tractarians, it is worth drawing attention to two other features on the nineteenth-century Anglican scene. First, many theologians who were not Tractarian were moving towards a sacrificial understanding of the eucharist. F. D. Maurice as early as 1838 "maintained that the character of the Eucharistic feast is sacrificial,"[17] although he is not precise on *how* it is sacrificial. Similarly, Frederick Meyrick in 1885 rejected much of the Tractarians' teaching on the eucharist, but accepted that the eucharist is a sacrifice, and his definition is worth quoting:

"It is a sacrifice inasmuch as it is *an offering made to God* as an act of religious worship—a spiritual sacrifice, as being a *sacrifice of prayer and praise to God* for the benefits received by the sacrifice of the death of Christ; a material sacrifice, in so far as the bread and wine are regarded as *gifts of homage to God in acknowledgement of His creative and sustaining power;* a commemorative sacrifice, inasmuch as it *commemorates the great sacrifice of the cross*—the words 'commemorative sacrifice' meaning in this acceptation a commemoration of the sacrifice. But it is not a sacrifice of Christ to His Father, whereby God is propitiated and man's sins expiated."[18]

More clearheaded than Richard Wilberforce, Meyrick manages to define in such a way as to do justice both to liturgical presentation and to theological concept, and it is interesting that he begins his definition by asserting that all worship is sacrificial.

Secondly, the condemnation of Anglican Orders in 1896 caused many but not all Anglicans much consternation. This dispute needs to be set against the background of the history of the Anglican Ordinal. The Bull of Leo XIII states that the form of ordination must express "the Sacred Order of Priesthood *or* its grace and power, which is chiefly the power of consecrating and of offering the true body and blood of the Lord," whereas most Anglicans took it to mean "The Sacred Order of priesthood *and* its grace and power. . . ."[19] Nonetheless, the fact remains that the Bull was based on a precritical knowledge of the history of the Roman Pontifical itself, and was written during the era when the imperative formulae that we discussed in a previous chapter were still taken to be the most significant parts of the rite. It was up to later writers (like Gregory Dix) to emphasize the corporate mind of the Church rather than what may or may not have been Cranmer's thinking, and to do so at a time when the ordination prayers of Hippolytus and their derived documents as well as Serapion could be pondered and sifted.[20] The whole controversy provoked Darwell Stone to write his *History of the Doctrine of the Holy Eucharist*, which is a mine of information presented in a clear manner, in which the author's opinions play second part to voluminous quotations from ancient and modern writers.[21]

FORETASTE 2: THE CATHOLIC APOSTOLICS

Edward Ratcliff once called out for a proper study to be made of the so-called Irvingite liturgy, a task that was completed a few years ago.[22] Although hard to classify, the Catholic Apostolics belong to the Romantic Movement of the nineteenth century, an assignation which no longer is regarded as pejorative. Founded in the 1830s as a result of private prayer meetings at Albury Park (Guildford), the home of the wealthy M.P., Henry Drummond, the new Church included from 1834 a full complement of twelve "apostles," but it was not until 1842 that a formal liturgy was introduced. Between 1842 and 1880,[23] several editions of the *Liturgy and Other Divine Offices of the Church* were published in England, Scotland, and also in many parts of Europe, notably in the Protestant parts of Germany, in Switzerland and in Denmark. John Bate Cardale, the "pillar" of the apostles of the church, is regarded as the author of this liturgy, and manuscript notes point to his scholarship lying behind the compilation of a fascinating service book.

From a very early period in the history of this church, all worship is understood to be sacrificial. Thus, in 1834, a "word of prophecy" indicated that the hours of 6 A.M. and 5 P.M. should be set aside for daily prayer, which were to be understood to be antitypical of the worship in the Old Testament Tabernacle. (Such a sacrificial spirituality permeates the later writings of the church and enables the eucharist to be seen sacrificially in a manner reminiscent of the Byzantine liturgy.) Only in 1835 did the church adopt a weekly eucharist, and in 1838 an outline guide to the celebration of the eucharist was sent around to all local ministers. Some of the language used in it is similar to the later liturgy. Thus the understanding of all worship as spiritual sacrifice was able to seep through this church before the eucharist is defined too closely.

The later liturgy of the eucharist mentions sacrifice at certain strategic points.

1. The Absolution (at the Introit):
Mentions Christ as "Sacrifice and Propitiation."

2. The Prayer of Approach (after the Absolution):
". . . that we, approaching unto Thee with pure heart and undefiled conscience, *may offer unto Thee a sacrifice in righteousness*, and duly celebrate these holy mysteries to the glory of Thy Name. . . ."
(Cardale, in a commentary on the liturgy, acknowledges his sources for this prayer, something which he does not always do.)

3. Anthem after the Epistle:
Psalm 118:24–27 (This is the Common form; there are seasonal variants).
Psalm 118:27, "Bind the sacrifice with cords, even to the horns of the altar."

4. The Offertory (after Homily and Creed):
Proverbs 3:9, Malachi 3:10, Hebrews 13:16.

5. The Offertory Prayer:
"Accept, of Thine infinite goodness, the tithes and offerings of Thy people; which . . . we yield and dedicate to Thee."

6. The Great Entrance Anthem (invariable):
Psalm 43:3–4, Psalm 116:17–18.
Psalm 43:4, "Then will I go unto the altar of God"
Psalm 116:17, "I will offer to Thee the sacrifice of thanksgiving"

7. Orate Fratres
"*Celebrant:* Brethren, pray that *our sacrifice* may be acceptable to God the Father Almighty, through our Lord Jesus Christ.
"*People:* The Lord be with thy spirit. The Lord accept our sacrifice, and give unto us his blessing."

8. Prayer of Oblation before *Consecration:*
"Almighty and most merciful Father, *we offer and present unto Thee this bread and this cup,* in token that we are Thine; for all that we have is Thine; *and of Thine own gifts only can we give to Thee. We are unworthy to offer unto Thee* any sacrifice; yet, we beseech Thee, accept this our duty and service. . . .

"And here we present to Thee ourselves, *our souls and bodies,* and dedicate ourselves unto Thy service. . . .

"Send down Thy Holy Spirit upon us, and let the flesh and all its affections and lusts be destroyed in us, as by a consuming fire; that we may henceforth yield ourselves to Thee *a living sacrifice, holy and acceptable, which is our reasonable service.*"

184

(The prayer concludes with a petition for the efficacy of the eucharist, but in the first-person plural, and aloud.)

9. Prayer of Oblation after Consecration (follows dialogue, preface, Sanctus, consecration):

"Almighty God, we Thy servants, *calling to mind the most blessed Sacrifice* of Thy Son, showing forth His death, rejoicing in His resurrection and glorious presence at Thy right hand, and waiting for the blessed hope of his appearing and coming again, do *present unto Thee this reasonable and unbloody sacrifice* which Thou has instituted in Thy Church, the holy bread of everlasting life, and the cup of eternal salvation. Whereupon do Thou look, and *accept them upon Thine altar*, before Thy glorious high throne in heaven. *Have respect unto that Sacrifice once offered upon the cross*, once for all, a full, perfect, and sufficient sacrifice, oblation, and satisfaction for the sins of the whole world; and grant unto us, and unto all Thy people, the full benefits of the passion of Thy dear Son, remission of all our sins, and eternal life. Which things, O Lord, *we seek for all in the communion of Thy holy Church*; for whom, and for all for whom Thou wouldest be besought, *we offer this our sacrifice, and present to Thee our prayers.*"
(Special intentions follow on certain occasion.)

10. Incense Anthem (follows 9, and leads into intercessions):
"Incense and a pure offering, O Lord of hosts:
Thy holy Church presents unto Thy Name.
And when the cloud covers the Mercy-seat:
Look forth upon Thy people, and speak peace."

11. Precommunion Sentence (follows intercession):
"Christ our Passover . . ." 1 Corinthians 5:7–8.

Although the language is undoubtedly Cranmerian in style, the sacrificial scheme in this rite is nearer the East Syrian and West Syrian rites seen in earlier chapters. The logic is clear and at times openly betrays an anxiety to heal sixteenth-century wounds. Thus the Absolution (1) states a doctrine of atonement in traditional terms—Christ is the sacrifice. But the Prayer of Approach (2) refers to the whole eucharist as a sacrifice, and it comes suitably after the Absolution; the cleansed people proceed with their worship. The Anthem after the Epistle (3) affirms that all worship is sacrificial, and quotes from a pilgrimage psalm, in the context of the readings, so that even they are doxological. The Offertory (4) adapts Anglican usage, carefully mentioning tithing, which was a practice of the Catholic Apostolics. The Offertory Prayer (5) simply expresses that offering.

The Great Entrance (6) heightens the tone of the celebration, as the whole people move in heart and mind to the altar (cf. Mozarabic use of "I will go to the altar of God" immediately before the eucharistic dialogue, and Mozarabic use of *sacrificum* as the offertory chant). The *Orate fratres* (7) carefully adapts the 1570 Missal's priestly bidding, so that the sacrifice is undubitably "our"; the response by the congregation also carefully adapts the Sarum response, but without the close definition of roles that we saw in *The Priest to the Altar*.[24] The Prayer of Oblation before Consecration (8) is perhaps the most involved prayer of all, for it combines the presentation of the eucharistic gifts with the self-oblation of the worshippers, thus providing at least one example of Gregory Dix's suggestion that self-oblation originally belonged at the "offertory" in antiquity, even though this particular example is not an ancient one! Then in the Prayer of Oblation after Consecration (9) are combined the themes of anamnesis, the heavenly altar, the single sacrifice of Christ, and intercession for the people of God. This is, perhaps, the most alert piece of eucharistic theology Cardale compiled, because he brings together memorial, eternal offering, Calvary, and intercessions in an inspiring manner; the most original way in which the unique sacrifice of Christ is stressed is by placing it *after* the mention of the heavenly altar. The Incense Anthem (10) firmly posits incense in the context of intercessory prayer (Cardale is clear about this in his commentary), and the Pre-Communion Sentences (11) echo Cranmer in 1549, and place the words in a background that is eucharistic, but in order to stress the christological character of the celebration.

Two further aspects of this rite require our attention. First, Cardale draws a sharp distinction between the offering of "tithes and other offerings" at the "table of prothesis" (approximating to the Credence table) and the transfer of the gifts of bread and wine from the table of prothesis to the altar during the Great Entrance. In this, he is probably following Non-Jurors and Scottish Episcopalians,[25] although he emphasizes the point much more clearly. Secondly, in addition to a rich provision for the liturgical year, the Catholic Apostolic service book also contains a number of votive forms whose use are strictly regulated and that concern the pastoral needs and internal organization of the church.

Cardale's rite is carefully nuanced and provides at least one answer to the debate about eucharistic sacrifice. He seems to be saying that *if* the eucharist is a sacrifice, then so is all worship, and so is the whole eucharist. Into that general notion of eucharistic offering comes the forgiveness of sins, by which we are enabled to offer sacrifice. But the offering of bread and wine follows the offering of money, as the requirement of God upon his people. The bread and wine are associated closely with the people themselves so that self-oblation is separated from intercession, but it, too, is regarded as sacrificial. The bread and wine are presented for consecration, and then for intercession and communion. All in all, Cardale by sheer prolixity manages to hold together story, gift, and response, within a eucharist that is built upon considerable reflection upon typology and its relevance to Christian worship. (His ordination rites show similar interests.)

We have taken some time over discussing this rite because it was the first ecumenical liturgy, and therefore the first attempt by a group of Christians to fashion a liturgy that would do justice to the traditions of early Christianity, and at the same time contribute positively to the post-sixteenth-century eucharistic debates. Theologically, they make a subtle (although quaint) contribution to an ecumenical movement that had not yet begun; they worshipped at a single Sunday eucharist, presided over by the local "angel" (bishop), at which everyone was expected to communicate. In this sense their liturgy is prophetic and by many sources they point the way forward to the twentieth century. But in cold historical terms, they still belong to the nineteenth century and can parallel the attempts by the compilers of the *Directorium* and *The Priest to the Altar* in looking to the Christian medieval East and West for enrichment and stimulus. The Catholic Apostolics spread their influence immediately on the Scottish (Presbyterian) Church Service Society,[26] and also upon the liturgy that emanated from the Mercersburg tradition in Pennsylvania.[27] But their *method* was not really taken up until the western churches were giving their liturgies a new form of surgery after Vatican II.

ENRICHMENT

We have seen how at the Reformation the eucharist was "purified" in the various attempts to restore the worship of what was taken to be the eucharist of the primitive Church. But in the period since, particularly among the English-speaking churches, there was no real attempt made to enable the liturgy to express the doctrine of the Church as authority perceived it. This is particularly true of the Church of England, a fact that has repercussions today, notably in the very existence of the Act of Uniformity of 1662, which induced a kind of liturgical paralysis comparable to the decree of the Council of Trent in 1563, when all liturgical authority was placed in the hands of the Pope.[28] Both western Catholicism and Anglicanism thus entered an era of aridity in matters of liturgy, relieved only by the exceptions, such as the Neo-Gallican tradition in France, and the Non-Jurors and

Scottish Episcopalians in Anglicanism. The net result of the Tractarian Movement in England over eucharistic theology was to stir people to think about the eucharist in traditional terms, and the erudite work of Meyrick quoted earlier could not have been written without the tradition of Anglicanism and the reinterpretation of the Tractarians acting as a kind of gadfly. Theology has to develop, it cannot be stopped. Liturgy develops, too, but in ways more imperceptible than theology.

In 1901, Charles Gore, then a canon of Westminster, published what many regard as his finest book, *The Body of Christ*. Gore was in temperament a High Churchman, but his theology was what could be described as Liberal Catholic. He had the kind of mind that went all too swiftly to the heart of a matter, and when he wrote something afresh, there would inevitably come forth a new interpretation of a traditional view. What he has to say about eucharistic offering comes with a welcome clarity:

"First of all, the eucharist is a sacrifice because in it the Christian Church . . . exercises her privilege of sonship in free approach to the Father in the name of Christ. She comes before the Father with her material offerings of bread and wine, and those things wherein God has prospered her, bearing witness that all good things come from Him; and though He needs nothing from man, yet He accepts the recognition of His fatherhood from loyal and free hearts. She comes with her wide-spreading intercessions for the whole race of mankind, and for her members living and departed. She offers her glad sacrifice of praise and thanksgiving for all the blessings of creation and redemption. She solemnly commemorates the passion in word and in symbolic action, through the bread broken and the wine outpoured, the appointed tokens of Christ's sacrificed body and blood, reciting before God His own words and acts in instituting the holy eucharist. This is the church's sacrifice; and it is all that she can do."

And he goes on:

"Now the eucharist is a sacrifice in a second and deeper sense, for God has united the offerings of the church to the ever-living sacrifice of the great High Priest in the heavenly sanctuary, or has given His presence among them who is their propitiation and their spiritual food.
"Then once more, united afresh in one body to God by the communion in Christ's body and blood, the church offers herself, one with Christ as a body with its head, living in the same life and indwelt by the same Spirit: she offers herself that her whole fellowship, both the

living and the dead, having their sins forgiven through the propitiation of Christ, may be accepted with all their good works and prayers
'in the beloved.' And in the self-oblation of the church is the culmination of the sacrifice."[29]

There are times when Gore's lengthy style runs away with him, but
beneath these poignant periods (which are reminiscent of both the
Prayer Book rite *and* the Byzantine liturgy) lie some important points
of principle. It is not without significance that it is his discussion of
patristic eucharistic theology that provoked these definitions.[30] Gore
sees the eucharist as sacrificial in the sense that it is at once story, gift,
and response. Moreover, while he defines the first two in terms of the
"privilege of sonship," he uses the union of the heavenly and the
earthly as the means whereby self-oblation is effected in intercession
and service without giving rise to the charge of Pelagianism. We come
before God, not having earned his grace, but in order to use it in living out our faith in the world. Herein lies an important reinterpretation of Cranmer's rite, expanded with some eastern spirituality. He
even manages to redefine intercession, so that it is an expression of
social concern, and not an instance of the Church trying to alter God's
mind or remit sins for those in purgatory.
    A few years later, the Royal Commission of 1906 condemned Ro-
man practices in Church of England liturgy, but was careful to accept
a Caroline definition of eucharistic sacrifice.[31] The Anglo-Catholic
practices continued, with varying degrees of episcopal persecution.
Prayer Book revision was contemplated. In 1911, Walter Howard
Frere, like Gore, a member of the newly founded Community of the
Resurrection, published his influential *Principles of Liturgical Reform*,[32]
in which he admitted that the kind of reform of the eucharistic prayer
that he would really like was not yet possible; his preference for the
Scottish-American type of anaphora was well known. But he does
propose reunification of the separated pieces of the eucharistic prayer
of 1552–1662, so that we have something more akin to 1549. The
Lower House of Canterbury in 1914 decisively passed this idea,
which later came to be called the interim rite, and which subsequently
appeared in Anglo-Catholic missals. (The Scots, in 1912, had slightly
revised their liturgy, and incorporated it into a full Prayer Book; the
only difference, for our discussion, is that the offering clause in the
anamnesis is now no longer printed in capital letters.)[33] The Lower
House of York found the Frere proposal unacceptable because of the
interpretation that Anglo-Catholics would put on "this our sacrifice of
praise and thanksgiving" as the consecrated elements, following

closely upon the institution narrative as the words of consecration. (Such a fear was to reappear in 1966 over the Draft form of the Series 2 Eucharist.)

The form suggested by Frere had already appeared in the *Prayer Book Revised* (1913).[34] The later draft forms reflect a restlessness with the 1549 text and a yearning for the more traditional type of anaphora:

1920 begins like Cranmer, but adds a short anamnesis (including reference to the second coming, which the Scots had since 1912), and a general epiclesis, leading into doxology; the prayer of oblation follows communion.

1923 is similar to 1920, but lacks the epiclesis, and instead inserts the prayer of oblation (it also has reference to the second coming in the anamnesis).

1924A is more reminiscent of Scotland, but the epiclesis of the Spirit does not appear; it resembles 1549, but without the "Word" and "Spirit" before the institution narrative.

1924B resembles *A*, but inserts quaint references:
after "perpetual memory . . . *wherein we do proclaim* his death . . .";
"blessings" are not "procured" but "assured";
"offering ourselves to thee in communion with him" before the epiclesis.

1926 adds "and propitiation" after "sufficient sacrifice"; after the self-oblation, a 1549 clause: ". . . we pray thee to accept this oblation of thy Church, through the ministry of our great High Priest . . ." (NB, the change from "angel" to Christ himself).

1927–1928 is the most adventurous of all. Like all the versions from 1924A, it begins with post-Sanctus and continues with allusion to the one sacrifice of Christ (as Cranmer), but moves straight into the narrative. The anamnesis is similar to 1926, but includes the words "and set forth" after celebrate (the nearest the compilers could get to an offering verb and reminiscent of Bright's hymn). The epiclesis is comparable to Scottish, but not as strong. The prayer continues with the Cranmer petition for acceptance of the sacrifice and the self-oblation of the worshippers.

Frere's influence over the draft texts in their final stages is obvious. He had also been in touch with the South Africans over their draft liturgy, which in 1920 had incorporated the very eastern-looking formula at the anamnesis: ". . . we offer here unto thy divine majesty

190

these sacred gifts and creatures of thine own, this holy Bread of eternal life and this Cup of everlasting salvation."[35]

The South Africans (more Anglo-Catholic in their liturgical stance) could freely combine Byzantine and Roman material in their new liturgy. ("Of thine own" was deleted before the final form was agreed on in 1929, when a dubious-looking offertory prayer was added: "Bless, O Lord, we beseech thee, these thy gifts and sanctify them unto this holy use, that by them we may be fed unto everlasting life of soul and body.") The Scottish (1929) and American (1928) books remain as before (for our purposes).[36] Much more adventurous is the Bombay liturgy. The result of Ratcliff's "plea for a distinctive liturgy for the Indian church" in 1920, it was modeled on the liturgy of St. James, from 1923 onwards.[37] Many of the sacrificial features of James reappear, including the incense prayer at the start of the eucharist. The anaphora itself produces much of James's distinctive language, albeit in Cranmerian English, and this includes "do offer unto thee this our reasonable service and sacrifice" in the anamnesis. This bold step towards inculturation was well ahead of its time, although the use of James as a model meant that Addai and Mari (which had been in use in India for considerably longer) was turned aside in the interests of a more conventional Greek West Syrian pattern.[38] Although 1927–1928 retains 1662s functional placing of the elements on the table, other Anglican rites opt for more symbolic language, including American 1928, which, however, does not go for the full-blooded "Blessed art thou" prayer to bring to an end the offering of the alms and the bread and wine. What is of particular interest is that the Bombay liturgy,[39] even though modeled on James, keeps to the traditional Anglican order of dealing with money and bread and wine immediately before the intercession; radical restructuring is not yet in the air.

While other provinces of the Anglican Communion settled down to their new liturgies, England had to learn to live with an illegal but authorized Prayer Book of 1928. It was left to scholars like Walter Howard Frere and John Blomfield to define the pseudo-fourth-century West Syrian type of anaphora[40] to a skeptical liturgical readership. Frere held that consecration was effected by giving thanks over the gifts, but that the consecration was not to be tied to a particular "moment," and that an anaphora should contain an epiclesis, that sign of antiquity kept by the eastern churches. His book *The Anaphora* clearly marks the end of an era in which Cranmer was reinterpreted by various groups within Anglicanism, some of whom (if they lived outside England) were in a position to make that reinterpretation find expression in the *lex orandi* itself. Unfortunately, Anglo-Catholicism in England had put forward proposals in the "Green Book" that bore no chance of acceptance by other groups, and it was left to the Liberals and the Prayer Book Catholics to attempt to refashion things. The debates in Parliament in 1927 and 1928 left a great deal of bitterness behind.[41]

The Catholic Apostolic liturgy had already been used by the compilers of the Scottish Presbyterian (Church Service Society) *Euchologion* of 1867, which went into several editions. The Scots had long known the custom of the elders solemnly bringing in the elements to the table immediately before the eucharistic liturgy. This is kept, and emphasized. Three important borrowings from the Catholic Apostolic liturgy increase the importance of the eucharistic sacrifice after the reading of the warrant. A prayer of the veil precedes the eucharistic prayer (not, therefore, as a preparation for the whole service); the eucharistic prayer has a full catalogue of "mighty acts," and moves on to epiclesis, which refers to "thine own gifts of bread and wine which we set before thee" (eastern influences). The intercessions also borrow from this liturgy, but they are set after communion, a position that the compilers defend, and which is an interesting variant of the notion of self-oblation. These features remain in subsequent editions of the *Euchologion*, and eventually appear in the *Book of Common Order*[42] of 1940, which sealed the union of the United Free Church and the Established Church in 1929. Many nineteenth-century Scots Presbyterian theologians were ready for this enrichment, and it shows what can be done with liturgical freedom.

The rite contained in the English Presbyterian *Directory*[43] describes the praise of the Church in the Sanctus as "a sacrifice of love." Orchard's 1919 *Divine Service*,[44] however, owes much both to the Roman Missal and to the Catholic Apostolic eucharist. A prayer of the veil comes near the beginning (but after the *Gloria in excelsis*). The offering of money and the elements occupy the same position, and the minister may say silently an English translation of *Suscipe, sante pater* (in the first-person singular, whereas it is optional, silent, *and simplified* in the Catholic Apostolic rite). The offertory prayer combines Catholic Apostolic themes from the prayer of oblation before consecration, including self-offering. The eucharistic prayer, however, uses Roman and Cranmerian ideas:

"Wherefore . . . we thy servants, together with all thy people, offer unto thy most excellent Majesty, of thine own gifts, this pure, holy, and spotless sacrifice, the Bread of eternal life, and the Cup of everlasting salvation."

And the invitation to communion includes an optional formula which is reminiscent of Baxter's Savoy liturgy:

"Come, ye people . . . for the Lamb of God is set forth as a sacrifice for us." Much of this, and more, is included in the *Free Church Book of Common Prayer*,[45] where Roman influence is more obvious, including the use of the 1570 *Orate fratres*.

There is a piecemeal aspect to many of these revisions because while they undoubtedly move in a direction of enrichment, they still show signs of self-consciousness, as well as a lack of radical rethinking. For example, the Anglican prayers (including the Scottish) are still preoccupied with getting the consecration right, in the epiclesis, so that the whole prayer (preface as well) is not given full treatment. The same is true of the Scottish Presbyterian revisions, where enrichment, in the form of a full thanksgiving along Catholic Apostolic lines, comes after the well-worn Knoxian formulae of reading the narrative of institution *first*. This is not to make any value judgement on the Scots Presbyterian form, but simply to observe that the enrichment comes after the traditional material has been used and at the point where the long prayer would have taken place. The examples from the "Free" traditions demonstrate to what degree High Churchmen[46] in those churches were prepared to be innovative, perhaps taking inherent local freedom to limits not known before.

Theologically, we are seeing a greater openness to sacrificial ideas, particularly among the Scots Presbyterians. Their clever use of the prayer of the veil prefixes to the euchological part of the eucharistic action a prayer to God that the congregation may offer a sacrifice in righteousness. William Milligan, writing in 1891, perhaps expressed the High Church Calvinist view most succinctly when he asserted that: ". . . the eucharist is an oblation, in which the offerer, offering himself, lives, having accepted death."[47]

REFORM

When John Halliburton was asked to write on the Canon for a collection of essays on the Series 3 Eucharist, he began in a whimsical vein:

"In the 'Lives' of Hendrik Willem van Loon, there is a delightful sketch (by the author himself) of all the Bachs enjoying themselves at a family concert, while over the page he shows all the Breughels who (as he puts it) 'meanwhile were busy drawing.' One feels one could add a third picture of 'all the liturgists busy writing canons,' for in this age of liturgical renewal one's liturgically minded friends are just as likely to send an epiclesis or anamnesis through the post as they are a Christmas card."[48]

Halliburton exaggerates in order to make the point that in the second part of the twentieth century there has been an unprecedented preoccupation with the eucharistic prayer, which has shown itself in the number of official and unofficial prayers written by committees and gifted persons. If you look at the American Episcopal Prayer Book of 1979 and the United Methodist *At the Lord's Table* of 1981,[49] you will see a degree of liturgical creativity and flexibility that would have been unthinkable in either denomination half a century ago.

So many books have been written about the eucharist this century that it would be folly to try to summarize them. A few stand out as particularly helpful in the debate in western Christianity as it searches again for its origins and tries to adapt to a new kind of society. Michael Ramsey's *The Gospel and the Catholic Church* (1936) had a great impact on ecclesiology among many British and other Christians, and what he has to say about liturgy and eucharistic offering betrays the author's awareness of origins. Writing of the early period, he states: "It was by a gradual process that the language of sacrifice became applied to each of the main aspects of the Eucharist."[50] Earlier, Nugent Hicks had written *The Fullness of Sacrifice* (1930), in which he attempted to identify sacrifice not as yielding *blood* but *life*, and many New Testament words were given sacrificial overtones, including the word "do" in the command to repeat at the Last Supper narratives. While some of his conclusions have been questioned, he makes many useful observations on the development of the doctrine of sacrifice. Of the eucharist he says: "The two outstanding thoughts are those of offering and thanksgiving."[51] Hicks's understanding of offering was necessarily a wide one, and it is more than likely that he influenced Gregory Dix's thinking about the eucharist as it eventually appeared in 1945 in *The Shape of the Liturgy*.[52] Dix's fertile mind and alert imagination led him at times to romanticize on the "golden age" of the fourth-century Fathers, but he was at home among them. His theology of the eucharistic sacrifice was not always clear, particularly as he tended to exaggerate the importance of the offertory procession in antiquity, and then try to drive a wedge between that offering and the oblation in the eucharistic prayer. Interesting above many of his other speculations was the suggestion that self-oblation originally belonged at the offertory, precisely where the Catholic Apostolics (and later, American Lutherans) were to place it.[53] But Dix taught liturgists and others to think of liturgy in terms of a *philosophy* rather than a preoc-

194

cupation with *words*, which was a lesson Church of England people needed to absorb to get over the 1927–1928 debacle. When he propounds his theory of the four actions, he is deliberately placing the actions over and above the words so that word only interprets action, and action lies at the heart of the rite. Thus the taking is the offertory (which in due course gets a prayer of its own in antiquity); the blessing is the eucharistic prayer (which soon finds its own definite structures); the breaking is the fraction (which eventually holds together both functional and symbolic aspects); and the sharing is the communion (which is necessary for the meaning of the rite to be clear).

Dix exaggerated the importance of offertory and fraction, since it is the second and the fourth of the actions that are most salient; you take to bless, and you break to share. But like so many scholars who can communicate easily with people, he sold his ideas to a wide public. Scholars were alive to what the great little man had to say,[54] as witness Edward Ratcliff who wrote: "*The Shape of the Liturgy* should materially assist the much-to-be-desired reshaping of English liturgical studies."[55] It could be pushed even further to the extent of suggesting that the "fat green book" materially assisted the much-to-be-desired reshaping of western liturgy.

It would be true to say that nothing has ever been the same since, and ironical indeed that the first liturgy to be so reshaped was that of the United Church of South India, the result of a scheme of union that Dix himself virulently attacked.[56] Looking back on it now, it seems amazing that by 1950 a united liturgy could have been agreed upon that has a clear structure and also brings together the *riches* of the traditions that went into the union. The service opens with an act of praise, which may be either the *Gloria in excelsis*, or the Litany of the Lamb (from Rv 5 and 7), itself an act of sacrificial praise to the Lamb of God in heaven.

The eucharistic liturgy begins with three scriptural quotations, linking unity with the offering of sacrifice (Ps 133:1, 1 Cor 10:17, and Ps 27:6, the latter said by all), after which "the peace may be given." The compilers of the rite draw on ancient precedent, but perhaps the rationale for thus joining the notions of unity and sacrifice are derived from the Matthean warning about the need for reconciliation before offering the gift. The offertory does not distinguish between money and bread and wine—everything is brought forward. Then the presbyter (NB) says a prayer that combines the *Euchologion* prayer of the veil with offertory themes, but does not mention offering of sacrifice: ". . . accept and use us and these our gifts for thy glory. All that is in heaven and earth is thine, and of thine own do we give thee." The inclusion of self-oblation seems cleverly contrived to interpret the Dix views about offertory, which has just been performed by a procession. Having dispensed with offering, we go on to the eucharistic prayer, which is expanded in order to include a christological section when no preface is prescribed. There is a post-Sanctus, followed by material from the 1662 rite, up to the end of the institution narrative (but without the petition for consecration). James-style acclamations interpret the flow of the prayer as it moves into anamnesis and epiclesis; the former does not offer gifts, since this has happened already, but points to the "perfect redemption which thou has wrought for us in him," while the latter prays for the Holy Spirit on "us and these thine own gifts of bread and wine." The mixture of biblical and liturgical sources in these prayers bodes well for the future. After communion, there are two alternative prayers; the second is from the Prayer Book and the first is a rewrite of Cranmer's prayer of self-oblation, which keeps the main theme but inserts thanksgiving at the start.

The other prophetic liturgy also comes from an ecumenical quarter, that of the Taizé community. In 1959, Max Thurian published an important ecumenical study, *L'Eucharistie,*[57] with the subtitles *mémorial du Seigneur* and *sacrifice d'action de grâce et d'intercession.* Thurian's priorities are thus displayed for all to see, with the sacrifical aspects of the eucharist primarily in thanksgiving and intercession. Thus, in the Taizé liturgies,[58] we find a restructured liturgy along the lines of antiquity and a full intercession after the Creed, which begins: *"Tout d'abord,* nous te les offrons pour *ta sainte Eglise universelle. . . ."* The offertory prayer often includes reference to the memorial that the church presents, as well as reference to the one sacrifice of Christ, so that this prayer points *forward* to the eucharistic prayer and to the whole eucharistic celebration rather than points *back* to the placing of the gifts on the table. In the eucharistic prayer itself, the themes of sacrifice of praise are closely identified with eucharist in the epiclesis, and at the anamnesis we come across language such as "accomplishing the memorial" of Christ. *"Tout vient de toi et notre seule offrande est de rappeler tes merveilles et tes dons."* The prayer moves on to "present . . . as our thanksgiving and our intercession . . . the signs of the eternal sacrifice of Christ. . . ." The themes of praise and prayer abound in the remainder of this remarkable anaphora.

Thurian's theological rationale is at work behind this eucharistic prayer and the preceding intercession and offering; one is left in no doubt that the subtitles of his book form the basis of his thinking on eucharistic sacrifice as expressed in this liturgy. His solution is not very different from Cardale's in the Catholic Apostolic rite; if you are

196

going to see the eucharist as sacrificial, then you have to spread sacrificial language all through the liturgy, and juxtapose it occasionally with reference to the only sacrifice of Christ. The Armenian anaphoras, it seems, are not far wrong after all.

Recent Taizé liturgies[59] include Roman material, but it is noticeable how the Thurian offering of thanks recurs in the way the prayers are presented. Thurian's understanding of offering includes faith, intercession, gifts, as well as thanksgiving, and this is all carefully explained in the introduction and set out in the typography of the rite. On story, gift, and response, the Taizé rite carefully walks through difficult ground. We are left with something positive and original, without the sense that it has been so carefully worded that it offends no one, and pleases few.

A similar treatment is to be found in the 1964 Evangelical Mass[60] of the Michaels Brotherhood in Germany. The intercessions are made "in the fellowship of this altar." The "thanks offerings" (i.e., money) are brought to the altar and prayed over, and the same sequence takes place with the bread and the wine: "we bring this bread and wine celebrating thereby the remembrance. . . ." This second offertory prayer is lengthy and includes the themes of intercession (and self-oblation, by implication), as well as the one sacrifice of Christ. The Creed is also "offered" (in an eastern position). In the full eucharistic prayer the anamnesis relies heavily on Hebrews spirituality:

"Purified and reconciled . . . we enter joyfully into Thy sanctuary and approach the throne of Thy Grace in the power of this pure, holy, and all-sufficient Sacrifice. In the fellowship of this Holy Meal, we offer the sacrifice of our praise. . . ."

The Michaels Brotherhood is not typical of German Lutheranism or Calvinism, though one *Agende* did introduce a full eucharistic prayer in 1955.[61] It is interesting to note how the same themes of self-oblation at the offertory and thank offering in the anaphora are also found in the American *Lutheran Book of Worship* of 1978:

"Blessed are you, O Lord our God, maker of all things.
Through your goodness you have blessed us with these gifts.
With them we offer ourselves to your service
and dedicate our lives to the care and redemption of all
that you have made, for the sake of him who gave himself for us,
Jesus Christ our Lord."[62]

The most adventurous Scandinavian rite is the Swedish Lutheran of 1976, where thank offering is joined closely with gift offering:

"We thank you, Lord of heaven and earth . . .
you bring forth bread and wine.
You spread this table for us."[63]

It would seem that all things are possible, provided that the eucharistic action is clearly seen to be theocentric.

In the Roman Catholic Church, theological emphasis had been moving away from sacrifice through the writings of theologians such as de la Taille, who had loosened up thinking about the eucharist toward a more imprecise notion of offering, and Schillebeeckx, who more recently had performed a comparable task over eucharistic presence. Both men proved controversial among conservatives, but the ecumenical potential of their work is considerable.[64] By Vatican II, it was becoming clear that the search for the primitive and the need to recapture something of the meal characteristics of the eucharist were a priority. Liturgical groups had been formed after the Second World War, and the founding of the Trier and Paris liturgical institutes resulted in many European Catholics receiving a liturgical training in seminaries that was both scientific in its treatment of the past and pastoral in its orientation for the present-day needs of the Church.[65] Thus, by the time the Second Vatican Council met, the Constitution on the Sacred Liturgy was the first to be passed, largely because much of the groundwork had been achieved already. Some passages from it are worth quoting:

"From this it follows that every liturgical celebration, because it is an action of Christ the Priest and of His Body, which is the Church, is a sacred action surpassing all others. (7)"

"The rite of the Mass is to be revised in such a way that the intrinsic nature and purpose of its several parts, as well as the connection between them, may be more clearly manifested, and that devout and active participation by the faithful may be more easily achieved.

"For this purpose the rites are to be simplified, due care being taken to preserve their substance. Parts which with the passage of time came to be duplicated, or were added with little advantage, are to be omitted. Other parts which suffered loss through accidents of history are to be restored to the vigor they had in the days of the holy Fathers, as may seem useful or necessary. (50)"[66]

In 1964, a *Consilium* was set up by Pope Paul VI to implement this decree, and various ways of restoring the Roman Canon were considered, including one by Hans Küng that would delete intercession from the eucharistic prayer altogether. It was becoming clear that no really satisfactory solution could be found. Accordingly, Paul VI made the decision in June of 1966 that the Canon should be left substantially as it was, and that a study group should draw up two or three alternative eucharistic prayers. This was an entirely new departure, for it would place the Roman Catholic Church in the same position over anaphoras as many of the eastern churches. A prominent member of this study group was Cipriano Vagaggini, an Italian Benedictine, who had the ear of the Pope. There does not seem to have been fundamental unanimity in the group over how ancient sources should be employed. Agreement was reached at an early stage that there should be three prayers, one based on Hippolytus's *Apostolic Tradition*, which was already being used as the basis for new anaphoras elsewhere; another should incorporate some of the euchological patterns of the old Mozarabic use; and yet another should be based on the Alexandrian anaphora of Basil of Caesarea, whose archetype had recently been edited by Emmanuel Lanne. The study group was a list of liturgiological paladins: Johannes Wagner and Balthasar Fischer (Trier), Pierre-Marie Gy (Paris), and Bernard Botte (Louvain), among others.[67] Botte's own critical edition of Hippolytus had already been produced, and he had drawn attention in many articles to the importance that should be attached to Hippolytus, a notion that Gregory Dix had popularized many years before.[68] In the end, the ancient sources had to be rewritten in order to fit into what was called the *ingenium romanum*:[69]

Dialogue
Preface (variable or invariable)
Sanctus
Post-Sanctus
First epiclesis: consecration
Institution narrative
Anamnesis (with oblation)
Second epiclesis: communion
Intercession: living and departed
Doxology

Such an *ingenium* is only *romanum* if the old Roman Canon is reunited with its preface, if prayers on either side of the institution narrative are reinterpreted to be epicleses (of a sort), and if the intercessions are grouped together at the end of the prayer. But leaving such questions aside, it is clear that the methodology for the study group was dictated at a certain stage, which meant that Hippolytus had to have a Sanctus as well as a consecration epiclesis, and Alexandrian

Basil had to have a consecration epiclesis inserted before the institution narrative. While Hippolytus's anaphora had long remained unused (except by the Ethiopic Church, which had included a Sanctus in order to bring the prayer into line with its other anaphoras), Alexandrian Basil was in use among the Copts, and indeed was the basis for other versions, including the Byzantine version of Basil used by Orthodox throughout the world. What happened in Rome is the same process that we observed among Anglicans, Lutherans, and Presbyterians, the inability to absorb too much change in euchology. Let us look at these eucharistic prayers each in turn:[70]

E.P. I. The Roman Canon is given minimal surgical treatment in order to restore it to its earliest form. However, the prefaces are increased, from 16 (in 1570) to 82, and this includes mandatory use of a preface when none other is appointed. The story is being restored to where it belongs.[71]

E.P. II. Hippolytus's atonement theology is kept: "For our sake he opened his arms on the cross."
First epiclesis: "Let your Spirit come upon these gifts to make them holy. . . ."
Anamnesis:
"In memory of his death and resurrection,
we offer you, Father, this life-giving bread, this saving cup."
The intercessions are brief.[72]

E.P. III. Mozarabic, with eastern retouches. Post-Sanctus is a fine piece of writing:
"Father, you are holy indeed,
and all creation rightly gives you praise.
All life, all holiness comes from you
through your Son, Jesus Christ our Lord,
by the working of the Holy Spirit.
From age to age you gather a people to yourself,
so that from east to west
a perfect offering may be made
to the glory of your name." (NB Mal 1:11)

First epiclesis: "And so, Father, we bring you these gifts."

Anamnesis:
"Father, calling to mind the death your Son endured for
our salvation,
his glorious resurrection and ascension into heaven,
and ready to greet him when he comes again,

200

we offer you in thanksgiving this holy and living sacrifice.
Look with favor on your Church's offering,
and see the Victim whose death has reconciled us to yourself."

Intercession:
"May he make us an everlasting gift to you. . . .
"Lord, may this sacrifice, which has made our peace with you,
advance the peace and salvation of all the world."
The intercession ends eschatologically.[73]

E.P. IV. Post-Sanctus: a full account of salvation history,
as *Basil Alex.*[2]
First epiclesis:
"Father, may this Holy Spirit sanctify these offerings."

Anamnesis:
"Father, we now celebrate this memorial of our redemption.
We recall Christ's death, his descent among the dead, his resurrection,
and his ascension to your right hand:
and, looking forward to his coming in glory,
we offer you his body and blood,
the acceptable sacrifice which brings salvation to the whole world."

Second epiclesis:
"Lord, look upon this sacrifice which you have given to your Church;
and by your Holy Spirit, gather all who share this bread and wine
into the one body of Christ, a living sacrifice of praise."
Intercessions:
"Lord, remember those for whom we offer this sacrifice. . . ."[74]

Much has been made of the diversity of language in these anaphoras,
of which our quotations are only a selection. Eucharistic Prayer II has
the simplest sequence of ideas, even though it has been expanded in
order to be more conventional. The offering of thanks,[75] as Jounel sees
it, is the primary movement in this prayer. It is intriguing to note the
simplicity of the first epiclesis, "make them holy," recalling the starkness of the epiclesis in *Basil Alex*[1] ("make them holy of holies"). The
anamnesis does not just offer bread and cup but adds epithets, thus
departing from the simplicity of the original. Eucharistic Prayer III
(the real brainchild of Vagaggini),[76] however, revels in the idea of
sacrifice, but begins on the theme of the sacrifice of praise, in union
with Christ, so that the post-Sanctus places the whole eucharistic action in that context; the quotation from Malachi 1:11 is a delightful

patristic touch. Similarly, the anamnesis offers "in thanksgiving," a nuance from the *Testamentum Domini*, as well as an idea from Thurian's book.[77] The most christological unity of the prayer, however, lies in the juxtaposition of what the *Church* has to offer (the memorial, with the gifts), and the sacrifice of Calvary, "the Victim whose death has reconciled. . . ." Here we have the Roman Catholic Church, of all the churches the most traditionally confident about the Church's sacrifice, wrestling with the same problems we have seen before, that the Church's sacrifice can only be celebrated in the context of the one and only sacrifice of Christ himself. The notion of being caught up in the offering of Christ continues in the intercession with its theme of response. All in all, Vagaggini's prayer is theologically the most authentic because it does not do damage to one whole liturgical source, but brings together different ideas from various sources in order to express a coherent sequence of ideas.

Eucharistic Prayer IV is the most disappointing of all, however, since one hears again and again the old Alexandrian original[78] and is apt to find the new Roman version wanting. While the study group may be forgiven for allowing the first epiclesis (it comes neatly in the sequence of ideas just after the first mention of the Holy Spirit—a peculiarity of Basil anaphoras), the anamnesis includes for the first time the notion of the offering of Christ's body and blood. Of this high theological statement, Aidan Kavanagh (a Roman Catholic Benedictine of the Byzantine rite) has written:

"This is novel, and can hardly be said to retain 'a most definitely traditional character.' One who has some acquaintance with the medieval and reformation history of eucharistic controversy will recognize the inadequacy of such a position, and may be forgiven his disappointment that its tendentiousness has got into a Catholic formulary precisely at a time when it could have been diagnosed and avoided most easily."[79]

Now, any liturgical formula has to bear repetition and suggest ideas to a praying congregation. But even allowing for that, Kavanagh is correct, in our opinion, to criticize the deliberate rewriting of a time-honored eastern prayer that is itself in use among millions of Christians painfully separated from Rome, as well as many in communion with her as Eastern Catholics. Apart from seeming to correct Basil of Caesarea himself, the formula that has been included here states with a cold starkness an understanding of the eucharist that no doubt is how many Catholics have "heard" the eucharistic action for centuries, but that has not so far been included in a formulary. If by "we offer you his body and blood" the celebrant means "we here present, we here spread forth to thee" (in the words of William Bright's famous hymn), then the eucharist is a "pleading," or an offering of a memorial of the one sacrifice. But the problem with that kind of strong liturgical formula is that a legitimate complaint can be made to the effect that many Catholics will interpret it as being in some sense a repetition of Calvary. As Geoffrey Wainwright has written, commenting on this part of the prayer: "Are Catholics and Protestants as far apart as ever?"[80] Nonetheless, the fourth eucharistic prayer keeps the sacrificial theme for the intercessions, although once again Latin ideas have crept in—"look upon this sacrifice." It is as though the eastern original has been restructured and made to conform with western ideas *as well as* a western shape.

Before moving on to Anglican and Methodist prayers, it is worth pausing to discuss the offertory rites of the 1970 Missal. In the 1965 *Missa normativa*,[81] the proposal was that the offertory should be as simple as possible. The altar is prepared, and the priest recites two poetic formulae quietly:

"As this bread was scattered and then gathered and made one, so may your Church be gathered into your kingdom. Glory to you, O God, for ever" (cf. *Didache* 9, 4; for the bread).

"Wisdom has built a house for herself, she has mixed her wine, she has set her table. Glory to you, O God, for ever" (Prv 9:1–2; for the cup).

The priest then says, again quietly, the *In spiritu humilitatis* (Dn 3: 39b–40) and goes on to recite the *Super oblata*, which "is the only public prayer of the preparation of the gifts."[82] Instead of this simplicity, the new Missal has two *berakah*-style prayers that are manifestly popular (in other communions also) but that anticipate the eucharistic prayer; the *Orate fratres* has been kept, although simplified. The *Super oblata* have been largely rewritten, and many of them reflect an imprecision over eucharistic offering that could be interpreted to mean the whole eucharistic celebration, as David Holeton was later to suggest was the original intention of these prayers at the time of Leo the Great.[83] These rites have been criticized; the popularity of the *berakoth* often means that instead of being prayed quietly at a sung celebration, they are prayed aloud at the end of the offertory chant, thus giving the preparation of the table an importance that the authors of the *Missa normativa* had not intended. Once again we encounter the inability to cope with too much change, although some countries (notably Germany) have taken some liberties with the offertory in simplifying the *Orate fratres,* and thus restoring the rite to its draft starkness of 1965.[84] The whole picture adds up to a considerable enrichment from 1570, for in the 1970 Missal we see story back in the eucharistic prayer, gift remaining in the anamnesis (although the new Eucharistic Prayers II and III play down the theme of gift when compared with I, and certainly IV), and response most thoroughly worked out in III. For all the prayers, the offertory rites are simplified, where the focus is on the gifts themselves.

Anglican liturgical revision has been no less lively, nor any the less political. The story for the Church of England texts begins in 1965 and ends in 1980.[85] In 1965, the Alternative Services Measure was passed, which allowed the Church to permit alternative forms of prayers to be used. In that year, a draft form of eucharist ("Series 2") was placed before the Convocations with a dissentient vote from an Evangelical member of the Liturgical Commission. The eucharistic prayer was modeled on that of Hippolytus, and Ratcliff's theory that this prayer should end with the Sanctus had been sold to a few members of the Commission, who nevertheless wanted to keep the conventional formula in the middle of the prayer. But the significant feature is that the eucharistic prayer is a unity, with a full christological preface. The Evangelical protest centered around the anamnesis:

"Wherefore, O Lord, having remembrance his saving passion, his resurrection from the dead, and his glorious ascension into heaven, and looking for the coming of his kingdom, *we offer unto thee this bread and this cup.*"

The controversy that ensued resulted in the alteration in the final 1967 text of the offending words: *"with this bread and this cup, we make the memorial."* Ronald Jasper, as chairman of the Commission, had written cautiously about the draft formula:

"Inevitably no one will find here exactly what he wants to say. But we hope that everyone will find here a prayer which with some self-sacrifice he can use; and will allow others the same liberty of interpretation that he claims for himself."[86]

The controversy provoked a number of articles in *Theology,*[87] notable among which was one citing Caroline precedent for accepting words like "offer." (The draft form also allowed the scriptural quotation, "Thine, O Lord . . . ," at the presentation of the gifts, but this disap-

204

peared.) The self-oblation remained in its postcommunion position, as Cranmer in 1552.

In 1971, a draft form of "Series 3" was produced in modern English, thus taking up where New Zealand and Australia led the way.[88] Once again, great care had to be exerted to make the anamnesis agreeable to all. "Series 3" is a more lengthy liturgy as a whole than "Series 2" (which had been criticized for being too brief), and the anamnesis contains reference to the sacrifice "once and for all." The "Series 3" and "Series 2" prayers are substantially what make up Eucharistic Prayers 1 and 2 of "Rite A" in the 1980 *Alternative Service Book*. Anglo-Catholic pressure for a proper epiclesis in "Series 3" resulted in the insertion of "by the power of your Spirit" into the draft form, although Anglo-Catholics had opposed the epiclesis in the 1920s, long before it had become acceptable in the Roman Catholic Church.[89] The "Yours, Lord, is the glory" at the offertory also appeared in the "Series 3" form. But the two most significant additions to the 1980 book came from Anglo-Catholic pressure as well. The first was provision for the president to "praise God for his gifts in creation," followed by the response, "blessed be God for ever" (everyone knew that this was a reference to the Roman *berakoth*).[90] The other was in the form of a third and a fourth eucharistic prayer. The fourth delighted many Evangelicals, because it is lengthy and explicit on the atonement. The third was based on Hippolytus more closely than "Series 2" or "Series 3," but it also contained material from Roman Eucharistic Prayer II. The nearest that could be got to an offering formula in the anamnesis was:

"We thank you for counting us worthy to stand in your presence and serve you.
We bring before you this bread and this cup."[91]

One of the weaknesses of the English scene is that a General Synod was formed in 1970, resulting in legislation and revision committees that were Byzantine in complexity.[92] But most important of all is that, for all the care that was taken from 1966 until 1971 over eucharistic offering, in the last stages to the 1980 book, little time was really given to a proper dialogue between Anglo-Catholics and Evangelicals. In one way, the differences of opinion are reflected in other provinces of the Anglican Communion, but the dispute is wider in its implications. It would be safe to say that the Anglican-Roman Catholic International Commission's espousal of the dynamic notion of anamnesis enabled the Church of England (and no doubt other churches) to revise the liturgy in the light of that ecumenical agreement. The 1980 book leaves gift in a stronger position than in 1662, through the theophany theology still lingering ("in the presence of your divine majesty"), and in other communion epicleses; story revitalized in a full preface; and response still located in the postcommunion prayer. The kind of wider use of sacrificial language that we came across in the Taizé liturgy was not contemplated, but we shall meet it later on.

Australia and New Zealand began with modern English in 1966, and by the time of the 1978 *Australian Prayer Book* we come across some direct references to the world of nature and the covenant between God and humanity: "You have given us this earth to care for and delight in, and with its bounty you preserve our life." It is noteworthy that in the third eucharistic prayer, the epiclesis is lavish:

"We thank you for the outpouring of the Spirit upon your saints;
renew us, we pray, by the same Holy Spirit,
as we offer ourselves to you through Christ our Saviour
to serve you as a royal priesthood."

The anamnesis sections, while showing the same sort of sensitivity as England, repeatedly "thank God for the gift" of Christ, thus showing an awareness of the Thurian-Taizé theme. The Australian prayers are more lengthy than the English, and more overtly doxological.[93]

The United States of America, being an heir to the Scottish tradition, knows no sensitivity over eucharistic oblation. By 1970, American Episcopalians were ready for alternative eucharistic prayers, including provision for informal eucharists, where an anaphora could be improvised according to set themes. By 1976, when the *Draft Proposed Book of Common Prayer* was produced, the pattern of things to come was already clear. The "First Service" (in thou-form), allowed two old-style eucharistic prayers reminiscent of 1928.[94] In the "Second Service" (in you-form) are no less than four anaphoras, which demonstrate the truth of a remark made about American Episcopalian liturgies: "The current revision of the Book of Common Prayer in the United States has been pluralistic in approach."[95]

Prayer A is a successful attempt to get away from Cranmer's medieval and juridical description of the sacrifice of Christ and to depict it rather in visual and imaginative terms. The post-Sanctus includes the Hippolytan christological material: "He stretched out his arms upon the cross, and offered himself, in obedience to your will, a perfect sacrifice for the whole world." After the institution narrative there is an acclamation followed by: "We celebrate the memorial of our redemption, O Father, in this sacrifice of praise and thanksgiving. Recalling his death, resurrection, and ascension, we offer you these gifts." In the epiclesis (the American texts have only one epiclesis) the theme of self-oblation is expressed in terms suited to the context. Thus the American notion of eucharistic offering brings together story, gift, and response in a logical sequence, and avoids confusion at the offertory, which is functional and performed in silence.

Prayer B (which is a conflation of two prayers from the 1970 book) is focused on salvation history, but halts at the sacrifice of Christ in the post-Sanctus:

"In him, you have delivered us from evil, and made us worthy to stand before you.
In him, you have brought us out of error into truth, out of sin into righteousness, out of death into life."

After the acclamation: "And we offer our sacrifice of praise and thanksgiving to you, O Lord of all; presenting to you, from your creation, this bread and this wine." Then follows the epiclesis, which includes the theme of response: "Unite us to your Son in his sacrifice, that we may be acceptable through him." Thus, the same logical progression appears, with the mingling of story, gift, and response, this time with obvious quotation from the Greek West Syrian tradition. The internal unity of these anaphoras is clear because the institution narrative is part of the thanksgiving, and the epiclesis is the point at which thanksgiving moves into supplication. Once again, structure interprets sequence of ideas, and the themes of memorial and the unity of Christ's sacrifice are stressed, so that the Church is not Pelagian, nor does it repeat Christ's work.

Prayer C had originally appeared with the informal rite in the 1970 book, but it had become so popular that by 1976 it was included with the "Second Service." A brave attempt to write a responsorial anaphora in overtly modern and scientific imagery, it stands out on its own from the others. Building on the softer Christ-sacrifice theme of Prayer B, it tells the story of salvation history in cosmic terms, and so describes the work of Christ:

"And in the fullness of time, you sent your only Son . . .
to open for us the way of freedom and peace."
(All:)
"By his blood, he reconciled us,
By his stripes we are healed."

This is the only American anaphora to contain an epiclesis before the

207

narrative, where it uses language reminiscent of Roman and English prayers: "And so, Father, we who have been redeemed by him, and made a new people by water and the Spirit, now bring before you these gifts. Sanctify them. . . ." After the narrative:

"Remembering now his work of redemption, and offering to you this sacrifice of thanksgiving,"
(All:)
"We celebrate his death and resurrection,
as we await the day of his coming."

The latter part of the prayer expresses the theme of self-oblation: "Let the grace of this Holy Communion make us one body, one spirit in Christ, that we may worthily serve the world in his name."

Prayer D was the work of an informal ecumenical group,[96] drawing from Roman Catholic, Lutheran, Methodist, and Presbyterian liturgists, as well as Episcopalian. Based on the Alexandrian version of Basil, it remains more faithful to the original than Eucharistic Prayer IV. In the post-Sanctus, the work of Christ is expressed in dynamic terms:

"To the poor he proclaimed the good news of salvation;
To prisoners, freedom; to the sorrowful, joy,
To fulfil your purpose he gave himself up to death;
and, rising from the grave, destroyed death, and made the whole creation new."

In the anamnesis, the Alexandrian original is brought out:

"Father, we now celebrate this memorial of our redemption.
Recalling Christ's death and his descent among the dead,
proclaiming his resurrection and ascension to your right hand,
awaiting his coming in glory; and offering to you, from the gifts you have given us, this bread and this cup, we praise you and we bless you."

The present participle of the Grottaferrata G b VII text is kept for the offering verb. In the epiclesis, the theme of self-oblation leads naturally into intercession:

"Grant that all who share this bread and cup may become one body and one spirit, a living sacrifice in Christ, to the praise of your Name.

Remember, Lord, your one holy catholic and apostolic Church, redeemed by the blood of your Christ. Reveal its unity, guard its faith, and preserve it in peace."

Apart from the prenarrative epiclesis in Prayer C, these American prayers show an inner logic that stresses the story, the gifts, and the response of faith, which we have not seen since the various eastern anaphoras in an earlier chapter. But the American compositions are not "mere archeologism." They are so constructed as to keep the internal unity of the eucharistic prayer by stressing the once and for all nature of Christ's work and the way in which the eucharist is both the continuation of that work by Christ himself and the response of the Church in its worship and service. Of particular note is the ways in which the American books bring these themes together in two standard modern prayers (A and B), an aggressively contemporary one (C), and in a creatively-used antique model (D).

It would be impossible to summarize the anaphoral traditions of the rest of the Anglican Communion. Suffice it to observe American influence on the Canadian Order,[97] the dual (and separate) influence of Rome (Eucharistic Prayer II) and England on South Africa[98] (1975), and the interesting experiment in Korea to make the liturgy indigenous in alternative anaphoras (1973), where the Korean word *chesa* has connotations suited to the eucharist as communion-food-sacrifice.[99] One suspects that the Korean innovation may well point ahead to the future.

The Scottish Liturgy (1982)[100] provides yet one more variant. Roman offertory prayers are optional, but the old Scottish offertory rationale (with its bidding) persists. The eucharistic prayer, however, boldly adopts the invariable preface, which ends with the offering of praise, before the Sanctus. At the narrative, Jesus "offered" thanks; the anamnesis contains the most original synthesis we have so far seen: "Made one with him, we offer you these gifts and with them ourselves, a single, holy, living sacrifice." The compilers must have had an eye on the earlier Scottish tradition, patristic Syriac formulations, *and* ecumenical dialogue, although it must be remembered that strong formulations on eucharistic offering have been acceptable to Scottish Presbyterians as well for some time.

In 1936, the British Methodist *Book of Offices*[101] appeared as a liturgical attempt to bring together the various branches of Methodism that had united a few years before. The alternative order for communion has been studied recently by David Tripp, who discerns influence from the 1928 *Book of Common Order* of the United Free Church of Scotland. While provision is made for extempore prayer at that part that corresponds to the anaphora, the formulae that 1936 produced as samples show a distinctive manner of expressing all three of our

criteria; the story is linked to the eucharist; the response is the self-
oblation, before communion; the gifts are prayed over in an extended
form of the Prayer of Humble Access. The interesting feature of this
fine Free Church form is the *order* of the criteria. Gift may only be
appropriate after story and response have been made explicit. When
it comes to the 1975 *Methodist Service Book,*[102] a more liturgical framework is obvious. The elements are brought to the minister or else un-
covered. The eucharistic prayer stresses the intercession of Christ in
heaven, before the Sanctus. The bread and wine are given Jewish
treatment in the following way:

"We praise you, Lord God, King of the universe,
through our Lord Jesus Christ, who. . . ."

The anamnesis prays that the sacrifice of praise and thanksgiving may
be accepted, and the prayer ends on the note of self-oblation. The
post-communion prayer abstains from any mention of good works,
since the self-offering has aleady been mentioned. (Is this a deliberate
eschewal of incipient Pelagianism?)

The American United Methodist Church, on the other hand, has
produced a minister's book with numerous eucharistic prayers, including the ecumenical anaphora (Prayer D in the Episcopal Prayer
Book). Particularly fine is the lyrical prayer[103] composed by James
White, where images flow freely in and out of each other. Thus,
before the narrative:

"When his hour had come,
he drank the cup of suffering
and accepted the baptism of death.
Like a lamb,
he was led away from the living,
but, as your Son,
he was raised from the grave."

After the acclamation:

"Send, we pray, your Holy Spirit on us,
gathered here out of love for you,
and on this offering.
May your Spirit make real the signs
that through breaking bread
and drinking wine together
we may know Christ present among us."

This epiclesis goes on to pray for further sanctification of the communicants, thus bringing together the three criteria in a biblical and patristic manner. The prayer designated for general use contains an interesting anamnesis that recurs in other prayers in this book. It brings together the spirituality of the Wesley hymns and shows the acute sensitivity of this tradition to atonement and eucharist:

"Therefore, in remembrance of all your mighty acts in Jesus Christ, we ask you to accept this our sacrifice of praise and thanksgiving, which we offer in union with Christ's sacrifice for us, as a living and holy surrender of ourselves."[104]

The juxtaposition of self-oblation and Christ's sacrifice is no longer a self-conscious theme, but is brought beautifully into eucharistic liturgy.

The Scots Presbyterians, in their *Book of Common Order* (1979),[105] develop further the enrichment of 1940, this time not only including references to the presentation of the gifts, but also providing complete eucharistic prayers, so that the institution narrative can be part of that prayer. The language of anamnesis is heightened in one of the forms: "Wherefore, having in remembrance . . . , and pleading his eternal sacrifice, we thy servants set forth this memorial. . . ." A similarly adventurous approach is apparent in the service book of the English United Reformed Church (1980).[106]

In the Roman Catholic Church, two further tendencies are noticeable over eucharistic prayers. The first is the composition of local indigenous anaphoras, a challenge that Huub Oosterhuis took up in the 1960s,[107] and that earned some rebuke for allegedly defective christology. Although the Oosterhuis search for contemporaneity may now be on the wane, it is interesting how in the anamnesis his prayers almost invariably "present the sign of our faith," thus linking the eucharistic gifts more fully with the eucharistic action; he is probably sharing some ecumenical insights as well. Oosterhuis, and other writers of his kind, use flowing and often agonizing language, stretching traditional items like the institution narrative until they have more *midrash* than *verba Christi* within them. The theme of self-oblation is closely allied with the Suffering Servant figure of Christ himself. (A comparable tendency is to be seen in the Roman Catholic anaphora for India, which is more concerned to use old Indian myths in a Christianized way than to reproduce traditional eucharistic prayer units.)

The other tendency is one that has been aired recently in the work of the International Commission for English in the Liturgy. Two texts they have produced[108] have been published with a possible view

211

to seeking official approval from Rome for use in Roman Catholic Churches as alternative eucharistic prayers. These prayers are the anaphoras of Hippolytus and Basil of Caesarea (Alexandrian version), translated in such a way as to bear liturgical repetition. In other words, the method is not to alter the structure but to smoothen the language. (The Basil version contains many of the Coptic responses by the congregation.) Whether or not these prayers and others like them will gain official approval is another matter, but the aspirations of the Committee are to be welcomed, in their search for authenticity and in the ecumenical potential of their work.

The last word must be given to ecumenical eucharistic prayers, which we have already seen in the South Indian liturgy of 1950 (which was largely turned into you-language in 1972) and in the Prayer D of the American Episcopal Prayer Book.[109] The publication in 1982 of the Lima Statement by the Faith and Order Commission of the World Council of Churches provided a unique opportunity for the mainstream churches of the world to think once again about the meaning of baptism, eucharist, and ministry. Some of the language in the report is reminiscent of the ARCIC documents, to say nothing of the other dialogues between separated churches on the eucharist. (See below for a discussion of these.) The notion of anamnesis and the once and for all nature of the sacrifice of Christ are stressed. But the report also involves an unofficial liturgy, known to have been the work of Jean Tillard (Roman Catholic Dominican) and Max Thurian (Taizé community).[110] This rite was celebrated at the end of the Lima meeting in 1982 and also at a eucharist during the World Council of Churches Assembly in Vancouver in 1983, at which the Archbishop of Canterbury presided and was assisted by ordained ministers of various churches, adding color through their vesture as much as through their race. The liturgy itself brings together many of the insights that we have seen in this chapter, wherein story, gift, and response once more come together in a unity that is at once contemporary and timeless.

At the presentation of the gifts, there are adaptations of the Roman Catholic *berakoth*, together with the prayer for the unity of the Church from *Didache* 9. (The adaptations of the Roman formulae are of intrinsic interest and keep the Jewish character more faithfully.) The eucharistic prayer is a prolix formulation in the Taizé style, using Roman structure, with split epiclesis and with intercessions. Because of its historic character, it is worth quoting:[111]

212

Preface:
"At the last supper,
Christ bequeathed to us the eucharist, that we should celebrate
the memorial of the cross and resurrection, and receive his presence
as food."

First epiclesis:
"May the outpouring of this Spirit of Fire transfigure this
thanksgiving meal. . . ."

Anamnesis:
"Wherefore, Lord, we celebrate . . . we recall the birth and life of
your Son . . . we proclaim Christ's resurrection and ascension in
glory, where as our Great High Priest he ever intercedes for all
people. . . .

"United in Christ's priesthood, we present to you this memorial:
Remember the sacrifice of your Son and grant to people everywhere
the benefits of Christ's redemptive work."

Second epiclesis:
"Behold, Lord, this eucharist which you yourself gave to the Church
and graciously receive it, as you accept the offering of your Son
whereby we are reinstated in your Covenant. When we shall be fed
by Christ's body and blood, fill us with the Holy Spirit that we may
be one single body and one single Spirit in Christ, a living sacrifice to
the praise of your glory."

The intercessions resemble Eucharistic Prayer IV and the American
ecumenical prayer. Among the noteworthy features of the rite are the
expanded anamnesis (in line with old Syriac traditions and some recent theological developments) and the stress on "we present to you
this memorial," linking anamnesis with atonement in a way similar to
other "Catholic-minded" rites we have seen so far.

POSTSCRIPT
By way of postscript, it is worth observing several overall tendencies
in the churches of the West that we have discussed in this chapter.
An important point of renewal has been the *context* of celebration,
with the central westward-facing altar inevitably emphasizing the gift
aspect of the eucharist. Another area of convergence is in rites of ordination,[112] where the *Apostolic Tradition* of Hippolytus has been wide-
spread in its influence on new texts, so bringing East and West together as well. Thus the imprecise term "spiritual sacrifices" has

appeared again and again, and the Roman Catholic ordination of presbyters has been restored to some of its ancient simplicity, relegating the *porrectio instrumentorum* to a subsidiary place, with a cleverly worked out formula at the giving of the chalice and paten. Yet another area of convergence is in hymnody, where erstwhile separated traditions have freely mixed with each other, a process that began in the nineteenth century among the non-Roman Catholic churches, but that is now at a remarkable stage of development. Hymnody as a vehicle of popular piety is an essential ingredient in the modern eucharist, and the fact that the treasures of each other's past and present are being used in liturgies means that the spiritualities of the churches and the hymn writers are being shared. Many modern hymns bring together story, gift, and response in a profoundly sacrificial way, a notable example of which is Brian Wren's "Lord God, your love has called us here," with the image of Jesus washing the feet of the disciples. The fourth stanza deserves special attention:

"Then take the towel, and break the bread,
and humble us, and call us friends.
Suffer and serve till all are fed,
and show how grandly love intends
to work till all creation sings,
to fill all worlds, to crown all things."[113]

Recent ecumenical statements have based discussion around the revived interest in anamnesis. Thus the ARCIC Windsor Statement of 1971:

"The eucharistic memorial is no mere calling to mind of a past event or of its significance, but the Church's effectual proclamation of God's mighty acts. . . . In the eucharistic prayer the Church continues to make a perpetual memorial of Christ's death, and his members, united with God and one another, give thanks for all his mercies, entreat the benefits of his passion on behalf of the whole Church, participate in these benefits and enter into the movement of his self-offering."[114]

This kind of language repeats itself in other ecumenical documents, and it has its critics, both from a Protestant and a radical standpoint. For the former, too much stress is laid on the action of the Church. For the latter, the language is too confidently patristic in its style[115] and too far dissociated from the language of modern theology. In the

1979 Salisbury Elucidation, the Commission has this to say in its defense:

"The Commission believes that the traditional understanding of sacramental reality, in which the once-for-all event of salvation becomes effective in the present through the action of the Holy Spirit, is well expressed by the word anamnesis. We accept this use of the word which seems to do full justice to the Semitic background. Furthermore, it enables us to affirm a strong conviction of sacramental realism and to reject mere symbolism. However the selection of this word by the Commission does not mean that our common eucharistic faith may not be expressed in other terms.

"In the exposition of the Christian doctrine of redemption the word *sacrifice* has been used in two intimately associated ways. In the New Testament, sacrificial language refers primarily to the historical events of Christ's saving work for us. The tradition of the Church, as evidenced for example in its liturgies, used similar language to designate in the eucharistic celebration the *anamnesis* of this historical event. Therefore, it is possible to say at the same time that there is only one unrepeatable sacrifice in this historical sense, but that the eucharist is a sacrifice in the sacramental sense, provided that it is clear that this is not a repetition of the historical sacrifice."[116]

There can be no doubt about the meaning of this "Elucidation," even though the kind of language used is that of an ecumenical commission. One of the difficulties over religious language today is that it is hard to find the right kind of representative dialect in an age of theological pluralism. What is interesting is that the Lima Statement of the World Council of Churches fans out its notions of eucharistic sacrifice toward a similar approach to the one we have taken in this study:

(Of the Eucharist as Thanksgiving to the Father:) "The eucharist is the great sacrifice of praise by which the Church speaks on behalf of the whole creation. For the world which God has reconciled is present at every eucharist in the bread and wine, in the persons of the faithful, and in the prayers they offer for themselves and for all people."

(Of the Eucharist as Anamnesis or Memorial of Christ:) "The eucharist is the memorial of the crucified and risen Christ. . . . The biblical idea of memorial as applied to the eucharist refers to this present efficacy of God's work when it is celebrated by God's people in a liturgy.

"The *anamnesis* in which Christ acts through the joyful celebration of his Church is thus both representation and anticipation. It is not only a calling to mind of what is past and of its significance. It is the Church's effective proclamation of God's mighty acts and promises.

"Representation and anticipation are expressed in thanksgiving and intercession. . . . In thanksgiving and intercession, the Church is united with the Son, its Great High Priest and Intercessor (Rom 3:34, Heb 7:25). The eucharist is the sacrament of the unique sacrifice of Christ, who ever lives to make intercession for us.

"In Christ we offer ourselves as a living and holy sacrifice in our daily lives (Rom 12:1, 1 Pt 2:5); this spiritual worship, acceptable to God, is nourished in the eucharist. . . ."[117]

There is a richer treatment of eucharistic sacrifice in the Lima document than the ARCIC statements, although they share a common approach to the sixteenth-century controversies, which is paralleled in the work of the Roman Catholics and Lutherans in the U.S.[118] Lima language is found in the unofficial liturgy discussed earlier, which tries to do justice to past controversy but also tries to move forward, particularly in the dynamic approach to the eucharistic action and the anamnesis of the *whole* life of Christ. Moreover, the overtones of Church serving world in document and liturgy also point to contemporary developments in the life of the churches. All this and much more is expanded in recent publications edited by Max Thurian, whose style is apparent throughout. The worldwide Church owes a great deal to the Taizé community in the way it has worked out a parable of Christian unity.

In sum, therefore, this unprecedented era of liturgical reform has brought together the churches of the West in the way the eucharist is prayed and understood. Much work remains to be done. But current tensions may well be the result of different cultures moving forward in their own way, rather than reliving the battles of sixteenth-century Europe (although these do live on). It is worth drawing attention to the importance of the three criteria in many modern eucharistic liturgies, with story spread throughout the eucharistic prayer (whether in preface, post-Sanctus, or anamnesis); gift as a theme in which the elements are either offered to God, or else referred to as sacred gifts; and response giving rise to new types of epiclesis that speak of the work of sanctification, which at times lead into explicit intercession. One cannot help noticing, too, the problems caused by bringing one or other of these themes out of the eucharistic prayer, whether in emphasizing gift at the offertory (and expressing self-oblation), or self-oblation at the post-communion (as a response to sharing the feast). In these and other ways, new paths continue to be made out of constructive insights from the past. If twentieth-century liturgical reform demonstrates one thing, it certainly shows what can be done in common, to the extent that the way separated Christians worship at the eucharist in this century shows that they have more in common with each other now than they have with their own predecessors four centuries ago. *Deo gratias!*

Chapter Eight

Conclusion

"In liturgiology as in any other field, knowledge is a perception of relationships, and advances not so much by new facts but by a new explanation of those already known; not by the acquisition of new data,
but by the creation of new systems, the organization of already avail
able data within a new intelligibility framework."[1]

This is how Robert Taft describes the progress of liturgical studies,
and those who toil in our field of study do so with new insights to
material that is, much of it, familiar. In our panorama of liturgical
texts down the ages, our aim has been to look at this material with a
different perspective from before, because it is our conviction that liturgical texts will continue to yield new fruit when looked at and
sifted and compared through different conceptual frameworks. The
Jewish origin of the early Christian notion of eucharistic sacrifice already embodies in its spirituality our three criteria. These have occurred repeatedly, and in different guises, as Christian history has
moved on. Some of our analyses and comments may be open to
question, perhaps in the early period, where some scholars would like
more precision than we have allowed, whereas others would see
much less precision than we have suggested. For that early period of
origins, much depends on one's use of the available liturgical material, and whether that material is authentic, and how far it is to be
regarded as typical. But there is, nonetheless, much that can be
gleaned from history, both in our own continuing conversation with
the whole tradition and also for the continuing ecumenical dialogue.
What are these lessons?

1. VARIETY?
Linguistic variety is apparent through all of the eastern and some of
the western traditions. The Greek liturgies have different ways of
handling the notion of eucharistic offering, whether within a particular tradition (Basil Byzantine, Chrysostom, and James), or within the
linguistic orbit of Greek (Basil Alexandrian, Mark, perhaps also Syriac

anaphoras originally written in Greek). There is nothing mutually contradictory in what they have to say, but when one adds the peculiarities of the East Syrian anaphoras, the Armenian, as well as the Syriac traditions of the Jacobites and Maronites, then a multifarious scheme opens out. Indeed, it is not really possible to maintain the traditional divisions of West Syrian and East Syrian any longer; we should really speak of Greek and Syriac (and perhaps East Syrian), because the way offering is handled in all three is different. The Armenian prayers, moreover, will continue to fascinate liturgiologists. They belong as early cousins of Syriac and East Syrian in the first place, although, as we have seen, they do not simply borrow; they develop in their own way. In all these traditions, the anaphora is the supreme prayer of the eucharist, even though it is called by various names. It is where Semitic, Greek, Coptic, and Armenian meet together, in order to work out in varying ways the meaning of the eucharist. The anaphora manages to hold together story and response through the recitation of the mighty acts in Christ and the intercession of the congregation; there are various ways in which gift is handled, usually in close connection with the epiclesis, thus strengthening the communion-sacrifice background of the Christian eucharist.

In the West, our evidence is less substantial, since the available non-Roman texts do not give a full picture of the old Mozarabic, Gallican, and Milanese liturgies. But from what is available, another kind of variety is apparent, even though the Roman Canon dominates the scene in a way that cannot be said of the eucharistic prayer in any one of the eastern churches. The Canon in its early form itself gives way to a simple interpretation,[2] once notions of impetration are cast aside, and the dominant theme of offering is recognized as the fundamental rationale for the prayer. The eventual eclipse of the preface as story results in the first part of the eucharistic prayer virtually disappearing, so that we have only the general theme of praise (after the Sanctus), as the Church offers its sacrifice of praise and response to the mighty work of God in Christ. Perhaps the strongly christological character of the Canon made the proper prefaces redundant as expressions of the theology of the Church. But in the Canon, more than in the eastern prayers, the movement of the Church into the eternal sacrifice of Christ is given fullest liturgical expression. (The only exception in the East is in the Syriac anaphoras, which extend the anamnesis forward to the day of judgement and ask for the offering of the eucharist to be accepted.) From a comparative point of view, the Gallican and Mozarabic variable prayers within the anaphora result in a mixture of petition for acceptance of the offering and

219

epiclesis on the offering, or both. The mixture has its own charm. Because the Latin is so different from the austere periods of Rome, these traditions deserve more attention than they have gained from scholars, and form an indispensible link with the East, from where they may have gleaned some of their liturgical sources.

Although it is impossible to distinguish sharply between the ideas of "petition for acceptance" and "petition for the Holy Spirit to come on the gifts/offering," the anaphoras that opt for one of these approaches to the exclusion of the other betray a different kind of spiritual attitude in liturgical prayer. Thus, the three Greek West Syrian prayers that eventually become the standard Byzantine anaphoras rehearse the events of salvation with a logic that seems to say, "this is what you did, this is what we are doing in response to it, please send your Spirit on us, and on these gifts, as we pray for our continuing ecclesial life together. . . ." This type of prayer is more *confident* in its liturgical psychology because it is a prayer whose starting point and ending point is the action of the Church. The same use of salvation history is discernible in the Syriac anaphoras (even those that *do* include petition for the acceptance of the offering prior to the epiclesis), which anaphoras expand the anamnesis so that it moves either backward to Bethlehem or forward to judgment or both. The Church's use of history is bound up inextricably with its application of history to the eucharistic gifts, whether or not these gifts are to be formally offered, or whether what is offered is the whole eucharist. Perhaps the Syriac anaphoras keep hold of something primitive that other traditions either discard or never had in the first place. Their occasional redefinition of anamnesis should dispel any notion that this idea was a static one in antiquity.[3]

Can this anaphoral linguistic variety be termed theological? The answer to this question must be both yes and no. It is negative in the sense that the compilers of these many prayers did not deliberately set out to write anaphoras that differed in eucharistic theology from other anaphoras. Within the Syriac orbit, where the most numerous eucharistic prayers were written that are available to us today, it could be argued that theological variety was deliberately sought. We have noted a few anaphoras in which the christology is strongly sacrificial, whereas others are not. This results in prayers that color eucharistic offering in different ways. But such theological variety was more in the interests of variegation than any comprehensiveness, since the prayers do not seem to have been written in order to cater to differing theologies of the eucharist. Great eucharistic presidents (and the traditions that they developed, or that were associated with them) wrote down anaphoras in order to express the meaning of the eucharist in ways that were fundamentally faithful to the tradition with its conventions and structure, but that expressed it differently.[4] Nonetheless, the answer is yes—for us. It is impossible to read these ancient prayers, whether eastern or western, without seeing theological variety in the light of the eucharistic controversies that came to a head in the West during the sixteenth century, and that are being slowly healed. Our use of the past to better inform us of the whole Christian tradition sets our quest in a different context from, for example, a devout and learned Syrian Jacobite sitting down and comparing the many anaphoras of his own tradition, or a scholarly monk in seventh-century Spain looking at all the *Post pridies* that were then in use among the Mozarabics.

Taking this point further, it seems that the Greek West Syrian type of anaphora (represented by its possible archetype, Hippolytus' *Apostolic Tradition*) has dominated models of contemporary liturgical reform in the West, and unnecessarily so.[5] It is clear that the logic of story + Sanctus + story + narrative + anamnesis + gift offering + epiclesis (with or without intercessions) is a most selective use of tradition, almost cavalier in its approach to all the other available evidence. There is no doubt that liturgical reform has learned much from the full implications of story within the anaphora, so that this element no longer has to be carried within the liturgy by individual devotions, or reading/preaching, or hymnody, useful though all these elements are. But the way gift is handled in antiquity in the anaphora is much more subtle. Some anaphoras "offer" in the anamnesis, but this is immediately before an epiclesis that holds together both consecration of the gifts and consecration of the communicants. Moreover, the almost universal practice of anaphoral intercession (already present in the early Coptic version of Basil) demonstrates how the "living sacrifice" was brought into the eucharistic prayer, usually after the epiclesis, as the logical outcome of that petition for consecration. However, other anaphoras do not offer the gifts at the anamnesis. These include many of the Syriac and Armenian eucharistic prayers, which are acutely sensitive to the christological character of the prayer in their different ways. One can ask why they refrain from doing this, but the answer is likely to be more colored by the presuppositions of the questioner than by any light that the prayer may throw upon the quest, except that already within these anaphoras there is a more apparent theological reflection upon the relationship between the offering of Christ and the offering of the eucharist than that which we see in the fourth-century Greek West Syrian patterns.[6] (And if the au-

thenticity of the past tense "we presented" in the anamnesis of the
early Coptic Basil is accepted, then the origin of the "remembering
. . . we offer" movement of ideas is further clouded by uncertainty.)[7]
There is no doubt that the Syriac and Armenian anaphoras see the
eucharist as sacrificial, but their conventions are different, and they
obviously feel free to develop their own ways of expressing eucharistic sacrifice. These include stress on the unique character of Christ's
sacrifice and the "dynamic memorial" nature of the eucharist.

2. SHAPE?

The theory of Dom Gregory Dix concerning the "four-action shape"
of the eucharist becomes increasingly difficult to sustain for the East,
once we have studied the various anaphoras and the prayers preceding them. The prayer immediately prior to the anaphora is no offertory prayer, but is, rather, a *preparatory* prayer to the whole anaphora.[8] It is impossible to speak of a "taking" and a "blessing" and a
"breaking" and a "sharing" as an underlying structure of the eastern
rites except as these actions are recounted in the institution narrative.
The East does not yield to that kind of schematized view of the eucharistic liturgy. There is no moment of offertory of the gifts. It is possible that in Greek Mark (Egypt), the placing of the gifts was looked
back to through the offering of the "bloodless service" early on in the
thanksgiving. The past-tense verb in the anamnesis may refer to the
"bloodless service" rather than to the gifts. Eastern anaphoras refer
constantly to those who have offered gifts, so that they cannot be ac-
cused of undermining the theme of gift in the anaphora. Moreover,
the placing of the gifts on the altar inevitably amounted to a significant point in the liturgy, as the sign that the anaphora was about to
start. But the equation, take = offertory, is untenable.[9] This conclusion
is not new, but we have substantiated it through studying the different nuances of offering in the East.

In the West, the analysis can hold better, perhaps demonstrating
that Dom Gregory was in his heart a western Latin-minded Christian.
But the question is, when does the presentation of the gifts become
formally ritualized? Dix pushes this ritual action as far back as he can,
even to the raising of the bread and the wine at the Jewish solemn
meal, as the *berakah* begins. But one man's perceived ritual action is
not the same as the functional presentation of the gifts in Justin Martyr. The "offertory" began and continued in the West as a popular
(but often abused)[10] example of the kind of self-consciousness that the
Reformers were happy to throw out. Even the old Roman *Super oblata*
may originally have been not a prayer over the oblations, but rather a

general prayer of offering for the whole eucharist, perhaps even summing up the fore-Mass.

Dix's stress on the philosophy of liturgy, however, has enabled scholars and others to look at the internal unity of the eucharist in a fresh light. This quest has borne much fruit in western liturgical reform, so that secondary or dubious ingredients can be eliminated, in favor of self-apparent simplicity. But it has also helped to produce the comparative methodology in liturgical study developed by Matéos and Taft, which distinguishes between deep structures and surface structures and therefore sharpens Dix's quest considerably.[11] On this basis, our study has shown two things; first, that the deep structures of the anaphora remain thanksgiving (story) and supplication (response), and that gift offering is a deep structure as an underlying attitude to the eucharist, which, however, is only made explicit in certain traditions in antiquity. Secondly, it shows that the formal presentation of gifts is a surface structure performed and interpreted variously down the ages, especially in the West, both before and after the Reformation. Dix's own work, moreover, was that of the pioneer and was ahead of his time, but his theory on the shape of the eucharist was itself accompanied by a strong hierarchical consciousness that was more post-Nicene than ante-Nicene in the distinction between the deacons who "bring forward" and the presbyter who "brings up" the gifts, $\pi\rho o\sigma\phi\acute\epsilon\rho\omega$ $\grave\alpha\nu\alpha\phi\acute\epsilon\rho\omega$. Thus, in order to safeguard the priestly character of the eucharistic prayer, there must be a double oblation, a notion that was popular with many of Dix's Anglican predecessors in liturgical study (and practitioners, too). The people offer the gifts at the offertory, and the priest offers the gifts in the anaphora. We are already into the problem of duplication in the liturgy, when ceremonies have to be given subtle explanations. This may explain why the *Oratio super oblata* had to move away from offering the whole eucharist to offering the gifts in the context of the eucharist. Prayer writing can be a supremely flexible exercise. But the problem with the double oblation is that it is inherently self-conscious if the former is lay and the latter is priestly. A different philosophy was coined by John Bate Cardale, the author of the Catholic Apostolic Liturgy, who managed to hold together the offering of alms, the offering of gifts, and the presentation before God of the consecrated gifts prior to intercession. The whole activity (although unquestionably complex) is that of the whole church, and his experiment is a constructive use of tradition. The collection cannot be ignored in the liturgy, especially in an age that takes social responsibility and ecology seriously; on the other hand, the presentation of the collection is not the same as the presentation of the bread and the wine, and Michael Ramsey's caution against offertory processions ("a shallow and romantic sort of Pelagianism")[12] was a timely one.

But what of the collection? It has certainly had a checkered career. There is evidence of its survival in antiquity from New Testament[13] times, but its place in the liturgy has never been regular until the western Reformation, at which time it became something more acceptable to offer than bread and wine. It is, however, just as susceptible to the charge of Pelagianism as the presentation of eucharistic elements, particularly in what we are told is a consumer society. Nonetheless, it is an important aspect of congregational life that requires some form of ritualizing. The answer seems to be that if you have offertory prayers over money, then you cannot really avoid them over bread and wine if both are presented, as they usually are in modern Anglican worship. Alternatively, a more satisfactory solution is to trust the simple action of presenting all the gifts and to realize that you are only going to give thanks over the bread and wine. So the liturgy retains its clarity and avoids clutter through didactic and self-conscious prayer forms. Kavanagh has this to say on the subject:

". . . cash offering probably is more vigorously symbolic of a modern assembly's gift of itself than even the eucharistic gifts of bread and wine. This suggests that including the assembly's gifts of cash along with its gifts-in-kind ought to be standard procedure."[14]

Perhaps the whole thrust of Dix's repeated advocacy of ancient liturgical models is that we cannot turn the clock back in liturgy. We cannot do it in theology, although it is easier to attempt this exercise the further one gets away from spirituality. The corporate memory of a church is a vital clue to its own identity. Nonetheless, progress can be made and the quest for origins must continue to be high on the list of the scholar in any field of theology, liturgy included, and that quest needs to be mediated to the Church. As the twentieth-century West adjusts to a new set of priorities and does so increasingly as an ecumenical exercise, the notion of roles within the Church becomes more and more part of the life of the Christian community, so that clericalism is seen as something inherently wrong.[15] Some secular notions that creep into church life are equally unhelpful, like the one that asserts that everyone can do everything and therefore anyone can preside at the eucharist. Such is a lurking question in the minds of some of the people who present the bread and wine at the altar and dutifully return to their places while the priest begins the eucharistic prayer. Cynicism about motives and about special roles is inevitably part of the baggage that some bring to the eucharist. Dix's role definition does not help, particularly as the understanding of eucharistic offering that is to be perceived from the ancient prayers of the anaphora in both East and West repeatedly assumes that the offering is that of the whole congregation.

In this sense, perhaps Dix is himself being postmedieval in his discussion about who does what, for it is in the Middle Ages that the self-conscious prayers intrude on the understanding of the eucharist, or perhaps express that understanding as it evolved far away from the fourth and fifth centuries in the East. The offertory prayers that are couched in the first-person singular and the *Orate fratres* that sometimes (although not always) addresses only the assistants in the sanctuary and sometimes (although not always) gives rise to a response that sends the celebrant on to do the professional thing—these and their concomitant ceremonial tendencies are the background for the western Reformation. Perhaps Dix's neat distinctions about ministry are eisegetical rather than exegetical of antiquity and betray a medieval consciousness. The fact is that the prayers of the *Didache* reflect a Christian community with a high doctrine of the eucharist and a low doctrine of ordained ministry. This is not to suggest a yet more primitive blueprint for the continuing debate about ministry in the Church today. The historian has limits. But history can tease the enquirer with its variety and the idiosyncrasies that different ages produce and solidify. It could well be that the ease with which the solemn presentation of the gifts on the table *returned* to Anglican liturgy in reaction to Cranmer's 1552 rite is really an example of the conservatism of ritual activity; the popularity of the offertory processions in the western churches of the Reformation in this century, including Lutheran, shows this to be a stronger possibility. "Nothing in my hand I bring, simply to thy cross I cling"[16] is evidently not enough.

We have already seen how Dix's theory of self-oblation at the offertory does not find expression in antiquity, but has occurred with some infrequency since the Catholic Apostolic experiment in the nineteenth century. Of course, within a highly structured liturgy in which items move rigidly from one ingredient to another, the "moment" of self-oblation is plain for all to see. But the Catholic Apostolic liturgy (for all its complexity and structuralism) does move from one part to another with more freedom than many modern experimental rites. The philosophy of self-oblation at the offertory is a way of avoiding the charge of Pelagianism precisely because the prayer repeats that it is only in Christ that we are accepted, and the eucharist is a highly christological action of the Church.

225

The eucharist cannot avoid reflection upon christology, as we have seen repeatedly in our survey of prayer formulae through the ages. But self-oblation is more subtle than a bland liturgical action. While Cranmer's insistence that it needed such bald liturgical expression was a sound one, intercession is also part of that self-oblation, and there are numerous instances of anaphoras that include intercession as a consequence of epiclesis, including anaphoras that offer at the intercession but that do *not* offer in the anamnesis.[17] The contemporary debate on intercession and its relation to spirituality and action in the world means that questions need to be asked of those churches that still shun anaphoral intercession. This question also needs to be asked as a result of the frequent trivializing of "free" intercession as it now so frequently finds itself at the end of the liturgy of the word.[18] It is conceivable that anaphoral intercession developed into a full form because it was being abused and in decline in its position at the end of the word service.[19] But whatever the historical details of that decline and fall, the practice of anaphoral intercession as embodying the *specific* requests for eucharistic sanctification mixes well with the emphasis in twentieth-century theology on the Church as a pilgrim and serving community.[20]

However, it is impossible (at least for an Anglican) to read *The Shape of the Liturgy* without using history to inform the process of liturgical reform. Dix wrote his work during the Second World War, since which time western Christendom has changed its eucharistic worship almost beyond recognition. His discussion of offertory leads one to the conclusion that in the West you cannot really win, and that it is much more consistent with a primitive and imprecise notion of eucharistic offering that the gifts are placed on the altar in silence, as a functional act that has symbolic overtones. The real offering in the first part of the eucharist is that of intercession. This is what we need to rediscover, so that the word-service intercession could end with variable prayers like the *Super oblata* in the earliest stratum of the sacramentaries and the *Post nomina* in the Mozarabic books. This would make the junction of word and sacrament through peace a more flowing action and settle once and for all the confusion surrounding the presentation of the gifts in not a few modern rites, which only seems to make sense in prayer if it also includes self-oblation.

Allied to the intercessory and self-oblatory aspects of the eucharist is the question of the use of votive forms. Essentially pastoral in their original character, they become so dominant a theme in the Middle Ages that they are objectionable to the Reformers. Cranmer's marriage rite retains a theoretical link with the celebration of the eucharist, but there are no special collect and readings, presumably because the Sunday provisions are deemed enough, and because the older votive Masses of Trinity and marriage that are to be found in the Sarum Manual are regarded as suspect and unsatisfactory.[21] The Missal of 1570 greatly reduced on the votive Masses of many of the medieval missals; the 1970 Missal provides for real needs of contemporary Roman Catholics in a way that fastens onto the idea of eucharist as solemn intercession rather than priestly impetration.[22] Many churches of the Reformation have lost their fear of such pastoral eucharists; in this respect, the Catholic Apostolic rite led the way in the nineteenth century. What is less than satisfactory today is the growth in many churches of privatized eucharistic celebrations so geared to particular needs, and the desires and concerns of small, gathered congregations, that the eucharist loses its universality. In this respect, the temporal Mass must dominate the votive, whatever the circumstances.

For the eucharistic prayer, the offering of story and response can provide two essential foundations for the thanksgiving and the supplication, a philosophy propounded by Thurian, and also enshrined in the American Episcopal Prayer Book.[23] Both these foundations are invariably part of tradition and they point back to the two essential ingredients of the Jewish meal-thanksgiving as we find it in the earliest forms of Christian euchology. "Gift," however, has been handled variously. Some will continue to assert the need of the Greek West Syrian logic ("remembering . . . we offer . . . and we pray"), a logic that is easier to accept if the epiclesis is also Greek West Syrian (and not Alexandrian-Vatican II). This avoids the outcome of the split epiclesis, which results in the institution narrative no longer being a psychological focus within the whole prayer but rather as "the words of consecration."[24] Others will stress a theophany theology of eating and drinking solemnly in the presence of the Lord, perhaps pointing back to a notion far more primitive than Greek West Syria. Others again will want to stress the relationship between atonement and the heavenly ministry of Christ as it relates to the action of the eucharist, thus bringing in the kind of christological reflection that the Syriac anaphoras and the western Reformation have in different ways brought to bear upon the eucharist, whether in prayer, as in the former tradition, or in theology, preaching, hymnody, as in the latter. History shows that gift is the most elusive of the three, perhaps because it is the most obvious in the very fact of having bread and wine on the altar. Beautiful as many offertory prayers are (they seem made for expressing popular piety!), they frequently run the risk of anticipating and therefore down-grading the eucharistic prayer itself. The soteriological emphasis of the Reformation has resulted in anamnesis and related elements that are much more complex than the simple confidence of Alexandrian Basil (or the unitive ideas of Addai and Mari), so that gift finds expression in the eucharist, as it were, through the back door, because, apart from Christ, "the Church cannot offer or present anything to God except its utter poverty."[25] In other words, we are only beneficiaries.[26]

3. HUMAN SCIENCES?

The insights of social anthropology, while being unable to illuminate the whole of the Christian story, can provide some useful explanation to our quest for the inner meaning of the eucharist. Thus, social anthropology distinguishes between feeding and eating. Feeding expresses commensality, which is fundamental to the character of the Christian eucharist, and which history shows has been abused systematically as the individual has reacted against the community.[27] Similarly, the sacred meal is a way of feeding upon God and thereby reducing him to manageable chunks, not so much in the food itself but in the whole ritual action of the meal. Here we have echoes of the theology of eucharistic presence that evokes Jesus being "at the table" rather than "on the table." Many a modern epiclesis stresses this theme without dissolving into an ultra-Protestant vagueness. The anthropologist continues to look at other Christian rituals as embodying patterns that are well established, time-honored, and not immediately susceptible to any kind of liturgical reform.[28] The liturgiologist, on the other hand, can use these tools to see how far popular perceptions of the eucharist have traveled from any attainable antique ideal. The eating-together is a way of self-incorporation into the deity, and many of the perceptions of the deity rely on ritual conservatism, so that it is through the familiar and the routine that the worshipper can settle into the religious activity of the meal sacrifice. The "fact" of the deity and the "activity" of the worshippers correspond with the Christian insistence on the unrepeatability of Calvary and the work of Christ within us now. But another kind of sacrifice is the *piacular* one, which exists primarily to deal with pollution, and in this sense the penitential and saving aspects of the eucharist enter the picture. "Christ died for our sins"; hence the references to his saving work in the prayers of the eucharist, to the forgiveness of sins, and to pardon and renewal among the faithful worshippers. The eucharist, therefore, is both commensal and piacular. But it is also an oft-repeated routine. Thus its ritual pattern fits in well with the way in which anthropologists study Christian and non-Christian worship. The community gathers to recite its story and to enter into certain actions that recall that story, and that express a number of aspirations that will lead out of that worship into life. This, in turn, will bring them to repeat the activity in worship again and again.[29]

It was through such ideas as these that we have sought to broaden the usual understandings of eucharistic sacrifice when we chose story, gift, and response as three criteria for our comparative study of liturgical texts through the Christian era. These, it seemed, would help to place the much-debated issue into a new perspective and bring in some of the talents of the social anthropologist at a time when theologians have to converse more effectively not only with each other, but with other academic disciplines. We have noted already how of the three, gift is the most elusive, probably because of the wide-ranging symbolisms that are attached to food in different religious activities. This variety is also clear within the Christian tradition itself, whether or not in the liturgy. David Power has recently suggested how the bread and wine of the eucharist can be taken to point to the essential unity between humanity and the whole creation.[30] This probably lies behind the repeated affirmation in eastern eucharistic prayers that the intercession associates those who provide the eucharistic gifts with their aspirations and intentions. Such an ideal is a legitimate one, which only the most cynical can despise as Pelagian. For far too long the debate about the eucharist has centered on when and in what way who is being Pelagian. While many of the tendencies of the Middle Ages are not helpful to contemporary Christian worship, the same can be said of the sixteenth century, with its suspicious attitude to creation itself. Certainly, the twentieth century gives the enquirer a viewpoint that is wide and at least partially detached.[31]

But even the Reformers in their passionate desire to return to the practice of the primitive Church (an exercise that does not invariably result in the desired goal) managed to establish gift as the commensality of the Christians. The fundamental characteristic of the Christian eucharist is that it is about Christians eating and drinking together, in the context of the saving work of Christ (the piacular sacrifice). Their emphasis on nourishment in these ritual actions resulted in any "offertory" being superfluous. Perhaps the growing attachment to *le petit canon* in the preceding era was its own kind of eucharistic substitute, that we keep offering and keep offering, but only the priest actually eats and drinks. No one can attend a Scots Presbyterian communion without being impressed by the solemnity of the occasion. The two moments which catch the eye of the worshipper are when the elders go out to collect the bread and wine and solemnly bring them forward to the table, and when the elders bring the consecrated elements down to the people to be consumed as they sit together at table. What it lacks in paschal joy it certainly expresses in Calvary awe.

The story may be pliable, as interest in the acts of God in Christ vary and expand and adapt in formulation. The response may be variable, as Christian concerns vary from a general desire for sanctification and unity, to a host of local concerns, as well as the bald "living sacrifice" that surrenders all to Christ. Nonetheless, it is in gift that the link between the heavenly and the earthly, the eternal and the historical, the timeless and the time-ridden is made, and it is made elusively. Even Max Thurian, in his defense of the offertory rite, insists on the starkness of the action of placing the bread and the wine on the table.[32] With our renewed consciousness of being only part of a creation that runs the risk of eating itself out of business or of destroying itself out of mutual hatred and mistrust, the ecology of the eucharist has the potential for taking on new meanings in the future. There is no need to stand still and try to absorb everything that history may or may not have said already. The eucharist is as much about human perceptions as it is about the intentions of those who write the prayers and those who sing the tunes. Whatever our particular emphasis in the story, and whatever our particular interest in the response, the bread and the wine are still there, offered by Christ himself, in order that we may be fed by him.

4. TEXT AND CONTEXT?

Three points need to be made to emphasize the wider context in which reflection on the eucharist should take place. The first is christological. From both the traditional and the radical ends of the spectrum, there is a remarkable convergence on the eucharist as the action of the Church, as the continuing activity of God in Christ. On the one hand, scholars such as Gustaf Aulén (Lutheran) and Alasdair Heron (Reformed)[33] are anxious not to make Calvary so drastic that it seems to immobilize Christ. Thus, Aulén contends that the eucharist is the result of the intercessory work of Christ in heaven, which releases "the powers of life which are contained in the atonement." Heron will criticize Calvin's separation of Calvary and Supper as too radical in nature, and will suggest, in language strongly reminiscent of the oblatory formula in the 1982 Scots Episcopal anaphora, that the eucharist "is both a *receiving* of Christ as the Father's gift to us and a *sharing* in his offering to the Father of our nature, indeed of *us*."

On the other hand, Geoffrey Lampe (Anglican) and James Mackey

(Roman Catholic)[34] take a less orthodox approach. Lampe is more than happy with the language of sacrifice as long as it points to the eucharist as "an acted parable"; the eucharist, for him, is "the sacrament of a continuing re-enactment of Christ's sacrifice by God the Spirit in union with human spirits." Mackey has a still wider starting point; "experience of the reign of God . . . is an experience of giving up life," which leads both to hostility from those who reject it as well as a life of self-surrender from those who embrace it. The eucharist is, therefore, a vehicle of God's way of life as manifested in Jesus.

While the two approaches share a broad, ecclesial view of the eucharist, they have different ways of expressing it; while the "heavenly liturgy" approach has a long pedigree in theological interpretation, the liturgical formulations of the Church have invariably stopped short of defining *how* the eucharist shares in the intercession or self-offering of Christ. Eucharistic prayers can revel in the activity of heavenly praise and worship (Sanctus), and intercession (in extended forms of anamnesis), but their genius is that they *evoke* God's presence and power rather than attempt to *describe* it so precisely as to run the risk of *confining* it. Such is one more symptom of the nature of liturgical language at its best.

The second point has to do with pastoral setting. We have looked at many liturgical forms, but we have also tried to hint at the religious experience that produced them and the patterns of devotion that fed them. Perhaps Dix's antagonism to late medieval piety results from his being so bound up with a liturgical piety that is corporatist, and also somewhat priestly. There is always a gap between what is experienced by the president and the faithful, even though twentieth-century renewal is characterized by noble attempts to make that gap as small as possible. However, to describe any given piety is as slippery as a banana skin; yet it is impossible to think of the anaphora of Addai and Mari without imagining some picture of a small, third-century East Syrian church; to think of the Byzantine anaphora of Basil of Caesarea without imagining the Great Church of Hagia Sophia in Constantinople, with bishops, presbyters, and deacons processing through its great spaces; to think of the *Orate fratres* without imagining a thirteenth-century side altar in a northern French cathedral; to think of a Scandinavian Lutheran rite without imagining a seventeenth-century Danish baroque reredos, the pastor clad in lace-trimmed alb, red velvet chasuble, and white ruff, organ-music wafting like incense from a west gallery. Some of this, and much more, seemed to come together at the World Council of Churches eucharist in Vancouver in 1983. Context can be as important as text, particularly when a text is new or is being reinterpreted.

Context, too, suggests that in an age that has seen an almost unprecedented revival of eucharistic worship, we should, perhaps, beware lest the eucharist become the *only* act of worship that Christians do together. A sacrificial understanding of the eucharist that we are suggesting points to two salient lessons in this regard. One is that sacrifice, so far from embodying a triumphalistic view of the Church, rather expresses its complete dependence on Christ. The eucharistic sacrifice, the offering of the Church, is therefore a *serious* activity of the Church because of the One Offering that provokes the celebration to happen.

Another lesson concerns the view that all worship is sacrificial. Worship and life must live in a creative tension, as Christians strive to relate their vision of the kingdom to what they do from day to day. Noneucharistic worship, including the liturgy of the hours, should enhance the celebration of the eucharist. The offering of daily prayer, however structured or formalized, has so much to provide as a way of feeding the prayer life of ordinary Christians. It can serve as a link between eucharist and the life of service; it can also, perhaps, act as a safeguard against casual attitudes toward the Supper of the Lord. The sacrifice will never be entirely pure in this world. Nevertheless, the *Didache's* warning is an appropriate caution to sound, especially at a time when so many opportunities for spiritual and theological growth appear to be set before us.

The third point relates to the previous one and concerns language. We have noted a wide variety of sacrificial vocabulary, much of which either reflects or gives rise to considerable theological variations in the churches. The scene today is increasingly complex; on the one hand, German Roman Catholics use the word *bringen* (which has softer nuances than the English "offer") in eucharistic prayers, whereas newer churches seek to Christianize deep-rooted pagan words (e.g., Anglicans in Korea). All this serves to show that in liturgy, precise semantic definitions are not really accessible, nor (for that matter) entirely appropriate, especially when central aspects of the sacraments are being "carried" and celebrated in language that, at the end of the day, has to convey the inexpressible and also has to be appropriated by the piety of ordinary people.

5. THE FUTURE OUT OF THE PAST?

It would be easy to end our study on a bland note of confidence that all is well. Certainly it will have become apparent by now that

232

the liturgy through 2,000 years tells a more imprecise and more varied tale concerning eucharistic offering than other developments in theology have shown. But liturgy is not everything. Much depends on how we appropriate the best of Christian tradition and move on into the future in a world in which Christians need no longer be fighting rivals so much as uniting brothers and sisters in a society that knows other creeds. The movement of the Church as it reflects upon the meaning of Christ's death in its eucharistic worship and life will continue, whether in seminar room, sacristy, or social service. Liturgy has to carry the believing life of the Church, however, and one senses that the Lord has indeed set before us an open door. Even though liturgy is an inherently conservative exercise (Basil of Caesarea and Martin Luther worked with established models in their different ways), the models do change and they will continue to change, imperceptibly and self-consciously. That is the way in which liturgy behaves.

Through a study such as ours, however, the relationship between liturgy and the rest of theology comes out variously. It is clear that from the very beginning the Church accepted a general and imprecise notion of sacrifice when speaking of the eucharist. There were few incisive attempts at *defining* it until the time of Augustine, by which era the liturgy had developed from imprecision to a variety of ways of describing the Christian sacrifice of the eucharist. The early Fathers *explain* how the eucharist is sacrificial in a number of different ways, as do the later theologians of the medieval West. The western Reformation, however, forces the need to define closely *how* the eucharist is sacrificial, and *how* it is not, resulting in confident Catholic euchology and piety, and Reformed prayers that preach Calvary to the devout. But at no point, except perhaps in the Continental Reformation, is the influence of the theologian transparent and explicit in the *language* of the liturgy. Sometimes there are hints, as in Zwingli and Bucer. But even they realize that the language of liturgy is not the same as the language of the doctrinal treatise. When liturgy writers have had the chance to comment on their own work, they have done so through a mixture of quotation, allusion, and reflection; a salient example of this is Thurian and Tillard writing of the Lima Report. Other theologians allude to the liturgy in order to explain ideas that may be far from the mind of the original, as in the medieval West and many Anglicans from the seventeenth century onwards.

Indeed, one could take this conclusion further and note how Lutherans and Methodists have been content to include in hymnody theological insights that they have shunned in liturgical prayer. The Danish Lutheran hymnbook contains a composition by Grundtvig with a verse that refers to the eucharist as *takkesangens offerskål*. But the Danish Lutheran Church of the time would have been more than reluctant to include that kind of idea within a prayer recited by the priest.[35] Moreover, the depth of eucharistic spirituality that we have seen in the eucharistic hymns of the Wesleys brings us into a world that many Evangelical Methodists since that time would not wish to enter.

Some theologians have written forcefully against recent liturgical revision.[36] While much liturgical revision can be criticized for its political mechanisms and its lack of firm principles, the problem at issue is really twofold. On the one hand, the critics often display an attachment to older, unliturgical pieties, which may mix strangely with their own (perhaps radical) theology. On the other hand, there is something innately ambiguous about liturgical language, which Aidan Kavanagh has recently alluded to as "part equivocation and part rumor."[37] To go a stage further, one could almost say that liturgy, susceptible as it is to analysis of various kinds, is *its own language*, and the best developments (e.g., in revision) are those produced by an age that is spiritually mature and imaginatively motivated; that means (*inter alia*) one in which the liturgist is taken seriously. The study of origins is of tantamount importance here. While not every liturgist can study the early centuries, these remain the ones to which we have to return. For this writer at any rate, that quest has convinced him that sacrifice is a basic and necessary model for our understanding of the eucharist, but this understanding needs to be made wider than it has appeared in the past. This has been the main reason for our adoption of the three criteria, in order to do justice to the "spiritual sacrifice" of the Lord's Supper.

The ancient East cannot and should not answer all the problems that face the churches of the West, as they go forward in ecumenical dialogue and cooperation among themselves and with the venerable churches of the Orient. But one of the problems that we have inherited in the West is our preoccupation with "magic moments." This has resulted in our failure to understand the internal unity of the eucharistic prayer and our consequent failure to understand the inner dynamic of the eucharistic celebration, even the eucharist itself. From our discussion of the eastern and western liturgies down the ages, it is plain that the three criteria are alive and vibrant, even if from time to time they have become exaggerated or distorted, or deliberately set aside as no longer helpful.

When the story becomes one-sided in the way it is formulated and that story is closely identified with gift (as in the medieval West), then the eucharist begins to take on too many claims for itself and is expected to do more than it can or should, so that response is relegated to a pious psychological reflex. The offering of gift, whether before or during the anaphora, can serve to build up a dubious edifice that also has to carry too much. The real answer to the movement of offering the gifts in the eucharistic prayer is that originally they are offered in remembrance of Christ simply and solely in prayer for consecration (the East) or acceptance (the West). And while "gift" was in our opinion the last of the three to become explicit in the early anaphora, it cannot be denied that many Anglican, Lutheran, Methodist, and Presbyterian traditions have been able to include gift more explicitly within the eucharistic prayer, because that primitive logic, or something resembling it, has been clearly understood in the minds of successive liturgical theologians, drafters, and many others who have been able to live in an increasingly open-minded theological climate. Many Conservative Evangelicals hold out against this recovery, both because of their aversion to the whole notion of gift and also because of their innate fear of seeing the eucharist in dynamic terms. It is also apparent that one of the problems attendant to any solemn presentation of the gifts before the anaphora is that it amounts to an action that is a sitting-duck for the imaginative mystagogue; no wonder some traditions (as we have seen) hastily add self-oblation at the offertory. The East seems to understand things better in adhering to a prayer that looks forward to the anaphora in general terms.

Our conclusion is that the sacrificial metaphor is an appropriate way of describing the eucharist, although like images of Kingdom, Spirit, and Supper, it cannot claim the whole picture. The eucharist is too rich for a one-sided portrait, as historical and systematic studies have shown. But provided that the three criteria are held together in balance and provided that they are understood for what they mean, the eucharist can be seen as sacrificial, supremely because it is celebrated by the Easter community in the shadow of Calvary. What, then, of these criteria?

Story is sacrificial because we are recounting the mighty acts of God as events that have a bearing on us now, so that to recount the story in the eucharist is to proclaim realities that involve commitment by us as God is committed to us in the first place. This is why to "offer thanks" is more than mere verbalization. The conservatism of the liturgy in keeping to the venerable formula, "lift up your hearts," shows that the *eucharistia* has a solemnity about it that marks it off from any other liturgical proclamation. In an age that takes words for granted and analyzes them beyond measure, the sacrifice of proclamation before God is even more important for the eucharistic congregation to enter into and to appropriate.

Gift is also part of the sacrifice because we are feasting in the presence of God. The bread and wine assume a new context by the very fact of being set amid the actions and words of Christ, who is present in the power of the Holy Spirit. Whether or not expressly presented before the eucharistic prayer moves into petition for consecration, the basic intention of the community to be sanctified by solemnly eating and drinking already sets those elements apart. As signs of the faith of the Church and as signs of the fallen and restored creation, they are part of the drama that brings men and women together with God in the world that will one day be finished and completed. Twentieth-century theology's interest in creation and preservation is perhaps a reason why gift has slipped easily into eucharistic spirituality and liturgy.

Response is the work of Christ within us as we express the concerns of the Christian community. This starts with ourselves and often leads into intercession,[38] which is a solemn and sacrificial activity of the whole Church, not an exercise in giving God information. Epiclesis and intercession are linked inextricably, even if intercession comes only at the end of the word liturgy, because to ask for the blessing of the Spirit on the Church's life of faith is to begin to think of the ways in which the Church wishes to plead for that sanctification in specific instances. Charles Gore wrote that "in the self-oblation is the culmination of the sacrifice."[39] Intercession and self-oblation are so much part of the eucharistic action of the Church that they belong together, right at the heart of the celebration of the redeemed humanity, where we eat and drink the gifts of God and celebrate the story of that redemption in bread and wine.

For at the end of the day, it is incongruous, in discourse no less than piety, to separate sacrifice from presence in the eucharist, precisely because the bread and wine are vehicles of God's grace and at the same time are the fruit of destruction and recreation. Thus, bread is the result of crushing and baking corn, just as wine is the result of the fermentation of crushed grapes. Bread and wine alike are therefore intrinsic embodiments of that pattern of dying and living in Christ to which God is drawing us, inevitably, whenever we do this in remembrance of Him.

Notes

CHAPTER ONE

1. See below, pp. 194ff.

2. C. O. Buchanan, *Modern Anglican Liturgies* (Oxford, 1968), pp. 118ff. Colin Buchanan was the dissenter.

3. J. Dowden, *The Annotated Scottish Communion Office* (Oxford, 1922), pp. 161–163. See also below, pp. 149ff., 157ff.

4. P. F. Bradshaw, "The Liturgical Use and Abuse of Patristics," in K. W. Stevenson (ed.) *Liturgy Reshaped*, (SPCK, London, 1982), p. 143.

5. See below pp. 27ff., 38ff. See also K. W. Stevenson, " 'Anaphoral Offering': Some Observations on Eastern Eucharistic Prayers," *EL* 94 (1980), pp. 209–228, esp. pp. 223ff.

6. Charles Wheatly, *A Rational Illustration of the Book of Common Prayer, The Third Edition, Much Enlarg'd and Improv'd* (Rivington, 1720), see Chap. 6. See also K. W. Stevenson, "L'offrande eucharistique: la recherche sur les origines etablit-elle une différence de sens?," *LMD* 154 (1983), p. 37.

7. See below pp. 79ff.

8. See, for example, D. Forrester, J. McDonald, & G. Tellini, *Encounter with God*, (Clark, Edinburgh, 1983), pp. 17ff, compare H. Hubert & M. Mauss, *Sacrifice: Its Nature and Function*, tr. W. D. Halls (Chicago, 1964).

9. *Hom.* 29. 1 in Rom.

10. Gn. 4:1–16.

11. Hos 6:6.

12. *Missale Romanum* (Typis Polyglottis Vaticanis, 1970), praefatio communis IV, p. 436; English translation from *The Sacramentary* (Catholic Book, New York, 1974), p. 453. Source noted by A. Dumas, "Les sources du nouveau Missel Romain," *Notitiae* 60 (1971), p. 40. For this discussion on story, compare David N. Power, *Unsearchable Riches: The Symbolic Nature of Liturgy* (Pueblo, New York, 1984), pp. 108ff.

13. *PEER*, p. 23. See also G. J. Cuming, *Hippolytus—A Text for Students*, *GLS* 8 (Grove Books, 1976), p. 11.

14. *L'offrande*, passim. See also below pp. 45ff.

15. *Anaphoral Offering*, pp. 226–228. See also below pp. 50ff.

16. See below pp. 14ff.

17. K. W. Stevenson, " 'Ye shall pray for. . . .': The Intercession," in *Liturgy Reshaped*, pp. 32–36.

18. *The Book of Common Prayer* (Church Hymnal Corporation/Seabury Press, 1979), p. 375. See also L. L. Mitchell, "The Alexandrian Anaphora of St. Basil of Caesarea: Ancient Source of 'A Common Eucharistic Prayer,' " *ATR* 58 (1976), pp. 194–206.

19. T. J. Talley, "The Eucharistic Prayer: Tradition and Development," in *Liturgy Reshaped*, pp. 59–62. See also K. W. Stevenson, "Preghiere eucaristiche moderne della Communione anglicana," *Rivista Liturgica* 70 (1983), pp. 338ff.

20. See below pp. 22ff., 41ff.

21. J. L. Houlden, "Sacrifice and the Eucharist," in *Explorations in Theology*, (SCM, London, 1978), p. 80.

22. Particularly useful in writing this study have been the seminal works: G. Wain-

wright, *Eucharist and Eschatology* (Epworth, 1971); J. H. McKenna, *Eucharist and Holy Spirit, ACC* 57 (Mayhew-McCrimmon, Great Wakering, 1975); and R. F. Buxton, *Eucharist and Institution Narrative, ACC* 58 (Mayhew-McCrimmon, Great Wakering, 1976). Also, the following articles: H.-J. Schulz, "Structures de l'Eucharistie comme sacrifice et oblation," *LMD* 154 (1983), pp. 59–79; M. Arranz, "L'Economie du Salut dans la prière du Post-Sanctus des anaphores de type antiochéen," *LMD* 105 (1971), pp. 46–75; G. Kretschmar's article on eucharistic sacrifice in the *Theologische Realenzyklopoedie*; M. Green & E. Mascall's "Eucharistic Sacrifice—Some Interim Agreement," in *Growing into Union*, (SPCK, London, 1970), pp. 186–192. I also owe a debt to Gutaf Aulén's work of historical theology, *Eucharist and Sacrifice* (Oliver & Boyd, Edinburgh, 1958), as well as Hans Lietzmann's classic study of the eucharist, *Mass and Lord's Supper: A Study in the History of the Liturgy*, 11 fascicles (Brill, Leiden, 1953–1979).

CHAPTER TWO

1. A. J. B. Higgins, *The Lord's Supper in the New Testament*, Studies in Biblical Theology 6 (SCM, London, 1952), esp. pp. 24ff.

2. J. Jeremias, *The Eucharistic Words of Jesus* (SCM, London, 1966), pp. 249–255; see also D. R. Jones, "ἀναμνῆσις in the LXX and the Interpretation of I Cor. 11:25," *JTS* 6 (1955), pp. 183–91; see also F. L. Cirlot, *The Early Eucharist* (SPCK, London, 1939), pp. 222–225 on the dynamic interpretation of ποιεῖτε.

3. Jeremias, op. cit., pp. 237ff.

4. G. Dix, *The Apostolic Tradition of St. Hippolytus*, Church Historical Society, (SPCK, London, 1937), pp. 73–75; "Words like 'memorial,' 'remembrance,' etc. have for us a connotation of a purely mental and subjective recollection of something in fact *absent*. ἀναμνῆσις has on the contrary the sense of bringing before God something which has happened in the past in such a way that its *consequences take effect in the present*." Dix repeated this notion in other of his publications.

5. D. Gregg, *Anamnesis in the Eucharist, GLS* 5 (Grove Books, 1976), passim.

6. B. Lindars, *Jesus Son of Man* (SPCK, London, 1983), pp. 76ff.

7. R. Daly, *The Origins of the Christian Doctrine of Sacrifice* (Darton, Longman and Todd, 1978), pp. 1–4 (summary); the longer version of this book is *Christian Sacrifice, SCA* 18 (Catholic University of America, Washington, D. C., 1978).

8. W. Sanday, A. C. Headlam, *The Epistle to the Romans*, International Critical Commentary (T. & T. Clark, Edinburgh, 1895), p. 352.

9. Daly, *Christian Sacrifice*, pp. 276–285 (on the letter to the Hebrews); but Daly's notion of "spiritualization" is not without its critics, e.g. H. A. Attridge, review in *Journal of Biblical Literature* 100 (1981), pp. 145–147.

10. R. K. Yerkes, *Sacrifice in Greek and Roman Religions and Early Judaism* (Scribner, New York, 1952), pp. 150ff; this sacrifice was partly burnt, partly consumed.

11. The literature on the Jewish background to the eucharist is vast. Here are the main studies. L. Ligier, "From the Last Supper to the Eucharist," in L. C. Sheppard (ed.), *The New Liturgy* (Darton, Longman, and Todd, 1970), pp. 113–150; L. Ligier, "The Origins of the Eucharistic Prayer," *SL* 9 (1973), pp. 161–185; T. J. Talley, "The Eucharistic Prayer of the Ancient Church According to Recent Research: Results and Reflections," *SL* 11 (1976), pp. 138–158; H. Cazelles, "L'Anaphore et L'Ancien Testament," *Eucharisties d'Orient et d'Occident I*, Lex Orandi 46 (Éditions du Cerf, Paris, 1970), pp. 11–21. Texts in *PEER*, pp. 9–10 and *PE*, pp. 5–57.

12. P. F. Bradshaw, *Daily Prayer in the Early Church, ACC* 63 (SPCK, London, 1981), pp. 1ff.

13. J. Laporte, *La doctrine eucharistique chez Philon d'Alexandrie*, Théologie Historique

16 (Beauchesne, Paris, 1972), passim.; see also R. J. Ledogar, *Acknowledgment: Praise-Verbs in the Early Greek Anaphora* (Herder, Rome, 1968), pp. 119ff.

14. Talley, "The Eucharistic Prayer of the Ancient Church," pp. 155–157.

15. F. Young, *Sacrifice and the Death of Christ* (SPCK, London, 1975); the longer version is *The Use of Sacrificial Ideas in Greek Christian Writers from the New Testament to John Chrysostom* (Philadelphia, 1979).

16. H. Ringgren, *Israelite Religion* (SPCK, London, 1966), pp. 166ff.

17. A. M. Ramsey, *Jesus and the Living Past* (Oxford, 1980), p. 65.

18. E.g., Tob 12:8ff.; conversation with Prof. Barnabas Lindars: see above n. 13.

19. Young, *Sacrifice and the Death of Christ*, pp. 64ff.

20. Texts in *PEER*, pp. 14–16; *PE*, pp. 66–68. See also Talley, "The Eucharistic Prayer of the Ancient Church," pp. 146–150; J. P. Audet, *La Didachè: Instructions des Apôtres* (Librairie Lecoffre, Paris, 1958), pp. 372–424, 458–467; W. Rordorf & A. Tuilier, *La Doctrine des Douze Apôtres*, SC 248 (Editions du Cerf, Paris, 1978), pp. 38–48, 63–80, and critical text, pp. 174–183, 192–193.

21. Rordorf & Tuilier, *La Doctrine*, pp. 70ff; cf. S. Giet, *L'Énigme de la Didachè* (Editions Ophyrs, Paris, 1970), pp. 232–234.

22. J. Hazelden Walker, "Reflections on a New Edition of the Didache," *Vigiliae Christianae* 35, 1981, pp. 35–42; and "A pre-Marcan dating for the Didache," *Studia Biblica* (1978), pp. 403–411.

23. R. P. C. Hanson, *Eucharistic Offering in the Early Church*, GLS 19 (Grove Books, 1979), passim.

24. *PEER*, p. 40; *PE*, pp. 130–131 (Serapion); and *PEER*, p. 45, *PE*, pp. 126–127 (Deir Balyzeh papyrus).

25. R. Williams, *Eucharistic Sacrifice—The Roots of a Metaphor*, GLS 31 (Grove Books 1982), p. 15.

26. See Williams, *Eucharistic Sacrifice*, p. 13 n. 5; compare Daly, *Christian Sacrifice*, pp. 147–148. See C. Mohrmann, "Rationabilis-ΛΟΓΙΚΟΣ", *Revue Internationale des Droits de L'Antiquite* 5 (1950), pp. 225–234; but "reasonable" is the translation adapted by Jasper and Cuming in Ambrose and the Canon, see below, pp. 25f.

27. Acts 7:42, Heb 10:4, Mt 8:4.

28. E.g., Charles Hodge, *Commentary on Romans (1838)* (Banner of Truth, 1972), p. 384; but for the more dynamic view, compare R. J. McKelvey, *The New Temple* (Oxford Theological Monographs, Oxford University), 1969; I am indebted to the Rev. Martin Kitchen for drawing my attention to this point.

29. 1 Clement 44:4.

30. Williams, *Eucharistic Sacrifice*, pp. 18–20. The relevant texts in Ignatius are *Eph.* 9, *Magn.* 7, *Trall.* 7, *Philad.* 9, *Smyrn.* 6–7, *Rom.* 2.4.

31. Texts in *PEER*, pp. 18–20, and *PE*, pp. 68–75; quotation from 1 *Ap.* 63, 3; see also *Dialogue* 41,1–3; 117,1–3 (*PEER*, pp. 17–18).

32. Gregory Dix, *The Shape of the Liturgy* (New York, 1982), p. 150.

33. E.g., Origen, *In Joannem* 28, 6.

34. Tr. from Hanson, *Eucharistic Offering*, p. 9.

35. Williams, *Eucharistic Sacrifice*, p. 9.

36. See below pp. 69–70.

37. *De Oratione* 28, 3,4; tr. Hanson, *Eucharistic Offering*, p. 11, and Mark Santer.

38. See discussion in Hanson, *Eucharistic Offering*, pp. 11f., esp. p. 11, n. 40, where Hanson gives several citations, including *De Praescr. Haer.* 40:4; *Ad Uxorem*, II. 8:6; *De Exhort. Cast.* 10.5.

39. But cf. Young's three different kinds of sacrifice, outlined in *Sacrifice and the Death*

of Christ, pp. 21ff.; she tries to work this thesis on early eucharistic references in *The Use of Sacrificial Ideas in Greek Christian Writers from the New Testament to John Chrysostom*, pp. 239–284. Noteworthy in this discussion is her criticism of Dix's anamnesis theology (p. 278, n. 112).

40. Texts in *PEER*, pp. 22–25 (Bibliography on p. 21); *PE*, pp. 80–81; and Cuming, *Hippolytus: A Text for Students*, p. 11.

41. Tr. from *PEER*, p. 23; see B. Botte, *La Tradition Apostolique de saint Hippolyte*, LQF 39 (Aschendorff, Münster, 1963), pp. 16–17; see also G. J. Cuming (ed.), *Essays on Hippolytus*, GLS 15 (Grove Books 1978), pp. 47–50.

42. Dix, *The Apostolic Tradition of St. Hippolytus*, p. 9 and note; cf. B. Botte, "L'épiclèse de l'anaphore d'Hippolyte," *Recherches de théologie ancienne et médiévale* 14 (1947), pp. 241–251.

43. Dix, *The Shape of the Liturgy*, p. 264; cf. L. Ligier, "The Origins of the Eucharistic Prayer," *SL* 9 (1973), pp. 179–182.

44. *L'offrande*, pp. 22ff.; see also E. Mazza, "Omelie pasquali e birkat ha-mazon: fonti dell' anafora di Ippolito?," *EL* 97 (1983), pp. 454f. (whole article, pp. 409–481).

45. *L'offrande*, pp. 22f. & 35.; cf. "As an invocation on behalf of the worshippers, not specifying the effect on the elements, it seems quite plausible," Cuming, *Hippolytus* p. 11n.

46. See Hanson, *Eucharistic Offering*, p. 13, on Hippolytus.

47. *PE*, p. 221.

48. See below pp. 58ff.

49. W. H. Frere, *The Primitive Consecration Prayer*, Alcuin Club Prayer Book Revision Pamphlets VIII (Mowbrays, 1922), p. 12.

50. E.g. M. J. Moreton, *Made Fully Perfect* (Church Literature Assn., 1974), pp. 19–23, part of a critique of the Draft Series 3 rite for the Church of England.

51. See below our discussion of the use of participle in anamnesis-offering verb, p. 40 (and n. 7).

52. Text with notes, B. D. Spinks, *Addai and Mari—The Anaphora of the Apostles: A Text for Students*, GLS 24 (Grove Books, 1980); texts also in *PEER*, pp. 26–28, and *PE*, pp 375–380 (with *cushapas*). The two most important studies of Addai and Mari are W. F. Macomber, "The Oldest Known Text of the Anaphora of the Apostles Addai and Mari," *OCP* 32 (1966), pp. 335–371; and B. D. Spinks, "The Original Form of the Anaphora of the Apostles," in *EL* 91 (1977), pp 146–161.

53. E. C. Ratcliff, "The Original Form of the Anaphora of Addai and Mari: a Suggestion," *JTS* 30 (1928), pp. 23–32 (= A. H. Couratin & D. H. Tripp (eds.), *E. C. Ratcliff: Liturgical Studies* [SPCK, London, 1976], pp. 80–90).

54. *L'offrande*, p. 27 (correcting *Anaphoral Offering*, pp. 220–221); agreed with by B. D. Spinks, "Eucharistic Offering in the East Syrian Anaphoras," *OCP* 50 (1984), pp. 347–371.

55. *Sermo de Domino nostro*, 50, tr. Williams, *Eucharistic Sacrifice*, p. 21 (where the similarity with Addai and Mari dialogue is not noted).

56. Text in Spinks, *Addai and Mari*, p. 18.

57. Text in Spinks, *Addai and Mari*, pp. 20–22; Addai and Mari's use of "altar" can be paralleled with Ignatius, cf. Williams, *Eucharistic Sacrifice*, pp. 18–20.

58. Text in *PEER*, p. 29; *PE*, p. 410. For a discussion of this formula, see Talley, "The Eucharistic Prayer of the Ancient Church," *SL* 11 (1976), pp. 152–153.

59. Strenuously argued (for authenticity) by Spinks, "The Original Form of the Anaphora of the Apostles" (see n. 52). This view is now shared by W. F. Macomber, "The Ancient Form of the Anaphora of the Apostles," in *East of Byzantium, Syria and Armenia*

in the Formative Period (Dumbarton Oaks, Washington, D. C., 1982) pp. 73–88; and also by Talley, "The Eucharistic Prayer: Tradition and Development," in K. W. Stevenson (ed.), *Liturgy Reshaped*, pp. 48–64.

60. See below pp. 58f., 45ff.

61. See above n. 57.

62. See B. Botte, "L'Anaphore Chaldéenne des Apôtres," *OCP* 15 (1949), pp. 259–276.

63. See Talley, "The Eucharistic Prayer of the Ancient Church," pp. 152–155. An original contribution to the debate about the institution narrative concentrates on its *function* within the eucharistic prayer, H. Manders, "Sens et fonction du récit de l'Institution," *QLP* (1972), pp. 203–218, esp. pp. 208–212.

64. See above n. 54, art. cit.

65. Texts in *PEER*, p. 43 (but NB, mistaken omission of "sacrifice" after "reasonable," restored in our text), and *PE*, pp. 116–117.

66. See below pp. 53ff.

67. The most important study is by G. J. Cuming, "The Anaphora of St. Mark: A Study in Development," *Muséon* 95 (1982), pp. 115–129. Other studies include W. H. Bates, "Thanksgiving and Intercession in the Liturgy of St. Mark," in B. D. Spinks (ed.), *The Sacrifice of Praise* (C.L.V., Rome, 1981), pp. 107–119; and H. A. J. Wegman, "Une Anaphore Incomplète?," in R. Van Den Broek & M. J. Vermaseren (eds.), *Studies in Gnosticism and Hellenistic Religions* (Leiden, 1981), pp. 434–450. But see also B. D. Spinks, "A Complete Anaphora? A Note on *Strasbourg Gr. 254*," *Heythrop Journal* 25 (1984), pp. 51–59.

68. See above n. 26. See also M. H. Shepherd, "Eusebius and the Liturgy of St. James," *Yearbook of Liturgical Studies* 4 (1963), pp. 116f.

69. Athenagoras, *Legatio* 13.2; Methodius, *Symposium* 5.6; Origen, *Contra Celsum*, 8.21. A case could be made out for Athenagoras (if not also Methodius and Origen) having concern with *pagan* sacrifice, and the need to define Christian worship.

70. Cuming, "The Anaphora of St. Mark," pp. 119–121. I would further suggest translating "over" as "through," which is just possible with the Greek; compare with *sharar*, for which, see below p. 58, quotation 4.

71. *Anaphoral Offering*, pp. 226–228.

72. R.-G. Coquin, "L'anaphore alexandrine de saint Marc," *Muséon* 82 (1969), pp. 313, 317, 321f., 338, 342.

73. See below pp. 72, 78, 107f., 184ff.

74. J. Doresse & E. Lanne, *Un temoin archaïque de la liturgie copte de saint Basile*, Bibliothèque du Muséon 47 (Louvain, 1960); the text is to be found on pp. 14–33, consisting of the anaphora from just before the institution narrative to the Lord's Prayer just after the anaphora; B. Capelle included a study of the later Alexandrian version and the Byzantine version, comparing them with writings from Basil himself (pp. 45–74), stopping short of the institution narrative. See also John R. K. Fenwick, "An Investigation into the Common Origin of the Anaphoras of the Liturgies of St. Basil and St. James," Ph.D. dissertation, University of Bristol, 1985.

75. A. Raes, "Un nouveau document de la liturgie de S. Basile," *OCP* 26 (1960), pp. 401–411.

76. See Capelle's contribution, n. 74; see also H. Engberding, *Das eucharistische Hochgebet der Basileiosliturgie*, Textgeschichtliche Untersuchungen und kritische Ausgabe (Ashendorff, Münster, 1931).

77. Cf. "It remains outside the Trinitarian and Christological controversies, and is based on an epiphany theology of Christ . . . ," A. Houssiau, "The Alexandrine Anaphora of St. Basil," in *The New Liturgy*, p. 243. This also means that here we have at least

one anaphoral tradition whose *full* structure goes back to before the Council of Nicaea, and probably much earlier still. On the development of salvation history as a theme in the eastern anaphoras in general, see José Manuel Sánchez Caro, *Eucaristía e Historia de la Salvación,* Biblioteca de Autores Cristianos (Madrid, 1983). He also treats sacrifice in a wider manner than has been usual.

78. Texts in *PEER,* pp. 36f, and also Doresse/Lanne, *Un temoin archaïque de la liturgie copte de saint Basile,* pp. 21, 24ff. See also K. W. Stevenson, " 'Ye Shall Pray For': the Intercession," in *Liturgy Reshaped,* pp. 46f.

79. Text in *PEER,* p. 35. See below pp. 53, 58.

80. Text in *PEER,* p. 36.

81. Doresse & Lanne, *Un temoin archaïque de la liturgie copte de saint Basile,* p. 21; see *Anaphoral Offering,* pp. 225–227 and *L'offrande,* pp. 23ff.

82. Raes, "Un nouveau document de la liturgie de S. Basile," pp. 403f. But the earliest Byzantine version of Basil has the present participle form (see below p. 40). Are we to assume that Basil brought this with him from Cappadocia? Our preference is to adhere to the aorist reading, however it is to be interpreted; Gregory Dix was criticized for altering texts to suit his inclinations (see above n. 42) and it would be hazardous for us to follow suit, particularly as it would involve an alteration of *verb* as well as *tense.*

83. See below pp. 38ff.

84. Text in S. Brock & M. Vasey, *The Liturgical Portions of the Didascalia,* GLS 29 (Grove Books, 1982), p. 11 (Chapter 9); see also "offer the oblation" (Chapter 12), p. 16, of celebrating the eucharist; see below n. 99.

85. Text in Brock & Vasey, *The Liturgical Portions of the Didascalia,* p. 15 (Chapter 11); cf. "offer the oblation," Chapter 12.

86. Ibid., p. 3.

87. *Contra Celsum* 8.33; tr. Hanson, *Eucharistic Offering,* p. 16.

88. *Hom. in Leviticus* 9.1; tr. H. Bettenson, *The Early Christian Fathers* (Oxford, 1969), p. 251.

89. *Letters,* 14:4; tr. Hanson, *Eucharistic Offering,* p. 19.

90. J. Laurance, "Le président de l'Eucharistie selon Cyprien de Carthage: un nouvel éxamen," *LMD* 154, 1983, pp. 151–165 (an extract of Ph.D. dissertation, University of Notre Dame, Indiana, 1983). Laurance's main thesis is a discussion of the use of liturgical words in Cyprian; his interpretation of the passage quoted by Hanson (Letters 14.4) is that Cyprian begins by referring to the sacrifice of Christ, and only then refers to the eucharist.

91. *Dialogue* 41.1, 70.4, 117.3.

92. *Symposium* 3.8; discussed by O. Casel, *La Fête de Pâques dans l'Eglise des Pères,* Lex. Orandi 37 (Editions du Cerf, Paris, 1963), p. 80 (= Fr. tr. of *Art und Sinn der Ältesten Christlichen Österfeier* [Aschendorff, Münster 1938]).

93. *Demonstratio Evangelica* 1.38 (49); tr. Hanson, *Eucharistic Offering,* p. 22.

94. Williams, *Eucharistic Sacrifice,* pp. 21–23.

95. See above n. 55.

96. E.g. in Justin Martyr, of prayer, *Dialogue* 117.2.

97. Hence I disagree with H.-J. Schulz's assertion that Syro-Byzantine *and* Alexandrian anaphoras all have present-tense offering in anamnesis, art. cit., p. 69.

98. Compare with E. Mascall's view that eucharistic presence emerged out of eucharistic sacrifice (and not vice versa) in this period, *Corpus Christi,* Longmans, 1965, 2nd. ed., pp. 50ff.

99. But the *Didascalia Apostolorum* uses the term "offer the oblation," which may well refer to the *whole* eucharist, see above n. 84: this could be a "Syriac symptom," along

the lines of our interpretation of *Addai and Mari*. In general, see Power, op. cit., p. 137; on the "transfer" of Old Testament sacrificial terms "back to Christian worship."

CHAPTER THREE

1. *DS* I, p. 132.
2. See above Chapter 2, nn. 74, 76, 78. Text in *PE*, pp. 347–355 (*PEER* only gives the first part because Basil Alex[1] lacks this, pp. 34f.).
3. See above Chapter 2, n. 75.
4. On the meaning and development of this phrase, see A. Raes," ΚΑΤΑ ΠΑΝΤΑ ΚΑΙ ΔΙΑ ΠΑΝΤΑ—en tout et pour tout," *OC* 48 (1964), pp. 216–220.
5. Text in *PEER*, pp. 98–104; *PE*, pp. 230–243. Parallel texts of Basil Byz and Chrysostom (Barberini 336/Grottaferrata G b VII and Barberini 336, respectively) in *LEW*, pp. 321–337. Reconstructed compendium of all three versions, in different typescripts, in L. Bouyer, *Eucharist* (Notre Dame, 1968), pp. 292–296.
6. See above Chapter 2, p. 25.
7. But it appears in the modern ecumenical version, produced by a study group in the U. S.: see below pp. 207f. From conversations with members of this group, the deliberate use of the participle (reverting to an earlier tradition than current Greek usage) did involve *some* desire to "soften" the offering verb, but this is a quite different matter from the more organic development we are noting now.
8. This rests on the assumption that the narrative is part of the *thanksgiving*, and the epiclesis is part of the *supplication* in the eucharistic prayer. The Latin mind, however, is capable of discerning theological insufficiency in eastern euchology, as witness J. M. Hanssens' disquiet over the past-tense offering verb in Egypt, *Institutiones Liturgicae de Ritibus Orientalibus*, III, (Rome, 1932), p. 365.
9. H. Engberding, "Die syrische Anaphora der zwölf Apostel und ihre Paralleltexte," *OC* 3 (1937), pp. 213–247. But this has been challenged by G. Wagner, *Der Ursprung der Chrysostomusliturgie*, *LQF* 59 (Aschendorff, Münster 1973), pp. 43–50.
10. Text in *PEER*, pp. 89–91; *PE*, pp. 224–229.
11. The Coptic version of Mark keeps "sacrifice" after "reasonable," although the Greek version does not; see below pp. 53f.
12. Compare Armenian Ignatius, pp. 67ff.
13. Text in *PEER*, pp. 61–69; *PE*, pp. 244–261.
14. Compare J. H. McKenna, *Eucharist and Holy Spirit*, pp. 33–35; see also (in general) B. D. Spinks, "The Consecratory Epiclesis in the Anaphora of St. James," *SL* 11 (1976), pp. 19–38.
15. For the Syriac versions, see A. Raes, *Anaphorae Syriacae*, II, 2 (Rome, 1953), pp. 29–43; and *Renaudot* II, pp. 126–133. One of the manuscripts of the longer version reads present participle offering verb in anamnesis. On Armenian James, see below pp. 65f.
16. Texts in *PEER*, pp. 71–78; *PE*, pp. 82–95. The use of θυσία at the epiclesis may be a Syriac symptom.
17. R. C. D. Jasper, *The Search for an Apostolic Liturgy*, Alcuin Club Pamphlet XVIII, (Mowbrays, 1963). See below pp. 162ff., 179ff.
18. Text in *PE*, pp. 387–396; see the important article by B. D. Spinks, "Eucharistic Offering in the East Syrian Anaphoras." See also B. H. Jones, "The Formation of the Nestorian Liturgy," *ATR* 48 (1966), pp. 276–306.
19. See pp. 18f., 39f.
20. This may be an indirect source for the words "which we now offer unto thee" in the Scottish Liturgy of 1764; see below pp. 165f.

21. Spinks, art. cit., p. 361.

22. Spinks, art. cit., p. 362.

23. *L'offrande*, pp. 27–28.

24. F. E. Brightman, "The Anaphora of Theodore," *JTS* 31 (1930), pp. 160–164; Wagner, op. cit., pp. 51–63.

25. Text in *PE*, pp. 381–386. See also Spinks, art. cit.

26. Spinks, art. cit., p. 371.

27. Text in *PEER*, pp. 39–41; *PE*, pp. 128–133. See also F. E. Brightman, "The Sacramentary of Serapion of Thmuis," *JTS* 1 (1900), pp. 88–113; B. Botte, "L'Euchologe de Sérapion, est-il authentique?," *OC* 48 (1964), pp. 50–57; B. Capelle, "L'Anaphore de Sérapion: Essai d'exégèse," *Muséon* 59 (1946), pp. 425–443 (= *Travaux Liturgiques*, II) (Louvain, 1962), pp. 344–358; for a modern rehabilitation, see G. J. Cuming, "Thmuis Revisited: Another Look at the Prayers of Bishop Serapion," *Theological Studies* 41 (1980), pp. 568–575.

28. Capelle, *Travaux Liturgiques* II, p. 349; compare P. Rodopoulos, *The Sacramentary of Serapion* (Thessaloniki, 1967), p. 81. See also *Anaphoral Offering*, p. 226.

29. See above p. 26.

30. Texts in *PEER*, pp. 43–46 (Strasbourg, British Museum, Deir Balyzeh and Louvain Coptic) and *PE*, pp. 116–127 (Strasbourg, John Rylands, Deir Balyzeh); see also for bibliographies, but add Cuming, "The Anaphora of Mark." For full text, see *PEER*, pp. 48–54; *PE*, pp. 102–115 (Greek), pp. 135–139 (Latin tr. of Coptic); see C. A. Swainson, *The Greek Liturgies* (London, 1884), p. 31, for *Codex Rossanensis's* use of incense at start of intercessions.

31. Cuming, art. cit., pp. 118–121.

32. See Chapter 7, n. 87.

33. See Chapter 2, n. 72.

34. *Anaphoral Offering*, p. 226; *L'Offrande*, pp. 33–35.

35. G. Dix, *The Shape of the Liturgy*, pp. 227–228.

36. This is the implication of R.-G. Coquin, "L'anaphore alexandrine de saint Marc," *Eucharisties d'Orient et d'Occident*, II, pp. 51–82.

37. Text in *PE*, pp. 358–373. See also A. Gerhards, *Die griechische Gregoriosanaphora: Ein Beitrag zur Geschichte des Eucharistichen Hochgebets*, LQF 65 (Aschendorff, Münster, 1984), pp. 22–49 (text), and discussion of passages referred to in our discussion, p. 55 (Pre-Sanctus), pp. 79f. (Post-Sanctus), and pp. 83f. and 230 (anamnesis), where Gerhards notes cultic language of sacrifice. For the Jungmann theory, see pp. 176–179 (description) and pp. 238–242, 247–249 (rebuttal).

38. Text in *PE*, pp. 144–149.

39. Text in *PE*, pp. 150–152.

40. Text in *PE*, pp. 153–159; see also *Anaphoral Offering*, p. 224.

41. See *Anaphoral Offering*, p. 224.

42. Text in *PEER*, pp. 29–33; *PE* pp. 410–415; see also critical text, J.-M. Sauget, *Anaphorae Syriacae*, II, 3 (Rome 1972), pp. 284–323 (alternative incense prayer, pp. 324f). See also B. D. Spinks, "The original form of the Anaphora of the Apostles."

43. As suggested by Spinks, "Eucharistic Offering in the East Syrian Anaphoras."

44. Text in *PEER*, pp. 93–96; *PE*, pp. 265–268. Wagner's suggestion that it is a later adaptation of Chrysostom fits in with our study of the offering material; see above n. 9. On the various Syrian Jacobite/Maronite anaphoras, see Hanssens, op. cit., pp. 598–615, though this is dated in parts.

45. Text in *PE*, pp. 306–309.

46. Text in *Renaudot* II, pp. 163–169.

47. Compare with John Patriarch of Antioch, text in *Renaudot* II, pp. 475f.

48. Text in *Renaudot* II, pp. 261–267; compare with Armenian Ignatius, p. 67ff.

49. E. Lanne, *Le Grand Euchologe du Monastère Blanc*, Patrologia Orientalis XXVIII, 2, 1958, pp. 304–309; see also H. W. Codrington, *Anaphorae Syriacae*, III, 1 (Rome, 1981), pp. 12–42.

50. Themes from Heb. 8 and 9; see *Anaphoral Offering*, pp. 215f.

51. Text in H. G. Codrington, *Anaphorae Syriacae* I, 2 (Rome, 1940), pp. 158–201.

52. Text in A. Raes, *Anaphorae Syriacae* II, 3 (Rome, 1972), pp. 336–351. Raes' anxiety is expressed on p. 333.

53. Reference to the eucharist as "mysteries" also appears in Marutas of Tagrit (text in *Renaudot* II, p. 263) and Mark (text in *Renaudot* II, p. 179).

54. Text in *Renaudot* II, pp. 448–451.

55. Texts in *Renaudot* II, pp. 301–304 and pp. 310–316.

56. Text in W. de Vries, *Anaphorae Syriacae* I, 3 (Rome, 1944), pp. 272–279.

57. Text in A. Raes, *Anaphorae Syriacae* III, 1 (Rome, 1981), pp. 52–71.

58. Compare with Holy Doctors, text in *Renaudot* II, p. 413, where a similar expression is to be found in the epiclesis, as a benefit of communion.

59. Text in H. G. Codrington, *Anaphorae Syriacae* I, 1 (Rome, 1939), pp. 49–96.

60. Text in A. Rücker, *Anaphorae Syriacae* I, 1 (Rome, 1939), pp. 1–47; Timothy also separates anamnesis and oblation, for which, compare Chapter 7, n. 97 (*Anaphoral Offering*, p. 214).

61. Text in A. Raes, *Anaphorae Syriacae* II, 1 (Rome, 1951), pp. 92–103.

62. Text in *PE*, pp. 310–314.

63. Compare with some Armenian anaphoras, see pp. 65ff. This feature (and the following seven) are outlined in *L'offrande*, pp. 31f.

64. See above pp. 45ff.

65. H.-J. Schulz, *The Byzantine Liturgy*, Eng. trans. M. J. O'Connell, (Pueblo, New York, 1986) pp. 34ff.; G. Dix, *The Shape of the Liturgy*, pp. 264ff. Compare R. F. Taft, "Historicism Revisited," *SL* 14 (1982), pp. 97–109.

66. *Anaphoral Offering*, p. 228.

67. The classic work is on initiation, G. Winkler, *Das Armenische Initiationsrituale*, OCA 217 (Rome, 1982).

68. Text in *PE*, pp. 342–346; and (with study) A. Baumstark, "Denkmäler altarmenischer Messliturgie 3: Die armenische Rezension der Jakobusliturgie," *OC* 7–8 (1918), pp. 1–32. On the offering verb, see J.-P. Montmimy, "L'offrande sacrificielle dans l'anamnèse des liturgies anciennes," *Revue des sciences philosophiques et théologiques* 50 (1966), p. 393, n. 28; the whole article (pp. 385–406) is a useful summary of some offering material in early anaphoras.

69. Text in *PE*, pp. 337–341; and (with study) A. Rücker, "Denkmäler altarmenischer Messliturgie 4: Die Anaphora des Patriarches Kyrillos von Alexandreia," *OC* 3, (1926), pp. 143–157.

70. Text in *PE*, pp. 332–336; and (with study) P. Ferhat, "Denkmäler altarmenischer Messliturgie 2: Die angebliche Liturgie des hl. Katholikos Sahak," *OC* 3 (1913), pp. 16–31.

71. Text in *PE*, pp. 320–326, and *LEW*, pp. 435–444; this is the only anaphora still in use among Armenians.

72. Text in *PE*, pp. 327–331; and (with study) P. Ferhat, "Denkmäler altarmenischer Messliturgie 1: Eine dem hl. Gregor von Nazianz zugeschriebene Liturgie," *OC* 1 (1911), pp. 204–214. See also G. Winkler, "Zur Geschichte des armenischen Gottesdienstes im

Hinblick auf den in mehreren Wellen erfolgten grieschischen Einfluss," *OC* 58 (1974), pp. 157–161.

73. Text in French tr., A. Renoux, "L'anaphore arménienne de saint Grégoire l'Illuminateur," in *Eucharisties d'Orient et d'Occident* II, pp. 89–104.

74. Text (with study) in A. Rücker, "Denkmäler altarmenischer Messliturgie 5: Die anaphora des hl. Ignatius von Antiochen," *OC* 5 (1930), pp. 56–79.

75. This is the basic interpretation also taken by H.-J. Schulz, *Ökumenische Glaubenseinheit aus eucharistischer Überlieferung*, Konfessionskundliche und kontroverstheologische Studien 39 (Paderborn, 1976), esp. pp. 20–22. Schulz's work was subsequently reviewed in *OCP* 44 (1978), pp. 273–308 by B. Schultze, which Schulz in turn answered in two articles, "Liturgischer Vollzug und sakramentale Wirklichkeit des eucharistischen Opfers," *OCP* 45 (1979), pp. 245–266, and *OCP* 46 (1980), pp. 5–19. The issue between the two is the nature of the eucharistic offering. Schulz, rightly in our view, associates the offering in the Greek West Syrian type of anaphora with memorial, in a close fashion; for him the two are inextricably bound together. Schultze, on the other hand, attempts to assert a more Latin mentality on the eastern texts. Apart from the question of theological interpretation, there is also the issue of historical development; if the narrative-anamnesis is a later addition to an anaphora which consists of thanksgiving and supplication (preface and epiclesis), then it is hardly possible to trace a primitive oblation at an early date and invest it with great theological weight. See *Anaphoral Offering*, p. 210: "in recalling the saving acts of Christ, we offer the gifts to God, and ask him to send the Holy Spirit upon them." See also G. Ramis, "El memorial eucharistico," *EL* 96 (1982), pp. 200ff., where the same point is made.

76. See below pp. 76ff.

77. See above pp. 22ff. (Addai and Mari) and below pp. 48ff. (Nestorius and Theodore). But see J. M. Sánchez Caro, "La anáfora de Addai y Mari y la anáfora meronita šarrar: intento de reconstrucción de la fuente primitiva común," *OCP* 43 (1977), pp. 41–69. Sánchez Caro's reconstruction of Addai and Mari includes both narrative and anamnesis.

78. Lecture 5, The Eucharist; 7 and 8. Text in *PEER*, p. 58; *PE*, pp. 208–209.

79. G. J. Cuming, "Egyptian Elements in the Jerusalem Liturgy," *JTS* 25 (1974), pp. 117–124. This view has been countered by B. D. Spinks, "The Jerusalem Liturgy of the Catecheses Mystagogicae: Syrian or Egyptian?," a paper read at the International Conference on Patristic Studies, Oxford, September 1983.

80. But the preposition could also be translated "through"; see Chapter 2, n. 70.

81. Text in *PE*, pp. 210–213.

82. Text in *PEER*, pp. 86–87; *PE*, pp. 214–218 (full); see F. J. Reine, *The Eucharistic Doctrine and Liturgy of the Mystagogical Catecheses of Theodore of Mopsuestia*, SCA 2 (Catholic University of America, Washington, D. C., 1942), pp. 55–72, esp. pp. 58–72. Narsai uses similar language. In Homily XVII, "the priest now *offers* the mystery," and in Homily XXI, "with the *oblation* the priest *sends up* the prayer of the people" see R. H. Connolly (ed.), *The Liturgical Homilies of Narsai*, Texts and Studies VIII, 1 (Cambridge, 1909), pp. 7, 57. (Before the anaphora, the priest "asks prayer of the deacons that are round about him, that by his humility he may receive mercy from the merciful," Homily XVII, Connolly, op. cit., pp. 7–8); this parallels both the *Cushapa* tradition (see Spinks, art. cit., Chapter 5, n. 34, and text) and the response to the priest's bidding for prayer before the anaphora in James and the East Syrian liturgy; see below pp. 66–67.

83. *Ep.* 93; tr. H. Bettenson, *The Later Christian Fathers* (Oxford, 1970), p. 89.

84. *Or.* 26.16; *Or.* 2.95; tr. Bettenson, op. cit., pp. 123, 124.

85. *De prod. Jud.* 1.6; *Hom.* 17 in *Heb.* 3; tr. Bettenson, op. cit., pp. 173, 174. NB the

language of "completion," as in Basil; this also occurs in the second epiclesis of Greek Mark; it does not occur in any of the Greek West Syrian anaphoras, and is a yet more cultic expression for "celebrate the eucharist" than the formula "offer gifts." A full list of Chrysostom's liturgical allusions is not possible here, but on the theme of sacrifice, see *In Matt. Hom.* 25/26.3 and 82/83.4; *In Ep. I ad Cor. Hom.* 24, 5 and 41, 4–5; *In Ep. II ad Cor. Hom.* 2, 5 and 20, 3; and *Vidi Dominum* 6.2, 3, and 4. See Frans Van de Paverd, *Zur Geschichte der Messliturgie in Antiocheia und Konstantinopel gegen Ende des Vierten Jahrhunderts*, OCA 187 (Rome 1970), passim. In the last cited text (*Vidi Dominum* 6.4), the verb is as Basil Alex[1] and Greek Mark—$\pi\rho o\epsilon\theta\dot{\eta}\kappa\alpha\mu\epsilon\nu$.

86. *In Ps. 109 (110)*.4; *interpr. in XIV epp. S. Pauli; in Heb.* 8.4; tr. Bettenson, op. cit., pp. 276, 277. Cyril of Alexandria, in a prayer for the $\dot{\upsilon}\pi\alpha\pi\alpha\nu\tau\dot{\eta}$ (Presentation of Our Lord) refers to "he who offers and is offered, and receives and is distributed" (*orat. in occursum Domini* 5); this idea is paralleled in Augustine (see pp. 81f.); it is also used in a later Byzantine prayer (see p. 125). (The theme of eucharist-offering-commemoration is also to be found in the *Syriac Acts of Thomas*; see W. Wright (ed.), *Apocryphal Acts of The Apostles* [London, 1871], I (Syriac) p. 219; II (English), p. 190.)

87. F. Young, *From Nicaea to Chalcedon* (SCM, 1983), p. 267, where she cites the suggestion made by P. Canivet, *Histoire d'une entreprise apologétique de Vè siècle* (Paris 1958), p. 25, n. 3.

88. See Wagner, op. cit.; see also review article by G. J. Cuming, *Eastern Churches Review* 7 (1975), pp. 95–97.

89. See above n. 72.

90. See above n. 9 for Engberding's study in 1937. A. Raes, "L'Authenticité de la liturgie byzantine de S. Jean Chrysostom," *OCP* 24 (1958), pp. 5–16.

91. See above pp. 27ff.

92. R. H. Connolly, *The So-Called Egyptian Church Order and Derived Documents*, Texts and Studies, viii. 4, (Cambridge 1916). On Theodore, see above n. 24.

93. G. J. Cuming, "Pseudonymity and Authenticity, with Special Reference to the Liturgy of St. John Chrysostom," in E. Livingstone (ed.), *Studia Patristica* 15, (Akademie Verlag, Berlin, 1984), pp. 532–538. See also *Jungmann* I, p. 65, n. 9, for a reference to a conversation in 1942 between Jungmann and Engberding, in which Engberding insisted that his researches should only be taken as suggesting "une simple hypothèse."

94. Lev. 19.15; quoted by R. P. C. Hanson, "The Liberty of the Bishop to Improvise Prayer in the Eucharist," *Vigiliae Christianae* 15 (1961), p. 174 (see whole article, pp. 173–176).

CHAPTER FOUR

1. *De Sac.* 4. 14, 21, 27; text in *PEER*, pp. 112–114, *PE*, pp. 421–422. On Ambrose, see C. Mohrmann, "Le style oral du De Sacramentis de saint Ambroise," *Vigiliae Christianae* 6 (1952), pp. 168–177.

2. Buxton, *Eucharist and Institution Narrative*, e.g., pp. 21, 56, 111, 162f.; see also Manders, art. cit., Chapter 2, n. 63.

3. See Cuming, *Essays on Hippolytus*, pp. 46f.

4. R. A. Keifer, "The Unity of the Roman Canon: An Examination of Its unique Structure," *SL* 11, 1976, pp. 39–58.

5. See Yerkes, *Sacrifice in Greek and Roman Religions and Early Judaism*, pp. 59ff., for a discussion of pagan votive offerings; see also G. Willis, "Sacrificium laudis," in Spinks (ed.), *The Sacrifice of Praise*, pp. 73–87.

6. On the origin of the Sanctus, see B. D. Spinks, "The Jewish Origins for the Sanctus," *Heythrop Journal* XXI (1980), pp. 168–179.

7. See G. G. Willis, "The Connection of the Prayers of the Roman Canon," in *Essays on Early Roman Liturgy*, ACC 46 (SPCK, 1964), pp. 121–133; see also B. Botte, *Le Canon de la messe romaine*, Textes et Etudes Liturgiques 2 (Louvain, 1935).

8. Text in *PEER*, pp. 120–122; see also Botte, op. cit. pp. 32–46.

9. See P.-M. Gy, "Le Sanctus romain et les anaphores orientales," in *Mélanges Liturgiques offerts au R. P. Dom Bernard Botte*, Abbaye du Mont César (Louvain, 1972), pp. 167–174, esp. p. 173.

10. Willis, op. cit., pp. 123f., 127f.

11. Willis, op. cit., p. 127.

12. See above pp. 20ff.

13. See above pp. 116ff.

14. See W. H. Frere, *The Anaphora or Great Eucharistic Prayer*, Church Historical Society (SPCK, 1938), pp. 134–152; described by Bouyer as "Frere's sarcasm in regard to the Roman canon, which according to him has been carved up and disfigured, to the point that the ancient Roman eucharistic prayer (he is referring, of course to Hippolytus!) has become unrecognizable," *Eucharist*, p. 428. However, it cannot be denied that between Hippolytus and the Canon are some very real differences of structure and emphasis, particularly concerning that point at which thanksgiving moves into supplication.

15. Keifer, art. cit., pp. 54f.

16. Correspondence with the writer. I am indebted to Père Gy for much help in the course of this study.

17. *In Ps 38.25* and *de off.* 1. 238; tr. Bettenson, *The Later Christian Fathers*, p. 186.

18. See above pp. 70ff.

19. *De civ. Dei* 10, 5.6; tr. Bettenson, *The Later Christian Fathers*, pp. 243f.; compare similar language centering on the paradox of Christ's role in the eucharist, "himself offerer, himself the offering" (*ipse offerens, ipse et oblatio*), *de civ. Dei* 10, 21. The same idea is to be found in Cyril of Alexandria (see Chapter 3, n. 86), and later in a Byzantine rite prayer, see below p. 125 (and n. 87).

20. *Dial.* 4, 58, 59; tr. *DS* I, pp. 195f.

21. Keifer, art. cit., p. 55.

22. J. Deshusses, *Le Sacramentaire Grégorien* I, Spicilegium Friburgense 16 (Fribourg, 1971), nos. 25, 331, 381, 831, 836 (= Gr).

23. J. Deshusses, *Le Sacramentaire Grégorien* II, Spicilegium Friburgense 24 (Fribourg, 1979), see index, pp. 396f.

24. Dix, *The Shape of the Liturgy*, p. 744; but compare J. Fenwick's reaction to this oft-repeated paragraph, "intensely moving, but (dare one ask) is it right? Is it defensible to appropriate the sacrament for a particular 'cause'? Is there not a danger of divorcing the sacraments from our ecclesiology?" in "These Holy Mysteries," in C. O. Buchanan (ed.), *Anglo-Catholic Worship: An Evangelical Appreciation after 150 Years*, GLS 33, p. 16. I have no quarrel with the legitimacy of the votive Mass, provided that it does not become the staple eucharistic diet; see pp. 112f., 123ff., 226ff.

25. K. W. Stevenson, *Nuptial Blessing: A Study of Christian Marriage Rites*, ACC 64, (SPCK, 1982), pp. 35ff.

26. Willis, op. cit., p. 127; compare H. Ashworth, "The Influence of the Lombard Invasions on the Gregorian Sacramentary," *Bulletin of the John Rylands Library* 36 (1954), pp. 305–327.

27. G. G. Willis, "The variable prayers of the Roman Mass," in *Further Essays in Early Roman Liturgy*, ACC 50 (SPCK, 1968), pp. 122f. For the sake of consistency and ease, we shall use the title *Super oblata* throughout this study.

28. B. Capelle, "une messe de s. Leon pour l'Ascension," *EL* 67 (1953), pp. 200–209

(= *Travaux Liturgiques* II [Louvain, 1962], pp. 71–78); F. L. Cross, "Pre-Leonine Elements in the Proper of the Roman Mass," *JTS* 50 (1949), pp. 191–197.

29. Willis, op. cit., p. 122.; see also *Jungmann*, II, pp. 90ff.

30. D. R. Holeton, "The sacramental language of S. Leo the Great. A study of the words 'munus' and 'oblata,' " *EL* 92 (1978), pp. 115–165.

31. M. P. Ellebracht, *Remarks on the Vocabulary of the Ancient Orations in the Missale Romanum*, Nijmegen, 1966, p. 163; see also J. A. G. Gimeno, *Las oraciónes sobre las Ofrendas en el Sacramentário Leoniano: Texto y Doctrína*, Consejo Superior de Investigaciónes Científicas (Madrid, 1965), pp. 25ff., 65ff., 149ff.

32. L. C. Mohlberg (ed.), *Sacramentarium Veronense*, Rerum ecclesiasticarum documenta; series maior: Fontes I (Rome, 1956) (= V), no. 14.

33. V 76, 100, 115, 142, 174, 181, 183, 208, 243, 253, 258, 262, 270, 293, 297, 309, 333, 342, 357, 360, 375, 411, 421, 433, 457, 463, 464, 583, 639, 708, 711, 714, 727, 739, 748, 817 (*nostra devotio*), 836, 854, 856, 868, 874, 895, 1010, 1041, 1070, 1093, 1098, 1165, 1240, 1246, 1254, 1259.

34. V 28, 68, 95, 149, 201, 216, 220, 276, 288, 299, 304, 306, 616, 756, 759, 889, 943, 1065, 1230.

35. V 33, 89, 91, 111, 216, 261, 318, 373, 433, 481, 511, 541, 595, 985, 1136; these are striking examples; this third category seems to predominate.

36. V 457.

37. V 728.

38. V 463, 705, 868.

39. V 868, 1047.

40. L. Eizenhöfer (ed.), *Liber Sacramentorum Aecclesiae ordinis anni circuli*, Rerum ecclesiasticarum documenta; series maior: Fontes V (Rome, 1960) (= GeV). Of the nouns *munus, oblatio, sacrificium, hostia,* and *mysterium*, it is (still) *munus* which occurs most frequently, but there is a tendency to combine with other nouns (e.g., GeV I, 10, 14, 38, 45 (where *munus* occurs twice); for the "inner qualities," see GeV I 27 b) and III 50.

41. For *mysterium gerimus*, see GeV I 37 b), 37 d), and 45. For *pro*, see GeV II 36, 53, 65.

42. See A. Chavasse, "L'oraison *super sindonem* dans la liturgie romaine," *Revue Bénédictine* 70 (1960), pp. 313–323.

43. *Munus* is still the most frequent noun (although *sacrificium* comes a close second); *munus* frequently occurs with *oblatum/oblata*, as Gr 172, 176, 253, 278, 313; *celebrare* occurs intermittently, e.g., Gr 605, 700, 707.

44. See above n. 23; the derivative texts are to be found in J. Deshusses, *Le Sacramentaire Grégorien* III, Spicilegium Friburgense 28 (Fribourg, 1982).

45. Gr 1302, 1305, 1318, 1324.

46. Gr 1282 (priest's own votive Mass), 2076, 2079, 2154, 2182, 2185, 2189, 2222, 2227, 2725, 2792, 3069. 3135.

47. For the epiclesis, Gr 2134; incense, 2128; general prayer, 3016.

48. See also A. Dumas (ed.), *Liber Sacramentorum Gellonensis*, Corpus Christianorum: Series Latina, CLIX (Textus), CLIXA (Introductio, Tabulae, et Indices) (Turnholti, Brepols, 1981), especially the "table synoptique" in the latter volume, pp. 8–138.

49. See below pp. 112ff.

50. See *Jungmann* I, pp. 60ff; Dix, *The Shape of the Liturgy*, pp. 578ff.

51. A. Paredi, G. Fassi (eds.), *Sacramentarium Bergomense*, Edizione "Monumenta Bergomensia" (Bergamo, 1929) (= Berg.).

52. Berg. 59.

53. Berg. 105, 164, 188.

54. Berg. 272, 657.

55. *Exp. brev. antiq. lit. Gall.* I; tr. *DS* I, p. 198.

56. L. C. Mohlberg (ed.), *Missale Gothicum*, Rerum ecclesiasticarum documenta; series maior: Fontes V (Rome, 1961) (= Go).

57. Go 15, 108, 207.

58. Go 88, 100, 154. See also J. Pinell, *"Legitima eucharistia.* Cuestiones sobre le anámnesis y la epíclesis en el antiguo rito galicano," in *Mélanges Botte,* pp. 445–460.

59. Go 154. In general, see J. A. Frendo, *The Post Secreta of the Missale Gothicum and the Eucharistic Theology of the Gallican Anaphora* (Malta, 1977), pp. 54–58; but his treatment is insufficiently critical of different eucharistic themes.

60. Go 100, 527.

61. Go 110, 205.

62. E. A. Lowe (ed.), *The Bobbio Missal,* Henry Bradshaw Society 58 (London, 1920) (= Bo).

63. Bo 61, 82, 260, 410, 490.

64. L. C. Mohlberg (ed.), *Missale Gallicanum Vetus,* Rerum ecclesiasticarum documenta; series maior: Fontes III (Rome, 1958) (= MGV).

65. MGV 206, 327, 346; for this latter, see Chapter 4, pp. 90f., 96f.

66. L. C. Mohlberg (ed.), *Missale Francorum,* Rerum ecclesiasticarum documenta; series maior: Fontes II (Rome, 1961) (= MF).

67. MF 143, 153.

68. *De fid. cath.* II 27, 1, 3; *de eccl. off.* I, 15, 3; tr. *DS* I pp. 198f.

69. M. Férotin (ed.), *Liber mozarabicus sacramentorum,* Monumenta ecclesiastica liturgica VI (Paris, 1912) (= Moz).

70. Moz 627, (for "sweet-smelling odour," compare Phil 4:18) Moz 193.

71. For *holocaustum,* see Moz 125, 188, 270, 284, 288, 306, 369, 745, 763, 772, 781, 1075, 1333; on the Maronite ordination rite, see pp. 103f.; the classic holocaust psalm text is Ps 20:3–5, which Amalarius of Metz uses as the response to the *Orate fratres.*

72. Moz 663. See also W. S. Porter, *The Gallican Rite* (Mowbrays, 1958), pp. 33ff.

73. Texts of dialogue, *Inlatio,* and *Post pridie* in *PEER,* pp. 110f; other sample texts of variable prayers are to be found in *PE,* pp. 497–513.

74. Moz 297.

75. Moz 116.

76. Conversation with David Tripp. Whereas the early Roman sacrifice vocabulary is pagan (e.g., *munus,* etc.), Mozarabic terms are increasingly Old Testament (e.g., holocaust).

77. See below p. 115.

78. When the narrative ceases to be part of thanksgiving, but is in what we may term the "supplication series" of the anaphora, its function becomes entirely different. This has important theological and pastoral implications, as well as literary ones. I am reminded of Aidan Kavanagh's *obiter dictum* in the course of a lecture in which he said that "much theological hay can be made out of the Roman Canon's preoccupation with supplication."

79. I am indebted to James Crichton for help over this elusive point. It is not so much a question of when impetration begins to be used by the theologians as when impetration becomes the pastoral norm for the setting of the eucharist. On these grounds, the Carolingian votive Mass is a good candidate. See the important study by C. Vogel, "La multiplication des messes solitaires au moyen âge. Essai de statistique," *Revue des Sciences Réligieuses* 55 (1981), pp. 206–213.

80. D. Sicard, *La liturgie de la mort dans l'Eglise latine des origines à la réforme carolin-*

gienne, LQF 63 (Aschendorff, Münster, 1978), p. 174, quoting P.-M. Gy, "les funerailles d'après le rituel de 1614," *LMD* 44 (1955), p. 81. On funeral rites through the ages, see G. Rowell, *The Liturgy of Christian Burial*, ACC 59 (SPCK, 1977).

81. Tertullian, *De Cor.* III; Cyprian, *Ep.* 1, 2; Chrysostom, *In I Cor.* 41, 5; Ambrose, *De obitu* Val. 56; Augustine, *Conf.* IX, 32. See Sicard, op. cit., pp. 174ff (and notes).

82. *PE*, p. 357; compare Basil Alex[1]: "Give them rest in your presence; preserve us who live here in your faith, guide us to your kingdom, and grant us your peace at all times. . . ." (*PEER*, p. 37). On Basil Alex[1] and Basil Alex[2], see above pp. 37ff. and above pp. 57, 72.

83. *PE's* Latin translation reproduces that of *Renaudot*, I, p. 71.

84. Text in *PE*, pp. 242–243.

85. See above pp. 41–42.

86. On Addai and Mari, see above p. 23; on *sharar*, see above pp. 58f. Armenian Athanasius similarly does not distinguish ("Through this give rest to all those who aforetime have fallen asleep in Christ. . . . We beseech thee that in this holy sacrifice remembrance be made of the mother of God . . . ," *PE*, pp. 324ff., *LEW*, pp. 439ff.); similar language appears in Armenian Gregory Nazianzus, *PE*, pp. 330f.

87. See below p. 136.

88. Sicard, op. cit., pp. 399ff. This ties in with any interpretation on the development of the requiem Mass as a regular part of eucharistic life, in contrast to its use at (or soon after) a funeral. It is noteworthy that the Supplement contains 9 Masses of the dead (Gr 463–470); the derivative documents contain many more (Gr 2804–3073; Mass sets 212–267) including some Masses for both the living and the dead (Gr 3074–3139, Mass sets 268–278).

89. See Sicard's discussion, op. cit., pp. 239–248; see also pp. 248–257 for his theological reflections, which bring out the paschal character of the early prayers, whose *secondary* aspect is to pray for forgiveness to God.

90. *Gr* 3059.

91. See above n. 88; but Sicard does not question the later developments.

92. *Carmen* XI, 11. 49–68 (see H. Waddell [ed.], *Mediaeval Latin Lyrics* (Penguin, 1952), pp. 46–47); discussed in J. A. Baker, *The Foolishness of God* (DLT, 1970), pp. 389ff.

CHAPTER FIVE

1. Cuming, *Hippolytus: A Text for Students*, p. 12; NB Phil 4:18, again; see also Bradshaw's discussion of the text here, *Essays on Hippolytus*, pp. 33ff.

2. Cuming, *Hippolytus: A Text for Students*, p. 13.

3. Bradshaw, *Essays on Hippolytus*, p. 36 and nn., esp. W. H. Frere, "Early Forms of Ordination," in H. B. Swete (ed.), *Essays on the Early History of the Church and the Ministry* (Macmillan, 1918), pp. 283f.; cited by Bradshaw, p. 36, n. 1.

4. P.-M. Gy, "Ancient Ordination Prayers," *SL* 13 (1979), p. 84 (whole article, pp. 70–93).

5. H. Denzinger, *Ritus Orientalium* II (Stahl, Würzburg, 1864) pp. 13 (presbyter), 24 (bishop).

6. J. Goar, *Euchologion, sive Rituale Graecorum* (Venice, 1730), p. 243 (Byzantine), Denzinger, op. cit., p. 90 (Syrian Jacobite).

7. Gy, art. cit., pp. 74f.; see also M. Black, *Rituale Melchitarum*, Bonner Orientalistische Studien 22 (Stuttgart, 1939), p. 68.

8. Denzinger, op. cit., pp. 234, 236.

9. Denzinger, op. cit., pp. 309, 311.

10. Denzinger, op. cit., pp. 152, 153, 154 (where in the latter "holocaust" imagery is used of the eucharist).

11. H. B. Porter, *The Ordination Prayers of the Ancient Western Churches, ACC* 49 (SPCK, 1967), pp. 24–27 (Leonine Sacramentary).

12. Boone Porter, op. cit., pp. 50f.

13. Boone Porter, op. cit., pp. 62–65; the ordination prayer has "*in tabernaculum templi*" of the Old Testament priesthood; and the declaration after ordination has "*accedere ad altare dei*"; on the "altar of God" in the dialogue before the eucharistic prayer, see above p. 95.

14. Boone Porter, op. cit. pp. 52f.

15. See Boone Porter, op. cit. p. 53, n. 1.

16. C. Vogel & R. Elze, *Le Pontifical Romano-Germanique du Dixieme Siècle*, Studi e Testi 226 (Vatican, 1963), no. 35; M. Andrieu, *Le Pontifical Romain au moyen âge*, Studi e Testi 86–88 (Vatican, 1959), I, p. 136 (12th cent. Roman Pontifical), II, p. 347 (Pontifical of Curia), III, p. 370 (Pontifical of Durandus).

17. See above n. 16: but ref. to Vogel & Elze is no. 36.

18. P. de Puniet, *Le Pontifical Romain; histoire et commentaire*, 2 vols., (Louvain, 1930–1931).

19. Taft, *The Great Entrance, OCA* 200 (Rome, 1975), pp. 257–275.

20. Taft, *The Great Entrance*, p. 365; see *LEW*, pp. 319–320.

21. See above p. 55.

22. J. Matéos, *La célébration de la parôle dans la liturgie byzantine, OCA* 191, Rome 1971, p. 179; but see also H. Engberding, "Die ΕΥΧΗ ΤΗΣ ΠΡΟΣΚΟΜΙΔΗΣ der byzantinischen Basileioseliturgie und ihre Geschichte" *Muséon* 79, 1966, pp. 287–313; discussed by Taft, p. 365. Engberding suggests that the sources are more than two.

23. Taft, *The Great Entrance*, pp. 365ff.

24. *LEW* pp. 47–48; James' own material consists of small insertions (e.g. allusion to Zechariah's offering of incense, and the attitude of the worshippers).

25. Taft, *The Great Entrance*, pp. 372f.

26. tr Taft, *The Great Entrance*, p. 357.

27. *loc. cit.*

28. See above pp. 85ff. (on Western *super oblata*) and p. 109f (on Syriac prayer of the veil).

29. See *LEW*, pp. 309, 313, 316–317 (*Basil Byz*; prothesis, trisagion, prayer of faithful); 31, 33, 40 (James; prothesis, trisagion, prayer of faithful); 115, 118 (Mark; introduction, trisagion (not prayer of faithful); for 'heavenly altar' in *Basil Byz* prothesis (p. 309) see later Chrysostom, pp. 360f.; for 'reasonable altar' in Mark, see p. 115. On the origin of the Chrysostom Trisagion prayer, see A. Jacob, 'Zum Eisodosgebet der byzantinischen Chrysostomusliturgie,' *Ostkirchliche Studien* 15, 1966, pp. 35–38.

30. For incense prayers, see *LEW* pp. 32 (James), and 116, 118, 123 (Mark; where common themes recur, as to be expected); see also p. 359 (later Chrysostom; compare Armenian, p. 419). On Mark and *sharar*'s use of anaphoral intercession, see above pp. 53, 58. See Matéos, *La célébration*, p. 137 on incense-prayer in Chrysostom, which Matéos regards as Syrian in origin.

31. *LEW*, p. 73.

32. *LEW*, pp. 250 (prayer to Christ), 251 and 282 (incense), 268 (prayer quoted).

33. *LEW*, p. 83 (Syriac James) and 272 (East Syrian); there are signs of duplication in the latter, where there is (first of all) a dialogue, and then a priestly prayer; after the deacon's response, the priest affirms, 'This offering is offered for all the living and the dead. . . . ,' which echoes the dialogue before the eucharistic prayer (see p. 23) but

here this version comes before the diptychs, which precede the eucharistic prayer. (See also S. Y. H. Jammo, *La structure de la messe chaldéenne*, OCA 207, Rome 1979, pp. 165–167). See Taft, *The Great Entrance*, pp. 286ff.

34. B. D. Spinks, 'Sacerdoce et offrande dans les "Koushapé" des anaphores syriennes orientales,' *LMD* 154, 1983, pp. 107–126.

35. *Renaudot* II, pp. 275, 450f., 347, and 409f.

36. *Renaudot* II, pp. 261, 309f., 321.

37. e.g. James Bordaya, *Renaudot* II, p. 333; Philoxenus of Mabug, *Renaudot* II, p. 300; Thomas of Heraclea, *Renaudot*, p. 383.

38. *LEW*, pp. 417, 418 (quotations from the prayer of Gregory of Narek).

39. *LEW*, p. 419.

40. *LEW*, pp. 423, 430; the new material is almost nonexistent.

41. *LEW*, pp. 432f.

42. R. F. Taft, "The structural analysis of liturgical units: an essay in methodology," *Worship* 54 (1978), p. 329.

43. See parallel texts provided by Brightman, *LEW*, pp. 309ff. But the fact that they do not appear until the ninth century begs two questions. First, our evidence before that date is sporadic—Barberini 336 is our earliest text of the full liturgy of John Chrysostom. Secondly, prayers such as those we have discussed immediately prior to the anaphora could be much older, since they were probably based on long-standing oral traditions, as presidential prayers of preparation before the eucharistic prayer begins. See Spinks, art. cit. in n. 34.

44. Texts in *PEER*, pp. 119f.

45. *Jungmann* II, pp. 41ff.; Willis, "The Offertory Prayers and the Canon of the Roman Mass," in *Essays on Early Roman Liturgy*, pp. 107–110; see B. Botte, C. Mohrmann (eds.), *L'Ordinaire de la Messe*, Études Liturgiques 2 (Abbaye du Mont César, Louvain, 1953), pp. 68–73; see also V. Fiala, "Les prières d'acceptation de l'offrande et le genre littéraire du canon romain," in *Eucharisties d'Orient et d'Occident* I, Lex Orandi 46 (Éditions du Cerf, 1970), pp. 117–133. The most thorough study is by P. Tirot, "Histoire des prières d'offertoire dans la liturgie romaine du VIIè au XVIè siècle," *EL* 98 (1984), pp. 148–197, and pp. 323–391.

46. Parallel texts of the British rites in W. Maskell, *The Ancient Liturgy of the Church of England* (Pickering, 1844), pp. 22–33, (Sarum, Bangor, York, Hereford, with 1570 Roman); for a late medieval French rite, see that of the abbey of St. Martin, Ainay, Lyon, in *Martène*, (Ordos in vol. I, cap. IV, art. XII), Ordo XXXIII; see A.-G. Martimort, *La documentation liturgique de Dom Edmond Martène*, Studi e Testi 279 (Vatican, 1978), p. 321.

47. Noted by *Jungmann*, II, pp. 62ff.

48. See Tirot, art. cit., pp. 341ff.

49. See texts in *Martène*, Ordos IV (containing the important *Missa Illyrica*), XXXVII; see also Tirot, art. cit., pp. 154ff.

50. The *Missa Illyrica* and an eleventh-century S. Denys book (= *Martène's* Ordos IV and V) both contain alternatives; the former has five versions (two ordinary, one weekday, two for himself), whereas the S. Denys has four (one ordinary, one in honor of the saints, one for himself, one for the dead). Later books expand on this. See also Tirot, art. cit., pp. 162ff.

51. *Martène*, Ordo XVI; see above n. 46.

52. See texts quoted by *Jungmann* II, pp. 82ff. See *Martène*, Ordo XVI for lengthy text. An 11th century book from St. James, Liège (= *Martène's* Ordo XV) contains in the response, 'immola sacrificium' (also in Gregorienmünster, Ordo XVI); a 14th century Rouen book (= *Martène's* Ordo XXVI) has a special form for requiem masses); a later

14th century Rouen book (= *Martène's* Ordo XXVII) has 'holocaust,' as does a 15th century Toul book (= *Martène's* Ordo XXXI). Amalarius of Metz has a psalmic response, Ps. 20: 3–5, with the holocaust imagery. I suspect that this antedates the spread of the Roman rite in Gaul, and goes right back to old Gallican/Mozarabic terminology; see above pp. 95ff. On the role of the priest at marriage, see Stevenson, *Nuptial Blessing*, pp. 75, 83, 90; see also K. W. Stevenson, 'The Marriage Rites of Mediaeval Scandinavia: a fresh look,' *EL* 97 (1983), pp. 550–557. See also Tirot, art. cit., pp. 193ff.

53. See *Jungmann* II, pp. 84ff. n. 16 for quotations from various texts.

54. *Ep.* 41.

55. *Cap.* 1, 5; *De ord. bapt.* 18.

56. Paschasius, De corp. et sang. Dom. 8, 1, 2; Rabanus, *De sac. ord.* 19; Ratramnus, *De corp. et sang. Dom.* 99, 100.

57. *Ep.* 1, 3, 4.

58. Fulbert, *Ep.* 5; Lanfranc, *De corp. et sang. Dom.* 18, 19.

59. Durandus of Troarm, *De corp. et sang. Christi,* 9; Witmund, 3, 51.

60. Peter Damien, *Exp. in ca. Missae* 2, 8, 12; Anselm, *Orat.* 35.

61. Alger of Liège, *De Sac. Missae.* See also M. Shaeffer, "Twelfth century Latin Commentaries on the Mass: The Relationship of the Priest to Christ and to the People," *SL* 15, 1982–1983, pp. 76–86; part of Ph.D. dissertation, University of Notre Dame, Indiana, 1983.

62. E.g., Honorius, *Brev. Tract. de sacram. alt.* 88, 90.

63. *Summ. Sent.* 6, 9.

64. *Sent.* 4, 12, 7; Lombard also emphasizes that it is "we offer" and not "I offer."

65. *De Sac. Myst.* 3; 5,6.

66. *De sacram. Euch.* 5.

67. *Summa Theol.* II, 85, 1ff.

68. See B. Capelle, "Les oraisons de la messe du saint sacrement," *QLP* (1946), pp. 61–71 (= *Travaux Liturgiques* III, Louvain, pp. 242–251).

69. See Oberman and Courtenay, eds., *Gabrielis Biel Canonis Misse Exposito,* II, p. 340. I am indebted to Thomas J. Talley for drawing my attention to this.

70. See O. B. Hardison, *Christian Rite and Christian Drama in the Middle Ages,* (Johns Hopkins, Baltimore, 1969), pp. 37–79; see also *Jungmann* I, pp. 74ff.

71. *Eclog. de officio missae,* passim; see Hardison, op. cit., pp. 37ff.

72. *De Exp. missae,* passim.

73. Hardison, op. cit., p. 47.

74. *Sermo* 5.

75. See Shaeffer, n. 61.

76. E.g. *In Gen.* 6, 32.

77. *Rat. Div. Off.,* passim; see also *Jungmann* I, 11, pp. 109ff.

78. T. F. Simmons (ed.), *Lay-Folks Mass-Book,* Early English Text Society 71 (London, 1879), p. 26.

79. J. Wickham Legg (ed.), *Tracts on the Mass,* Henry Bradshaw Society 27, p. 23; Gregory Dix makes much of Langforde's cross-centered penitential and individualistic piety, *The Shape of the Liturgy,* pp. 605ff.

80. F. Clark, *Eucharistic Sacrifice and the Reformation* (Blackwells, Oxford, 1st ed. 1960, 2nd ed. 1967); the most searching review (unanswered by the second edition, in our opinion) was by E. Mascall, *Theology* 44 (1961), pp. 310–316. Clark's confidence in "the" Catholic view of eucharistic sacrifice would appear to be questioned, at least from a liturgical point of view, by the variety of material discussed in this study.

81. See *Jungmann* II, pp. 359ff.

82. See above, pp. 118f.; Aquinas's theology is soberly expressed and unaffected by dramatic liturgical commentary.

83. Maximus, *Quaest. et dubia* 41, *Schol. in eccl.* 3 2,3; *Historia Ecclesiastica* 28, 29, 31a, 48; *Protheoria*, 6f., 18f, 23; see R. Bornert, *Les Commentaires Byzantines de la Divine Liturgie du VIIè au XVè siècle*, Archives de l'Orient Chrétien 9 (Paris, 1966), p. 107 (Maximus), pp. 148, 263 (*Historia Ecclesiastica*), pp. 183, 188, 200 (*Protheoria*), pp. 208, 209 (Psellos). See also N. Cabasilas, *A Commentary on the Divine Liturgy* (tr. J. M. Hussey, P. A. McNulty), (SPCK 1966), pp. 25ff., 65ff. (esp. pp. 80–82, where the sacrificial character of the eucharist is lavishly defined, "without the bloody immolation"). See also N. Bulgaris, *A Holy Catechism* (Constantinople, 1861), pp. 50ff., 198ff. It is interesting to note that the Protheoria describes the Cherubim as offering praise to God with the full verb προσφέρουσι. A similar heightening of sacrificial terminology is discernible in the Armenian Commentary by Chosrov, see S. Salaville, "L' 'Explication de la messe de l'Arménien Chosrov (950)," *Échos d'Orient* 39 (1940), pp. 349–382, where see the discussion on the dismissal of noncommunicants, p. 356.

84. Discussed by Taft, *The Great Entrance*, pp. 84–88 (*Sermo de paschate et de ss. eucharistia*, 8).

85. Discussed by Taft, *The Great Entrance*, pp. 135f. See also A. L. Townsley, "Eucharistic doctrine and the Liturgy in late Byzantine painting," *OC* 1974, pp. 138–153.

86. Discussed fully by Taft, *The Great Entrance*, pp. 119–148, with citations to E. Lanne, "La prière de la Grande Entrée," in *Miscellanea Liturgica in onore di S. E. il Cardinale G. Lercaro*, II, Rome 1967, pp. 303–312.

87. See above, Chapter 3 n. 86; compare with Augustine, Chapter 4 n. 19.

88. Dix, *The Shape of the Liturgy*, pp. 546ff.; see also R. F. Taft, "How Liturgies Grow: The Evolution of the Byzantine 'Divine Liturgy,' " *OCP* 43, 1977, pp. 355–378. While Dix is open to criticism, he pioneered the modern movement towards seeing liturgy as not just texts but embodiments of *meaning*.

89. See above n. 49.

90. See *Jungmann* II, pp. 97ff. n. 2. Compare the 1519 *Missale Aquilensis*, where, after the Creed, the offertory prayers begin ominously with the direction, *sequitur canon minor* (fo. 174 v). I am grateful to Père Gy and Thomas J. Talley for help here.

91. Here are the three alternative *Suscipe sancta trinitas* from the Sacramentary of Séez:
1. "Receive, Holy Trinity, this oblation, which I offer to you for myself, a sinner, and for the salvation of our congregation, and for the whole Christian people, and for all of us who are giving alms, and for those also who have commended themselves in our prayers; and who have memory of us in their prayers; so that we here may receive forgiveness of sins, and may merit eternal rewards in the future."
2. "Receive, Holy Trinity, this oblation, which I offer first of all, as is right, in memory of the Incarnation, Nativity, Passion, Resurrection, and Ascension of our Lord Jesus Christ, and in honor of all your saints, who have pleased you from the beginning of the world, and whose names and relics are contained here, and those whose festival is celebrated on the earth, that they may be profited in honor, and we in salvation, so that they may deign to intercede in heaven for us who make their commemoration on earth."
3. "Receive, Holy Trinity, this oblation, which I offer for the soul of your servant, so that, through the help which you provide, he may merit the forgiveness of sins, and also the great joys of everlasting life."

Text in E. Lodi, *Enchiridion Euchologicum Fontium Liturgicorum, EL Subsidia* 15, Edizioni Liturgiche, Rome, 1979, pp. 1623f.

92. See the "strong" role of the priest apparent in many of the medieval tropes, N. K. Rasmussen, "Quelques réflexions sur la théologie des tropes," in G. Iversen (ed.), *Research on Tropes, Proceedings of a Symposium Organized by the Royal Academy of Literature, History and Antiquities and the Corpus Troporum* (Almqvist and Wiksell, Stockholm, 1982), pp. 86–88 (whole article, pp. 77–88).

CHAPTER SIX

1. *Summa Theologica*, 3a, 79, 5.

2. Lecture delivered at Salisbury-Wells Theological College, May 1973.

3. *Luther's Works*, 36, p. 35.

4. T. H. Schattauer, "Some Roman Catholic Approaches to Luther on the Mass as Sacrifice," a paper read at Notre Dame University, May 1982; see also Schattauer's S.T.M. thesis, "Eucharistic Sacrifice in Luther's Writings on the Mass," Yale Divinity School, 1980.

5. *Luther's Works*, 35, p. 52.

6. R. Prenter, "Eucharistic Sacrifice according to the Lutheran Tradition," *Theology* 68 (1964), pp. 286–295 (= R. Prenter, *Theologie und Gottesdienst*, (Aros, Århus 1977), pp. 195–207, see p. 197).

7. See above n. 5.

8. Texts in *PEER*, pp. 136–140; *CDI*, pp. 33–39 (see also pp. 29–33).

9. Y. Brilioth, *Eucharistic Faith and Practice, Evangelical and Catholic*, (SPCK, 1930), pp. 95ff.; L. D. Reed, *The Lutheran Liturgy* Fortress, Philadelphia, 1st ed. 1947, 2nd ed. 1959 (revised), pp. 69ff. (ref. to 1959 ed.).

10. Text in *PEER*, p. 144; *CDI* pp. 114–116.

11. Texts in *CDI*, p. 55, pp. 77f. It would appear that Bugenhagen envisages the preface to be optional and sung in Latin.

12. G. Wainwright, *Doxology, The Praise of God in Worship, Doctrine and Life*, (Epworth, 1980), pp. 269–329.

13. B. D. Spinks, *Luther's Liturgical Criteria and his Reform of the Canon of the Mass*, GLS 30 (Grove Books, 1982), passim.

14. See the important article by I. Pahl, "Das eucharistische hochgebet in den Abendmahlsordnungen der Reformationskirchen," *QLP* 1972, pp. 219–244.

15. Texts in *PEER*, pp. 130–133, *CDI*, pp. 185–188 (see also pp. 181–185).

16. Text in *PEER*, pp. 134–135, *CDI*, pp. 189–198.

17. Text in *CDI*, pp. 311–317; see W. Maxwell, *The Liturgical Portions of the Genevan Service Book*, (Oliver & Boyd, Edinburgh, 1931), pp. 25–32; and J. M. Barkley, " 'Pleading his eternal sacrifice' in the Reformed Liturgy," in *The Sacrifice of Praise*, pp. 127–130. The Worms German Mass of 1524 had a simpler *Orate Fratres* (*CDI*, p. 17), which disappeared.

18. See texts in *CDI*, pp. 317–329.

19. Text in *PEER*, pp. 146–152; *CDI*, pp. 329–336.

20. Texts in *PEER*, pp. 153–156 and *CDI*, pp. 355–362; compare Poullain, pp. 362–367; see also pp. 347–355.

21. *Calvin's Commentaries: The Epistle of Paul the Apostle to the Hebrews and the First and Second Epistles of St. Peter*, (Clark, Edinburgh, 1963), p. 139; quoted by Williams, *Eucharistic Sacrifice*, p. 3.

22. J. Calvin, *Institutes* IV, 17, 43.

23. Texts in *PEER*, pp. 179–181; *CDI*, pp. 472–479; see also Maxwell, op. cit., pp.

50–52.

24. See B. D. Spinks, *From the Lord and "The Best Reformed Churches": A Study of the Eucharistic Liturgy in the English Puritan and Separatist Traditions, 1550–1633, EL Subsidia* 33 (Edizioni Liturgiche, Rome, 1984), pp. 76–83 (see also pp. 45–84 for a full discussion of Knox's rite).

25. G. Dix, *The Shape of the Liturgy*, p. 656; see C. Dugmore, review in *JTS* 46 (1945), p. 111; and *The Mass and the English Reformers* (Macmillan 1958), pp. 163–171; see also G. J. Cuming, *A History of Anglican Liturgy* (Macmillan, 2nd ed. 1982), p. 81. On the Dix debate, see K. W. Stevenson, *Gregory Dix—25 Years On, GLS* 10 (Grove Books, 1977), pp. 31–33. See also C. O. Buchanan, *What Did Cranmer Think He Was Doing?*, *GLS* 7 (Grove Books, 1976), passim.

26. Text in *PEER*, pp. 158–161, and Cuming, op. cit., pp. 286–304.

27. Texts in *PEER*, pp. 167–174; *CDI*, pp. 395–406; see also G. J. Cuming, *The Godly Order, ACC* 65 (SPCK, 1983), pp. 91–98.

28. See also F. E. Brightman, *The English Rite* II (Rivingtons, 1915), pp. 682–703.

29. See *Jungmann*, II, pp. 10–17.

30. E. C. Whitaker, *Martin Bucer and the Book of Common Prayer, ACC* 55 (Mayhew-McCrimmon, Great Wakering), 1974, pp. 36–37.

31. See Brightman, op. cit., p. 688.

32. See Cuming, *The Godly Order*, pp. 96–97.

33. Ibid., pp. 104f.

34. Ibid., pp. 104f; see also Brightman, op. cit., p. 694.

35. F. E. Brightman, *The English Rite*, I (Rivingtons 1915), p. xlix.

36. Cuming, *The Godly Order*, pp. 92ff.

37. See Dix, *The Shape of the Liturgy*, p. 661.

38. Whitaker, op. cit., pp. 62f.

39. Texts in *PEER*, pp. 176–178; *CDI*, pp. 406–408; see above n. 28; see also Cuming, *The Godly Order*, pp. 110–121.

40. E.g. Horton Davies, *Worship and Theology in England: I, From Cranmer to Hooker* (Princeton University Press, 1970), pp. 178ff.

41. See above n. 25.

42. Dix, *The Shape of the Liturgy*, pp. 605ff., where he compares with Baxter's rite: the comparison is good fun, but it does not quite come off.

43. Subsequent controversy was to elicit from him the charge that Cranmer's eucharistic doctrine was of a "real absence," see "Dixit Cranmer et non Timuit," *Church Quarterly Review* 290 (1948), pp. 150, 167, 176.

44. See above n. 2.

45. See above nn. 28, 39; see also Cuming, *A History of Anglican Liturgy*, pp. 102ff.

46. Text in *PEER*, pp. 182–186; *CDI*, pp. 409–413. See also G. Donaldson, *The Making of the Scottish Prayer Book of 1637* (Edinburgh University Press, 1954), pp. 27–59; Buxton, *Eucharist and Institution Narrative*, pp. 145ff. (Buxton returns to this theme, "This rite deserves far more attention than it has ever received in England," from his essay "The Shape of the Eucharist," in *Liturgy Reshaped*, p. 88; see also review by L. Weil, *Worship* 57 [1983], p. 562.)

47. See Donaldson, op. cit., pp. 67ff.

48. W. Laud, *Speech Delivered in the Starr-Chamber on Wednesday, June 14th, 1637*, Works, 3, 344.

49. Buxton, *Eucharist and Institution Narrative*, p. 148.

50. G. J. Cuming (ed.), *The Durham Book* (Oxford University Press, 1969); see also Cuming, *A History of Anglican Liturgy*, p. 115.

51. For "offer up," see Cuming, *The Durham Book*, pp. 146f. For the meaning of "oblations," see J. Dowden, *Further Studies in the Prayer Book* (Methuen, 1908), pp. 176–222.

52. Texts in *PEER*, pp. 199–203; *CDI*, pp. 414–425.

53. E. Cardwell, *A History of Conferences* (Oxford University Press, 1840), pp. 320f., see also Cuming, *The Godly Order*, pp. 142–152.

54. Text in I. Breward (ed.), *The Westminster Directory*, GLS 21 (Grove Books, 1980), pp. 21–23; also *PEER*, pp. 187–192; *CDI*, pp. 486–489.

55. See Buxton, *Eucharist and Institution Narrative*, who even suggests that "the essential eucharistic theology of the Westminster Directory's rite is . . . arguably 'higher' than that of the Prayer Book it replaced," p. 139.

56. Text in *CDI*, pp. 490–493; see also P. Hall (ed.), *Reliquiae Liturgicae* IV (Bath, 1847). I am indebted to Rev. Gordon Wakefield for help over the spirituality and eucharistic theology of the Puritans. See also B. D. Spinks, *Freedom or Order?: The Eucharistic Liturgy in English Congregationalism, 1645–1980*, Pittsburgh Theological Monographs New Series 8 (Pickwick, Pittsburgh, 1984), pp. 61–65.

57. Stevenson, *Nuptial Blessing*, pp. 156f.

58. The analysis of E. C. Ratcliff, "Puritan Alternatives to the Prayer Book: The *Directory* and Richard Baxter's *Reformed Liturgy*," in *The English Prayer Book, 1549–1662* (SPCK, 1963), pp. 75ff. Also in Couratin, Tripp (eds.), *E. C. Ratcliff: Liturgical Studies*, pp. 234ff.

59. See Barkley, art. cit., pp. 123–140, for study of this theme in Reformed liturgies. The crucial point is that some of the Puritans had a higher doctrine of eucharistic sacrifice than some Anglicans (notably Cranmer himself); their distaste for any lingering liturgical clothing, in the way of vestments and elaborate liturgical language (indeed, for some of them, the notion of a set liturgy at all) must not be confused with their eucharistic theology. The 1689 *Book of Comprehension* included some High Church suggestions, among which were a Proper Preface for Good Friday, and an insertion to the Prayer of Humble Access which made reference to being "wash'd and cleansed by the Sacrifice of his most precious Body and bloud"; but this latter seems to be an attempt to improve upon the old prayer's partiality to Christ's "body" and "blood" performing separate tasks; see T. J. Fawcett, *The Liturgy of Comprehension 1689*, ACC 54 (Mayhew-McCrimmon, Great Wakering), 1973, pp. 110, 243.

60. Dix, *The Shape of the Liturgy*, p. 624, "the real eucharistic action goes on separately, even if simultaneously, within each man's mind."

61. For a summary, see P. F. Bradshaw, "The Reformers and the Ordination Rites," *SL* 13 (1979), pp. 94–107.

62. E. C. Ratcliff, "The English Usage of Eucharistic Consecration 1548–1662," *Theology* 60 (1957), pp. 229–236, 273–280 (also in *E. C. Ratcliff: Liturgical Studies*, pp. 203–221; the Johnson case is discussed on pp. 213–217). See also Buxton, *Eucharist and Institution Narrative*, pp. 89–92.

63. *A Reply unto M. Harding's Answer*, I, 734f. Discussed by Buxton, *Eucharist and Institution Narrative*, pp. 92–94; Buxton also discusses several of the Anglican writers which we deal with in these and the following pages.

64. *Sermons*, Parker Society, pp. 410–415.

65. *Laws of Ecclesiastical Polity* IV, xi. 10.

66. See *DS* II, p. 251.

67. *Minor Works*, (*Library of Anglo-Catholic Theology* II) pp. 20f.

68. Mountague, *Apello Caesarem* (1625) p. 286; Morton, *Of the Institution of the Sacrament of the Blessed Body and Blood of Christ* (1631) VI, vii, 3. The same kind of "self-

oblation" may be behind George Herbert's poems, "An Offering" and "Clasping of Hands."

69. *A Replication to the Bishop of Chalcedon's Survey of the Vindication of the Church of England from Criminous Schism,* 1656, IX, 6 (= LACT II, p. 276).

70. On Laud, see above n. 48.

71. *Considerationes Modestae et Pacificae* (1658) III.i.10, 12 and ii.2.

72. *Holy Living,* IV, X, 5; *The Great Exemplar* III, xv. Taylor in the latter passage goes on to defend the eucharistic sacrifice as impetratory in the same way that Bramhall does, but it is clear that by impetratory they mean no more than "strong intercession." On Taylor's eucharistic theology, see H. B. Porter, *Jeremy Taylor, Liturgist, ACC* 61 (SPCK, 1979), pp. 61ff.; see also W. J. Grisbrooke, *Anglican Liturgies of the Seventeenth and Eighteenth Centuries, ACC* 40 (SPCK, 1958), pp. 26ff.

73. Text in Grisbrooke, *Anglican Liturgies,* p. 195. Taylor breaks up his service into separate units, an aspect particularly noticeable during his "anaphora"; in this he has a lot in common with the nineteenth-century Catholic Apostolic rite, see pp. 175ff.

74. *A Rationale or Practical Exposition on the Book of Common Prayer,* 1722, pp. 166, 181f. Another important Restoration divine is Daniel Brevint, who was made Dean of Lincoln in 1681. His emphasis on eucharistic sacrifice (and perhaps his Lincolnshire connection, too) is influential on Wesley (see p. 00); in his *Christian Sacrament and Sacrifice,* he makes such bold statements as, ". . . this Sacrifice which by a *real Oblation* [his italics] was not to be offered more than once, is by an eucharistical and devout commemoration to be offered up every day," p. 74. See also Chapter 7, for his reappearance again in nineteenth-century devotional manuals, along with Andrewes and others.

75. See Buxton, *Eucharist and Institution Narrative,* pp. 156ff.

76. See Buxton, *Eucharist and Institution Narrative,* pp. 106–109, and see nn. pp. 242f

77. *A Rational Illustration of the Book of Common Prayer* (1710) p. 111; and 3rd ed., (1720) p. 255; discussed by Buxton, *Eucharist and Institution Narrative,* pp. 161–164; noted in *L'offrande,* p. 37.

78. *The Unbloody Sacrifice,* I, p. 304.

79. Ibid. I, pp. 86, 360, 402, 418.

80. See below pp. 185ff. Johnson's second volume is an historical survey of ancient literature; his interest in typology and his attachment to the narrative as consecratory (thereby making any subsequent oblation, whether verbal or ritual, one of consecrated gifts) are both influential on the Catholic Apostolic rite.

81. *Companion to the Festival and Fasts of the Church of England* (1703) p. 340.

82. *A Review of the Doctrine of the Eucharist* (1737) pp. 66ff. See Buxton, *Eucharist and Institution Narrative,* pp. 173ff.

83. See above, n. 72.

84. Texts in Grisbrooke, *Anglican Liturgies,* pp. 211ff. (first), 226ff. (second), 233ff. (third); see also Grisbrooke's discussion, p. 47.

85. Text in Grisbrooke, *Anglican Liturgies,* pp. 249–261 (quotation, p. 257); see also discussion on pp. 59ff.; Whiston's expanded anamnesis may be the result of his reading of ancient liturgies; like Johnson, he was interested in typology.

86. Text in Grisbrooke, *Anglican Liturgies,* pp. 265–271 (quotations, pp. 268f); see also p. 67. For Apostolic Constitutions, see above pp. 161f. For capitalization, see 1764 Scottish rite, pp. 165f.

87. Text in Grisbrooke, *Anglican Liturgies,* pp. 278–296 (quotations, pp. 286, 289); see also Cuming, *A History of Anglican Liturgy,* pp. 141ff.

88. Text in Grisbrooke, *Anglican Liturgies,* pp. 301–316 (offertory, p. 306, anamnesis, pp. 310ff.); a significant alteration in 1734 is that the institution narrative (and not the

anamnesis) is preceded by "wherefore, having in remembrance"—is this the final apo-gee of the narrative as no longer "magic words," or is it a desire to hold together an expanding anaphora?

89. Text in Grisbrooke, *Anglican Liturgies*, pp. 319–332 (quotations, pp. 325, 327).

90. Text in Grisbrooke, *Anglican Liturgies*, pp. 335–348 (quotation, p. 343); see also J. Dowden, *The Annotated Scottish Communion Office*, pp. 54f., 64–71, on the origin of the book, and pp. 151f. (note on the offertory sentence as a prayer, with the "offering up" of the elements), p. 160 (note on the omission of "there" between "made" and "a full sacrifice"), pp. 161–165 (note on the offering formula in the anamnesis). Gadderar, who knew many of the English Non-Jurors, had these words inserted into the rite in various editions from 1755 onwards; it was left to his episcopal, scholarly colleague, Rattray, to seal this.

91. See above pp. 40f., 48. The East Syrian anaphora of Nestorius also uses the subor-dinate clause in this way, see p. 48.

92. See F. C. Eeles, *Traditional Ceremonial and Customs Connected with the Scottish Lit-urgy*, ACC 17 (Longmans, 1910), pp. 59–63 (offertory), 63–67 (anaphora); in the latter included the tradition in some places of offering the paten and chalice at the oblatory words in the anamnesis; the writer remembers seeing celebrants doing this in the East-ern manner, crossing over the arms in so doing, doubtless in direct imitation, and also to ease tender muscles.

93. M. Hatchett, *The Making of the First American Book of Common Prayer* (Seabury, 1982), pp. 1–4, 42, 98, 100ff., 107ff.

94. M. Hatchett, op. cit., p. 111 (quotation of Seabury).

95. See W. McGarvey, *Liturgiae Americanae* (Philadelphia, 1895), pp. 238–242 for par-allel texts; see also S. Hart, *Bishop Seabury's Communion-Office* (Whitaker, New York, 1883), pp. 8 (offertory), 12 (anamnesis).

96. E. Echlin, *The Anglican Eucharist in Ecumenical Perspective: Doctrine and Rite from Cranmer to Seabury* (Seabury, 1968), p. 235; see passim for discussion of evolution of 1789 book.

97. See J. E. Rattenbury, *The Eucharistic Hymns of John and Charles Wesley* (Epworth, 1948), pp. 195–249 for full text.

98. Wesley was influenced by Daniel Brevint's eucharistic theology contained in *The Christian Sacrament and Sacrifice* (1673); see above n. 74 on Brevint. John Wesley pub-lished an abbreviation of Brevint's work with the *Hymns on the Lord's Supper*. On Wes-ley's piety, see T. Dearing, *Wesleyan and Tractarian Worship* (Epworth, 1966), pp. 7ff. (I owe much to Raymond George's paper, "Mr. Wesley's Abridgement," read at the third Meeting of the Society for Liturgical Study, Spode House, September 1981.)

99. Quoted in Rattenbury, op. cit., p. 82.

100. No. 137 (ibid., p. 239), stanzas 1 and 4.

101. No. 116, stanza 5; no. 117 stanza 2 (ibid., p. 232). No. 116 ("Victim divine") is supposed to have been a versification of Brevint's work, see Horton Davies, *Worship and Theology in England: III From Watts and Wesley to Maurice* (Princeton, 1961), p. 208.

102. No. 147 (ibid., p. 242).

103. An important feature of "self-oblation" in Methodist spirituality is in the Cove-nant Service, see D. H. Tripp, *The Renewal of the Covenant in the Methodist Tradition* (Epworth, 1969), passim; see his references to the post communion prayer of oblation, pp. 127, 160.

104. See Cuming, *A History of Anglican Liturgy*, pp. 137ff., where Cuming (rightly, in our view) sees Wesley's adaptations of the Prayer Book to be "the final realization of Baxter's ideals" (p. 137).

105. *Sacrosancti Oecumenici Concilii Tridentini Canones et Decreta* (Mechliniae, 1847), Sessio XXII, Capit. II and IX (pp. 183f., 188f.).; key quotations are (from II) ". . . in divino hoc sacrificio . . . idem ille Christus continetur, et incruente immolatur. . . . Quare non solum pro fidelium vivorum peccatis . . . sed pro defunctis . . ."; and (from IX), "Si quis dixerit, in missa non offerri Deo verum et proprium sacrificium; aut quod offerri non sit aliud, quam nobis Christum ad manducandum dari; anathema sit" (Canon 1). (For a discussion of the extension of hands at *Hanc Igitur* as sacrificial, see *Jungmann* II, pp. 186f.)

106. T. Klauser, *A Short History of the Western Liturgy* (Oxford, 1969), pp. 117ff. For the offertory prayers and Canon, see *PEER*, pp. 119–122, but the "Amens" were inserted at the end of each paragraph in the Canon, making them separate units.

107. See *DS* II, pp. 362ff., for texts and discussion.

108. E.g. the hymn writers Johann Frank and Ernst Moritz Arndt (Germany) and Thomas Kingo and Nikolai Grundtvig (Denmark).

109. See Chapter 7, n. 42.

110. *Apology of the Augsburg Confession*, XXIV, 88; noted by H.-J. Schulz, art. cit., p. 59.

CHAPTER SEVEN

1. W. Palmer, *Origines Liturgicae* I (Oxford University Press, 1839), pp. 79, 80, 85ff.

2. See A. Härdelin, *The Tractarian Understanding of the Eucharist*, Studia Historico-Ecclesiastica Upsaliensia 8 (Uppsala, 1965), pp. 200ff.

3. *Tract 81*, pp. 11f., 30, 37, 55, 60; compare *The Holy Eucharist, a Comfort to the Penitent*, pp. 21ff.; see Härdelin, op. cit., pp. 212ff. on Pusey's later teaching.

4. See Härdelin, op. cit., p. 213, n. 76, for (undated) letter from Pusey to Manning.

5. R. I. Wilberforce, *The Doctrine of the Holy Eucharist* (Mozley, 1853), pp. 367ff., 373ff.

6. *Eucharistica: Meditations and Prayers on the Most Holy Eucharist from Old English Divines*, with an Introduction by Samuel, Lord Bishop of Oxford (Suttaby, 1849); quotations include Andrewes, Sparrow, Laud, and others.

7. J. Purchas (ed.), *Directorium Anglicanum* (Masters, 1858), p. 41n.

8. Ibid., pp. 42, n. 2 (prothesis prayer, compare *LEW* 311, Chrysostom Liturgy), 47 (alms and oblations, the latter reinterpreted; also the Hereford offertory "Suscipe sancta trinitas," untranslated, for which see Maskell, *The Ancient Liturgy*, p. 23), 50–53 (Canon), 53f. (Latin prayers from Canon). The criteria for the preference for the *Hereford* offertory prayer may be that it simply prays for the salvation of all, whereas the form used in Sarum, Bangor, and York mentions Mary and the saints, and the eucharist offers "for" (*pro*) the salvation of the living and departed.

9. P. G. Medd (ed.), *The Priest to the Altar* (1861), no page numbering; for the *Orate fratres* response, see Maskell, op. cit., p. 30; Hereford does not have a response, and York has Ps 20:1–3; Bangor has the same as Sarum. For the epiclesis in *Apostolic Constitutions*, see above p. 45; this is one of the anaphoras that refers to the gifts as "sacrifice," which is certainly the meaning here, though not, as we have argued, in early antiquity.

10. The "ancient use of York" is York's response to the *Orate fratres;* the editors of this book clearly like late medieval offertory material; see above n. 9.

11. O. Shipley (ed.), *The Ritual of the Altar* (Longmans, 1870), pp. 26–32 (offertory), 61–73 (Canon).

12. *Mediaeval Hymns and Sequences translated by J. M. Neale* (Masters, 1852).

13. M. Frost (ed.), *Historical Companion to Hymns Ancient and Modern* (Clowes, 1962), p. 349 (no. 395).

14. Ibid., p. 351 (no. 400).

15. Ibid. pp. 349f. (no. 397).

16. Ibid. pp. 350f. (nos. 398, 399).

17. *The Kingdom of Christ* II (Rivingtons, 1838), pp. 126ff.

18. *The Doctrine of the Church of England on the Holy Communion* (Rivingtons, 1885), p. 241.

19. See P. F. Bradshaw, *The Anglican Ordinal, ACC* 53 (SPCK, 1971), pp. 144ff.

20. G. Dix, *The Question of Anglican Orders* (Dacre, 1944); see also Bradshaw, op. cit., pp. 152f.

21. D. Stone, *A History of the Doctrine of the Holy Eucharist*, 2 Vols. (Longmans, 1909). My indebtedness to this book, for its copious quotations, is considerable.

22. E. Peaston, *The Prayer Book Tradition in the Free Churches* (Clarke, 1964), where Ratcliff writes (in the Foreword, p. x), "The Catholic Apostolic prayer book, *The Liturgy and other Divine Offices of the Church*, has never received the notice which it merits. . . ."

23. K. W. Stevenson, "The Catholic Apostolic Eucharist," Ph.D. dissertation, University of Southampton, 1975. See also K. W. Stevenson, "The Catholic Apostolic Church—Its History and Its Eucharist," *SL* 13 (1979), pp. 21–45, and "The Liturgical Year in the Catholic Apostolic Church," *SL* 14 (1982), pp. 128–234; see also D. H. Tripp, "The Liturgy of the Catholic Apostolic Church—A Minor Chapter in Ecumenical History," *Scottish Journal of Theology* 24 (1969), pp. 437–454. (See also section on this rite, by K. W. Stevenson, forthcoming in *Coena Domini II*, Spicilegium Friburgense series, under the editorship of I. Pahl.) The material referred to and quoted is taken from *The Liturgy and Other Divine Offices of the Church* (Pitmans, 1880), pp. 1ff. At the presentation of the gifts on the altar, Cardale recommends in his commentary on the rite that a prayer from the Ambrosian Missal "may be fitly offered by the Celebrant to God in secret, although the singing of the anthem of Introit (no. 6 in our scheme) hinders its being uttered aloud." See J. B. Cardale, *Readings upon the Liturgy and Other Divine Offices of the Church* I (Bosworth, 1874), p. 140, with citation to *Martène*, I, ix, xii, Ordo III; Cardale's translation is exact, "Receive, O most merciful Father, this holy bread (*or* this chalice), that it may become the Body (*or* Blood) of Thine only-begotten, in the Name of the Father . . ."; once again, we have selective use of traditional material. The main sources are worth noting (numbering taken from our text): 2. *Prayer of Approach.* For "that . . . righteousness," compare "prayer of veil" in the liturgy of James (*LEW*, p. 49). 7. *Orate fratres.* See p. 184. 8. *Prayer of Oblation before Consecration.* For "we offer . . . cup," compare anamnesis in *Apostolic Constitutions* VIII (*PE* pp. 92f.). For "for all . . . Thee," compare 1 Chr 29:14 and anamnesis in Basil Alex² and Basil Byz (*PE*, pp. 352f., 236f.) and Chrysostom (*PE*, pp. 226f.). For "we are unworthy . . . service" compare 1662 Prayer Book prayer of oblation. For "And here . . . bodies" compare the same. For "that we may henceforth . . . service" compare same, but NB epiclesis preceding it. 9. *Prayer of Oblation after Consecration.* For "do present . . . Church" compare Greek Mark ("we presented": *PE*, pp. 114f.), Greek Mark and James ("reasonable and unbloody": *PE*, pp. 102f., 248f.), and Basil Byz ("And he left us memorials of his saving passion, these things which we have set forth according to his commandments": *PE*, pp. 236f.). For "whereupon . . . heaven," compare Roman Canon, *Supplices te rogamus.* For "Have respect . . . world," compare Roman Canon, *Supra quae* and Prayer Book Consecration Prayer. For "Which things . . . prayers," compare Roman Canon, *Memento, Domine, famulorum* and *Communicantes.* 10. *Incense Anthem.* Line 1—Mal 1:11—at long

last. NB the prayer's position at the juncture between oblation and intercession. Compare Greek Mark and *Sharar*. Other sources noted in dissertation. See also Stevenson, "The Catholic Apostolic Church—Its History and its Eucharist," pp. 35ff. (NB Cardale not only separates the offering of money from the presentation of the gifts at the altar, but he does this latter in Byzantine fashion, by having the gifts placed on the table of prothesis *before* the eucharist begins, and then transferring them from the table of prothesis to the altar at the Greater Introit.)

24. The Sarum response is *"spiritus sancti gratia illuminet cor tuum . . ."* (see Maskell, *The Ancient Liturgy of the Church of England*, p. 30; also the Bangor form). For *The Priest to the Altar*, see above pp. 179f.

25. See above pp. 149ff., 161ff.

26. See *Euchologion*, Church Service Society (Edinburgh, Blackwood 1867), first of several eds.), pp. 45–61; the obvious examples of influence from the Catholic Apostolic rite are in the "prayer of access," the "eucharistic prayer," and the "invocation," pp. 52–55; in the first, we have "offer unto Thee a sacrifice in righteousness," in the second, a full thanksgiving series, and in the third, the full epiclesis, which includes "these Thine own gifts of bread and wine which we set before Thee." See also E. Bersier, *Liturgie à l'usage des églises réformées* (Paris, 1874), passim; see Stevenson, dissertation, pp. 374f.

27. J. M. Maxwell, *Worship and Reformed Theology: The Liturgical Lessons of Mercersburg*, Pittsburgh Theological Monographs Series 10 (Pickwick, Pittsburgh, 1976), esp. pp. 435ff.; influence also noted and studied in Stevenson dissertation.

28. See above pp. 171f.

29. C. Gore, *The Body of Christ* (Murray, 1901), pp. 210–213.

30. Compare "material offerings" with presentation of gifts; "wide-spread intercessions" with prayer for whole state of Christ's Church; "sacrifice of praise" with preface; "solemnly commemorates the passion" with consecration; "self-oblation" with prayer of oblation after communion. But there is also a restlessness with the Prayer Book order in the wider context in which Gore places his discussion and in the elaborate way in which he reinterprets Cranmer's rite. Nonetheless, his statement is the most systematic we have so far seen, from an Anglican point of view.

31. See Cuming, *A History of Anglican Liturgy*, pp. 165ff.

32. W. H. Frere, *Some Principles of Liturgical Reform* (Murray, 1911), pp. 186ff.

33. *The Scottish Liturgy* (Cambridge University Press, Edinburgh, 1912), pp. 10ff; note also the addition of "and looking for his coming again with power and great glory" at the anamnesis (p. 15), perhaps influenced by the Catholic Apostolic rite; this was the first Anglican liturgy remodeled to include an eschatological section here.

34. See Cuming, *The Godly Order*, pp. 168ff.; texts, pp. 182–189. See also R. C. D. Jasper (ed.), *Walter Howard Frere: His Correspondence on Liturgical Revision and Construction*, ACC 39 (SPCK, 1954), pp. 56–190 for full documentation of Frere's role.

35. Ibid., pp. 203–229; quotation p. 210.

36. Texts in *LiE*, pp. 41ff. (Scottish), 55ff. (American).

37. *The Eucharist in India—a Plea for a Distinctive Liturgy for the Indian Church* (Longmans, 1920), pp. 39–69 (article by Ratcliff).

38. See B. D. Spinks, "The Anaphora for India: Some Theological Objections to an Attempt at Inculturation," *EL* 95 (1981), pp. 529ff.

39. Text in *LiE*, pp. 98ff.; the anamnesis contains the offering of "our reasonable service and sacrifice," an Anglican periphrastic use of ancient material.

40. W. H. Frere, *The Anaphora*; J. Blomfield, *The Eucharistic Canon* (SPCK, 1930). See

pp. vii–viii, for Lowther Clarke's Introduction, which bears the marks of the anti-epiclesis lobby after the English 1927–1928 battle.

41. The greatest irony of all is that King George V and Queen Mary were, apparently, in favor of the proposed revisions; see K. Rose, *King George V* (Weidenfeld and Nicholson, 1983), p. 364: "Both the King and Queen, however, favoured the Revised Prayer Book which failed to gain parliamentary approval in 1927 and again in 1928, and regretted that the Commons had been stampeded by a cry of 'No Popery.'"

42. G. Burnet, *The Holy Communion in the Reformed Church of Scotland* (Oliver & Boyd, Edinburgh, 1960), pp. 57f. See above n. 26 for *Euchologion*. The influence on the *Euchologion* can be traced through the 1923 *Prayers for Divine Service* (Church of Scotland) as well as the 1928 *Book of Common Order* (United Free Church of Scotland), to the 1940 *Book of Common Order* (Oxford University Press) pp. 117ff. The features which can be noted are (1) the preparatory prayer before the anaphora, (2) the full thanksgiving, (3) the anamnesis/epiclesis, with reference to the gifts "which we set before thee." See below p. 211 for recent rites.

43. *Directory for Public Worship for use in the Presbyterian Church of England* (Publications Committee of the Presbyterian Church), 1923, p. 91; the prayer in question is an interesting blend of thanksgiving, invocation, and self-oblation, which leads into Sanctus.

44. *The Order of Divine Service for Public Worship* (Oxford University Press, 1919); strongly influenced by W. E. Orchard; pp. 122 (prayer of the veil), pp. 126ff., (offertory and anaphora).

45. *A Free Church Book of Common Prayer* (Dent, 1929), pp. 112ff (offertory and anaphora); this was compiled by a group of "Free Catholics."

46. The significant recurring factor is the gradual readiness of traditions of varying kinds (from eighteenth-century Scottish Episcopalians, through to nineteenth-century Scottish Presbyterians) to introduce a stronger element of oblation into their liturgies, even if adapted or toned down, in order to express Reformation insight.

47. *The Ascension and Heavenly Priesthood of our Lord* (Macmillan, 1891), p. 266.

48. J. Halliburton, "The Canon of Series 3," in R. C. D. Jasper (ed.), *The Eucharist Today: Studies on Series 3* (SPCK, 1974), p. 95.

49. *The Book of Common Prayer 1979* (Seabury, 1979), pp. 333–336, 340–343 (anaphoras in Rite One), 361–363, 367–375 (four anaphoras in Rite Two); *At The Lord's Table: A Communion Service Book for Use by the Minister*, Supplemental Worship Resources 9, (Abingdon, Nashville, 1981). See below pp. 206ff., 210f.

50. A. M. Ramsey, *The Gospel and the Catholic Church* (Longmans, 1936), p. 115.

51. N. Hicks, *The Fullness of Sacrifice* (SPCK, 1946, 3rd ed), p. 279; Hicks pursues his material with a relentlessness few books have bettered; it was said that he had a face that could stop a train.

52. G. Dix, *The Shape of the Liturgy*; see also K. W. Stevenson, *Gregory Dix—25 Years On*, pp. 23ff.

53. Dix, *The Shape of the Liturgy*, pp. 118ff; see above pp. 185ff. (Catholic Apostolic) and p. 197 (American Lutheran).

54. J. Jungmann's remark on Dix's courage and overall treatment is kind and perceptive "darin liegt das Reizvolle, freilich auch das Gewagte des Buches," *Zeitschrift für Katholische Theologie* 70 (1948), p. 224.

55. E. C. Ratcliff, review in *Theology* 48 (1945), p. 131.

56. Text in *LiE*, pp. 209–222; for offertory, see p. 218; for anaphora, see pp. 218–220.

57. M. Thurian, *L'Eucharistie* (Delachaux/Niestlé, Neuchâtel, 1959); eucharistic sacrifice remained an interest among French Reformed theologians in the seventeenth cen-

tury, in a way comparable to some Anglicans, see P.-Y. Emery, *Le sacrifice eucharistique selon les théologiens réformées français du XVIIè siècle* (Delachaux/Niestlé, Neuchâtel, 1959).

58. *Eucharistie à Taizé* (Taizé, 1963), pp. 42 (intercession), 49 (anamnesis); eastern source for the latter is obvious.

59. *Eucharistie à Taizé* (Taizé, 1971), passim.

60. Text in *SL* 4 (1965), pp. II-c-1-20; see pp. 7 (intercession), 9 (offertory), 12–15 (anaphora).

61. *Agende für die evangelisch-lutherische Kirchen*, I (Stauder, Kassel, 1955); the German liturgical revival owes a great deal to Löhe; see H.-C. Schmidt-Lauber, "La riscoperta della Preghiera eucaristica nelle Chiese evangeliche," *Rivista Liturgica* 70 (1983), pp. 291–310. (Catholic Apostolic influence is also likely.)

62. *Lutheran Book of Worship* (Augsburg Publishing House/Board of Publication, Lutheran Church in America, Philadelphia, 1978), p. 68.

63. *Gudstjänstordning I Ritual* (Tempte, Lund, 1976), p. 30 (from eucharistic prayer C).

64. E. Schillebeeckx, *Christ the Sacrament of the Encounter with God* (New York & London, 1963), passim; see also J. M. Powers, *Eucharistic Theology* (Burns and Oates/Herder, 1967), pp. 130ff., where Powers discusses Schillebeeckx's (and other modern theological) influence on Vatican II. See also the classic, M. de La Taille, *Mysterium Fidei* (Paris, 1915), which helped broaden Roman Catholic perspectives.

65. See B. Botte, *Le mouvement liturgique, Témoignages et souvenirs* (Desclée, Tournai, 1973), pp. 77ff.

66. A. Flannery (ed.), *Vatican Council II: The Conciliar and Post-Conciliar Documents* (Liturgical Press, Collegeville, 1975), pp. 5, 17. See also P.-M. Gy's annotated text in *LMD* 76 (1963), pp. 40ff., 84ff.

67. For an account of the work of the study group, see A. Bugnini, *La riforma liturgica (1948–1975), EL Subsidia* 30 (Edizioni Liturgiche, Rome 1983), pp. 441–479; see also Botte, *Le mouvement liturgique*, pp. 181ff.

68. Botte's edition of the Apostolic Tradition appeared in 1946, *Hippolyte de Rome, La Tradition Apostolique, SC* 11, Éditions du Cerf, Paris, 1946. For Dix, see Stevenson, *Gregory Dix—25 Years On*, pp. 8–10. (The full *LQF* edition appeared in 1963.)

69. See H.-C. Schmidt-Lauber, "The Eucharistic Prayers in the Roman Catholic Church Today," *SL* 11, 1976, pp. 159ff.

70. The literature on the new eucharistic prayers is prodigious. See articles in *LMD* 94, 1968; essays in Sheppard (ed.), *The New Liturgy*; and B. Kleinheyer, *Erneuerung des Hochgebetes* (Pustet, Regensburg, 1968). Texts in *Missale Romanum*, 1970, pp. 456–460 (*EP* II), 461–465, (*EP* III), 466–471 (*EP* IV); these correspond with *The Sacramentary*, pp. 548–551, 552–555, 556–560.

71. How the Roman Canon was to be revised was a matter of considerable debate; see C. Vagaggini, *The Canon of the Mass and Liturgical Reform* (Chapman, 1967), pp. 84ff.

72. See P. Jounel, "La composition des nouvelles prières eucharistiques," *LMD* 94 (1968), pp. 45–53; B. Botte, "The Short Anaphora," in Sheppard (ed.), *The New Liturgy*, pp. 194–199.

73. See P. Jounel, art. cit., pp. 53–61; L. Bouyer, "The Third Eucharistic Prayer," in Sheppard (ed.), *The New Liturgy*, pp. 203–212. See also B. Botte, "Sacrificium vivum," *Didaskalia* 1 (1971), pp. 5–9, where he notes the Syriac reemphasis on thanksgiving in the anamnesis. Power criticizes the translation of *hostia* by "victim," op. cit., pp. 214 and 216, n. 2: "polysemy has given way to univocity".

74. See P. Jounel, art. cit., pp. 61–72; J. Gelineau, "The Fourth Eucharistic Prayer," in

Sheppard (ed.), *The New Liturgy*, pp. 213–227 (this essay is followed by A. Houssiau on Basil Alex,[1] "The Alexandrine Anaphora of St. Basil," pp. 228–243).

75. All the commentators remark on the proper role of the thanksgiving in the first part of the eucharistic prayer; see A. Dumas, "Les nouvelles préfaces du Missel romain," *LMD* 94, 1968, pp. 159–172; and A. Rose, "The New Prefaces," in Sheppard (ed.), *The New Liturgy*, pp. 244–258. See also Jounel, art. cit. on EP II. This trend is more apparent in the 1975 Children's and Reconciliation EP's issued by Rome, though handling of oblation themes is much the same as the 1970 models; see *Eucharistic Prayers for Masses with Children and Masses for Reconciliation* (Mayhew-McCrimmon, Great Wakering, 1975).

76. See Vagaggini, op. cit., pp. 124–129. For Mal 1:11, see above pp. 15ff.

77. See above n. 73. On thanksgiving, see also P.-M. Gy, "L'Eucharistie dans la tradition de la prière et de la doctrine," *LMD* 137 (1979), pp. 81–102, esp. pp. 85–92; and L.-M. Chauvet, "La dimension sacrificielle de l'Eucharistie," *LMD* 123 (1975), pp. 47–78, where the author links memorial closely with sacrifice.

78. See above n. 75; compare with Vagaggini's suggested text, op. cit., pp. 130–138. See H. A. J. Wegman, "The Rubrics of the Institution-Narrative in the Roman Missal 1970," in P. Jounel, R. Kaczynski, G. Pasqualetti (eds.), *Liturgia Opera Divina e Umana*, *EL Subsidia* 26 (Edizioni Liturgiche, Rome, 1982), pp. 319–328, on use of *hostia* in the new rubrics.

79. Quoted by T. Talley, "The Eucharistic Prayer: Tradition and Development," in Stevenson (ed.), *Liturgy Reshaped*, pp. 60f.; see Kavanagh's article *in toto*, "Thoughts on the New Eucharistic Prayers," *Worship* 43 (1969), pp. 2–12; see also R. Albertine, "Problem of the (Double) Epiclesis in the New Roman Eucharistic Prayer," *EL* 91 (1977), pp. 193–202. See H.-J. Schulz's treatment in *Ökumenische Glaubenseinheit aus eucharistscher Überliferung*, pp. 56–72. But Vagaggini's draft text reads: "et gratias agentes offerimus tibi hoc sacrificium incruentum de tuis donis ac datis: Hostiam puram, Hostiam sanctam, immaculatam hanc Hostiam pro saeculi vita" (we thank you, we offer you this bloodless sacrifice, the gift which you yourself have given us: the pure Victim, the holy, blameless Victim, the Victim given that the world might live), op. cit., p. 135. The final text gets rid of "bloodless sacrifice" and the Latin repetitious victim imagery; even so, granted that the *ingenium romanum* dictated a double epiclesis, the anamnesis here could have been left well alone, in the original Coptic form; see K. W. Stevenson, "Preghiere eucaristiche moderne della Communione anglicana," pp. 337f (on American Episcopal use of the same source).

80. G. Wainwright, *Doxology*, p. 272; see his whole treatment in eirenical vein, pp. 271–274.

81. See F. McManus, "The Berakah Award and Response: The Genius of the Roman Rite Revisited," *Worship* 54 (1980), pp. 360–378; his discussion of the 1965 rite is on pp. 365ff.

82. Art. cit., p. 372.

83. See above pp. 85ff. On the sources for these prayers, see A. Dumas, "Les sources du nouveau Missel Romain," *Notitiae* 1971, pp. 37–42 (60), pp. 74–77 (61), pp. 94–95 (62), pp. 134–136 (63), pp. 276–280 (65), pp. 409–410 (66). The *context* of this prayer has been altered, being now audible, and following on a simplified (and overtly corporate) offertory rite.

84. See H.-J. Schulz, art. cit., pp. 71ff.; he draws attention to the study by E. Lengeling of the evolution of the new Roman offertory rite, and Lengeling's criticism of German tendencies to play it down, *Die neue Ordnung der Eucharistiefeier. Allgemeine Einführung in das römische Messbuch* (Münster, 1971), pp. 24, 29, 33ff, 39, 218ff. In general,

266

see N. K. Rasmussen, "Les rites de présentation du pain et du vin," *MD* 100, 1969, pp. 44–58; see also L. Cornet, "Nouvel offertoire et Berakoth," *QLP* (1978), pp. 97–111. The offertory prayers become popular outside the Roman Church.

85. See C. O. Buchanan, "Series 3 in the Setting of the Anglican Communion," in Jasper (ed.), *The Eucharist Today*, pp. 8–33; and "Liturgical Revision in the Church of England in Retrospect," in Stevenson (ed.), *Liturgy Reshaped*, pp. 146–156; see also Stevenson, art. cit., n. 79. For a complete selection of Anglican texts from 1975 to the present, see C. O. Buchanan (ed.), *Latest Anglican Liturgies*, ACC 66 (SPCK/Grove, 1984).

86. *Alternative Services: Second Series* (SPCK, 1966), p. 147; see also *MAL*, passim, for other Anglican rites in this "interim" stage.

87. See J. L. Houlden, "Good Liturgy or Even Good Battlefield: 'We Offer This Bread and This Cup': 1," *Theology* 69 (1966), pp. 433–437; A. H. Couratin, "The Tradition Received: 'We Offer This Bread and This Cup': 2," ibid., pp. 437–442; M. J. Moreton, "The Early Liturgies: 'We Offer This Bread and This Cup': 3," ibid., pp. 442–447; G. Cuming, "The English Rite: 'We Offer This Bread and This Cup': 4," ibid., pp. 447–452. The four articles make an interesting ensemble. Houlden's parting shot was never really heeded: "The better placed the disagreement, the stronger the chance of ultimate harmony or at least of willing sympathy" (ibid., p. 437). Couratin thumps the patristic tub and shows greater understanding of his opponents than many Anglo-Catholics would: "The prayer is capable of expressing the doctrine of the historic Churches, but in no way enforces it" (ibid., p. 442). Moreton gratuitously translates Egyptian past-tense verbs as present, without any discussion (ibid., pp. 443f.). Cuming extensively quotes from Anglican divines, ending with the telling paragraph, which it is worth quoting in full:

"This brief historical survey shows that the idea of offering the bread and the cup as a representative memorial has been accepted in the Anglican Communion, if not *semper, ubique,* or *ab omnibus,* at any rate for most of the time, in many places, and by very many people. The New World has redressed the balance of the Old, and the mother Church finds herself almost alone in maintaining the posture of 1552." (ibid., p. 452). I find myself in total agreement.

C. O. Buchanan & R. T. Beckwith replied in "This Bread and this Cup: An Evangelical Rejoinder," *Theology* 70 (1967), pp. 265–271.

88. For tabular view of main English anaphoras for the Church of England, see C. O. Buchanan, *The Development of the New Eucharistic Prayers of the Church of England*, GLS 20 (Grove Books, 1979), passim.

89. See Cuming, *A History of Anglican Liturgy*, pp. 175–179, and *The Godly Order*, pp. 177ff.

90. *Alternative Service Book*, 1980, p. 129; this entire section is confused and confusing: for an Evangelical assessment, see C. O. Buchanan, *The End of the Offertory*, GLS 14 (Grove Books, 1978). Anglo-Catholic enthusiasm for the Roman *berakoth* ("Blessed are you") can be paralleled in the Tractarian Missals; insert Roman material in order to make the Anglican original acceptable. There is even provision in *ASB* for singing a hymn *after* the presentation of the gifts, which exalts this preparatory action out of all proportion to the rest of the eucharistic liturgy.

91. Ibid., p. 138; texts of four EP's are to be found in ibid., pp. 130–132 (EP 1) pp. 133–135 (EP 2), pp. 136–138 (EP 3), and pp. 139–141 (EP 4). See also *LAL*, pp. 9ff.

92. See Stevenson, art. cit., p. 322; see also Buchanan's essay in *Liturgy Reshaped*, above, n. 85.

93. *An Australian Prayer Book* (Sydney, 1978), pp. 159, 164 (quotations); see other anaphoras, pp. 145ff, 159ff, 161ff; see also *LAL*, pp. 224ff., 232ff.

94. See American texts in *FAL*, pp. 122–171; and *LAL*, pp. 133ff; see also n. 49 for citations to Prayer Book.

95. H. B. Porter, "An American Assembly of Anaphoral Prayers," in Spinks (ed.), *The Sacrifice of Praise*, p. 196 (essay, pp. 181–195); see also M. Hatchett, *Commentary on the American Prayer Book* (Seabury 1980), pp. 346–377, esp. pp. 367–369. The offering verb in the anamnesis is now in the main clause; compare other rites.

96. See above Chapters 2 and 3 on the Basil tradition, pp. 22ff., 41ff. See also Mitchell, art. cit.; and Talley's remarks, "The Eucharistic Prayer: Tradition and Development," in Stevenson (ed.), *Liturgy Reshaped*, p. 63.

97. *Proposed Third Canadian Eucharist* (1979), pp. 21ff; see *The Book of Alternative Services of the Anglican Church of Canada* (Anglican Book Centre, Toronto, 1985), pp. 193ff. (EP1), pp. 196ff. (EP2), pp. 198ff. (EP3), 201ff. (EP4), pp. 204ff. (EP5); see also *LAL*, pp. 96ff.; a feature of the new Canadian rite is the (optional) provision for *super oblata* prayers, written in line with Holeton's theory (see above pp. 85ff.). EP 1 separates anamnesis from oblation, along the lines of Timothy; see Chapter 3, n. 60; noted in *Anaphoral Offering*, p. 214.

98. Texts in *FAL*, pp. 221–226 (offertory and anaphora); the second EP is from English Series 3, the third is Roman EP II; the Roman offertory prayers appear, preceded by a *berakah* over alms, in the same style.

99. Texts in *FAL*, pp. 307–310 (simple offertory, with three EP's).

100. See *The Scottish Liturgy 1982* (Representative Church Council, Edinburgh, 1982), pp. 6–9 and 18. See also *LAL*, pp. 51–56ff. The "Experimental Liturgy" of 1977 did not contain all these features, but the anamnesis was sharpened in 1982; the rationale was to bring together "the self-offering of the Head and the self-offering of the Body" (correspondence with Dr. G. Tellini). For other Anglican rites, see *MAL*, *FAL*, and *LAL*, passim.

101. *The Book of Offices* (Methodist Publishing House, 1936), pp. 32–35 ("1662" Order) and pp. 37–39 (Alternative Order); see also D. H. Tripp, "Behind the 'Alternative Order,'" *Proceedings of the Wesley Historical Society* 43 (1981), pp. 4–8, where Tripp demonstrates influence from the United Free Church of Scotland *Book of Common Order* of 1928; see n. 42.

102. *The Methodist Service Book* (Methodist Publishing House, 1975), pp. B 12ff. See also D. H. Tripp, "Il rinnovamento della Preghiera eucaristiche nelle Chiese metodiste," *Rivista Liturgica* 70 (1983), pp. 353–373.

103. See above n. 49; texts, ibid., pp. 20–21 (= EP 5).

104. Ibid., passim. Only a few of the 22 EP's in this book do not use this anamnesis. EP 6 is the "Common Eucharistic Prayer" (Episcopal Prayer D), ibid. pp. 22–23. These prayers also frequently "offer" thanks at the narrative, as Scottish Episcopal rite, n. 99. (On *offering* thanks, see above p. 18.) The quoted anamnesis goes back to the 1972 *The Sacrament of the Lord's Supper, an Alternate Text.*

105. Text in *The Book of Common Order 1979* (St. Andrew Press, Edinburgh, 1979), p. 10 (First Order), which is an anaphora preceded by both a "prayer of the veil" (as we have already seen) *and* a simple prayer offering the bread and cup (pp. 7ff.). The big change with this book is that the eucharist is the first service to appear in the contents of the book.

106. See *A Book of Services*, United Reformed Church (St. Andrew Press, Edinburgh, 1980), pp. 26–37, with offertory (money and bread and wine, together, with a prayer over them), and three EP's (the first two offering the sacrifice of praise at the anamnesis,

the third using the Oosterhuis formula, "we present this sign of our faith"); compare H. Oosterhuis, *Open Your Hearts* (Sheed and Ward, 1972), pp. 9, 13, 17. Before the union of Congregational and Presbyterian to form the United Reformed Church, in England, the Congregational Church produced *An Order of Public Worship* (Oxford University Press, 1970), with a similar format, of offertory (p. 16), followed by EP's (pp. 18–25), this time no less than five (preceded by the narrative), the last of which is a rendering of Hippolytus' anaphora, in traditional language. Once again, sacrificial language has been appropriated into the Reformed tradition, with no fear of offertory, nor of subsequent offering of praise, self, and (sometimes) gift, in the EP. See also Spinks, *Freedom or Order?*, pp. 251–255; see also pp. 206ff.

107. See J. B. Ryan, *The Eucharistic Prayer: A Study in Contemporary Liturgy* (Paulist Press, New York, 1974), passim; texts in Oosterhuis, *Open Your Hearts* (see above n. 106), which contains ten "table prayers." Ryan's study treats of other authors. Oosterhuis' compositions earned waspish rebukes from B. Botte, see *Le mouvement liturgique. Témoignages et souvenirs*, p. 182 (where Botte takes him to task for describing Christ as an "unforgettable man"); see also Botte, "La libre composition des prières liturgiques," *QLP* 1974, pp. 211–215, and 1975, p. 60. Botte was addressing the pendulum-swing against rigidity that followed Vatican II.

108. *Eucharistic Prayer of Hippolytus: Text for Consultation* (ICEL, Washington, 1983); *Eucharistic Prayer of St. Basil: Text for Consultation* (ICEL, Washington, 1985).

109. Text in *FAL*, pp. 286f.; and *Book of Common Prayer 1979*, pp. 372–376 (American Episcopal), *At the Lord's Table*, pp. 22–23 (American Methodist), *The Holy Eucharist: Third Canadian Order*, pp. 32–35 (Canadian Anglican).

110. Text in M. Thurian (ed.), *Ecumenical Perspectives on Baptism, Eucharist and Ministry*, Faith and Order Paper 116 (World Council of Churches, Geneva, 1983), pp. 236–246, with commentary, pp. 225–236. See also the copiously annotated text and commentary, F. Schulz, *Die Lima-Liturgie* (Stauda, Kassel, 1983).

111. Quotations in Thurian, op. cit., pp. 242ff. For a comprehensive selection of modern (and less modern) texts, see M. Thurian & G. Wainwright (eds.), *Baptism and Eucharist: Ecumenical Convergence in Celebration* (World Council of Churches, Geneva, 1983); of particular interest are the new texts for India and Zaire (RC), pp. 186ff. and 205ff.

112. See P. F. Bradshaw, "Ordination: Recent Developments," in C. Jones, G. Wainwright, E. Yarnold (eds.), *The Study of Liturgy* (SPCK, 1978), pp. 342–349. For the text of the new Roman Catholic rite, see *De Ordinatione Diaconi, Presbyteri, et Episcopi* (Typis Polyglottis Vaticanis, 1968), pp. 38ff. (ordination prayer) and p. 46 (formula at giving of paten and chalice); see B. Kleinheyer, "L'ordination des prêtres," (*LMD* 98, 1969), pp. 95–112.

113. *Hymns Ancient and Modern: New Standard*, no. 489; compare Pratt Green's hymn, "An upper room" (ibid., no. 434), whose third stanza begins, "And after supper he washed their feet/for service, too, is sacrament."

114. Anglican-Roman Catholic International Commission, *The Final Report* (CTS/SPCK, 1982), p. 14.

115. See J. H. S. Kent, "Christian Theology in the Eighteenth to the Twentieth Centuries," in H. Cunliffe-Jones, *A History of Christian Doctrine*, (Clark, Edinburgh, 1978), pp. 578f.

116. *The Final Report*, pp. 19f.

117. *Baptism, Eucharist, and Ministry*, Faith and Order Paper 111 (World Council of Churches, Geneva, 1982), pp. 11–12.

118. See *Modern Eucharistic Agreement* (SPCK, 1973), pp. 37–39 (American Lutheran-

Roman Catholic Statement: The Eucharist as Sacrifice, 1967), pp. 57ff. (Group of Les Dombes, Doctrinal Agreement on the Eucharist, 1973), pp. 81ff. (Faith and Order Statement, Louvain, 1971).

CHAPTER EIGHT

1. R. F. Taft, book review, *OCP* 49 (1983), p. 46. See further discussion in A. Kavanagh, *On Liturgical Theology*, (Pueblo, New York, 1984), pp. 129ff.

2. See above pp. 79ff.

3. See above pp. 61ff., 68f.

4. R. P. C. Hanson, art. cit.; see also P. F. Bradshaw, "Authority and Freedom in the Early Liturgy," in K. W. Stevenson (ed.), *Authority and Freedoom in Liturgy, GLS* 17 (Grove Books, 1979), pp. 4–10; the fullest account and exploration of this subject is A. Bouley, *From Freedom to Formula, SCA* 21 (Catholic University of America Press, Washington, D.C. 1981).

5. P. F. Bradshaw, "The Liturgical Use and Abuse of Patristics," in *Liturgy Reshaped*, pp. 138f.

6. The heart of the controversy between H.-J. Schulz and B. Schultze concerns the internal unity of the eucharistic prayer; many-sided as the eastern anaphoras are, they all stress thanksgiving in such a powerful manner that offering is seen in a wider perspective. It is for this reason that we favor Schulz's analysis; see above p. 68 (and n. 75).

7. See J. R. K. Fenwick, "The significance of similarities in the anaphoral intercession sequence in the Coptic anaphora of St. Basil and other ancient liturgies," forthcoming in *Studia Patristica* (a Communication read at the Ninth International Conference on Patristic Studies, Oxford, September 1983); recent scholarship is attaching increasing importance on Basil Alex[1].

8. See above pp. 16f.

9. K. W. Stevenson, *Gregory Dix—25 Years On*, pp. 23f.

10. M. B. Moreton, "Offertory Processions?," a paper read at the Eighth International Conference on Patristic Studies, Oxford, September 1979.

11. See Taft, art. cit., Chapter 5, n. 42; see also Kavanagh, op. cit., pp. 129ff.

12. A. M. Ramsey, *Durham Essays and Addresses*, (SPCK, 1956), p. 18; this remark became notorious and has been frequently quoted. The best critique of the offertory procession is from W. J. Grisbrooke who (*inter alia*) insists that the elements should be provided by the people (an eastern insight, doubtless connected with the prayers for the "offerers" we saw earlier); see "Oblation at the Eucharist; I. The Theological Issues," *SL* 3 (1964), pp. 227–239, and "Oblation at the Eucharist; II. The Liturgical Issues," *SL* 4 (1965), pp. 37–55 (esp. pp. 48ff.). I have found these articles of great importance.

13. K. F. Nickle, *The Collection: A Study in Paul's Strategy*, Studies in Biblical Theology 48 (SCM, 1966).

14. A. Kavanagh, *Elements of Rite: A Handbook of Liturgical Style* (Pueblo, New York, 1982), p. 65.

15. P. F. Bradshaw, "Modèles de ministère: le rôle des laïcs dans la liturgie," (*LMD* 154, 1983), pp. 127–150; see also his *Liturgical Presidency in the Early Church, GLS* 36 (Grove Books, 1983), passim.

16. The first two lines of stanza 3 of Toplady's hymn, "Rock of ages, cleft for me," *Hymns Ancient and Modern: New Standard*, 1983, no. 135.

17. See above pp. 59ff., 64ff., 68f.; see also *L'offrande*, pp. 31f.

18. See Stevenson, " 'Ye shall pray for . . .': The Intercession," in *Liturgy Reshaped*, pp. 32–47, esp. pp. 36–40.

19. P. De Clerck, *La "prière universelle" dans les liturgies latines anciennes, LQF* 62

(Aschendorff, Münster, 1977), (summary of conclusions, pp. 305ff).

20. The classic statement of this theme comes, appropriately, from L. Newbigin, *The Household of God* (SCM, 1953), p. 25. But anaphoral intercession continues to have its critics, e.g. Schmidt-Lauber, art. cit. in *SL*, pp. 173ff.

21. K. W. Stevenson, *Nuptial Blessing: A Study of Christian Marriage Rites*, pp. 138ff; see pp. 79ff on the British Manuals; Anglican pressure for a nuptial eucharist proper came from the later Tractarians, p. 236, n. 38.

22. *Missale Romanum*, 1970, contains 15 votive Mass topics and 46 themes for "missae et orationes ad diversa"; this represents a rearrangement and a considerable reduction from the provisions of *Missale Romanum*, 1570.

23. See above pp. 206ff. on the influence of Max Thurian and the American Episcopal Prayer Book texts.

24. The net result of defining the narrative as containing the "words of consecration" is that the offering formula in the anamnesis can be interpreted in such a way that what is offered is the consecrated body and blood of the Lord. I suspect that this western and unprimitive liturgical mystagogy is what lies behind B. Schultze's criticism of H.-J. Schulz; see above pp. 202f. (and n. 79).

25. M. Thurian, "The eucharistic memorial: sacrifice of praise and supplication," in M. Thurian (ed.), *Ecumenical Perspectives on Baptism, Eucharist and Ministry*, p. 101.

26. See classical Anglican Evangelical anxieties expressed by C. Buchanan, *ARCIC and Lima on Baptism and Eucharist*, Grove Worship Series 86 (Grove Books, 1983), p. 12: compare Frieder Schulz's *fehlende Stimme*, op. cit., pp. 29–32.

27. P. Evans-Pritchard, *The Nuer* (Oxford, 1940); this is still the standard field study by a social anthropologist.

28. E.g. Mary Douglas, *Purity and Danger*, (Routledge & Kegan Paul, London), 1966; see discussion by C. Walsh, "Liturgy and Symbolism: A Map,'" in K. W. Stevenson (ed.), *Symbolism and the Liturgy* I, GLS 23 (Grove Books, 1980), pp. 17–26, esp. pp. 18–20 (he also discusses Victor Turner, pp. 20ff.).

29. M. F. C. Bourdillon & M. Fortes (eds.), *Sacrifice* (Academic Press for the Royal Anthropological Institute, 1980). See also E. Durkheim, *The Elementary Forms of the Religious Life* (tr. J. W. Swain) (Allen & Unwin, London, 1915), p. 378.

30. D. N. Power, "Words that crack: the uses of 'sacrifice' in eucharistic discourse," *Worship* 53 (1979), pp. 386–404, esp. pp. 398f. The theology and creation theme is taken up by many writers, including A. Richardson, *An Introduction to the Theology of the New Testament* (London & New York, 1958), pp. 385f.

31. See G. Wainwright, *Eucharist and Eschatology*, pp. 104–110; also *Doxology*, pp. 23–28.

32. See Thurian, ibid., p. 102.

33. See Aulén, *Eucharist and Sacrifice*, p. 153; A. Heron, *Table and Tradition: Towards an Ecumenical Understanding of the Eucharist* (Handsel, Edinburgh, 1983), pp. 169ff. See also K. W. Stevenson, "Eucharistic Sacrifice—What Can We Learn from Christian Antiquity?," in C. O. Buchanan (ed.), *Essays on Eucharistic Sacrifice in the Early Church*, GLS 40 (Grove Books, 1984), pp. 31f, and nn. (for whole essay, pp. 26–33).

34. See G. W. H. Lampe, *God as Spirit* (Oxford University Press, 1977), pp. 167ff.; J. P. Mackey, *Jesus—the Man and the Myth* (SCM, 1979, pp. 151ff).

35. *Den Danske Salmebog* (København, 1953). no. 247. ('*I al sin glans nu stråler solen*'), from stanza 5, a verse laden with the theme of eucharistic praise; *takkesangens offerskål* means literally "thanksong's drink-offering" ('skål' being the traditional Danish drinking greeting); on Grundtvig's place in theology in general, see A. M. Allchin, *The Kingdom of Love and Knowledge* (Darton, Longman and Todd, 1979), pp. 71–89.

271

36. J. L. Houlden, "Liturgy and her companions: a theological appraisal," in R. C. D. Jasper (ed.), *The Eucharist Today*, pp. 168–176; see also K. W. Stevenson, "Stretching Worship," *Theology* 697 (1981), pp. 12–17.

37. See Kavanagh, op. cit., passim (quotation from preface, p. ix); see also critique of Wainwright, pp. 123ff.

38. The use of incense at the intercession (as we have seen above in Greek Mark and *Sharar*, pp. 53, 58) needs looking at also. Is it really part of the ministry of foot-washing to cense clergy elaborately according to *rank?* By all means cense the whole people of God (as a mark of respect), as well as the bread and wine, the gospel-book, and other important externals. But the *biblical* symbolism of incense is prayer in the presence of God. See E. G. C. F. Atchley, *A History of the Use of Incense*, ACC 13 (Longmans, 1909), passim. We suggest that Mark and *Sharar* keep something western Christianity could well appropriate.

39. C. Gore, *The Body of Christ*, p. 213. A similar movement of ideas is apparent in one of the few entirely new *Super oblata* in the *Missale Romanum*, 1970, for the Baptism of Our Lord (p. 168):

"Suscipe munera, Domine,
in dilecti Filii tui revelatione delata,
ut *fidelium tuorum oblatio in eius sacrificium transeat,*
qui mundi voluit peccata miseratus obtuere."

(Noted in *L'offrande*, p. 42, n. 27.)

Appendix One

An Overview of History

1. A. New Testament—anamnesis of the death of Christ (1 Cor 11: 25)
   the living sacrifice (Rom 12:1)
   spiritual sacrifices (1 Pt 2:5)
   B. Jewish background: sacrificial character of *berakah*
   C. *Didache* 14: the sacrifice must be pure (+ Mal 1:11)

2. Hippolytus' *Apostolic Tradition*

   offering of thanks

   "remembering . . . we offer you the bread and the cup . . ."

   "send the Holy Spirit upon the offering of your holy Church . . ."

   Anaphora of *Addai and Mari*

   ("offering" in dialogue); offering of praise and thanks

   "the commemoration of the body and the blood . . . which we offer to you . . ."

   "may your Holy Spirit come and rest on this offering . . ."

3. Roman Canon

   "accept . . . these gifts . . . accept this offering . . . make this offering . . . blessed . . ."

   "remembering . . . we offer to . . . a pure victim . . . to your altar on high . . ."

   Basil/Chrysostom

   offering of thanks

   "remembering . . . we offer"

   Syrian Jacobite/ Maronite

   offering of thanks

   "remembering . . ."

273

Holy Spirit on gifts set forth prayer for offerers	Holy Spirit on gifts/oblations "receive offering for . . ." prayer for offerers

4. Medieval West (Roman)
   1. Offertory prayers
   2. Allegorical interpretation of Mass
   3. Cross-centered piety
   4. Decrease in communicants
   5. Increase of "mass offered for . . ."

   Medieval East (Byzantine)
   1. Great Entrance of gifts: ≠ offertory
   2. Preanaphoral prayer: ≠ offertory
   3. Ceremonial interpretations: ≠ sacrificial
   4. Other "sacrificial" prayers in liturgy: *imprecise*

5. Reformers
   A. Christ died once for all: delete all sacrificial language except "sacrifice of praise" and "living sacrifice": story and response?
   B. Luther, Calvin, Cranmer performed this in different ways/emphases
   C. Placing of gifts on table: explicit? implicit? functional? symbolic?
   D. Solemn eating and drinking in presence of God: sacrificial "flavor"

6. Post-Reformers
   A. Anglican reflection
      1637 Prayer Book: symbolic placing of gifts; reunited eucharistic prayer
      Theological/liturgical scholarship: High and Middle Church
   B. John Wesley
      Daily communicant at university: = "High Church" Puritan
      1745 *Hymns on the Lord's Supper*: strong on sacrifice
   C. Roman Catholic emphasis on presence and sacrifice; in reaction to Reformation
   D. Nineteenth century revival of historical study
      Catholic Apostolic rite (1842–1880) = first ecumenical liturgy

7. Modern Western Rites

274

RC 1970	MSB 1975	AmEp BCP 1979	ASB 1980
simplified offertory prayers	no offertory prayers	no offertory prayers	offertory prayers optional
rich new prefaces	full eucharistic prayer	several eucharistic prayers	four eucharistic prayers
"remembering . . . we offer"	"remembering . . ."	"remembering . . . we offer"	"remembering . . ."
"living sacrifice"	"living sacrifice"	"living sacrifice"	"living sacrifice"
Eucharistic Prayer IV problem	hymnody	Prayer D	controversy

A. Recovery of anamnesis, key of eucharistic action (cf. ARCIC and Lima Statements)
B. Clarification of shape of eucharist; but what of cash offering?
C. Theological developments: christology/pneumatology/eschatology/ecology
D. Politics of liturgical revision: liturgy developing self-consciously, not organically
E. The phenomenon of the complex anamnesis: atonement vs. eucharist; cf. U.S. United Methodist

Notes

1. Tripartite structure of Jewish *berakah:* blessing/thanksgiving/supplication.
Whole prayer has sacrificial flavor: story (acts of God) and response (act of Church).
Early Christian eucharistic prayers inherit this spiritual tradition.
Importance of right relationships.

2. Two archetypes: anamnesis belongs with institution narrative as liturgical unit, but Addai and Mari probably lacks this.
Oblatory language at epiclesis could be earlier: the *whole* eucharist.
Hippolytus = the first to make gift explicit in anaphora.

3. Roman Canon emphasizes offering: Basil/Chrysostom locate offering within total thanksgiving: Syriac prayers reticent on specific offering of gifts.
Both eastern traditions strong on sacrificial character of intercession.
East and West treat intercession and departed differently.

4. Roman and Byzantine differ on meaning of prayers and actions immediately before anaphora: Roman emphasizes offering, Byzantine emphasizes preparatory character.
NB variety in non-Roman Western and non-Byzantine Eastern rites.

5. Liturgies of Reformers written specifically in order to express "correct" theology. "Horizontal" dimension emphasized.
NB imaginative liturgical work of marginals (Richard Baxter).
6. 1637 conservatism could have been due to the "corporate memory" of offertory. Wesley's eucharistic hymns strong on sacrifice: to redress the balance (in Prayer Book). Different results of liturgical scholarship in sixteenth, nineteenth, and twentieth centuries.
7. RC 1970 = Missal of Paul VI
MSB 1975 = Methodist Service Book (British)
AmEp BCP 1979 = Book of Common Prayer (American Episcopal)
ASB 1980 = Alternative Service Book (Church of England)
RC 1970: Preface restores story to full importance; Eucharistic Prayer III sacrificial, within wide context; Eucharistic Prayer IV offers body and blood at anamnesis, rewriting Basil Alex.[1]
MSB 1975 and ASB 1980 allow gifts to be brought to table, or already there.
AmEp BCP 1979 includes reference to money, as does ASB 1980.
AmEp BCP 1979 avoids confusion of gifts and money by having no offertory prayers. ASB 1980 flexible at offertory.
AmEp BCP 1979 includes Prayer D (= ecumenical version of Basil Alex[1]); also allows certain degree of extemporizing in Rite Three (informal use).
All include the theme of "living sacrifice" of the eucharistic community.
But consensus on essential in all these modern (and other modern) rites.

Appendix Two

Lamb Imagery

The description of Jesus as the Lamb is one among several that appear in the pages of the New Testament. At the beginning of the fourth gospel, John the Baptist describes Jesus as the Lamb who takes away the sins of the world (Jn 1:29, 36); in the Acts of the Apostles, Philip explains the (new) meaning of the Lamb led to slaughter (Is 53:7) when catechizing the eunuch (Acts 8:32); and the author of the first letter of Peter refers to Christ as a lamb without blemish (1 Pt 1: 19). In the book of Revelation, however, Jesus is constantly described (and worshipped) as the Lamb (Rev 5:6, 8, 12; 6:16; 7:10, 14, 17; 12: 11; 13:8; 14:1, 4, 10; 15:3; 17:14; 19:7; 21:9, 14, 22, 23, 27; and 22:1, 3). But even if Massey Shepherd's theory that the paschal liturgy forms the background to Revelation is to be accepted,[1] the connotation of Jesus as the Lamb is first and foremost a christological one, not eucharistic. Jesus is a new kind of lamb, for in the Jewish system, no

276

lamb had atoning power. For the new religion to employ and adapt this image would be natural and obvious.

It should therefore come as no surprise that some Christian hymns include references to Christ as the Lamb. In the early versions of the *Gloria in excelsis* analyzed by Capelle,[2] Jesus is the Lamb who takes away the sins of the world, and to whom prayer is addressed for mercy and forgiveness, but the texts vary. *Apostolic Constitutions VII* prays to the Father first and refers to the sin (not sins) of the world; the *Codex Alexandrinus* prays to Christ and refers to the sins (not sin) of the world. (Capelle regards the special features of *Apostolic Constitutions* as betraying Arian symptoms at this point.)[3] When we come to the Agnus Dei, however, we are on slightly different ground because the context is more specifically eucharistic. The antecedent is probably to be found in the East, in the (Greek) liturgy of St. James, where at the fraction the priest exclaims:

"Behold the Lamb of God, who takest away the sins of the world, slaughtered for the life and salvation of the world."[4]

Such a combination of Jn 1:29 and Is 53:7 is a new use of scripture, and may have been introduced as a comment on a traditional liturgical action, the breaking of the bread. (A comparable expression seems to have been included in the Byzantine liturgy, but later dropped.)[5] When Sergius I introduced Agnus Dei during his pontificate (687–701), he was probably responsible for adapting this liturgical tradition of the East to suit the needs of the Roman Church.[6] It becomes a chant to be sung during the lengthy business of breaking the bread for communion.[7] The *Gloria in excelsis* no doubt suggested the formula. Both Jungmann and Bishop regard the chant as primarily one of adoration to Christ present in the sacrament.[8] I would myself prefer to interpret it as a christological hymn, whose eucharistic setting is more to do with the bread being broken (and by analogy, with the Lamb being slain) than with Christ present in the sacrament. When the fraction and the Agnus Dei become separated later on in the West, the chant probably does become a general eucharistic hymn in the function it serves in the liturgy.

Function is the key word, for the Agnus Dei reappears in two Gallican books around the same time, together with a rich "Lamb" preface:

"Lamb of God, who takes away the sins of the world, look upon us and have mercy on us, you who have become

277

both victim and priest for us, both reward and redeemer. Saviour of the world, guard from all evil those whom you have redeemed."

". . . who was led for us as a sheep for the slaughter and as a lamb was dumb before the shearer. For this is the Lamb of God, your only-begotten Son, who has taken away the sin of the world; who did not refrain from offering himself for us, and defends us before you with intercession that does not cease, because he never dies, though he was immolated, he lives for ever, though he was killed. For Christ is our Passover that is sacrificed; let us not immolate him in the old leaven, nor in the blood of fleshly victims, but in unleavened bread of sincerity and truth."[9]

The first prayer appears in the *Missale Gothicum* as the *Post secreta* for Maundy Thursday; in other words, it makes up a variable part of the anaphora, which follows on the institution narrative. The paschal character of the Maundy Thursday Mass of the Last Supper no doubt suggested its use here.[10] (The Gallican rite had no Agnus Dei in the way the Roman rite did.) The second prayer occurs as the *Immolacio* for the Wednesday after Easter. Many of the sacramentaries have Lamb image prefaces at Easter, but this one is particularly strong in its language and eucharistic in its overtones.

In the *Missale Gallicanum Vetus*, however, both these prayers occur together on the Wednesday after Easter. The first prayer is a collect, the second retains the same function as the *Gothicum*, namely that of an *Immolacio* (preface). The second prayer appears in a reedited (or perhaps independent) form in the eighth-century Gelasian books, and once more, on Easter Wednesday.[11] The association with Easter Wednesday continues much later, for in the 1736 de Vintimille Missal of Paris, and in the 1781 Missal of S. Vanne, both these two prayers are rewritten into a *Super oblata*, for the same day.[12]

Clearly, the theme of Christ as the Lamb of God was of interest to liturgical minds at the time; at Rome, for the breaking of the bread (as in Greek James); in the *Gothicum*, as an anamnetic prayer in the anaphora on Maundy Thursday; in the *Gallicanum Vetus*, as a collect for Easter Wednesday. Indeed, the Mozarabic Sacramentary uses it as an *Illatio* (preface) for Easter Tuesday, in a different form.[13]

In this connection, it is also worth noting that Easter hymns such as *"Ad cenam agni providi"* [14] are celebrations of the Easter victory of Christ, whose allusions to the "feast" are probably meant to mean the entire paschal celebration, only eucharistic by implication. The versions of the Agnus Dei written by Nikolaus Decius and Martin Luther are purely doxological,[15] nothing to do with the fraction, because in

278

the Lutheran rite, the Agnus Dei is sung during the administration of communion. However, in Baxter's "Savoy" liturgy, we encounter yet one more use; at the fraction, the minister says:

"Behold the sacrificed Lamb of God,
that taketh away the sins of the world."[16]

Baxter's eucharistic theology was typical of the seventeenth-century English-speaking world, Anglican and Puritan, as Cranmer's was of the early sixteenth. Neither is medieval Catholic, but they are significantly different from one another. Baxter here expresses a call to the faithful to adore the heavenly Lamb and to approach the eucharistic table in penitence and faith.

In the Eastern eucharistic prayers, Lamb christology is not unknown, but the Byzantine rite from at least the eighth century associates the incisions made in the eucharistic bread at the prothesis with the immolation of the Lamb (and the priest recites Is 57:3 as words of interpretation). Byzantines and Copts refer to the bread as the "Lamb" throughout the eucharistic liturgy.[17] But this, once again, is by way of analogy, not an abstruse anticipation of consecration, since it would be hard to locate a "moment" of immolation in these rich and venerable rites. The Lamb is, after all, a deeply traditional way of depicting Christ in eastern spirituality and iconography.

Turning to the Roman rite, it was not until 1585 in Aix-en-Provence that Jn 1:29 ("*ecce agnus dei . . .*") was used for the first time before communion.[18] Modern euchology tends to employ other christological imagery, although James White's subtle interweaving of these themes in the American United Methodist "lyrical" eucharistic prayer is a notable exception.[19] All in all, however, the old Frankish prayers quoted earlier point to the essential paradox of eucharistic sacrifice; the Lamb has been slain, and yet lives for ever, to be worshipped, adored, and served.[20]

Notes

1. M. H. Shepherd, *The Paschal Liturgy and the Apocalypse*, Ecumenical Studies in Worship 6 (Lutterworth, 1960), pp. 92ff.

2. B. Capelle, "Le texte du 'Gloria in excelsis,' " *Revue de l'Histoire Ecclésiastique* 44 (1949), pp. 439–457 (= *Travaux Liturgiques* II, pp. 176–191).

3. See. J. Jungmann, *The Place of Christ in Liturgical Prayer* (Chapman, 1965), pp. 259–262 and nn.

4. *LEW*, p. 62; see also above p. 108.

5. Noted by Jungmann, *The Place of Christ*, p. 260, n. 1.

6. G. Iversen, *Corpus Troporum: Tropes de l'Agnus Dei,* Acta Universitatis Stockholmiensis: Studia Latina Stockholmiensia XXVI (Almqvist and Wiksell, Stockholm, 1980), pp. 195ff.

7. For the subsequent history of the Agnus Dei, see *Jungmann,* pp. 261–269; see also Iversen, op. cit., passim.

8. Jungmann, *The Place of Christ,* p. 259; E. Bishop, *Liturgica Historica* (Oxford 1918), p. 145 (noted by Jungmann, p. 259, n. 2).

9. *Go* 211 and 296; *MGV* 212 and 214; the second prayer becomes Preface 43 (Paschal: III) in the 1969 *Missale Romanum.* (*MGV* 212 reads sin, as *Apostolic Constitutions* VII.)

10. See Frendo, *The "Post Secreta" of the "Missale Gothicum,"* pp. 32–34; but Frendo seems to miss the essential point, that the Agnus Dei is being subjected to quite distinct liturgical *uses* at this stage in its history.

11. A. Dumas, *Liber Sacramentorum Gellonensis: Textus,* 760 (p. 107); see also the accompanying volume, *Introductio, Tabulae et Indices,* p. 39, for *"table synoptique."*

12. See F. Brovelli, "Per uno studio dei messali francesi del XVIII secolo. Saggi di analisi," *EL* 97 (1983), p. 518 (no. 153, and nn.).

13. *Moz* 679.

14. M. Frost (ed.), *Historical Companion to Hymns Ancient and Modern,* p. 208.

15. "O Lamm Gottes, unschuldig" (Decius, 1522), and "Christe, du Lamm Gottes" (Luther, 1528).

16. See B. Spinks, *Freedom or Order?,* pp. 64f.; see above pp. 154f., on Baxter's rite.

17. *LEW,* p. 356; cf. p. 309 (*Barberini 336*), which alludes to the Lamb sacrificed for the world, but without the biblical quotation; for Greek Mark, see *LEW,* p. 145.

18. *Jungmann* II, p. 303 and nn. Jn 1:29 is, however, used in the ninth century Celtic rite, just before Communion; see G. F. Warner, *The Stowe Missal,* p. 18.

19. See above p. 210 for quotation from "lyrical" prayer.

20. I am indebted to the Rev. Charles Brock for his paper, "The Relation of the Absolution to the *Agnus Dei,*" read at the Fifth Meeting of the British Society for Liturgical Study, Oxford, September 1984.

Bibliography

Albertine, R. "Problem of the (Double) Epiclesis in the New Roman Eucharistic Prayers," *EL* 91 (1977), pp. 193–202.

Allchin, A. M. *The Kingdom of Love and Knowledge* (Darton, Longman and Todd, 1979).

Anaphorae Syriacae, I–III (Rome, 1939–1981).

Andrieu, M. *Le Pontifical Romain au moyen âge*, Studi e Testi 86–88 (Vatican, 1959).

Anglican-Roman Catholic International Commission, *The Final Report* (Catholic Truth Society/SPCK, 1982).

Arranz, M. "L'Economie du Salut dans la prière du Post-Sanctus des anaphores de type antiochéen," *LMD* 105 (1971), pp. 46–75.

Ashworth, H. "The influence of the Lombard invasions on the Gregorian Sacramentary," *Bulletin of the John Rylands Library* 36 (1954), pp. 305–327.

Atchley, E. G. C. F. *A History of the Use of Incense*, ACC 13 (Longmans, 1909).

Audet, J. P. *La Didachè: Instructions des Apôtres* (Librairie Lecoffre, Paris, 1958).

Aulén, G. *Eucharist and Sacrifice* (Oliver & Boyd, Edinburgh, 1958).

Baker, J. A. *The Foolishness of God* (Darton, Longman and Todd, 1970).

Baptism, Eucharist, and Ministry, Faith and Order Paper 111 (World Council of Churches, Geneva, 1982).

Barkley, J. M. " 'Pleading his eternal sacrifice' in the Reformed Liturgy," in B. D. Spinks (ed.), *The Sacrifice of Praise*, EL Subsidia 19 (Edizioni Liturgiche, Rome, 1981), pp. 123–140.

Bates, W. H. "Thanksgiving and Intercession in the Liturgy of St. Mark," in B. D. Spinks (ed.), *The Sacrifice of Praise*, EL Subsidia 19 (Edizioni Liturgiche Rome, 1981), pp. 109–119.

Baumstark, A. "Denkmäler altarmenischer Messliturgie 3: Die armenische Rezension der Jakobus-liturgië, *OC* 7–8 (1918), pp. 1–32.

Bettenson, H. *The Early Christian Fathers* (Oxford, 1969).

———. *The Later Christian Fathers* (Oxford, 1970).

Black, M. *Rituale Melchitarum*, Bonner Orientalistische Studien 22 (Stuttgart, 1939).

Blomfield, J. *The Eucharistic Canon* (SPCK, 1930).

Bornert, R. *Les Commentaires Byzantines de la Divine Liturgie du VIIè au XVè siècle*, Archives de l'Orient Chrétien 9 (Paris, 1966).

Botte, B. *Le Canon de la messe romaine*, Textes et Etudes Liturgiques 2 (Louvain, 1935).

————. *Hippolyte de Rome, La Tradition Apostolique*, SC 11 (Editions du Cerf, Paris, 1946).

————. "L'épiclèse de l'anaphore d'Hippolyte," *Recherches de théologie ancienne et médiévale* 14 (1947), pp. 241–251.

————. "L'Anaphore Chaldéenne des Apôtres," *OCP* 15 (1949), pp. 259–276.

———— & C. Mohrmann, eds. *L'Ordinaire de la Messe*, Etudes Liturgiques 2 (Abbaye du Mont César, Louvain, 1953).

————. *La Tradition Apostolique de saint Hippolyte*, LQF 39, (Aschendorff, Münster, 1963).

————. "L'Euchologe de Sérapion, est-il authentique?" *OC* 48 (1964), pp. 50–57.

————. "Sacrificium vivum," *Didaskalia* 1 (1971), p. 5–9.

————. *Le mouvement liturigique: Témoignages et souvenirs* (Desclée, Tournai, 1973).

————. "La libre composition des prières liturgiques," *QLP* (1974), pp. 211–215.

Bouley, A. *From Freedom to Formula*, SCA 21 (Catholic University of America Press, Washington D.C., 1981).

Bourdillon, M. F. C. & M. Fortes, eds. *Sacrifice* (Academic Press for the Royal Anthropological Institute, 1980).

Bouyer, L. *Eucharist* (Notre Dame, 1968).

Bradshaw, P. F. *The Anglican Ordinal*, ACC 53 (SPCK, 1971).

————. "The Reformers and the Ordination Rites," *SL* 13 (1979), pp. 94–107.

————. *Daily Prayer in the Early Church*, ACC 63 (SPCK, 1981) (-Oxford University Press, New York, 1982).

————. "The Liturgical Use and Abuse of Patristics," in K. W. Stevenson (ed.), *Liturgy Reshaped* (SPCK, London, 1982), pp. 134–145.

————. "Modèles de ministère: le rôle des laïcs dans la liturgie," *LMD* 154 (1983), pp. 127–150.

————. *Liturgical Presidency in the Early Church*, GLS 36 (Grove Books, 1983).

Breward, I. ed. *The Westminster Directory*, GLS 21 (Grove Books, 1980).

Brightman, F. E. *Liturgies Eastern and Western, I: The Eastern Liturgies* (Oxford, 1896).

————. "The Sacramentary of Serapion of Thmuis," *JTS* 1 (1900), pp. 88–113.

————. *The English Rite I & II* (Rivingtons, 1915).

————. "The Anaphora of Theodore", *JTS* 31 (1930), pp. 160–164.

Brilioth, Y. *Eucharistic Faith and Practice, Evangelical and Catholic* (SPCK, 1930).

Brock, S. & M. Vasey. *The Liturgical Portions of the Didascalia*, GLS 29 (Grove Books, 1982).

Brovelli, F. "Per uno studio dei messali francesi del XVIII secolo. Saggi di analisi," *EL* 97 (1983), pp. 482–549.

Buchanan, C. O., ed. *Modern Anglican Liturgies* (Oxford, 1968).

————, ed. *Further Anglican Liturgies* (Grove Books, 1975).

————. *What Did Cranmer Think He Was Doing?* GLS 7 (Grove Books, 1976).

————. *The End of the Offertory*, GLS 14 (Grove Books, 1978).

————. *The Development of the New Eucharistic Prayers of the Church of England*, GLS 20 (Grove Books, 1979).

————. "Liturgical Revision in the Church of England in Retrospect," in K. W. Stevenson, ed., *Liturgy Reshaped* (SPCK, London, 1982), pp. 146–156.

————, ed. *Anglo-Catholic Worship: An Evangelical Appreciation after 150 Years* GLS 33 (Grove Books, 1983).

————. *ARCIC and Lima on Baptism and Eucharist*, Grove Worship Series 86 (Grove Books, 1983).

————, ed. *Latest Anglican Liturgies*, ACC 66 (SPCK/Grove, 1985).

Buchanan, C. O. & R. T. Beckwith. "This Bread and This Cup—An Evangelical Rejoinder," *Theology* 70 (1967), pp. 265–271.

Bugnini, A. *La riforma liturgica—1948-1975*, EL Subsidia 30 (Edizioni Liturgiche, Rome, 1983).

Bulgaris, N. *A Holy Catechism*, (Constantinople, 1861).

Burnet, G. *The Holy Communion in the Reformed Church of Scotland* (Oliver & Boyd, Edinburgh, 1960).

Buxton, R. F. *Eucharist and Institution Narrative*, ACC 58 (Mayhew-McCrimmon, Great Wakering, 1976).

———. "The Shape of the Eucharist: A Survey and Appraisal," in K. W. Stevenson, ed., *Liturgy Reshaped* (SPCK, London, 1982) pp. 83–93.

Cabasilas, N. *A Commentary on the Divine Liturgy*, tr. J. M. Hussey, P. A. McNulty (SPCK, 1966).

Capelle, B. "L'Anaphore de Sérapion: Essai d'exégèse," *Muséon* 59 (1946), pp. 425–443 (= *Travaux Liturgiques II*, [Louvain, 1962], pp. 344–358).

———. "Les oraisons de la messe du saint sacrement," *QLP* 1946, pp. 61–71 (= *Travaux Liturgiques III* [Louvain, 1967], pp. 242–251).

———. "Le texte du 'Gloria in excelsis,'" *Revue de l'Histoire Ecclésiastique* 44 (1949), pp. 439–457 (= *Travaux Liturgiques II*, pp. 176–191).

———. "Une messe de S. Léon pour L'Ascension," *EL* 67 (1953), pp. 200 – 209 (= *Travaux Liturgiques II* [Louvain, 1962], pp. 71–78).

Cardale, J. B. *Readings upon the Liturgy and Other Divine Offices of the Church I* (Bosworth, 1874).

Cardwell, E. *A History of Conferences* (Oxford University Press, 1840).

Casel, O. *La Fête de Pâques dans l'Eglise des Pères*, Lex Orandi 37 (Editions du Cerf, Paris, 1963).

Cazelles, H. "L'Anaphore et L'Ancient Testament," *Eucharisties d'Orient et d'Occident I*, Lex Orandi 46 (Éditions du Cerf, Paris, 1970), pp. 11–21.

Chauvet, L.-M. "La dimension sacrificielle de l'Eucharistie," *LMD* 123 (1975), pp. 47–78.

Chavasse, A. "L'oraison *super sindonem* dans la liturgie romaine," *Revue Bénédictine* 70 (1960), pp. 313–323.

Cirlot, F. L. *The Early Eucharist* (SPCK, 1939).

Clark, F. *Eucharistic Sacrifice and the Reformation* (Blackwells, Oxford, 1st ed. 1960, 2nd ed. 1967).

Connolly, R. H., ed. *The Liturgical Homilies of Narsai*, Texts and Studies VIII, 1 (Cambridge, 1909).

———. *The So-Called Egyptian Church Order and Derived Documents*, Texts and Studies, VIII, 4, (Cambridge, 1916).

Coquin, R.-G. "L'anaphore alexandrine de saint Marc," *Muséon* 82 (1969), pp. 307–338.

———. "L'anaphore alexandrine de saint Marc," *Eucharisties d'Orient et d'Occident, II*, pp. 51–82.

Cornet, L. "Nouvel offertoire et Berakoth," *QLP* (1978), pp. 97–111.

Couratin, A. H. "The Tradition Received: 'We Offer This Bread and This Cup': 2," *Theology* 69 (1966), pp. 437–442.

Cross, F. L. "Pre-Leonine Elements in the Proper of the Roman Mass," *JTS* 50 (1949), pp. 191–197.

Cuming, G. J. "The English Rite: 'We offer this Bread and this Cup': 4," *Theology* 69 (1966), pp. 447–452.

———, ed. *The Durham Book* (Oxford University Press, 1969).

———. "Egyptian Elements in the Jerusalem Liturgy," *JTS* 25 (1974), pp. 117–124.

———. *Hippolytus—A Text for Students*, GLS 8 (Grove Books, 1976).

———, ed. *Essays on Hippolytus*, GLS 15 (Grove Books, 1978).

———. "Thmuis Revisited: Another Look at the Prayers of Bishop Sarapion," *Theological Studies* 41 (1980), pp. 568–575.

———. "The Anaphora of St. Mark: A study in Development," *Muséon* 95 (1982), pp. 115–129.

———. *A History of Anglican Liturgy*, (Macmillan, 2nd ed. 1982).

———. *The Godly Order*, ACC 65 (SPCK, 1983).

———. "Pseudonymity and Authenticity, with Special Reference to the Liturgy of St John Chrysostom," in E. Livingstone, ed., *Studia Patristica* 15 (Akademie Verlag, Berlin, 1984), pp. 532–538.

Cunliffe-Jones, H., ed. *A History of Christian Doctrine* (T. & T. Clark, Edinburgh, 1978).

Daly, R. *The Origins of the Christian Doctrine of Sacrifice* (Darton Longman and Todd, 1978).

———. *Christian Sacrifice*, SCA 18 (Catholic University of America Press, Washington D.C., 1978).

Davies, H. *Worship and Theology in England: III, From Watts and Wesley to Maurice* (Princeton University Press, 1961).

———. *Worship and Theology in England: IV, From Newman to Martineau* (Princeton University Press, 1962).

———. *Worship and Theology in England: V, The Ecumenical Century* (Princeton University Press, 1965).

———. *Worship and Theology in England: I, From Cranmer to Hooker* (Princeton University Press, 1970).

————. *Worship and Theology in England: II, From Andrewes to Baxter and Fox* (Princeton University Press, 1975).

Dearing, T. *Wesleyan and Tractarian Worship* (Epworth, 1966).

De Clerck, P. *La "prière universelle" dans les liturgies latines anciennes*, LQF 62 (Aschendorff, Münster, 1977).

Denzinger, H. *Ritus Orientalium I & II* (Stahl, Würzburg, 1864).

Deshusses, J. *Le Sacramentaire Grégorien I*, Spicilegium Friburgense 16 (Fribourg, 1971).

————. *Le Sacramentaire Grégorien II*, Spicilegium Friburgense 24 (Fribourg, 1979).

————. *Le Sacramentaire Grégorien III*, Spicilegium Fribrugense 28 (Fribourg, 1982).

Dix, G. *The Apostolic Tradition of St. Hippolytus* (Church Historical Society, SPCK, 1937).

————. *The Question of Anglican Orders* (Dacre, 1944).

————. *The Shape of the Liturgy* (Dacre, 1945; revised ed. New York, 1982).

Donaldson, G. *The Making of the Scottish Prayer Book of 1637* (Edinburgh University Press, 1954).

Doresse, J. & E. Lanne. *Un témoin archaïque de la liturgie copte de saint Basile*, Bibliothèque du Muséon 47 (Louvain, 1960).

Douglas, M. *Purity and Danger: An Analysis of Concepts of Pollution and Taboo* (Routledge and Kegan Paul, London, 1966).

Dowden, J. *Further Studies in the Prayer Book* (Methuen, 1908).

————. *The Annotated Scottish Communion Office* (Oxford, 1922).

Dugmore, C. *The Mass and the English Reformers* (Macmillan, 1958).

Dumas, A. "Les nouvelles préfaces du Missel romain," *LMD* 94 (1968), pp. 159–172.

————. "Les sources du nouveau Missel Romain," *Notitiae* (1971), pp. 37–42 (60), pp. 74–77 (61), pp. 94–95 (62), pp. 134–136 (63), pp. 276–280 (65), pp. 409–410 (66).

————. *Liber Sacramentorum Gellonensis*, Corpus Christianorum: Series Latina CLIX, CLIXA (Turnholti, Brepols, 1981).

Durkheim, E. *The Elementary Forms of the Religious Life*, tr. J. W. Swain (Allen & Unwin, London, 1915).

Echlin, E. *The Anglican Eucharist in Ecumenical Perspective: Doctrine and Rite from Cranmer to Seabury* (Seabury, 1968).

Eeles, F. C.. *Traditional Ceremonial and Customs Connected with the Scottish Liturgy*, ACC 18, (Longmans, 1910).

Eizenhöfer, L., ed. *Liber Sacramentorum Aecclesiae ordinis anni circuli*, Rerum ecclesiasticarum documenta; series maior: Fontes V (Rome, 1960).

Ellebracht, M. P. *Remarks on the Vocabulary of the Ancient Orations in the Missale Romanum* (Nijmegen, 1966).

Eméry, P.-Y. *Le sacrifice eucharistique selon les théologiens réformées français du XVIIè siècle* (Delachaux/Niestlé, Neuchatel, 1959).

Engberding, H. *Das eucharistische Hochgebet der Basileiosliturgie, Textgeschichtliche Untersuchungen und kritische Ausgabe* (Ashendorff, Münster, 1931).

————. "Die syrische Anaphora der zwölf Apostel und ihre Paralleltexte," *OC* 3 (1937), pp. 213–247.

————. "Die ΕΥΧΗ ΤΗΣ ΠΡΟΣΚΟΜΙΔΗΣ der byzantinischen Basileioseliturgie und ihre Geschichte," *Muséon* 79 (1966), pp. 287–313.

The Eucharist in India—a Plea for a Distinctive Liturgy for the Indian Church (Longmans, 1920).

Eucharistica: Meditations and Prayers on the Most Holy Eucharist from Old English Divines, with an Introduction by Samuel, Lord Bishop of Oxford (Suttaby, 1849).

Evans-Pritchard, P. *The Nuer* (Oxford, 1940).

Fawcett, T. J. *The Liturgy of Comprehension 1689*, ACC 54 (Mayhew-McCrimmon, Great Wakering, 1973).

Fenwick, J. R. K. "The Significance of Similarities in the Anaphoral Intercession Sequence in the Coptic Anaphora of St. Basil and Other Ancient Liturgies," a paper read at the 9th International Conference on Patristic Studies, Oxford, September 1983.

————. "An investigation into the Common Origin of the Anaphoras of the Liturgies of St. Basil and St. James," Ph.D. dissertation, University of Bristol, England, 1985.

Ferhat, P. "Denkmäler altarmenischer Messliturgie 1: Eine dem hl. Gregor von Nazianz zugeschriebene Liturgie," *OC* 1 (1911), pp. 204–214.

————. "Denkmäler altarmenischer Messliturgie 2: Die angebliche Liturgie des hl. Katholikos Sahak," *OC* 3 (1913), pp. 16–31.

Férotin, M., ed. *Liber mozarabicus sacramentorum*, Monumenta ecclesiastica liturgica VI (Paris, 1912).

287

Fiala, V. "Les prières d'acceptation de l'offrande et le genre littéraire du canon romain," in *Eucharisties d'Orient et d'Occident I*, Lex Orandi 46 (Editions du Cerf, 1970), pp. 117–133.

Flannery, A., ed. *Vatican Council II: The Conciliar and Post-Conciliar Documents* (Liturgical Press, Collegeville, 1975).

Forrester, D., J. McDonald, & G. Tellini. *Encounter with God* (T. & T. Clark, Edinburgh, 1983).

Frendo, J. A. *The Post Secreta of the Missale Gothicum and the Eucharistic Theology of the Gallican Anaphora* (Malta, 1977).

Frere, W. H. *Some Principles of Liturgical Reform* (Murray, 1911).

———. "Early Forms of Ordination," in H. B. Swete, ed., *Essays on the Early History of the Church and the Ministry* (Macmillan, 1918).

———. *The Primitive Consecration Prayer*, Alcuin Club Prayer Book Revision Pamphlets VIII (Mowbrays, 1922).

———. *The Anaphora or Great Eucharistic Prayer* (Church Historical Society, SPCK, 1938).

Frost, M., ed. *Historical Companion to Hymns Ancient and Modern* (Clowes, 1962).

Gerhards, A. *Die griechische Gregoriosanaphora: Ein Beitrag zur Geschichte des Eucharistischen Hochgebets*, LQF 65 (Aschendorff, Münster, 1984).

Giet, S. *L'Enigme de la Didachè* (Editions Ophyrs, Paris, 1970).

Gimeno, J. A. G. *Las oraciónes sobre las Ofrendas en el Sacramentário Leoniano: Texto y Doctrína* (Consejo Superior de Investigaciónes Científicas, Madrid, 1965).

Goar, J. *Euchologion sive Rituale Graecorum* (Venice, 1730).

Gore, C. *The Body of Christ* (Murray, 1901).

Gray, D. C. The Influence of Tractarian Principles on Parish Worship, 1839–1849," *Alcuin* (1984), pp. 1–15.

———. "The Evolution of the Parish Communion in the Church of England," Ph.D. dissertation, University of Manchester, England, 1985.

Gregg, D. *Anamnesis in the Eucharist*, GLS 5 (Grove Books, 1976).

Grisbrooke, W. J. *Anglican Liturgies of the Seventeenth and Eighteenth Centuries*, ACC 40 (SPCK, 1958).

———. "Oblation at the Eucharist: I The Theological Issues," *SL* 3 (1964), pp. 227–239.

288

————. "Oblation at the Eucharist: II The Liturgical Issues," *SL* 4 (1965), pp. 37–55.

Gy, P.-M. "Le Sanctus romain et les anaphores orientales," in *Mélanges Liturgiques offerts au R. P. Dom Bernard Botte* (Abbaye du Mont César, Louvain, 1972), pp. 167–174.

————. "Ancient Ordination Prayers," *SL* 13 (1979), pp. 70–93.

————. "L'Eucharistie dans la tradition de la prière et de la doctrine," *LMD* 137 (1979), pp. 81–102.

Hall P., ed. *Reliquiae Liturgicae I–V* (Bath, 1847).

Halliburton, R. J. "The Canon of Series 3," in R. Jasper, ed., *The Eucharist Today*, (SPCK, 1973) pp. 95–129.

Hammerschmidt, E. *Die koptische Gregoriosanaphora*, Berliner byzantinische Arbeiten 8 (Berlin, 1957).

Hänggi A. & I. Pahl, eds. *Prex Eucharistica*, Spicilegium Friburgense 12 (Fribourg University, 1968).

Hanson, R. P. C. "The liberty of the bishop to improvise prayer in the eucharist," *Vigiliae Christianae* 15 (1961), pp. 173–176.

————. *Eucharistic Offering in the Early Church*, GLS 19 (Grove Books, 1979).

Hanssens, J. M. *Institutiones Liturgicae de Ritibus Orientalibus, III* (Rome, 1932).

Härdelin, A. *The Tractarian Understanding of the Eucharist*, Studia Historico-Ecclesiastica Upsaliensia 8 (Uppsala, 1965).

Hardison, O. B. *Christian Rite and Christian Drama in the Middle Ages* (Johns Hopkins, Baltimore, 1969).

Hart, S. *Bishop Seabury's Communion-Office* (Whitaker, N.Y., 1883).

Hatchett, M. *Commentary on the American Prayer Book* (Seabury, 1980).

————. *The Making of the First American Book of Common Prayer* (Seabury, 1982).

Heron, A. *Table and Tradition; Towards an Ecumenical Understanding of the Eucharist* (Handsel, Edinburgh, 1983).

Hicks, N. *The Fullness of Sacrifice* (SPCK, 3rd ed. 1946).

Higgins, A. J. B. *The Lord's Supper in the New Testament*, Studies in Biblical Theology 6 (SCM, 1952).

Holeton, D. R.. "The Sacramental Language of S. Leo the Great. A study of the words 'munus' and 'oblata,' " *EL* 92 (1978), pp. 115–165.

Houlden, J. L. "Good Liturgy or Even Good Battlefield: 'We offer this Bread and this Cup': 1," *Theology* 69 (1966), pp. 433–437.

———. *Explorations in Theology* (SCM, 1978).

Hubert H. & M. Mauss. *Sacrifice: Its Nature and Function*, tr. W. D. Halls (Chicago, 1964).

Iversen, G. *Corpus Troporum IV: Tropes de l'Agnus Dei*, Acta Universitatis Stockholmiensis: Studia Latina Stockholmiensia XXVI (Almqvist and Wiksell International, Stockholm, 1980).

Jacob, A. "Zum Eisodosgebet der byzantinischen Chrysostomusliturgie," *Östkirchliche Studien* 15 (1966), pp. 35–38.

Jammo, S. Y. H. *La structure de la messe chaldéenne*, OCA 207 (Rome, 1979).

Jasper, R. C. D., ed. *Walter Howard Frere: His Correspondence on Liturgical Revision and Construction*, ACC 39 (SPCK, 1954).

———. *The Search for an Apostolic Liturgy*, Alcuin Club Pamphlet XVIII (Mowbrays, 1963).

———, ed. *The Eucharist Today: Studies on Series 3* (SPCK, 1974).

Jasper, R. C. D. & G. J. Cuming, eds. *The Prayers of the Eucharist: Early and Reformed* (Oxford University Press, New York, 2nd ed. 1980).

Jeremias, J. *The Eucharistic Words of Jesus* (SCM, 1966).

Jones, B. H. "The Formation of the Nestorian Liturgy," *ATR* 48 (1966), pp. 276–306.

Jones, C., G. Wainwright, & E. Yarnold, eds. *The Study of Liturgy* (SPCK, 1978).

Jones, D. R. "Ἀνάμνησις in the LXX and the Interpretation of I Cor. 11:25," *JTS* 6 (1955), pp. 183–191.

Jounel, P. "La composition des nouvelles prières eucharistiques," *LMD* 94 (1968), pp. 45–53.

Jungmann, J. (*Missarum Sollemnia,*) The Mass of the Roman Rite, Its Origins and Development 2 vols., (Benziger Bros. New York, 1950).

———. *The Place of Christ in Liturgical Prayer* (Chapman, 1965).

Kavanagh, A. "Thoughts on the New Eucharistic Prayers," *Worship* 43 (1969), pp. 2–12.

———. *Elements of Rite: A Handbook of Liturgical Style* (Pueblo, New York, 1982).

————. *On Liturgical Theology* (Pueblo, New York, 1984).

Keifer, R. A. "The Unity of the Roman Canon: An Examination of Its Unique Structure," *SL* 11 (1976), pp. 39–58.

Klauck, H.-J. *Herrenmahl und Hellenistischer Kult*, Neutestamentliche Abhandlungen 15 (Aschendorff, Münster, 1982).

Klauser, T. *A Short History of the Western Liturgy* (Oxford University Press, 1969).

Kleinheyer, B. *Erneuerung des Hochgebetes* (Pustet, Regensburg, 1968).

————. "L'ordination des prêtres," *LMD* 98 (1969), pp. 95–112.

Lampe, G. W. H. *God as Spirit* (Oxford University Press, 1977).

Lanne, E. *Le Grand Euchologe du Monastère Blanc*, Patrologia Orientalis XXVIII, 2, 1958.

————. "Le prière de la Grande Entrée," in *Miscellanea Liturgica in onore di S. E. il Cardinale G. Lercaro, II* (Rome, 1967), pp. 303–312.

Laporte, J. *La doctrine eucharistique chez Philon d'Alexandrie*, Théologie Historique 16 (Beauchesne, Paris, 1972).

Laurance, J. "Le président de l'Eucharistie selon Cyprien de Carthage: un nouvel examen," *LMD* 154 (1983), pp. 151–165

Ledogar, R. J. *Acknowledgement: Praise-Verbs in the Early Greek Anaphora* (Herder, Rome, 1968).

Legg, J. W., ed. *Tracts on the Mass*, Henry Bradshaw Society 27 (London, 1904).

Lengeling, E. *Die neue Ordnung der Eucharistiefeier. Allgemeine Einführung in das römische Messbuch* (Münster, 1971).

Lietzmann, H. *Mass and Lord's Supper: A Study in the History of the Liturgy*, 11 fascicles (Brill, Leiden, 1953–1979).

Ligier, L. "The Origins of the Eucharistic Prayer," *SL* 9 (1973), pp. 161–185.

Lindars, B. *Jesus Son of Man* (SPCK, 1983).

Lodi, E. *Enchiridion Euchologicum Fontium Liturgicorum*, EL Subsidia 15 (Edizioni Liturgiche, Rome, 1979).

Lowe, E. A., ed. *The Bobbio Missal*, Henry Bradshaw Society 58 (London, 1920).

Mackey, J. P *Jesus—The Man and the Myth* (SCM, 1979)

Macomber, W. F. "The Oldest Known Text of the Anaphora of the Apostles Addai and Mari," *OCP* 23 (1966), pp. 335–371.

———. "The Ancient Form of the Anaphora of the Apostles," in *East of Byzantium, Syria and Armenia in the Formative Period* (Dumbarton Oaks, Washington D.C., 1982), pp. 73–88.

Manders, H. "Sens et fonction due récit de l'institution," *QLP* (1972), pp. 208–218.

Martène, E. *De Antiquis Ecclesiae Ritibus*, 4 vols. (Antwerp, 1764).

Martimort, A.-G. *La documentation liturgique de Dom Edmond Martène*, Studi e Testi 279 (Vatican, 1978).

Mascall, E. *Corpus Christi* (Longmans, 2nd ed. 1965).

Maskell, W. *The Ancient Liturgy of the Church of England* (Pickering, 1844).

Matéos, J. *La célébration de la parôle dans la liturgie byzantine*, OCA 191 (Rome, 1971).

Maurice, F. D. *The Kingdom of Christ*, I & II (Rivingtons, 1838).

Maxwell, J. M. *Worship and Reformed Theology: The Liturgical Lessons of Mercersburg*, Pittsburgh Theological Monographs Series 10 (Pickwick, Pittsburgh, 1976).

Maxwell, W. *The Liturgical Portions of the Genevan Service Book* (Oliver & Boyd, Edinburgh, 1931).

Mazza, E. "Omelie pasquali e birkat ha-mazon: fonti dell'anafora di Ippolito?," *EL* 97 (1983), pp. 409–481.

McGarvey, W. *Liturgiae Americanae* (Philadelphia Church Publishing Company, Philadelphia, 1895).

McKelvey, R. J. *The New Temple: The Church in the New Testament*, Oxford Theological Monographs (Oxford, 1969).

McKenna, J. H. *Eucharist and Holy Spirit*, ACC 57 (Mayhew-McCrimmon, Great Wakering, 1975).

McManus, F. "The Berakah Award and Response: The Genius of the Roman Rite Revisited," *Worship* 54 (1980), pp. 360–378.

Medd, P. G., ed. *The Priest to the Altar* (Rivingtons, 1861).

Mitchell, L. L. "The Alexandrian Anaphora of St. Basil of Caesarea: Ancient Source of 'A Common Eucharistic Prayer,' " *ATR* 58 (1976), pp. 194–206.

Modern Eucharistic Agreement (SPCK, 1973).

292

Mohlberg, L. C., ed. *Sacramentarium Veronense,* Rerum ecclesiasticarum documenta; series maior: Fontes I (Rome, 1956).

———, ed. *Missale Gallicanum Vetus,* Rerum ecclesiasticarum documenta; series maior: Fontes III (Rome 1958).

———, ed. *Missale Francorum,* Rerum ecclesiasticarum documenta; series maior: Fontes II (Rome, 1961).

———, ed. *Missale Gothicum,* Rerum ecclesiasticarum documenta; series maior: Fontes V (Rome, 1961).

Mohrmann, C. "Rationabilis -ΛΟΓΙΚΟΣ" Revue Internationale des Droits de l'Antiquite 5 (1950), pp. 223–234.

———. "Le style oral du De Sacramentis de saint Ambroise," *Vigiliae Christiane* 6 (1952), pp. 168–177.

Montmimy, J.-P. "L'offrande sacrificielle dans l'anamnèse des liturgies anciennes," *Revue des sciences philosophiques et théologiques* 50 (1966), pp. 385–406.

Moreton, M. J. "The Early Liturgies: 'We Offer This Bread and This Cup': 3," *Theology* 69 (1966), pp. 442–447.

———. *Made Fully Perfect* (Church Lit. Assn., 1974).

Neale, J. M. *Mediaeval Hymns and Sequences* (Masters, 1852).

Newbigin, L. *The Household of God* (SCM, 1953).

Nickle, K. F. *The Collection: A Study in Paul's Strategy,* Studies in Biblical Theology 48 (SCM, 1966).

Oberman, H. A. & W. J. Courtenay, eds., *Gabrielis Biel Canonis Misse Expositio* (Franz Steiner Verlag, GMBH: Wiesbaden, 1965) P. II, p. 340.

Oosterhuis, H. *Open Your Hearts* (Sheed & Ward, 1972).

Pahl, I. "Das eucharistische hochgebet in den Abendmahlsordnungen der Reformationskirchen," *QLP* (1972), pp. 219–244.

———, ed. *Coena Domini I,* Spicilegium Friburgense 29 (Fribourg University, 1983).

Palmer, W. *Origines Liturgicae,* I & II (Oxford University Press, 1839).

Paredi, A & G. Fassi, eds. *Sacramentarium Bergomense,* Edizione "Monumenta Bergomensia" (Bergamo, 1929).

Paverd, F. van de. *Zur Geschichte der Messliturgie in Antiocheia und Konstantinopel gegen Ende des Vierten Jahrhunderts,* OCA 187 (Rome, 1970).

Peaston, E. *The Prayer Book Tradition in the Free Churches* (Clarke, 1964).

Porter, H. B., *The Ordination Prayers of the Ancient Western Churches*, ACC 49 (SPCK, 1967).

————. *Jeremy Taylor, Liturgist*, ACC 61 (SPCK, 1979).

————. "An American Assembly of Anaphoral Prayers," in B. D. Spinks (ed.), *The Sacrifice of Praise*, EL Subsidia 19 (Edizioni Liturgiche, Rome, 1981), pp. 181–195.

Porter, W. S. *The Gallican Rite* (Mowbrays, 1958).

Power, D. N. "Words That Crack: The Uses of 'Sacrifice' in Eucharistic Discourse," *Worship* 53 (1979), pp. 386–404.

————. *Unsearchable Riches: The Symbolic Nature of Liturgy* (Pueblo, New York, 1984).

Powers, J. M. *Eucharistic Theology* (Burns and Oates/Herder, 1967).

Prenter, R. "Eucharistic Sacrifice according to the Lutheran Tradition," *Theology* 68 (1964), pp. 286–295 (= R. Prenter, *Theologie und Gottesdienst*, [Aros, Århus 1977], pp. 195–207).

de Puniet, P. *Le Pontifical Romain: histoire et commentaire*, I & II (Louvain, 1930–1931).

Purchas, J., ed. *Directorium Anglicanum* (Masters, 1858).

Raes, A. "L'authenticité de la liturgie byzantine de S. Jean Chrysostom," *OCP* 24 (1958), pp. 5–16.

————. "Un nouveau document de la liturgie de S. Basile," *OCP* 26 (1960), pp. 401–411.

————. "ΚΑΤΑ ΠΑΝΤΑ ΚΑΙ ΔΙΑ ΠΑΝΤΑ—en tout et pour tout," *OC* 48 (1964), pp. 216–220.

Ramis, G. "El memorial eucharistico," *EL* 96 (1982), pp. 189–208.

Ramsey, A. M. *The Gospel and the Catholic Church* (Longmans, 1936).

————. *Durham Essays and Addresses* (SPCK, 1956).

————. *Jesus and the Living Past* (Oxford, 1980).

Rasmussen, N. K. "Les rites de présentation du pain et du vin," *LMD* 100 (1969), pp. 44–58.

————. "Quelques réflexions sur la théologie des tropes," in G. Iversen, ed., *Research on Tropes: Proceedings of a Symposium Organized by the Royal Academy of Literature, History, and Antiquities, and the Corpus Troporum* (Almqvist & Wiksell, Stockholm, 1982) pp. 77–88.

Ratcliff, E. C. "The Original Form of the Anaphora of Addai and Mari—a

Suggestion," *JTS* 30 (1928), pp. 23-32 (= A. H. Couratin and D. H. Tripp, eds., *E. C. Ratcliff: Liturgical Studies* [SPCK, 1976], pp. 80-90).

————. "The English Usage of Eucharistic Consecration 1548-1662," *Theology* 60 (1957), pp. 229-236, 273-280 (= *E. C. Ratcliff: Liturgical Studies*, pp. 203-221).

————. "Puritan Alternatives to the Prayer Book: The Directory and Richard Baxter's Reformed Liturgy," in *The English Prayer Book, 1549-1662* (SPCK, 1963), pp. 56-81 (= *E. C. Ratcliff: Liturgical Studies*, pp. 222-243).

Rattenbury, J. E. *The Eucharistic Hymns of John and Charles Wesley* (Epworth, 1948).

Reed, L. D.. *The Lutheran Liturgy* (Fortress, Philadelphia, 1st ed. 1947, 2nd ed., 1959).

Reine, F. J. *The Eucharistic Doctrine and Liturgy of the Mystagogical Catecheses of Theodore of Mopsuestia*, SCA 2 (Catholic University of America, Washington, D.C., 1942).

Renaudot, E. *Liturgiarum Orientalium Collectio*, 2 vols. (Frankfurt, 1847).

Renoux, A. "L'anaphore arménienne de saint Gregoire l'illuminateur," in *Eucharisties d'Orient et d'Occident* II, pp. 89-104.

Richardson, A. *An Introduction to the Theology of the New Testament* (London & New York, 1958).

Ringgren, H. *Israelite Religion* (SPCK, 1966).

Rodopoulos, P. *The Sacramentary of Serapion* (Thessaloniki, 1967).

Rordorf, W. & A. Tuiller, eds. *La Doctrine des Douze Apôtres*, SC 248 (Editions du Cerf, Paris, 1978).

Rose, K. *King George V* (Weidenfeld & Nicholson, 1983).

Rowell, G. *The Liturgy of Christian Burial*, ACC 59 (SPCK, 1977).

Rücker, A. "Denkmäler altarmenischer Messliturgie 4: Die Anaphora des Patriarches Kyrillos von Alexandreia," *OC* 3 (1926), pp. 143-157.

————. "Denkmäler altarmenischer Messliturgie 5: Die anaphora des hl. Ignatius von Antiochen," *OC* 5 (1930), pp. 56-79.

Ryan, J. B. *The Eucharistic Prayer: A Study in Contemporary Liturgy* (Paulist Press, New York, 1974).

Salaville, S. "L' 'Explication de la messe' de l'Arménien Chosrov 950," *Echos d'Orient* 39 (1940), pp. 349-382.

Sánchez Caro, J. M. "La anáfora de Addai y Mari y la anáfora meronita šarrar: intento de reconstrucción de la fluenta primitiva común," *OCP* 43 (1977), pp. 41–69.

————. *Eucaristía e Historia de la Salvación,* Biblioteca de Autores Cristianos, (Madrid, 1983).

Sanday, W. & A. C. Headlam. *The Epistle to the Romans, International Critical Commentary* (T. & T. Clark, Edinburgh, 1895).

Schattauer, T. H. "Eucharistic Sacrifice in Luther's Writings on the Mass," Yale Divinity School, STM thesis, 1980.

————. "Some Roman Catholic Approaches to Luther on the Mass as Sacrifice," a paper read at Notre Dame University, May 1982.

————. The Koinonikon of the Byzantine Liturgy: An Historical Study," *OCP* 49 (1983), pp. 91–129.

Schillebeeckx, E. *Christ the Sacrament of the Encounter with God* (New York & London, 1963).

Schmidt-Lauber, H.-C. "The Eucharistic Prayers in the Roman Catholic Church Today," *SL* 11 (1976), pp. 159ff.

————. "La riscoperta della Preghiera eucharistica nelle Chiese evangeliche," *Rivista Liturgica* 70 (1983), pp. 291–310.

Schulz, F. *Die Lima-Liturgie* (Stauda, Kassel, 1983).

Schulz, H.-J. *Ökumenische Glaubenseinheit aus eucharistischer Überlieferung,* Konfessionskundliche und kontroverstheologische Studien 39 (Paderborn, 1976).

————. *The Byzantine Liturgy,* Eng. tr. M. J. O'Connell, (Pueblo, New York, 1986).

————. "Structures de l'Eucharistie comme sacrifice et oblation," *LMD* 154 (1983), pp. 59–79.

Shaeffer, M. "Twelfth Century Latin Commentaries on the Mass: The Relationship of the Priest to Christ, and to the People," *SL* 15 (1982–1983), pp. 76–86.

Shepherd, M. H. *The Paschal Liturgy and the Apocalypse,* Ecumenical Studies in Worship 6 (Lutterworth, 1960).

————. "Eusebius and the Liturgy of St. James," *Yearbook of Liturgical Studies,* 4 (1963), pp. 109–125.

Sheppard, L. C. ed. *The New Liturgy* (Darton, Longman, & Todd, 1970).

Shipley, O., ed. *The Ritual of the Altar* (Longmans, 1870).

Sicard, D. *La liturgie de la mort dans l'Eglise latine des origines à la réforme caro-lingienne*, LQF 63 (Aschendorff, Münster, 1978).

Simmons, T. F., ed. *Lay-Folks Mass Book*, Early English Text Society 71 (London, 1879).

Spinks, B. D. "The Consecratory Epiclesis in the Anaphora of St. James," *SL* 11 (1976), pp. 19–38.

———. "The Original Form of the Anaphora of the Apostles," *EL* 91 (1977), pp. 146–161.

———. "The Jewish Origins for the Sanctus," *Heythrop Journal* 21 (1980), pp. 168–179.

———. *Addai and Mari—The Anaphora of the Apostles: A Text for Students*, GLS 24 (Grove Books, 1980).

———. "The Cleansed Leper's Thankoffering before the Lord: Edward Crad-dock Ratcliff and the Pattern of the Early Anaphora," in B. D. Spinks (ed), *The Sacrifice of Praise*, EL Subsidia 19 (Edizioni Liturgiche, Rome, 1981), pp. 161–178.

———. "The Anaphora for India: Some Theological Objections to an Attempt at Inculturation," *EL* 95 (1981), pp. 529–549.

———. *Luther's Liturgical Criteria and His Reform of the Canon of the Mass*, GLS 30 (Grove Books, 1982).

———. "Sacerdoce et offrande dans les 'Koushapé' des anaphores syriennes orientales," *LMD* 154 (1983), pp. 107–126.

———. "The Jerusalem Liturgy of the Catecheses Mystagogicae: Syrian or Egyptian?," a paper read at the Ninth International Conference on Patristic Studies, Oxford, September 1983.

———. "A Complete Anaphora? A Note on *Strasbourg Gr. 254*," *Heythrop Journal* 25 (1984), pp. 51–59.

———. "Eucharistic Offering in the East Syrian Anaphoras," *OCP* 50 (1984), pp. 347–371.

———. *Freedom or Order?: The Eucharistic Liturgy in English Congregationalism 1645-1980*, Pittsburgh Theological Monographs New Series 9 (Pickwick Publications, Pittsburgh, 1984).

———. *From the Lord and "The Best of Reformed Churches": A Study of the Eu-charistic Liturgy in the English Puritan and Separatist Traditions: 1550-1633*, EL Subsidia 33 (Edizioni Liturgiche, Rome, 1984).

Stevenson, K. W. "The Catholic Apostolic Eucharist," Ph.D. dissertation, University of Southampton, 1975.

————. *Gregory Dix—25 Years On*, GLS 10 (Grove Books, 1977).

————, ed. *Authority and Freedom in Liturgy*, GLS 17 (Grove Books, 1979).

————. "The Catholic Apostolic Church—Its History and its Eucharist," *SL* 13 (1979), pp. 21–45.

————. " 'Anaphoral Offering': Some Observations on Eastern Eucharistic Prayers," *EL* 94 (1980), pp. 209–228.

————, ed. *Symbolism and Liturgy* I, GLS 23 (Grove Books, 1980).

————. "Stretching Worship," *Theology* 83 (1981), pp. 12–17.

————, ed. *Symbolism and Liturgy* II, GLS 25 (Grove Books, 1981).

————. "Ye Shall Pray For: The Intercession," in K. W. Stevenson (ed.), *Liturgy Reshaped* (SPCK, London, 1982), pp. 32–47.

————. *Nuptial Blessing: A Study of Christian Marriage Rites*, ACC 64 (SPCK, London, 1982) (= Oxford University Press, New York, 1983).

————. "The Liturgical Year in the Catholic Apostolic Church," *SL* 14 (1982), pp. 128–134.

————. "L'offrande eucharistique: la recherche sur les origines, établit-elle une différence de sens?" *LMD* 154 (1983), pp. 81–106 (= Eucharistic Offering: Does Research into Origins Make any Difference?" *SL* 15, [1982–1983], pp. 87–103).

————. "Preghiere eucharistiche moderne della Communione anglicana," *Rivista Liturgica* 70 (1983), pp. 311–340.

————. "The Marriage Rites of Mediaeval Scandinavia: A Fresh Look," *EL* 97 (1983), pp. 550–557.

————. "Eucharistic Sacrifice—What Can We Learn from Christian Antiquity?," in C. O. Buchanan, ed., *Essays on Eucharistic Sacrifice in the Early Church*, GLS 40 (Grove Books, 1984), pp. 26–33.

Stone, D. *A History of the Doctrine of the Holy Eucharist*, I & II (Longmans, 1909).

Swainson, C. A. *The Greek Liturgies* (London, 1884).

Taft, R. F. *The Great Entrance*, OCA 200 (Rome, 1975).

————. "How Liturgies Grow: The Evolution of the Byzantine 'Divine Liturgy'," *OCP* 43 (1977), pp. 355–378.

————. "The Structural Analysis of Liturgical Units: An Essay in Methodology," *Worship* 54 (1978), pp. 314–329.

————. "Historicism Revisited," *SL* 14 (1982), pp. 97–109.

de La Taille, M. *Mysterium Fidei* (Paris, 1915).

Talley, T. J. "The Eucharistic Prayer of the Ancient Church According to Recent Research: Results and Reflections," *SL* 11 (1976), pp. 138–158.

———. "The Eucharistic Prayer: Tradition and Development," in K. W. Stevenson, ed., *Liturgy Reshaped* (SPCK, London, 1982), pp. 48–64.

Thurian, M. *L'Eucharistie* (Delachaux/Niestlé, Neuchâtel, 1959).

———, ed. *Ecumenical Perspectives on Baptism, Eucharist, and Ministry*, Faith and Order Paper 116 (World Council of Churches, Geneva, 1983).

Thurian, M. & G. Wainwright, eds. *Baptism and Eucharist: Ecumenical Convergence in Celebration* (World Council of Churches, Geneva, 1983).

Tirot, P. "Histoire des prières d'offertoire dans la liturgie romaine du VIIè au XVIè siècle," *EL* 98 (1984), pp. 148–197, 323–391.

Townsley, A. L. "Eucharistic Doctrine and the Liturgy in Late Byzantine Painting," *OC* 58 (1974), pp. 138–153.

Tripp, D. H. *The Renewal of the Covenant in the Methodist Tradition* (Epworth, 1969).

———. "The Liturgy of the Catholic Apostolic Church—A Minor Chapter in Ecumenical History," *Scottish Journal of Theology* 24 (1969), pp. 437–454.

———. "Behind the 'Alternative Order,' " *Proceedings of the Wesley Historical Society* 43 (1981), pp. 4–8.

———. "Shape and Liturgy," in K. W. Stevenson, ed., *Liturgy Reshaped* (SPCK, London, 1982), pp. 65–82.

———. "Il rinnovamento della Preghiera eucharistische nelle Chiese metodiste," *Rivista Liturgica* 70 (1983), pp. 353–373.

Vagaggini, C. *The Canon of the Mass and Liturgical Reform* (Chapman, 1967).

Vogel, C. & R. Elze. *Le Pontifical Romano-Germanique du Dixième Siècle*, Studi e Testi 226 (Vatican, 1963).

———. "La multiplication des messes solitaires au moyen âge. Essai de statistique," *Revue des Sciences Réligieuses* 55 (1981), pp. 206–213.

Waddell, H., ed. *Mediaeval Latin Lyrics* (Penguin, 1952).

Wagner, G. *Der Ursprung der Chrysostomusliturgie*, LQF 59, (Aschendorff, Münster 1973).

Wainwright, G. *Eucharist and Eschatology* (Epworth, 1971).

———. *Doxology, The Praise of God in Worship, Doctrine and Life* (Epworth, 1980).

Walker, J. H. "A Pre-Marcan Dating for the Didache," *Studia Biblica* (1978), pp. 403–411.

———. "Reflections on a New Edition of the Didache," *Vigiliae Christianae* 35 (1981), pp. 35–42.

Warner, G. F. *The Stowe Missal*, Henry Bradshaw Society 31 (1915).

Wegman, H. A. J. "The Rubrics of the Institution-Narrative in the Roman Missal of 1970," in P. Jounel, R. Kaczynski, G. Pasqualetti, eds., *Liturgia Opera Divina e Umana*, EL Subsidia 26 (Edizioni Liturgiche, Rome, 1982), pp. 319–328.

———. "Une anaphore incomplète?" in R. Van Den Broek & J. J. Vermaseren, eds., *Studies in Gnosticism and Hellenistic Religions* (Brill, Leiden, 1981) pp. 432–450.

Wheatly, C. *A Rational Illustration of the Book of Common Prayer, The Third Edition, Much Enlarg'd and Improv'd* (Rivingtons, 1720).

Whitaker, E. C. *Martin Bucer and the Book of Common Prayer*, ACC 55 (Mayhew-McCrimmon, Great Wakering, 1974).

Wigan, B., ed. *The Liturgy in English* (Oxford, 2nd ed. 1964).

Williams, R. *Eucharistic Sacrifice: The Roots of a Metaphor*, GLS 31 (Grove Books, 1982).

Willis, G. G. *Essays in Early Roman Liturgy*, ACC 46 (SPCK, 1964).

———. *Further Essays in Early Roman Liturgy*, ACC 50 (SPCK, 1968).

———. "Sacrificium laudis," in Spinks (ed.), *The Sacrifice of Praise*, pp. 73–87.

Winkler, G. "Zur Geschichte des armenischen Gottesdienstes im Hinblick auf den in mehreren Wellen erfolgten griechischen Einflüss," *OC* 58 (1974), pp. 154–172.

———. *Das Armenische Initiationsrituale*, OCA 217 (Rome, 1982).

Wright, W., ed. *Apocryphal Acts of the Apostles*, I & II (London, 1871).

Index of Authors Cited

Cirlot, F. L., 238n.2
Clark, Alan, Bishop, 130, 148–149
Clark, Francis, 124, 254n.80
Clarke, Lowther, 263–264n.40
Codrington, H. G., 245nn.51,59
Comber, Thomas, 159
Connolly, R. H., 72, 246n.82;
    247n.92
Coquin, R.-G., 241n.72; 244n.36
Cornet, L., 267n.85
Cosin, John, 151, 157
Couratin, A. H., 266n.87
Crichton, James, 250n.79
Cross, F. L., 248–249n.28
Cuming, Geoffrey J., ix, 21, 25, 26,
    47, 72, 144, 145, 237n.13;
    239n.26; 240nn.40,42,45;
    241nn.67,70; 244nn.27,30,31;
    246n.79; 247nn.88,93,3;
    251nn.1,2; 257nn.25,26,27,
    32,36,39,45,50; 258nn.51,57;
    260n.104; 263nn.31,34;
    267nn.87,89
Cunliffe-Jones, H., 269n.115

Daly, Robert, 11, 12, 238nn.7,9;
    239n.26
Davies, Horton, 257n.40; 260n.101
Dearing, T., 260n.98
Denzinger, H., 251nn.5,8,9;
    252n.10
Deshusses, J., 248nn.22,23; 249n.44
Dix, Gregory, 10, 18, 20, 56, 84,
    112, 122, 127, 129, 138, 142,
    144–145, 147, 155, 183, 186,
    194, 195, 199, 222, 223, 225,
    226, 231, 238n.4; 239–
    240nn.32,39,42,43; 242n.82;
    244n.35; 245n.65; 248n.24;
    249n.50; 254n.79; 255n.88;
    257nn.25,37,42; 258n.60;
    262n.20; 264nn.52,53,54;
    265n.68; 270n.9
Donaldson, Gordon, 149f.,
    257nn.46,47

Douglas, Mary, 271n.28
Dowden, John, 151, 237n.3;
    258n.51
Drummond, Henry, 183
Dugmore, C., 257n.25
Dumas, A., 237n.12; 249n.48;
    266n.75; 266n.83; 280n.11
Durkheim, E., 271n.29

Echlin, E., 167, 260n.96
Eeles, F. C., 260n.92
Eizenhöfer, L., 249n.40
Ellebracht, M. P., 249n.31
Elze, R., 252nn.16,17
Emery, P.-Y., 264–265n.57
Engberding, H., 27, 38, 72,
    241n.76; 243n.9; 247nn.90,93;
    252n.22
Evans-Pritchard, P., 271n.27

Fassi, G., 249n.51
Fawcett, T. J., 258n.59
Fenwick, John R. K., 241n.74,
    248n.24; 270n.7
Ferhat, P., 245nn.70,72
Férotin, M., 258n.69
Fiala, V., 253n.45
Fischer, Balthasar, 199
Forrester, D., 237n.8
Frendo, J. A., 250n.59; 280n.10
Frere, Walter Howard, 22, 79,
    189ff., 240n.49; 248n.14;
    251n.3; 263nn.32,40

Gelineau, J., 265–266n.74
George, Raymond, 260n.98
Gerhards, A., 57, 244n.37
Gimeno, J. A. G., 249n.31
Goar, J., 251n.6
Gore, Charles, 188f., 236,
    263nn.29,30; 272n.39
Green, M., 238n.22
Gregg, David, 10, 238n.5

304

57,59; 241n.67; 243nn.14,18;
244nn.21,22,25,26,42,43;
246nn.79,82; 247n.5; 248n.25;
253nn.34,43; 256n.13;
257n.24; 258n.56; 263n.38;
268–269n.106; 280n.16
Stevenson, Kenneth W., vii, viii,
237nn.4,5,6,14,17,19;
240nn.44,45,54; 240–241n.59;
242n.78; 244nn.23,34;
245n.63; 253–254n.52;
257n.25; 258n.57; 262n.23;
263n.26; 265n.68; 266n.79;
267n.92; 270nn.9,18;
271nn.21,28,33; 272n.36
Stone, Darwell, 38, 183, 262n.21
Swainson, C. A., 244n.30
Sweeney, Beryl, x
Swete, H. B., 251n.3

Taft, Robert, 105, 106, 111, 126,
218, 223, 245n.65;
252nn.19,20,22,23,25,26;
253nn.33,42; 255nn.84,85,86,
88; 270nn.1,11
Taille, M. de la, 198; 265n.64
Talley, T. J., 237n.19; 238n.11,
239nn.14,20; 240–241nn.58,59;
241n.63; 254n.69; 255n.90;
266n.79; 268n.96
Taylor, Vincent, 168
Tellini, G., 237n.8; 268n.100
Thurian, Max, 196, 202, 206, 212,
216, 227, 230, 233; 264–
265n.57; 269n.110;
271nn.23,25,32
Tillard, Jean, 212, 233
Tirot, P., 113, 253nn.45,48,50
Townsley, A. L., 255n.85

Tripp, D. H., 260n.103
Tuilier, A., 239nn.20,21.

Vaggagini, Cipriano, 109, 201, 202,
265n.71; 266nn.76,79
Vermaseren, M. J., 241n.67
Vogel, C., 250n.79; 252n.16
Vries, W. de, 245n.56

Wagner, George, 49, 72, 243n.9;
244n.44; 247n.88
Wagner, Johannes, 199
Wainwright, Geoffrey, ix, 203, 237–
238n.22; 256n.12; 266n.80;
271n.31; 272n.37
Wakefield, Gordon, 258n.56
Walker, Joan H., 15, 239n.22
Walsh, C., 271n.28
Warner, G. F., 280n.18
Waterland, Daniel, 161
Wegman, H. A. J., 241n.67;
266n.78
Weil, N., 257n.46
Wheatly, Charles, 3, 159, 160,
237n.6
Whitaker, E. C., 257n.30
White, James, 210
Wilberforce, R. I., 261n.5
Williams, Rowan, 19, 33–34,
239nn.25,26,30,35; 240n.55;
242n.94; 256n.21
Willis, G., 77, 85, 113, 247n.5;
248nn.7,9,10,16,26,27;
249n.29; 253n.45
Winkler, Gabrielle, 72, 245nn.67,72
Wright, W., 247n.86

Yerkes, R. K., 238n.10; 247n.5
Young, F., 239nn.15,19,39; 240;
247n.87

General Index

bloodless service, 56, 68f., 83
Catholic Apostolic rite of, 184–185
and Calvary, 8
Christ's presence in, 116, 135
Christian life and, 19
as Christian sacrifice, 16
christological reflection on, 230
as commemoration of passion of our Lord, 90
and commemoration of departed, 2, 26f., 42, 47
and commemoration of saints, 27–28
and commemoration of the living, 42
as commensal, 228f.
as commitment to God, 12
communion, and, 21, 24, 65, 81
consecration and, 2, 8, 22, 25, 27, 36, 38ff., 47, 55, 80, 81, 82, 84, 89, 122, 124, 136, 159ff., 167, 178, 191
context of, as story, 7
as corporate offering of the whole Church, 115
Cranmer's views of, 3, 141ff.
and criteria of "story," "gift," and "response." See eucharistic prayer
as "deified body and blood" of Christ, 67
difference from pagan and Jewish cults, 15
Dix's "four-action shape" of, 222
draft form of ("Series 2" and "Series 3") 204ff.
Eastern notion of, ix
eschatology and, ix
gift, as material of, 7
as "gift of Christ," 70
Gore's view of, 188ff.
heavenly intercession of Christ and, 8
heavenly ministry of Christ and, 16, 176

High Church Anglican view of, 3
as immolation, 87
as intercession, 81, 117
Jewish liturgical background of, 12ff.
language of sacrifice and, 194
as life of God in the faithful, 82
as "likenesses" of the body and blood of Christ, 40
as "living sacrifice" of the Church, 6–7
meal and, 13f., 20, 135, 145, 228
as memorial of Christ, 153. See memorial
as memorial of offering of Christ, 50, 67, 70, 82, 93, 118f.
memorial reality of, 72, 214
as memorial-sacrifice, 119
as "mysteries," 62
as "mystic institution," 61
oblation in, 166
as offering, 2, 6, 102, 155. See offering
as "offering" of the Church, 21
as offering a memorial, 33
as offering of New Covenant, 19
as "offering the offerer," 33
as offering of whole congregation, 225
as "pleading," 155
as preached assurance of faith, 137f.
as prefiguring future glory, 118–119
presence of Christ in, 37, 116f., 129, 153f., 157, 175f., 198
as prophetic sign of the Kingdom, 48
reality of, 19
as remitting sins of the dead, 101
as representing the passion of Christ, 118
response as action of, 7
Roman Canon and, 3
Roman Catholic theology of, 170ff.

312

prayers over, 86f., 90. 110
preparation of, 128, 132, 203, 212
presentation of, 6, 32, 41, 85f., 103, 108, 174, 204, 212, 222f., 235
reception of, from God, 132
Reformation view of, 7
in Roman Canon, 7, 80ff.
sacerdotal, 104
as sacred, 216
as sacrifice, 6, 33, 80, 111
sanctification of, by the Spirit, 27, 83. *See also* eucharist; offering; sacrifice
and "story," 166
Gloria in excelsis, 120, 195, 277
The Gospel and the Catholic Church (1936), of Michael Ramsey, 194
Great Entrance, 90, 113, 125ff., 173, 185, 186
Gregorian University, 130
Gregory the Great, Pope, 77, 82ff., 96, 116, 123

hand-laying, 13
Henley, John, liturgy of, 162–163, 165
Hermann von Wiede, 142, 144
Hierarchia Ecclesiastica, of Pseudo-Dionysius the Areopagite, 69
Hildebert, of Tours, 117, 121
Hincmar of Reims, 116
Hippolytus, 2, 5–6, 9, 17, 20ff.
Historia Ecclesiastica of Germanus, 125
A History of the Doctrine of the Holy Eucharist, of Darwell Stone, 38, 183
Hoffmeier, Christian J. S., x
holocaust, 9, 13, 94ff., 104, 106, 115
Holy Ghost, *See* Holy Spirit
Holy Spirit, ix, 8, 18, 20ff., 40, 43f., 47f., 51, 53f., 60ff., 66ff., 72,

80, 83, 91, 93, 96, 106, 125, 153, 220, 236
Holy Teachers, 109
Honorius of Autun, 117, 121
Hooker, Richard, 157
Hugh of St. Victor, 118, 123
hymnody, 8, 124, 135, 155–156, 214, 221, 227, 233
Lutheran, 172
Hymns, Ancient and Modern, New Standard, xi, 181
Hymns on the Lord's Supper, 167f.
hymns, writers of,
    William Bright, 181–182, 190
    George Hugh Bourne, 181
    William Chatterton, 182
    John Mason Neale, 181
    John and Charles Wesley, 8, 167f., 210, 234
    James White, 210
    Brian Wren, 214

idolaters, 140
Ignatius of Antioch, 17–18, 19, 36
incense, 27, 33, 56, 58, 88ff., 104, 107f. 111, 113, 186
    of a godly life, 110
India, anaphora for, 211
Innocent I, Pope, and letter to Decentius of Gubbio, 77ff.
Innocent III, Pope (Lothar Conti), 118
Institutes, of Calvin, 140ff.
institution narrative, ix, 6, 20, 22, 24, 26, 28, 39ff., 46, 50, 52f., 56f., 61f., 99, 118, 132, 134, 135, 137, 139ff., 146, 151ff., 160, 163, 193, 221f.
    anamnesis and, 21, 35, 68, 97
    and consecration, 8, 75, 128, 156, 178, 227
    and intercession, 48
    and *midrash*, 211
    as offering, 48, 49
    Qui pridie, 79f., 100f.

Leo XIII on Anglican Orders and, 182f.
Luther on, 131ff.
Principles of Liturgical Reform, of Walter H. Frere, 189f.
procession, 86, 90, 174, 194f.
Protheoria, of Nicholas of Andida, 125
prothesis, 105, 107, 108, 110f., 125, 177f., 180, 279
Purgatory, 189
Puritans, 150, 153
Pusey, Edward, 176

Rabanus, Maurus, 116
Ratherius of Verona, 116–117
Rational Illustration of the Book of Common Prayer (1720), 3, 159
Rationale, of Anthony Sparrow, 159–160
Ratramnus of Corbie, 116
Rattray, Thomas, liturgy of, 164ff.
reading, 135, 141, 148, 221
real presence of Christ, 117
in bread and wine, 119
Reformation, Protestant, vii, 1, 6f., 15, 124, 129ff., 149, 173
English, 176
Reformers, 124, 129ff., 172
and rejection of sacrificial character of eucharist, 129ff.
"response," as action of eucharist, 7f., 36, 147
focused in postcommunion event and intercession, 147
as psychological devotion of faithful, 7
See also gift; "story," s/v eucharistic prayer
Ritual of the Altar, of Orby Shipley, 180
Roman Canon, 6, 36, 68, 76ff., 91, 95, 97, 113f., 116f., 120, 139, 144, 147, 151, 171ff., 219
anamnesis in, 79
and Anglican rite, 177ff.

commemoration of saints in, 79
communicantes, 78ff., 100
consecration in, 80f.
Deus qui humanae substantiae, 112–113
development of, 128
dispensed with, by Luther, 139
Eucharistic Prayer I, 200ff.
gift sacrifice theme in, 80ff., 97–98
and Greek epiclesis, 94
John Halliburton on, 193–194
Hanc igitur, 74, 77ff., 84ff., 101, 144
in spiritu humilitatis, 112ff.
institution narrative (*Qui pridie*) in, 79f., 100f.
intercession in, 80, 81
Ite missa est, 83
memento, 77ff., 100, 144
Nobis quoque, 144
Offerimus tibi, 112ff.
offering and, 74, 219
offering of body and blood of Christ in, 79ff.
and Old Gelasian Sacramentary, 77, 78
Orate fratres, 98, 113ff., 122, 127f., 161, 179, 203f., 225, 231
Per intercessionem, 112, 113
Post pridie, 98, 221
praise in, 219
prayer for acceptance of sacrifice in, 80
prayer for departed in, 79
prefaces, 78, 97, 123, 130, 132, 134ff., 200, 219
Quam oblationem, 77ff.
Qui pridie (Institution narrative), 79f., 100f.
Sanctus in, 78, 122, 134, 139, 219
and similarities to *Strasbourg Mark*, 36
"story" in, 200
and "stratum three" prayers, 97–98, 135

and offering of gifts, 223
in Roman Missal of 1970, 203
vocabulary of, 85, 94
supplication, 8, 16, 24, 92, 99, 110, 227
for communion, 139
for the living, 59
for the people, 52f., 69
sacrificial character of, 69
as story and response, 35
Swedish rite, 134ff., 197f.
Symon of Thessalonica, 125
Syria, 15
Syriac language, 102
Syriac rites, 107, 110, 128, 145

table, 93, 139ff., 145, 147, 149, 151, 160, 161, 163, 176, 228, 230
of prothesis, 186
used in remembrance of Christ's death, 141
Taizé, community of, 196, 206, 216
Taylor, Jeremy, 151, 158, 161
Tertullian, 19, 99
Testament of Levi, 26, 35, 52
thanksgiving, 63, 67, 69, 80, 83, 92, 120, 132, 141, 153f., 196, 227
and anamnesis, 22
christological, 53f.
and commemoration and oblation, 24
as *Eucharistia*, 152
for redemption, 20
representation and anticipation, 216
sacrificial character of, 12, 18, 24
and supplication, 24, 60, 207
in *Testamentum Domini*, 22
Theodore of Mopsuestia, 120
Theodoret of Cyrrhus, 71
Theodulf of Orleans, 116
Thomas Aquinas, 118f., 124, 129, 170
Thorndike, Herbert, 157
tithes, 95, 184ff.
Toul, rite of, 115

Tractarians, Anglican, 175ff., 188
on eucharist as sacrifice, 182
on eucharistic presence, 175f.
transubstantiation, 141, 176
Trier, liturgical institute at, 198
Trinity, Holy, 67, 110, 112f., 154
Trisagion, 107f., 110f.
typology, 93, 104, 117

Unbloody Sacrifice, of John Johnson, 160
unconsecrated elements, veneration of, 125
United Church of South India, liturgy of, 195f.
Urmiah version of Nestorius, 58

variability, principle of, 89
Vasquez, Gabriel, 171
Vatican II, Council. *See* Second Vatican Council
vernacular piety, 122ff., 132, 138, 147
vestments, 139, 145, 177
Visigothic-Latin language, 102
Visigothic rite (5–6 centuries), 74, 113
vocabulary of prayers in Mozarabic Sacramentary, 94–95

washing of hands, 113
Washington, George, 167
water, 54, 112
Wesley, Charles, 168ff.
Wesley, John, 167ff.
Westminster Directory, 152ff.
Wheatley, Charles, 3, 159–160, 237n.6
Whiston, William, liturgy of, 162
White, James, 279
White, William, 166f.,
Wilberforce, R., 176f., 182
Wilberforce, Samuel, 177
wine, 5, 34, 38f., 55f., 70, 83, 93, 95, 112, 119, 136, 141, 161
mixed with water, 18, 61

pouring of, 159. *See also* bread
   and wine
Wied, Hermann von, 142
William of Auvergne, 118
Witmund of Aversa, 117
Wittenberg, Germany, 1
World Council of Churches, Lima
   report, vii, 233
World Council of Churches
   Assembly in Vancouver (1983),
   212, 231
worship
   living offering of, 111
   and New Covenant, 11

preaching as, 4
popular piety and, 3, 123
Reformers' notion of, 147
as sacrificial, ix, 4, 108, 156f.,
   183, 232
spiritual (pure), 161
Wren, Matthew, 151

Zwingli, Ulrich, 129, 136ff., 149,
   155, 174, 233
   and replacement of Canon, 137f.
   and repudiation of eucharistic
   presence, 138
Zikkaron (anamnesis), 10, 13